50% OFF
Online GED Prep Course!

By Mometrix University

Dear Customer,

We consider it an honor and a privilege that you chose our GED Study Guide. As a way of showing our appreciation and to help us better serve you, we are offering **50% off our online GED Prep Course**. Many GED courses cost hundreds of dollars. As our valued customer, **you will only pay $19.99 each month**, which is 50% off our regular monthly price of $39.99.

We have structured our online course to perfectly complement your printed study guide. Our GED Prep Course contains **over 140 lessons** that cover all the most important topics, **180+ video reviews** that explain difficult concepts, **700 practice questions** to ensure you feel prepared, and **digital flashcards**, so you can fit in some studying while you're on the go.

Online GED Prep Course

Topics Covered:

- Reasoning Through Language Arts
    - Reading Comprehension
    - Critical Thinking
    - Writing
- Mathematical Reasoning
    - Number Operations
    - Algebra, Functions, and Patterns
    - Measurement and Geometry
- Science
    - Physical Science
    - Earth and Space Science
- Social Studies
    - History and Government
    - Economics

Course Features:

- GED Study Guide
    - Get content that complements our best-selling study guide.
- 3 Full-Length Practice Tests
    - With over 700 practice questions, you can test yourself again and again.
- Mobile Friendly
    - If you need to study on the go, the course is easily accessible from your mobile device.
- GED Flashcards
    - Our course includes a flashcard mode consisting of over 400 content cards to help you study.

To receive this discount, simply head to our website: www.mometrix.com/university and add the course to your cart. At the checkout page, enter the discount code: **ged50off**

If you have any questions or concerns, please don't hesitate to contact us at universityhelp@mometrix.com.

Sincerely,

GED

Test Prep
2020 & 2021

**GED Secrets Study Guide
All Subjects**

Full-Length Practice Test

**Step-by-Step
Preparation Video
Tutorials**

Written and edited by the Mometrix High School Equivalency Test Team

Printed in the United States of America

This paper meets the requirements of ANSI/NISO Z39.48-1992 (Permanence of Paper).

Mometrix offers volume discount pricing to institutions. For more information or a price quote, please contact our sales department at sales@mometrix.com or 888-248-1219.

Paperback
ISBN 13: 978-1-5167-1239-7
ISBN 10: 1-51671-239-0

DEAR FUTURE EXAM SUCCE

First of all, **THANK YOU** for purchasing Mometrix study materials!

Second, congratulations! You are one of the few determined test-takers who a. whatever it takes to excel on your exam. **You have come to the right place.** We study materials with one goal in mind: to deliver you the information you need in a concise and easy to use.

In addition to optimizing your guide for the content of the test, we've outlined our recomn. steps for breaking down the preparation process into small, attainable goals so you can make you stay on track.

We've also analyzed the entire test-taking process, identifying the most common pitfalls and showing how you can overcome them and be ready for any curveball the test throws you.

Standardized testing is one of the biggest obstacles on your road to success, which only increases the importance of doing well in the high-pressure, high-stakes environment of test day. Your results on this test could have a significant impact on your future, and this guide provides the information and practical advice to help you achieve your full potential on test day.

Your success is our success

We would love to hear from you! If you would like to share the story of your exam success or if you have any questions or comments in regard to our products, please contact us at **800-673-8175** or **support@mometrix.com**.

Thanks again for your business and we wish you continued success!

Sincerely,
The Mometrix Test Preparation Team

Need more help? Check out our flashcards at:
http://mometrixflashcards.com/GED

TABLE OF CONTENTS

Introduction

Thank you for purchasing this resource! You have made the choice to prepare yourself for a test that could have a huge impact on your future, and this guide is designed to help you be fully ready for test day. Obviously, it's important to have a solid understanding of the test material, but you also need to be prepared for the unique environment and stressors of the test, so that you can perform to the best of your abilities.

For this purpose, the first section that appears in this guide is the **Secret Keys**. We've devoted countless hours to meticulously researching what works and what doesn't, and we've boiled down our findings to the five most impactful steps you can take to improve your performance on the test. We start at the beginning with study planning and move through the preparation process, all the way to the testing strategies that will help you get the most out of what you know when you're finally sitting in front of the test.

We recommend that you start preparing for your test as far in advance as possible. However, if you've bought this guide as a last-minute study resource and only have a few days before your test, we recommend that you skip over the first two Secret Keys since they address a long-term study plan.

If you struggle with **test anxiety**, we strongly encourage you to check out our recommendations for how you can overcome it. Test anxiety is a formidable foe, but it can be beaten, and we want to make sure you have the tools you need to defeat it.

1

Secret Key #1 – Plan Big, Study Small

There's a lot riding on your performance. If you want to ace this test, you're going to need to keep your skills sharp and the material fresh in your mind. You need a plan that lets you review everything you need to know while still fitting in your schedule. We'll break this strategy down into three categories.

Information Organization

Start with the information you already have: the official test outline. From this, you can make a complete list of all the concepts you need to cover before the test. Organize these concepts into groups that can be studied together, and create a list of any related vocabulary you need to learn so you can brush up on any difficult terms. You'll want to keep this vocabulary list handy once you actually start studying since you may need to add to it along the way.

Time Management

Once you have your set of study concepts, decide how to spread them out over the time you have left before the test. Break your study plan into small, clear goals so you have a manageable task for each day and know exactly what you're doing. Then just focus on one small step at a time. When you manage your time this way, you don't need to spend hours at a time studying. Studying a small block of content for a short period each day helps you retain information better and avoid stressing over how much you have left to do. You can relax knowing that you have a plan to cover everything in time. In order for this strategy to be effective though, you have to start studying early and stick to your schedule. Avoid the exhaustion and futility that comes from last-minute cramming!

Study Environment

The environment you study in has a big impact on your learning. Studying in a coffee shop, while probably more enjoyable, is not likely to be as fruitful as studying in a quiet room. It's important to keep distractions to a minimum. You're only planning to study for a short block of time, so make the most of it. Don't pause to check your phone or get up to find a snack. It's also important to **avoid multitasking**. Research has consistently shown that multitasking will make your studying dramatically less effective. Your study area should also be comfortable and well-lit so you don't have the distraction of straining your eyes or sitting on an uncomfortable chair.

The time of day you study is also important. You want to be rested and alert. Don't wait until just before bedtime. Study when you'll be most likely to comprehend and remember. Even better, if you know what time of day your test will be, set that time aside for study. That way your brain will be used to working on that subject at that specific time and you'll have a better chance of recalling information.

Finally, it can be helpful to team up with others who are studying for the same test. Your actual studying should be done in as isolated an environment as possible, but the work of organizing the information and setting up the study plan can be divided up. In between study sessions, you can discuss with your teammates the concepts that you're all studying and quiz each other on the details. Just be sure that your teammates are as serious about the test as you are. If you find that your study time is being replaced with social time, you might need to find a new team.

Secret Key #2 – Make Your Studying Count

You're devoting a lot of time and effort to preparing for this test, so you want to be absolutely certain it will pay off. This means doing more than just reading the content and hoping you can remember it on test day. It's important to make every minute of study count. There are two main areas you can focus on to make your studying count:

Retention

It doesn't matter how much time you study if you can't remember the material. You need to make sure you are retaining the concepts. To check your retention of the information you're learning, try recalling it at later times with minimal prompting. Try carrying around flashcards and glance at one or two from time to time or ask a friend who's also studying for the test to quiz you.

To enhance your retention, look for ways to put the information into practice so that you can apply it rather than simply recalling it. If you're using the information in practical ways, it will be much easier to remember. Similarly, it helps to solidify a concept in your mind if you're not only reading it to yourself but also explaining it to someone else. Ask a friend to let you teach them about a concept you're a little shaky on (or speak aloud to an imaginary audience if necessary). As you try to summarize, define, give examples, and answer your friend's questions, you'll understand the concepts better and they will stay with you longer. Finally, step back for a big picture view and ask yourself how each piece of information fits with the whole subject. When you link the different concepts together and see them working together as a whole, it's easier to remember the individual components.

Finally, practice showing your work on any multi-step problems, even if you're just studying. Writing out each step you take to solve a problem will help solidify the process in your mind, and you'll be more likely to remember it during the test.

Modality

Modality simply refers to the means or method by which you study. Choosing a study modality that fits your own individual learning style is crucial. No two people learn best in exactly the same way, so it's important to know your strengths and use them to your advantage.

For example, if you learn best by visualization, focus on visualizing a concept in your mind and draw an image or a diagram. Try color-coding your notes, illustrating them, or creating symbols that will trigger your mind to recall a learned concept. If you learn best by hearing or discussing information, find a study partner who learns the same way or read aloud to yourself. Think about how to put the information in your own words. Imagine that you are giving a lecture on the topic and record yourself so you can listen to it later.

For any learning style, flashcards can be helpful. Organize the information so you can take advantage of spare moments to review. Underline key words or phrases. Use different colors for different categories. Mnemonic devices (such as creating a short list in which every item starts with the same letter) can also help with retention. Find what works best for you and use it to store the information in your mind most effectively and easily.

Secret Key #3 – Practice the Right Way

Your success on test day depends not only on how many hours you put into preparing, but also on whether you prepared the right way. It's good to check along the way to see if your studying is paying off. One of the most effective ways to do this is by taking practice tests to evaluate your progress. Practice tests are useful because they show exactly where you need to improve. Every time you take a practice test, pay special attention to these three groups of questions:

- The questions you got wrong
- The questions you had to guess on, even if you guessed right
- The questions you found difficult or slow to work through

This will show you exactly what your weak areas are, and where you need to devote more study time. Ask yourself why each of these questions gave you trouble. Was it because you didn't understand the material? Was it because you didn't remember the vocabulary? Do you need more repetitions on this type of question to build speed and confidence? Dig into those questions and figure out how you can strengthen your weak areas as you go back to review the material.

Additionally, many practice tests have a section explaining the answer choices. It can be tempting to read the explanation and think that you now have a good understanding of the concept. However, an explanation likely only covers part of the question's broader context. Even if the explanation makes sense, **go back and investigate** every concept related to the question until you're positive you have a thorough understanding.

As you go along, keep in mind that the practice test is just that: practice. Memorizing these questions and answers will not be very helpful on the actual test because it is unlikely to have any of the same exact questions. If you only know the right answers to the sample questions, you won't be prepared for the real thing. **Study the concepts** until you understand them fully, and then you'll be able to answer any question that shows up on the test.

It's important to wait on the practice tests until you're ready. If you take a test on your first day of study, you may be overwhelmed by the amount of material covered and how much you need to learn. Work up to it gradually.

On test day, you'll need to be prepared for answering questions, managing your time, and using the test-taking strategies you've learned. It's a lot to balance, like a mental marathon that will have a big impact on your future. Like training for a marathon, you'll need to start slowly and work your way up. When test day arrives, you'll be ready.

Start with the strategies you've read in the first two Secret Keys—plan your course and study in the way that works best for you. If you have time, consider using multiple study resources to get different approaches to the same concepts. It can be helpful to see difficult concepts from more than one angle. Then find a good source for practice tests. Many times, the test website will suggest potential study resources or provide sample tests.

Practice Test Strategy

If you're able to find at least three practice tests, we recommend this strategy:

UNTIMED AND OPEN-BOOK PRACTICE

Take the first test with no time constraints and with your notes and study guide handy. Take your time and focus on applying the strategies you've learned.

TIMED AND OPEN-BOOK PRACTICE

Take the second practice test open-book as well, but set a timer and practice pacing yourself to finish in time.

TIMED AND CLOSED-BOOK PRACTICE

Take any other practice tests as if it were test day. Set a timer and put away your study materials. Sit at a table or desk in a quiet room, imagine yourself at the testing center, and answer questions as quickly and accurately as possible.

Keep repeating timed and closed-book tests on a regular basis until you run out of practice tests or it's time for the actual test. Your mind will be ready for the schedule and stress of test day, and you'll be able to focus on recalling the material you've learned.

Secret Key #4 – Pace Yourself

Once you're fully prepared for the material on the test, your biggest challenge on test day will be managing your time. Just knowing that the clock is ticking can make you panic even if you have plenty of time left. Work on pacing yourself so you can build confidence against the time constraints of the exam. Pacing is a difficult skill to master, especially in a high-pressure environment, so **practice is vital**.

Set time expectations for your pace based on how much time is available. For example, if a section has 60 questions and the time limit is 30 minutes, you know you have to average 30 seconds or less per question in order to answer them all. Although 30 seconds is the hard limit, set 25 seconds per question as your goal, so you reserve extra time to spend on harder questions. When you budget extra time for the harder questions, you no longer have any reason to stress when those questions take longer to answer.

Don't let this time expectation distract you from working through the test at a calm, steady pace, but keep it in mind so you don't spend too much time on any one question. Recognize that taking extra time on one question you don't understand may keep you from answering two that you do understand later in the test. If your time limit for a question is up and you're still not sure of the answer, mark it and move on, and come back to it later if the time and the test format allow. If the testing format doesn't allow you to return to earlier questions, just make an educated guess; then put it out of your mind and move on.

On the easier questions, be careful not to rush. It may seem wise to hurry through them so you have more time for the challenging ones, but it's not worth missing one if you know the concept and just didn't take the time to read the question fully. Work efficiently but make sure you understand the question and have looked at all of the answer choices, since more than one may seem right at first.

Even if you're paying attention to the time, you may find yourself a little behind at some point. You should speed up to get back on track, but do so wisely. Don't panic; just take a few seconds less on each question until you're caught up. Don't guess without thinking, but do look through the answer choices and eliminate any you know are wrong. If you can get down to two choices, it is often worthwhile to guess from those. Once you've chosen an answer, move on and don't dwell on any that you skipped or had to hurry through. If a question was taking too long, chances are it was one of the harder ones, so you weren't as likely to get it right anyway.

On the other hand, if you find yourself getting ahead of schedule, it may be beneficial to slow down a little. The more quickly you work, the more likely you are to make a careless mistake that will affect your score. You've budgeted time for each question, so don't be afraid to spend that time. Practice an efficient but careful pace to get the most out of the time you have.

Secret Key #5 – Have a Plan for Guessing

When you're taking the test, you may find yourself stuck on a question. Some of the answer choices seem better than others, but you don't see the one answer choice that is obviously correct. What do you do?

The scenario described above is very common, yet most test takers have not effectively prepared for it. Developing and practicing a plan for guessing may be one of the single most effective uses of your time as you get ready for the exam.

In developing your plan for guessing, there are three questions to address:

- When should you start the guessing process?
- How should you narrow down the choices?
- Which answer should you choose?

When to Start the Guessing Process

Unless your plan for guessing is to select C every time (which, despite its merits, is not what we recommend), you need to leave yourself enough time to apply your answer elimination strategies. Since you have a limited amount of time for each question, that means that if you're going to give yourself the best shot at guessing correctly, you have to decide quickly whether or not you will guess.

Of course, the best-case scenario is that you don't have to guess at all, so first, see if you can answer the question based on your knowledge of the subject and basic reasoning skills. Focus on the key words in the question and try to jog your memory of related topics. Give yourself a chance to bring the knowledge to mind, but once you realize that you don't have (or you can't access) the knowledge you need to answer the question, it's time to start the guessing process.

It's almost always better to start the guessing process too early than too late. It only takes a few seconds to remember something and answer the question from knowledge. Carefully eliminating wrong answer choices takes longer. Plus, going through the process of eliminating answer choices can actually help jog your memory.

Summary: Start the guessing process as soon as you decide that you can't answer the question based on your knowledge.

How to Narrow Down the Choices

The next chapter in this book (**Test-Taking Strategies**) includes a wide range of strategies for how to approach questions and how to look for answer choices to eliminate. You will definitely want to read those carefully, practice them, and figure out which ones work best for you. Here though, we're going to address a mindset rather than a particular strategy.

Your chances of guessing an answer correctly depend on how many options you are choosing from.

How many choices you have	How likely you are to guess correctly
5	20%
4	25%
3	33%
2	50%
1	100%

You can see from this chart just how valuable it is to be able to eliminate incorrect answers and make an educated guess, but there are two things that many test takers do that cause them to miss out on the benefits of guessing:

- Accidentally eliminating the correct answer
- Selecting an answer based on an impression

We'll look at the first one here, and the second one in the next section.

To avoid accidentally eliminating the correct answer, we recommend a thought exercise called **the $5 challenge**. In this challenge, you only eliminate an answer choice from contention if you are willing to bet $5 on it being wrong. Why $5? Five dollars is a small but not insignificant amount of money. It's an amount you could afford to lose but wouldn't want to throw away. And while losing $5 once might not hurt too much, doing it twenty times will set you back $100. In the same way, each small decision you make—eliminating a choice here, guessing on a question there—won't by itself impact your score very much, but when you put them all together, they can make a big difference. By holding each answer choice elimination decision to a higher standard, you can reduce the risk of accidentally eliminating the correct answer.

The $5 challenge can also be applied in a positive sense: If you are willing to bet $5 that an answer choice *is* correct, go ahead and mark it as correct.

Summary: Only eliminate an answer choice if you are willing to bet $5 that it is wrong.

Which Answer to Choose

You're taking the test. You've run into a hard question and decided you'll have to guess. You've eliminated all the answer choices you're willing to bet $5 on. Now you have to pick an answer. Why do we even need to talk about this? Why can't you just pick whichever one you feel like when the time comes?

The answer to these questions is that if you don't come into the test with a plan, you'll rely on your impression to select an answer choice, and if you do that, you risk falling into a trap. The test writers know that everyone who takes their test will be guessing on some of the questions, so they intentionally write wrong answer choices to seem plausible. You still have to pick an answer though, and if the wrong answer choices are designed to look right, how can you ever be sure that you're not falling for their trap? The best solution we've found to this dilemma is to take the decision out of your hands entirely. Here is the process we recommend:

Once you've eliminated any choices that you are confident (willing to bet $5) are wrong, select the first remaining choice as your answer.

Whether you choose to select the first remaining choice, the second, or the last, the important thing is that you use some preselected standard. Using this approach guarantees that you will not be enticed into selecting an answer choice that looks right, because you are not basing your decision on how the answer choices look.

This is not meant to make you question your knowledge. Instead, it is to help you recognize the difference between your knowledge and your impressions. There's a huge difference between thinking an answer is right because of what you know, and thinking an answer is right because it looks or sounds like it should be right.

Summary: To ensure that your selection is appropriately random, make a predetermined selection from among all answer choices you have not eliminated.

Test-Taking Strategies

This section contains a list of test-taking strategies that you may find helpful as you work through the test. By taking what you know and applying logical thought, you can maximize your chances of answering any question correctly!

It is very important to realize that every question is different and every person is different: no single strategy will work on every question, and no single strategy will work for every person. That's why we've included all of them here, so you can try them out and determine which ones work best for different types of questions and which ones work best for you.

Question Strategies

READ CAREFULLY

Read the question and answer choices carefully. Don't miss the question because you misread the terms. You have plenty of time to read each question thoroughly and make sure you understand what is being asked. Yet a happy medium must be attained, so don't waste too much time. You must read carefully, but efficiently.

CONTEXTUAL CLUES

Look for contextual clues. If the question includes a word you are not familiar with, look at the immediate context for some indication of what the word might mean. Contextual clues can often give you all the information you need to decipher the meaning of an unfamiliar word. Even if you can't determine the meaning, you may be able to narrow down the possibilities enough to make a solid guess at the answer to the question.

PREFIXES

If you're having trouble with a word in the question or answer choices, try dissecting it. Take advantage of every clue that the word might include. Prefixes and suffixes can be a huge help. Usually they allow you to determine a basic meaning. Pre- means before, post- means after, pro - is positive, de- is negative. From prefixes and suffixes, you can get an idea of the general meaning of the word and try to put it into context.

HEDGE WORDS

Watch out for critical hedge words, such as *likely, may, can, sometimes, often, almost, mostly, usually, generally, rarely*, and *sometimes*. Question writers insert these hedge phrases to cover every possibility. Often an answer choice will be wrong simply because it leaves no room for exception. Be on guard for answer choices that have definitive words such as *exactly* and *always*.

SWITCHBACK WORDS

Stay alert for *switchbacks*. These are the words and phrases frequently used to alert you to shifts in thought. The most common switchback words are *but, although,* and *however*. Others include *nevertheless, on the other hand, even though, while, in spite of, despite, regardless of*. Switchback words are important to catch because they can change the direction of the question or an answer choice.

10

FACE VALUE

When in doubt, use common sense. Accept the situation in the problem at face value. Don't read too much into it. These problems will not require you to make wild assumptions. If you have to go beyond creativity and warp time or space in order to have an answer choice fit the question, then you should move on and consider the other answer choices. These are normal problems rooted in reality. The applicable relationship or explanation may not be readily apparent, but it is there for you to figure out. Use your common sense to interpret anything that isn't clear.

Answer Choice Strategies

ANSWER SELECTION

The most thorough way to pick an answer choice is to identify and eliminate wrong answers until only one is left, then confirm it is the correct answer. Sometimes an answer choice may immediately seem right, but be careful. The test writers will usually put more than one reasonable answer choice on each question, so take a second to read all of them and make sure that the other choices are not equally obvious. As long as you have time left, it is better to read every answer choice than to pick the first one that looks right without checking the others.

ANSWER CHOICE FAMILIES

An answer choice family consists of two (in rare cases, three) answer choices that are very similar in construction and cannot all be true at the same time. If you see two answer choices that are direct opposites or parallels, one of them is usually the correct answer. For instance, if one answer choice says that quantity x increases and another either says that quantity x decreases (opposite) or says that quantity y increases (parallel), then those answer choices would fall into the same family. An answer choice that doesn't match the construction of the answer choice family is more likely to be incorrect. Most questions will not have answer choice families, but when they do appear, you should be prepared to recognize them.

ELIMINATE ANSWERS

Eliminate answer choices as soon as you realize they are wrong, but make sure you consider all possibilities. If you are eliminating answer choices and realize that the last one you are left with is also wrong, don't panic. Start over and consider each choice again. There may be something you missed the first time that you will realize on the second pass.

AVOID FACT TRAPS

Don't be distracted by an answer choice that is factually true but doesn't answer the question. You are looking for the choice that answers the question. Stay focused on what the question is asking for so you don't accidentally pick an answer that is true but incorrect. Always go back to the question and make sure the answer choice you've selected actually answers the question and is not merely a true statement.

EXTREME STATEMENTS

In general, you should avoid answers that put forth extreme actions as standard practice or proclaim controversial ideas as established fact. An answer choice that states the "process should be used in certain situations, if…" is much more likely to be correct than one that states the "process should be discontinued completely." The first is a calm rational statement and doesn't even make a definitive, uncompromising stance, using a hedge word *if* to provide wiggle room, whereas the second choice is a radical idea and far more extreme.

11

BENCHMARK

As you read through the answer choices and you come across one that seems to answer the question well, mentally select that answer choice. This is not your final answer, but it's the one that will help you evaluate the other answer choices. The one that you selected is your benchmark or standard for judging each of the other answer choices. Every other answer choice must be compared to your benchmark. That choice is correct until proven otherwise by another answer choice beating it. If you find a better answer, then that one becomes your new benchmark. Once you've decided that no other choice answers the question as well as your benchmark, you have your final answer.

PREDICT THE ANSWER

Before you even start looking at the answer choices, it is often best to try to predict the answer. When you come up with the answer on your own, it is easier to avoid distractions and traps because you will know exactly what to look for. The right answer choice is unlikely to be word-for-word what you came up with, but it should be a close match. Even if you are confident that you have the right answer, you should still take the time to read each option before moving on.

General Strategies

TOUGH QUESTIONS

If you are stumped on a problem or it appears too hard or too difficult, don't waste time. Move on! Remember though, if you can quickly check for obviously incorrect answer choices, your chances of guessing correctly are greatly improved. Before you completely give up, at least try to knock out a couple of possible answers. Eliminate what you can and then guess at the remaining answer choices before moving on.

CHECK YOUR WORK

Since you will probably not know every term listed and the answer to every question, it is important that you get credit for the ones that you do know. Don't miss any questions through careless mistakes. If at all possible, try to take a second to look back over your answer selection and make sure you've selected the correct answer choice and haven't made a costly careless mistake (such as marking an answer choice that you didn't mean to mark). This quick double check should more than pay for itself in caught mistakes for the time it costs.

PACE YOURSELF

It's easy to be overwhelmed when you're looking at a page full of questions; your mind is confused and full of random thoughts, and the clock is ticking down faster than you would like. Calm down and maintain the pace that you have set for yourself. Especially as you get down to the last few minutes of the test, don't let the small numbers on the clock make you panic. As long as you are on track by monitoring your pace, you are guaranteed to have time for each question.

DON'T RUSH

It is very easy to make errors when you are in a hurry. Maintaining a fast pace in answering questions is pointless if it makes you miss questions that you would have gotten right otherwise. Test writers like to include distracting information and wrong answers that seem right. Taking a little extra time to avoid careless mistakes can make all the difference in your test score. Find a pace that allows you to be confident in the answers that you select.

12

KEEP MOVING

Panicking will not help you pass the test, so do your best to stay calm and keep moving. Taking deep breaths and going through the answer elimination steps you practiced can help to break through a stress barrier and keep your pace.

Final Notes

The combination of a solid foundation of content knowledge and the confidence that comes from practicing your plan for applying that knowledge is the key to maximizing your performance on test day. As your foundation of content knowledge is built up and strengthened, you'll find that the strategies included in this chapter become more and more effective in helping you quickly sift through the distractions and traps of the test to isolate the correct answer.

Now it's time to move on to the test content chapters of this book, but be sure to keep your goal in mind. As you read, think about how you will be able to apply this information on the test. If you've already seen sample questions for the test and you have an idea of the question format and style, try to come up with questions of your own that you can answer based on what you're reading. This will give you valuable practice applying your knowledge in the same ways you can expect to on test day.

Good luck and good studying!

Reading Comprehension

UNDERSTANDING LITERATURE

Reading literature is a different experience than reading non-fiction works. Our imagination is more active as we review what we have read, imagine ourselves as characters in the novel, and try to guess what will happen next. Suspense, surprise, fantasy, fear, anxiety, compassion, and a host of other emotions and feelings may be stirred by a provocative novel.

Reading longer works of fiction is a cumulative process. Some elements of a novel have a great impact, while others may go virtually unnoticed. Therefore, as novels are read with a critical eye to language, it is helpful to perceive and identify larger patterns and movements in the work as a whole. This will benefit the reader by placing characters and events in perspective, and will enrich the reading experience greatly. Novels should be savored rather than gulped. Careful reading and thoughtful analysis of the major themes of the novel are essential to a clear understanding of the work.

One of the most important skills in reading comprehension is the identification of **topics** and **main ideas.** There is a subtle difference between these two features. The topic is the subject of a text, or what the text is about. The main idea, on the other hand, is the most important point being made by the author. The topic is usually expressed in a few words at the most, while the main idea often needs a full sentence to be completely defined. As an example, a short passage might have the topic of penguins and the main idea *Penguins are different from other birds in many ways.* In most nonfiction writing, the topic and the main idea will be stated directly, often in a sentence at the very beginning or end of the text. When being tested on an understanding of the author's topic, the reader can quickly *skim* the passage for the general idea, stopping to read only the first sentence of each paragraph. A paragraph's first sentence is often (but not always) the main topic sentence, and it gives you a summary of the content of the paragraph. However, there are cases in which the reader must figure out an unstated topic or main idea. In these instances, the student must read every sentence of the text, and try to come up with an overarching idea that is supported by each of those sentences.

> **Review Video: Topics and Main Ideas**
> Visit mometrix.com/academy and enter code: 407801

While the main idea is the overall premise of a story, **supporting details** provide evidence and backing for the main point. In order to show that a main idea is correct, or valid, the author needs to add details that prove their point. All texts contain details, but they are only classified as supporting details when they serve to reinforce some larger point.

Supporting details are most commonly found in informative and persuasive texts. In some cases, they will be clearly indicated with words like *for example* or *for instance*, or they will be enumerated with words like *first*, *second*, and *last*. However, they may not be indicated with special words.

As a reader, it is important to consider whether the author's supporting details really back up his or her main point. Supporting details can be factual and correct but still not relevant to the author's point. Conversely, supporting details can seem pertinent but be ineffective because they are based on opinion or assertions that cannot be proven.

An example of a main idea is: "Giraffes live in the Serengeti of Africa." A supporting detail about giraffes could be: "A giraffe uses its long neck to reach twigs and leaves on trees." The main idea gives the general idea that the text is about giraffes. The supporting detail gives a specific fact about how the giraffes eat.

As opposed to a main idea, themes are seldom expressed directly in a text, so they can be difficult to identify. A **theme** is an issue, an idea, or a question raised by the text. For instance, a theme of William Shakespeare's *Hamlet* is indecision, as the title character explores his own psyche and the results of his failure to make bold choices. A great work of literature may have many themes, and the reader is justified in identifying any for which he or she can find support. One common characteristic of themes is that they raise more questions than they answer. In a good piece of fiction, the author is not always trying to convince the reader, but is instead trying to elevate the reader's perspective and encourage him to consider the themes more deeply. When reading, one can identify themes by constantly asking what general issues the text is addressing. A good way to evaluate an author's approach to a theme is to begin reading with a question in mind (for example, how does this text approach the theme of love?) and then look for evidence in the text that addresses that question.

PURPOSES FOR WRITING

In order to be an effective reader, one must pay attention to the author's **position** and purpose. Even those texts that seem objective and impartial, like textbooks, have some sort of position and bias. Readers need to take these positions into account when considering the author's message. When an author uses emotional language or clearly favors one side of an argument, his position is clear. However, the author's position may be evident not only in what he writes, but in what he doesn't write. For this reason, it is sometimes necessary to review some other texts on the same topic in order to develop a view of the author's position. If this is not possible, then it may be useful to acquire a little background personal information about the author. When the only source of information is the text, however, the reader should look for language and argumentation that seems to indicate a particular stance on the subject.

Identifying the **purpose** of an author is usually easier than identifying her position. In most cases, the author has no interest in hiding his or her purpose. A text that is meant to entertain, for instance, should be obviously written to please the reader. Most narratives, or stories, are written to entertain, though they may also inform or persuade. Informative texts are easy to identify as well. The most difficult purpose of a text to identify is persuasion, because the author has an interest in making this purpose hard to detect. When a person knows that the author is trying to convince him, he is automatically more wary and skeptical of the argument. For this reason, persuasive texts often try to establish an entertaining tone, hoping to amuse the reader into agreement, or an informative tone, hoping to create an appearance of authority and objectivity.

An author's purpose is often evident in the organization of the text. For instance, if the text has headings and subheadings, if key terms are in bold, and if the author makes his main idea clear from the beginning, then the likely purpose of the text is to inform. If the author begins by making a claim and then makes various arguments to support that claim, the purpose is probably to persuade. If the author is telling a story, or is more interested in holding the attention of the reader than in making a particular point or delivering information, then his purpose is most likely to entertain. As a reader, it is best to judge an author on how well he accomplishes his purpose. In other words, it is not entirely fair to complain that a textbook is boring: if the text is clear and easy to understand, then the author has done his job. Similarly, a storyteller should not be judged too harshly for getting some facts wrong, so long as he is able to give pleasure to the reader.

> **Review Video: Purpose**
> Visit mometrix.com/academy and enter code: 511819

The author's purpose for writing will affect his writing style and the response of the reader. In a **persuasive essay**, the author is attempting to change the reader's mind or convince him of something he did not believe previously. There are several identifying characteristics of persuasive writing. One is opinion presented as fact. When an author attempts to persuade the reader, he often presents his or her opinions as if they were fact. A reader must be on guard for statements that sound factual but which cannot be subjected to research, observation, or experiment. Another characteristic of persuasive writing is emotional language. An author will often try to play on the reader's emotion by appealing to his sympathy or sense of morality. When an author uses colorful or evocative language with the intent of arousing the reader's passions, it is likely that he is attempting to persuade. Finally, in many cases a persuasive text will give an unfair explanation of opposing positions, if these positions are mentioned at all.

An **informative text** is written to educate and enlighten the reader. Informative texts are almost always nonfiction, and are rarely structured as a story. The intention of an informative text is to deliver information in the most comprehensible way possible, so the structure of the text is likely to be very clear. In an informative text, the thesis statement is often in the first sentence. The author may use some colorful language, but is likely to put more emphasis on clarity and precision. Informative essays do not typically appeal to the emotions. They often contain facts and figures, and rarely include the opinion of the author. Sometimes a persuasive essay can resemble an informative essay, especially if the author maintains an even tone and presents his or her views as if they were established fact.

The success or failure of an author's intent to **entertain** is determined by those who read the author's work. Entertaining texts may be either fiction or nonfiction, and they may describe real or imagined people, places, and events. Entertaining texts are often narratives, or stories. A text that is written to entertain is likely to contain colorful language that engages the imagination and the emotions. Such writing often features a great deal of figurative language, which typically enlivens its subject matter with images and analogies. Though an entertaining text is not usually written to persuade or inform, it may accomplish both of these tasks. An entertaining text may appeal to the reader's emotions and cause him or her to think differently about a particular subject. In any case, entertaining texts tend to showcase the personality of the author more so than do other types of writing.

When an author intends to **express feelings,** she may use colorful and evocative language. An author may write emotionally for any number of reasons. Sometimes, the author will do so because she is describing a personal situation of great pain or happiness. Sometimes an author is attempting to persuade the reader, and so will use emotion to stir up the passions. It can be easy to identify this kind of expression when the writer uses phrases like *I felt* and *I sense*. However, sometimes the author will simply describe feelings without introducing them. As a reader, it is important to recognize when an author is expressing emotion, and not to become overwhelmed by sympathy or passion. A reader should maintain some detachment so that he or she can still evaluate the strength of the author's argument or the quality of the writing.

In a sense, almost all writing is descriptive, insofar as it seeks to describe events, ideas, or people to the reader. Some texts, however, are primarily concerned with **description**. A descriptive text focuses on a particular subject, and attempts to depict it in a way that will be clear to the reader. Descriptive texts contain many adjectives and adverbs, words that give shades of meaning and create a more detailed mental picture for the reader. A descriptive text fails when it is unclear or vague to the reader. On the other hand, however, a descriptive text that compiles too much detail can be boring and overwhelming to the reader. A descriptive text will certainly be informative, and it may be persuasive and entertaining as well. Descriptive writing is a challenge for the author, but when it is done well, it can be fun to read.

WRITING DEVICES

Authors will use different stylistic and writing devices to make their meaning more clearly understood. One of those devices is comparison and contrast. When an author describes the ways in which two things are alike, he or she is **comparing** them. When the author describes the ways in which two things are different, he or she is **contrasting** them. The "compare and contrast" essay is one of the most common forms in nonfiction. It is often signaled with certain words: a comparison may be indicated with such words as *both, same, like, too,* and *as well*; while a contrast may be indicated by words like *but, however, on the other hand, instead,* and *yet*. Of course, comparisons and contrasts may be implicit without using any such signaling language. A single sentence may both compare and contrast. Consider the sentence *Brian and Sheila love ice cream, but Brian prefers vanilla and Sheila prefers strawberry*. In one sentence, the author has described both a similarity (love of ice cream) and a difference (favorite flavor).

> **Review Video: Compare and Contrast**
> Visit mometrix.com/academy and enter code: 171799

One of the most common text structures is **cause and effect**. A cause is an act or event that makes something happen, and an effect is the thing that happens as a result of that cause. A cause-and-effect relationship is not always explicit, but there are some words in English that signal causality, such as *since, because,* and *as a result*. As an example, consider the sentence *Because the sky was clear, Ron did not bring an umbrella*. The cause is the clear sky, and the effect is that Ron did not bring an umbrella. However, sometimes the cause-and-effect relationship will not be clearly noted. For instance, the sentence *He was late and missed the meeting* does not contain any signaling words, but it still contains a cause (he was late) and an effect (he missed the meeting). It is possible for a single cause to have multiple effects, or for a single effect to have multiple causes. Also, an effect can in turn be the cause of another effect, in what is known as a cause-and-effect chain.

Authors often use analogies to add meaning to the text. An **analogy** is a comparison of two things. The words in the analogy are connected by a certain, often undetermined relationship. Look at this analogy: moo is to cow as quack is to duck. This analogy compares the sound that a cow makes with the sound that a duck makes. Even if the word 'quack' was not given, one could figure out it is the correct word to complete the analogy based on the relationship between the words 'moo' and 'cow'.

Some common relationships for analogies include synonyms, antonyms, part to whole, definition, and actor to action.

Another element that impacts a text is the author's point of view. The **point of view** of a text is the perspective from which it is told. The author will always have a point of view about a story before he draws up a plot line. The author will know what events they want to take place, how they want the characters to interact, and how the story will resolve. An author will also have an opinion on the topic, or series of events, which is presented in the story, based on their own prior experience and beliefs.

The two main points of view that authors use are first person and third person. If the narrator of the story is also the main character, or *protagonist*, the text is written in first-person point of view. In first person, the author writes with the word *I*. Third-person point of view is probably the most common point of view that authors use. Using third person, authors refer to each character using the words *he* or *she*. In third-person omniscient, the narrator is not a character in the story and tells the story of all of the characters at the same time.

> **Review Video: Point of View**
> Visit mometrix.com/academy and enter code: 383336

A good writer will use **transitional words** and phrases to guide the reader through the text. You are no doubt familiar with the common transitions, though you may never have considered how they operate. Some transitional phrases (*after, before, during, in the middle of*) give information about time. Some indicate that an example is about to be given (*for example, in fact, for instance*). Writers use them to compare (*also, likewise*) and contrast (*however, but, yet*). Transitional words and phrases can suggest addition (*and, also, furthermore, moreover*) and logical relationships (*if, then, therefore, as a result, since*). Finally, transitional words and phrases can demarcate the steps in a process (*first, second, last*). You should incorporate transitional words and phrases where they will orient your reader and illuminate the structure of your composition.

> **Review Video: Transitional Words and Phrases**
> Visit mometrix.com/academy and enter code: 197796

TYPES OF PASSAGES

A **narrative** passage is a story. Narratives can be fiction or nonfiction. However, there are a few elements that a text must have in order to be classified as a narrative. To begin with, the text must have a plot. That is, it must describe a series of events. If it is a good narrative, these events will be interesting and emotionally engaging to the reader. A narrative also has characters. These could be people, animals, or even inanimate objects, so long as they participate in the plot. A narrative passage often contains figurative language, which is meant to stimulate the imagination of the reader by making comparisons and observations. A metaphor, which is a description of one thing in terms of another, is a common piece of figurative language. *The moon was a frosty snowball* is an example of a metaphor: it is obviously untrue in the literal sense, but it suggests a certain mood for the reader. Narratives often proceed in a clear sequence, but they do not need to do so.

An **expository** passage aims to inform and enlighten the reader. It is nonfiction and usually centers around a simple, easily defined topic. Since the goal of exposition is to teach, such a passage should be as clear as possible. It is common for an expository passage to contain helpful organizing words, like *first, next, for example,* and *therefore*. These words keep the reader oriented in the text. Although expository passages do not need to feature colorful language and artful writing, they are often more effective when they do. For a reader, the challenge of expository passages is to maintain steady attention. Expository passages are not always about subjects in which a reader will naturally be interested, and the writer is often more concerned with clarity and comprehensibility than with engaging the reader. For this reason, many expository passages are dull. Making notes is a good way to maintain focus when reading an expository passage.

A **technical** passage is written to describe a complex object or process. Technical writing is common in medical and technological fields, in which complicated mathematical, scientific, and engineering ideas need to be explained simply and clearly. To ease comprehension, a technical passage usually proceeds in a very logical order. Technical passages often have clear headings and subheadings, which are used to keep the reader oriented in the text. It is also common for these passages to break sections up with numbers or letters. Many technical passages look more like an outline than a piece of prose. The amount of jargon or difficult vocabulary will vary in a technical passage depending on the intended audience. As much as possible, technical passages try to avoid language that the reader will have to research in order to understand the message. Of course, it is not always possible to avoid jargon.

A **persuasive** passage is meant to change the reader's mind or lead her into agreement with the author. The persuasive intent may be obvious, or it may be quite difficult to discern. In some cases, a persuasive passage will be indistinguishable from an informative passage: it will make an assertion and offer supporting details. However, a persuasive passage is more likely to make claims based on opinion and to appeal to the reader's emotions. Persuasive passages may not describe alternate positions and, when they do, they often display significant bias. It may be clear that a persuasive passage is giving the author's viewpoint, or the passage may adopt a seemingly objective tone. A persuasive passage is successful if it can make a convincing argument and win the trust of the reader.

A persuasive essay will likely focus on one central argument, but it may make many smaller claims along the way. These are subordinate arguments with which the reader must agree if he or she is going to agree with the central argument. The central argument will only be as strong as the subordinate claims. These claims should be rooted in fact and observation, rather than subjective judgment. The best persuasive essays provide enough supporting detail to justify claims without overwhelming the reader. Remember that a fact must be susceptible to independent verification: that is, it must be something the reader could confirm. Also, statistics are only effective when they take into account possible objections. For instance, a statistic on the number of foreclosed houses would only be useful if it was taken over a defined interval and in a defined area. Most readers are wary of statistics, because they are so often misleading. If possible, a persuasive essay should always include references so that the reader can obtain more information. Of course, this means that the writer's accuracy and fairness may be judged by the inquiring reader.

Opinions are formed by emotion as well as reason, and persuasive writers often appeal to the feelings of the reader. Although readers should always be skeptical of this technique, it is often used in a proper and ethical manner. For instance, there are many subjects that have an obvious emotional component, and therefore cannot be completely treated without an appeal to the emotions. Consider an article on drunk driving: it makes sense to include some specific examples that will alarm or sadden the reader. After all, drunk driving often has serious and tragic consequences. Emotional appeals are not appropriate, however, when they attempt to mislead the reader. For instance, in political advertisements it is common to emphasize the patriotism of the preferred candidate, because this will encourage the audience to link their own positive feelings about the country with their opinion of the candidate. However, these ads often imply that the other candidate is unpatriotic, which in most cases is far from the truth. Another common and improper emotional appeal is the use of loaded language, as for instance referring to an avidly religious person as a "fanatic" or a passionate environmentalist as a "tree hugger." These terms introduce an emotional component that detracts from the argument.

HISTORY AND CULTURE

Historical context has a profound influence on literature: the events, knowledge base, and assumptions of an author's time color every aspect of his or her work. Sometimes, authors hold opinions and use language that would be considered inappropriate or immoral in a modern setting, but that was acceptable in the author's time. As a reader, one should consider how the historical context influenced a work and also how today's opinions and ideas shape the way modern readers read the works of the past. For instance, in most societies of the past, women were treated as second-class citizens. An author who wrote in 18th-century England might sound sexist to modern readers, even if that author was relatively feminist in his time. Readers should not have to excuse the faulty assumptions and prejudices of the past, but they should appreciate that a person's thoughts and words are, in part, a result of the time and culture in which they live or lived, and it is perhaps unfair to expect writers to avoid all of the errors of their times.

Even a brief study of world literature suggests that writers from vastly different cultures address similar themes. For instance, works like the *Odyssey* and *Hamlet* both tackle the individual's battle for self-control and independence. In every culture, authors address themes of personal growth and the struggle for maturity. Another universal theme is the conflict between the individual and society. In works as culturally disparate as *Native Son*, the *Aeneid*, and *1984*, authors dramatize how people struggle to maintain their personalities and dignity in large, sometimes oppressive groups. Finally, many cultures have versions of the hero's (or heroine's) journey, in which an adventurous person must overcome many obstacles in order to gain greater knowledge, power, and perspective. Some famous works that treat this theme are the *Epic of Gilgamesh*, Dante's *Divine Comedy*, and *Don Quixote*.

Authors from different genres (for instance poetry, drama, novel, short story) and cultures may address similar themes, but they often do so quite differently. For instance, poets are likely to address subject matter obliquely, through the use of images and allusions. In a play, on the other hand, the author is more likely to dramatize themes by using characters to express opposing viewpoints. This disparity is known as a dialectical approach. In a novel, the author does not need to express themes directly; rather, they can be illustrated through events and actions. In some regional literatures, like those of Greece or England, authors use more irony: their works have characters that express views and make decisions that are clearly disapproved of by the author. In Latin America, there is a great tradition of using supernatural events to illustrate themes about real life. In China and Japan, authors frequently use well-established regional forms (haiku, for instance) to organize their treatment of universal themes.

RESPONDING TO LITERATURE

When reading good literature, the reader is moved to engage actively in the text. One part of being an active reader involves making predictions. A **prediction** is a guess about what will happen next. Readers are constantly making predictions based on what they have read and what they already know. Consider the following sentence: *Staring at the computer screen in shock, Kim blindly reached over for the brimming glass of water on the shelf to her side.* The sentence suggests that Kim is agitated and that she is not looking at the glass she is going to pick up, so a reader might predict that she is going to knock the glass over. Of course, not every prediction will be accurate: perhaps Kim will pick the glass up cleanly. Nevertheless, the author has certainly created the expectation

21

Copyright © Mometrix Media. You have been licensed one copy of this document for personal use only. Any other reproduction or redistribution is strictly prohibited. All rights reserved.

that the water might be spilled. Predictions are always subject to revision as the reader acquires more information.

Test-taking tip: To respond to questions requiring future predictions, the student's answers should be based on evidence of past or present behavior.

Readers are often required to understand text that claims and suggests ideas without stating them directly. An **inference** is a piece of information that is implied but not written outright by the author. For instance, consider the following sentence: *Mark made more money that week than he had in the previous year.* From this sentence, the reader can infer that Mark either has not made much money in the previous year or made a great deal of money that week.

Often, a reader can use information he or she already knows to make inferences. Take as an example the sentence *When his coffee arrived, he looked around the table for the silver cup.* Many people know that cream is typically served in a silver cup, so using their own base of knowledge they can infer that the subject of this sentence takes his coffee with cream. Making inferences requires concentration, attention, and practice.

> **Review Video: Inference**
> Visit mometrix.com/academy and enter code: 379203

Test-taking tip: While being tested on his ability to make correct inferences, the student must look for contextual clues. An answer can be *right* but not *correct*. The contextual clues will help you find the answer that is the best answer out of the given choices. Understand the context in which a phrase is stated. When asked for the implied meaning of a statement made in the passage, the student should immediately locate the statement and read the context in which it was made. Also, look for an answer choice that has a similar phrase to the statement in question.

A reader must be able to identify a text's **sequence**, or the order in which things happen. Often, and especially when the sequence is very important to the author, it is indicated with signal words like *first*, *then*, *next*, and *last*. However, sometimes a sequence is merely implied and must be noted by the reader. Consider the sentence *He walked in the front door and switched on the hall lamp.* Clearly, the man did not turn the lamp on before he walked in the door, so the implied sequence is that he first walked in the door and then turned on the lamp. Texts do not always proceed in an orderly sequence from first to last: sometimes, they begin at the end and then start over at the beginning. As a reader, it can be useful to make brief notes to clarify the sequence.

> **Review Video: Sequence**
> Visit mometrix.com/academy and enter code: 489027

In addition to inferring and predicting things about the text, the reader must often **draw conclusions** about the information he has read. When asked for a *conclusion* that may be drawn, look for critical "hedge" phrases, such as *likely*, *may*, *can*, *will often*, among many others. When you are being tested on this knowledge, remember that question writers insert these hedge phrases to cover every possibility. Often an answer will be wrong simply because it leaves no room for exception. Extreme positive or negative answers (such as always, never, etc.) are usually not correct. The reader should not use any outside knowledge that is not gathered from the reading passage to answer the related questions. Correct answers can be derived straight from the reading passage.

LITERARY GENRES

Literary genres refer to the basic generic types of poetry, drama, fiction, and nonfiction. Literary genre is a method of classifying and analyzing literature. There are numerous subdivisions within genre, including such categories as novels, novellas, and short stories in fiction. Drama may also be subdivided into comedy, tragedy, and many other categories. Poetry and nonfiction have their own distinct divisions.

Genres often overlap, and the distinctions among them are blurred, such as that between the nonfiction novel and docudrama, as well as many others. However, the use of genres is helpful to the reader as a set of understandings that guide our responses to a work.

The generic norm sets expectations and forms the framework within which we read and evaluate a work. This framework will guide both our understanding and interpretation of the work. It is a useful tool for both literary criticism and analysis.

Review Video: Literary Genres
Visit mometrix.com/academy and enter code: 587617

Fiction is a general term for any form of literary narrative that is invented or imagined rather than being factual. For those individuals who equate fact with truth, the imagined or invented character of fiction tends to render it relatively unimportant or trivial among the genres. Defenders of fiction are quick to point out that the fictional mode is an essential part of being. The ability to imagine or discuss what-if plots, characters, and events is clearly part of the human experience.

Prose is derived from the Latin and means "straightforward discourse." Prose fiction, although having many categories, may be divided into three main groups:

- **Short stories**: a fictional narrative, the length of which varies, usually under 20,000 words. Short stories usually have only a few characters and generally describe one major event or insight. The short story began in magazines in the late 1800s and has flourished ever since.
- **Novels**: a longer work of fiction, often containing a large cast of characters and extensive plotting. The emphasis may be on an event, action, social problems, or any experience. There is now a genre of nonfiction novels pioneered by Truman Capote's *In Cold Blood* in the 1960s. Novels may also be written in verse.
- **Novellas**: a work of narrative fiction longer than a short story but shorter than a novel. Novellas may also be called short novels or novelettes. They originated from the German tradition and have become common forms in all of the world's literature.

Many elements influence a work of prose fiction. Some important ones are:

- Speech and dialogue: Characters may speak for themselves or through the narrator. Dialogue may be realistic or fantastic, depending on the author's aim.
- Thoughts and mental processes: There may be internal dialogue used as a device for plot development or character understanding.
- Dramatic involvement: Some narrators encourage readers to become involved in the events of the story, whereas others attempt to distance readers through literary devices.
- Action: This is any information that advances the plot or involves new interactions between the characters.
- Duration: The time frame of the work may be long or short, and the relationship between described time and narrative time may vary.

- Setting and description: Is the setting critical to the plot or characters? How are the action scenes described?
- Themes: This is any point of view or topic given sustained attention.
- Symbolism: Authors often veil meanings through imagery and other literary constructions.

Fiction is much wider than simply prose fiction. Songs, ballads, epics, and narrative poems are examples of non-prose fiction. A full definition of fiction must include not only the work itself but also the framework in which it is read. Literary fiction can also be defined as not true rather than nonexistent, as many works of historical fiction refer to real people, places, and events that are treated imaginatively as if they were true. These imaginary elements enrich and broaden literary expression.

When analyzing fiction, it is important for the reader to look carefully at the work being studied. The plot or action of a narrative can become so entertaining that the language of the work is ignored. The language of fiction should not simply be a way to relate a plot—it should also yield many insights to the judicious reader. Some prose fiction is based on the reader's engagement with the language rather than the story. A studious reader will analyze the mode of expression as well as the narrative. Part of the reward of reading in this manner is to discover how the author uses different language to describe familiar objects, events, or emotions. Some works focus the reader on an author's unorthodox use of language, whereas others may emphasize characters or storylines. What happens in a story is not always the critical element in the work. This type of reading may be difficult at first but yields great rewards.

The **narrator** is a central part of any work of fiction, and can give insight about the purpose of the work and its main themes and ideas. The following are important questions to address to better understand the voice and role of the narrator and incorporate that voice into an overall understanding of the novel:

- Who is the narrator of the novel? What is the narrator's perspective, first person or third person? What is the role of the narrator in the plot? Are there changes in narrators or the perspective of narrators?
- Does the narrator explain things in the novel, or does meaning emerge from the plot and events? The personality of the narrator is important. She may have a vested interest in a character or event described. Some narratives follow the time sequence of the plot, whereas others do not. A narrator may express approval or disapproval about a character or events in the work.
- Tone is an important aspect of the narration. Who is actually being addressed by the narrator? Is the tone familiar or formal, intimate or impersonal? Does the vocabulary suggest clues about the narrator?

> **Review Video: The Narrator**
> Visit mometrix.com/academy and enter code: 742528

A **character** is a person intimately involved with the plot and development of the novel. Development of the novel's characters not only moves the story along but will also tell the reader a lot about the novel itself. There is usually a physical description of the character, but this is often omitted in modern and postmodern novels. These works may focus on the psychological state or motivation of the character. The choice of a character's name may give valuable clues to his role in the work.

Characters are said to be flat or round. Flat characters tend to be minor figures in the story, changing little or not at all. Round characters (those understood from a well-rounded view) are more central to the story and tend to change as the plot unfolds. Stock characters are similar to flat characters, filling out the story without influencing it.

Modern literature has been greatly affected by Freudian psychology, giving rise to such devices as the interior monologue and magical realism as methods of understanding characters in a work. These give the reader a more complex understanding of the inner lives of the characters and enrich the understanding of relationships between characters.

Another important genre is that of **drama**: a play written to be spoken aloud. The drama is in many ways inseparable from performance. Reading drama ideally involves using imagination to visualize and re-create the play with characters and settings. The reader stages the play in his imagination, watching characters interact and developments unfold. Sometimes this involves simulating a theatrical presentation; other times it involves imagining the events. In either case, the reader is imagining the unwritten to re-create the dramatic experience. Novels present some of the same problems, but a narrator will provide much more information about the setting, characters, inner dialogues, and many other supporting details. In drama, much of this is missing, and we are required to use our powers of projection and imagination to taste the full flavor of the dramatic work. There are many empty spaces in dramatic texts that must be filled by the reader to fully appreciate the work.

When reading drama in this way, there are some advantages over watching the play performed (though there is much criticism in this regard):

- Freedom of point of view and perspective: Text is free of interpretations of actors, directors, producers, and technical staging.
- Additional information: The text of a drama may be accompanied by notes or prefaces placing the work in a social or historical context. Stage directions may also provide relevant information about the author's purpose. None of this is typically available at live or filmed performances.
- Study and understanding: Difficult or obscure passages may be studied at leisure and supplemented by explanatory works. This is particularly true of older plays with unfamiliar language, which cannot be fully understood without an opportunity to study the material.

Critical elements of drama, especially when it is being read aloud or performed, include dialect, speech, and dialogue. Analysis of speech and dialogue is important in the critical study of drama. Some playwrights use speech to develop their characters. Speeches may be long or short, and written in as normal prose or blank verse. Some characters have a unique way of speaking which illuminates aspects of the drama. Emphasis and tone are both important, as well. Does the author make clear the tone in which lines are to be spoken, or is this open to interpretation? Sometimes there are various possibilities in tone with regard to delivering lines.

Dialect is any distinct variety of a language, especially one spoken in a region or part of a country. The criterion for distinguishing dialects from languages is that of mutual understanding. For example, people who speak Dutch cannot understand English unless they have learned it. But a speaker from Amsterdam can understand one from Antwerp; therefore, they speak different dialects of the same language. This is, however, a matter of degree; there are languages in which different dialects are unintelligible.

Dialect mixtures are the presence in one form of speech with elements from different neighboring dialects. The study of speech differences from one geographical area to another is called dialect geography. A dialect atlas is a map showing distribution of dialects in a given area. A dialect continuum shows a progressive shift in dialects across a territory, such that adjacent dialects are understandable, but those at the extremes are not.

Dramatic dialogue can be difficult to interpret and changes depending upon the tone used and which words are emphasized. Where the stresses, or meters, of dramatic dialogue fall can determine meaning. Variations in emphasis are only one factor in the manipulability of dramatic speech. Tone is of equal or greater importance and expresses a range of possible emotions and feelings that cannot be readily discerned from the script of a play. The reader must add tone to the words to understand the full meaning of a passage. Recognizing tone is a cumulative process as the reader begins to understand the characters and situations in the play. Other elements that influence the interpretation of dialogue include the setting, possible reactions of the characters to the speech, and possible gestures or facial expressions of the actor. There are no firm rules to guide the interpretation of dramatic speech. An open and flexible attitude is essential in interpreting dramatic dialogue.

Action is a crucial element in the production of a dramatic work. Many dramas contain little dialogue and much action. In these cases, it is essential for the reader to carefully study stage directions and visualize the action on the stage. Benefits of understanding stage directions include knowing which characters are on the stage at all times, who is speaking to whom, and following these patterns through changes of scene.

Stage directions also provide additional information, some of which is not available to a live audience. The nature of the physical space where the action occurs is vital, and stage directions help with this. The historical context of the period is important in understanding what the playwright was working with in terms of theaters and physical space. The type of staging possible for the author is a good guide to the spatial elements of a production.

Asides and soliloquies are devices that authors use in plot and character development. **Asides** indicate that not all characters are privy to the lines. This may be a method of advancing or explaining the plot in a subtle manner. **Soliloquies** are opportunities for character development, plot enhancement, and to give insight to characters' motives, feelings, and emotions. Careful study of these elements provides a reader with an abundance of clues to the major themes and plot of the work.

Art, music, and literature all interact in ways that contain many opportunities for the enrichment of all of the arts. Students could apply their knowledge of art and music by creating illustrations for a work or creating a musical score for a text. Students could discuss the meanings of texts and decide on their illustrations, or a score could amplify the meaning of the text.

Understanding the art and music of a period can make the experience of literature a richer, more rewarding experience. Students should be encouraged to use the knowledge of art and music to illuminate the text. Examining examples of dress, architecture, music, and dance of a period may be helpful in a fuller engagement of the text. Much of period literature lends itself to the analysis of the prevailing taste in art and music of an era, which helps place the literary work in a more meaningful context.

Informational Sources

Informational sources often come in short forms like a memo or recipe, or longer forms like books, magazines, or journals. These longer sources of information each have their own way of organizing information, but there are some similarities that the reader should be aware of.

Most books, magazines, and journals have a **table of contents** at the beginning. This helps the reader find the different parts of the book. The table of contents is usually found a page or two after the title page in a book, and on the first few pages of a magazine. However, many magazines now place the table of contents in the midst of an overabundance of advertisements, because they know readers will have to look at the ads as they search for the table. The standard orientation for a table of contents is the sections of the book listed along the left side, with the initial page number for each along the right. It is common in a book for the prefatory material (preface, introduction, etc.) to be numbered with Roman numerals. The contents are always listed in order from the beginning of the book to the end.

> **Review Video: Table of Contents**
> Visit mometrix.com/academy and enter code: 279693

A nonfiction book will also typically have an **index** at the end so that the reader can easily find information about particular topics. An index lists the topics in alphabetical order. The names of people are listed with the last name first. For example, *Adams, John* would come before *Washington, George*. To the right of the entry, the relevant page numbers are listed. When a topic is mentioned over several pages, the index will often connect these pages with a dash. For instance, if the subject is mentioned from pages 35 to 42 and again on 53, then the index entry will be labeled as *35-42, 53*. Some entries will have subsets, which are listed below the main entry, indented slightly, and placed in alphabetical order. This is common for subjects that are discussed frequently in the book. For instance, in a book about Elizabethan drama, William Shakespeare will likely be an important topic. Beneath Shakespeare's name in the index, there might be listings for *death of, dramatic works of, life of*, etc. These more specific entries help the reader refine his search.

> **Review Video: Index**
> Visit mometrix.com/academy and enter code: 836890

Many informative texts, especially textbooks, use **headings** and **subheadings** for organization. Headings and subheadings are typically printed in larger and bolder fonts, and are often in a different color than the main body of the text. Headings may be larger than subheadings. Also, headings and subheadings are not always complete sentences. A heading announces the topic that will be addressed in the text below. Headings are meant to alert the reader to what is about to come. Subheadings announce the topics of smaller sections within the entire section indicated by the heading. For instance, the heading of a section in a science textbook might be *AMPHIBIANS*, and within that section might be subheadings for *Frogs, Salamanders*, and *Newts*. Readers should always pay close attention to headings and subheadings, because they prime the brain for the information that is about to be delivered, and because they make it easy to go back and find particular details in a long text.

SOURCES OF INFORMATION

Books, journals, and magazines offer a lot of information to a reader at once. Other types of informational sources are targeted at a specific audience for a more limited purpose. One such type of informational source is the labeling of foods and medicines. The Food and Drug Administration has strict mandates for the information that must be included on these labels. For instance, a **food label** must list the corresponding food's number of calories, total fat, cholesterol, sodium, protein, and carbohydrates, among others. Also, a food label will usually contain a list of the vitamins that can be found in the product. Most importantly, a food label lists the serving size, which is the portion of the product for which the vitamin and nutrient values are true.

Some food manufacturers use odd serving sizes to make it look as if a product is healthier than it is. When making a comparison, one should always calculate the amount of nutrients per unit of measure (grams or fluid ounces, for example) to account for these serving size distortions.

Medicine labels contain a wealth of information that can be used to make comparisons and informed purchases. Every medicine label must have detailed and comprehensive instructions regarding dosage, including how much and how often the medicine should be taken. A label will also include warning information, and what to do in case of overdose or adverse reaction. Medicine labels will have a complete list of ingredients, but will isolate the active ingredients, which are those that accomplish the advertised purpose of the product. Often, generic versions of a medicine have the same active ingredients as more expensive name-brand versions. Finally, a label will specify when a medication should not be taken by certain people, like the elderly or pregnant women. When comparing medicines, it is important to isolate the most crucial information: dosage schedule, active ingredients, and counter-indications.

A slightly different type of informational source is a **memo**. Memos are generally short, official messages written by and for members of the same organization. They usually contain a plan of action, a request for information on a specific topic, or a response to such a request. There is a standard format for these documents. It is typical for there to be a heading at the top indicating the author, date, and recipient. In some cases, this heading will also include the author's title and the name of his or her institution. Below this information will be the body of the memo. Many memos are organized with numbers or bullet points, which make it easier for the reader to identify key ideas.

Announcements are another type of written communication that gives information to readers. People post announcements for all sorts of occasions. Many people are familiar with notices for lost pets, yard sales, and landscaping services. In order to be effective, these announcements need to contain all of the information the reader requires to act on the message. For instance, a lost pet announcement needs to include a good description of the animal and a contact number for the owner. A yard sale notice should include the address, date, and hours of the sale, as well as a brief description of the products that will be available there. When composing an announcement, it is important to consider the perspective of the audience: what will they need to know in order to respond to the message? Although a posted announcement should try to use color and decoration to attract the eye of the passerby, it must also convey the necessary information.

Classified advertisements, or **ads**, are used to sell or buy goods, to attract business, to make romantic connections, and to do countless other things. They are an inexpensive, and sometimes free, way to make a brief pitch. Classified ads used to be found only in newspapers or special advertising circulars, but there are now many famous online listings as well. The style of these ads has remained basically the same. An ad usually begins with a word or phrase indicating what is being sold or sought. Then, the listing will give a brief description of the product or service. Because space is limited and costly in newspapers, classified ads there will often contain abbreviations for common attributes.

For instance, two common abbreviations are *bk* for *black*, and *obo* for *or best offer*. Classified ads will then usually conclude by listing the price (or the amount the seeker is willing to pay), followed by contact information like a telephone number or email address.

A student must be able to find information in various sources. A **road atlas** is one such source that is designed specifically for drivers. It is a collection of maps that are useful for finding the distances between places, the correct roads and highways for reaching a given destination, and the relative positions of places in a certain geographic area. Most road atlases have a table at the beginning that illustrates the distance in miles between any two major cities. These tables are set up like a grid, with cities listed along the left and top sides. To find the distance between two places, follow the row of the first place perpendicular from the left until it intersects with the column of the second place. Some atlases have similar tables indicating the estimated travel time from one location to another.

Almost all maps contain a key, or legend, that defines the symbols used on the map for various landmarks. This key is usually placed in a corner of the map. It should contain listings for all of the important symbols on the map. Of course, these symbols will vary depending on the nature of the map. A road map uses different colored lines to indicate roads, highways, and interstates. A legend might also indicate the different dots and squares that are used to indicate towns of various sizes. The legend may contain information about the map's scale, though this may be elsewhere on the map. Many legends will contain special symbols, such as a picnic table indicating a campground.

Another source of information is the **card catalog**. Although rarely seen in the physical world anymore, card catalogs they still exist in most libraries in an online, digital format. These catalogs contain a wealth of information about the contents of the library. A typical card catalog entry contains the title, name of the author, year of publication, publisher, number of pages, and reference number in the Library of Congress. Most importantly, perhaps, card catalogs contain a brief summary of the book, so that a potential reader or researcher can get an idea of its contents. Many online card catalogs allow easy navigation to books on the same subject, by the same author, or close by on the library shelves. In any case, the card catalog entry will contain the library call number so that the researcher can find the book.

> **Review Video: Card Catalog**
> Visit mometrix.com/academy and enter code: 615004

An **owner's manual** is the appropriate source of information for a purchased product. An owner's manual is mainly devoted to the operation and maintenance of the product. It will often begin with a brief outline of the product's parts and method of operation. Most manuals will contain the products specifications: that is, the precise details about its components and features. For the most part, though, the owner's manual will be devoted to the routine repairs and care that a non-expert owner can be expected to provide. In the owner's manual for a car, for instance, there will be instructions for tasks like changing the oil, replacing windshield wipers, and presetting stations on the radio. An owner's manual is unlikely to contain instructions for complex repairs that require special equipment. Finally, the owner's manual will often detail the service warranty associated with the product.

The **Yellow Pages** of the phone book contain commercial listings for businesses that provide services to the general public. The listings are organized according to the type of service being offered: there are sections for florists, auto mechanics, and pizza restaurants. These categories are placed in alphabetical order, and within each category, the listings are in alphabetical order. A basic listing in the yellow pages will include the name of the business, the address, and the phone number. However, some merchants elect to pay extra and have large advertisements alongside their listing in the yellow pages. For instance, a restaurant might buy enough space to print their entire menu.

Sometimes informational and technical passages will require the reader to follow a set of directions. For many people, especially those who are tactile or visual learners, this can be a difficult process. It is important to approach a **set of directions** differently than other texts. First of all, it is a good idea to scan the directions to determine whether special equipment or preparations are needed. Sometimes in a recipe, for instance, the author fails to mention that the oven should be preheated first, and then halfway through the process, the cook is supposed to be baking. After briefly reading the directions, the reader should return to the first step. When following directions, it is appropriate to complete each step before moving on to the next. If this is not possible, it is useful at least to visualize each step before reading the next.

REFERENCE MATERIALS

Knowledge of reference materials such as dictionaries, encyclopedias, and manuals are vital for any reader. **Dictionaries** contain information about words. A standard dictionary entry begins with a pronunciation guide for the word. The entry will also give the word's part of speech: that is, whether it is a noun, verb, adjective, etc. A good dictionary will also include the word's origins, including the language from which it is derived and its meaning in that language. This information is known as the word's etymology.

> **Review Video: Dictionaries**
> Visit mometrix.com/academy and enter code: 897395

Dictionary entries are in alphabetical order. Many words have more than one definition, in which case the definitions will be numbered. Also, if a word can be used as different parts of speech, its various definitions in those different capacities may be separated. A sample entry might look like this:

WELL: (adverb) 1. in a good way (noun) 1. a hole drilled into the earth

The correct definition of a word will vary depending on how it is used in a sentence. When looking up a word found while reading, the best way to determine the relevant definition is to substitute the dictionary's definitions for the word in the text, and select the definition that seems most appropriate.

Encyclopedias used to be the best source for general information on a range of common subjects. Many people took pride in owning a set of encyclopedias, which were often written by top researchers. Now, encyclopedias largely exist online. Although they no longer have a preeminent place in general scholarship, these digital encyclopedias now often feature audio and video clips. A good encyclopedia remains the best place to obtain basic information about a well-known topic. There are also specialty encyclopedias that cover more obscure or expert information. For instance, there are many medical encyclopedias that contain the detail and sophistication required by doctors. For a regular person researching a subject like ostriches, Pennsylvania, or the Crimean War, an encyclopedia is a good source.

A **thesaurus** is a reference book that gives synonyms of words. It is different from a dictionary because a thesaurus does not give definitions, only lists of synonyms. A thesaurus can be helpful in finding the meaning of an unfamiliar word when reading. If the meaning of a synonym is known, then the meaning of the unfamiliar word will be known. The other time a thesaurus is helpful is when writing. Using a thesaurus helps authors to vary their word choice.

Review Video: Thesaurus
Visit mometrix.com/academy and enter code: 391773

A **database** is an informational source that has a different format than a publication or a memo. They are systems for storing and organizing large amounts of information. As personal computers have become more common and accessible, databases have become ever more present. The standard layout of a database is as a grid, with labels along the left side and the top. The horizontal rows and vertical columns that make up the grid are usually numbered or lettered, so that a particular square within the database might have a name like A3 or G5. Databases are good for storing information that can be expressed succinctly. They are most commonly used to store numerical data, but they also can be used to store the answers to yes-no questions and other brief data points. Information that is ambiguous (that is, has multiple possible meanings) or difficult to express in a few words is not appropriate for a database.

Often, a reader will come across a word that he does not recognize. The reader needs to know how to identify the definition of a word from its context. This means defining a word based on the words around it and the way it is used in a sentence. For instance, consider the following sentence: *The elderly scholar spent his evenings hunched over arcane texts that few other people even knew existed.* The adjective *arcane* is uncommon, but the reader can obtain significant information about it based on its use here. Based on the fact that few other people know of their existence, the reader can assume that arcane texts must be rare and only of interest to a few people. And, because they are being read by an elderly scholar, the reader can assume that they focus on difficult academic subjects. Sometimes, words can even be defined by what they are not. For instance, consider the following sentence: *Ron's fealty to his parents was not shared by Karen, who disobeyed their every command.* Because someone who disobeys is not demonstrating *fealty*, the word can be inferred to mean something like obedience or respect.

When conducting research, it is important to depend on reputable **primary sources**. A primary source is the documentary evidence closest to the subject being studied. For instance, the primary sources for an essay about penguins would be photographs and recordings of the birds, as well as accounts of people who have studied penguins in person. A secondary source would be a review of a movie about penguins or a book outlining the observations made by others. A primary source should be credible and, if it is on a subject that is still being explored, recent. One way to assess the credibility of a work is to see how often it is mentioned in other books and articles on the same subject. Just by reading the works cited and bibliographies of other books, one can get a sense of what are the acknowledged authorities in the field.

Review Video: Primary Sources
Visit mometrix.com/academy and enter code: 383328

The Internet was once considered a poor place to find sources for an essay or article, but its credibility has improved greatly over the years. Still, students need to exercise caution when performing research online. The best sources are those affiliated with established institutions, like universities, public libraries, and think tanks. Most newspapers are available online, and many of them allow the public to browse their archives. Magazines frequently offer similar services. When obtaining information from an unknown website, however, one must exercise considerably more caution. A website can be considered trustworthy if it is referenced by other sites that are known to be reputable. Also, credible sites tend to be properly maintained and frequently updated. A site is easier to trust when the author provides some information about him or herself, including some credentials that indicate expertise in the subject matter.

Critical Thinking Skills

OPINIONS, FACTS, & FALLACIES

Critical thinking skills are mastered through understanding various types of writing and the different purposes that authors have for writing the way they do. Every author writes for a purpose. Understanding that purpose, and how they accomplish their goal, will allow you to critique the writing and determine whether or not you agree with their conclusions.

Readers must always be conscious of the distinction between fact and opinion. A **fact** can be subjected to analysis and can be either proved or disproved. An **opinion**, on the other hand, is the author's personal feeling, which may not be alterable by research, evidence, or argument. If the author writes that the distance from New York to Boston is about two hundred miles, he is stating a fact. But if he writes that New York is too crowded, then he is giving an opinion, because there is no objective standard for overpopulation. An opinion may be indicated by words like *believe*, *think*, or *feel*. Also, an opinion may be supported by facts: for instance, the author might give the population density of New York as a reason for why it is overcrowded. An opinion supported by fact tends to be more convincing. When authors support their opinions with other opinions, the reader is unlikely to be moved.

Facts should be presented to the reader from reliable sources. An opinion is what the author thinks about a given topic. An opinion is not common knowledge or proven by expert sources, but it is information that the author believes and wants the reader to consider. To distinguish between fact and opinion, a reader needs to look at the type of source that is presenting information, what information backs-up a claim, and whether or not the author may be motivated to have a certain point of view on a given topic. For example, if a panel of scientists has conducted multiple studies on the effectiveness of taking a certain vitamin, the results are more likely to be factual than if a company selling a vitamin claims that taking the vitamin can produce positive effects. The company is motivated to sell its product, while the scientists are using the scientific method to prove a theory. If the author uses words such as "I think...", the statement is an opinion.

> **Review Video: Fact or Opinion**
> Visit mometrix.com/academy and enter code: 870899

In their attempt to persuade, writers often make mistakes in their thinking patterns and writing choices. It's important to understand these so you can make an informed decision. Every author has a point of view, but when an author ignores reasonable counterarguments or distorts opposing viewpoints, she is demonstrating a **bias**. A bias is evident whenever the author is unfair or inaccurate in his or her presentation. Bias may be intentional or unintentional, but it should always alert the reader to be skeptical of the argument being made. It should be noted that a biased author may still be correct. However, the author will be correct in spite of her bias, not because of it. A **stereotype** is like a bias, except that it is specifically applied to a group or place. Stereotyping is considered to be particularly abhorrent because it promotes negative generalizations about people. Many people are familiar with some of the hateful stereotypes of certain ethnic, religious, and cultural groups. Readers should be very wary of authors who stereotype. These faulty assumptions typically reveal the author's ignorance and lack of curiosity.

> **Review Video: Bias and Stereotype**
> Visit mometrix.com/academy and enter code: 644829

33

Sometimes, authors will **appeal to the reader's emotions** in an attempt to persuade or to distract the reader from the weakness of the argument. For instance, the author may try to inspire the pity of the reader by delivering a heart-rending story. An author also might use the bandwagon approach, in which he suggests that his opinion is correct because it is held by the majority. Some authors resort to name-calling, in which insults and harsh words are delivered to the opponent in an attempt to distract. In advertising, a common appeal is the testimonial, in which a famous person endorses a product. Of course, the fact that a celebrity likes something should not really mean anything to the reader. These and other emotional appeals are usually evidence of poor reasoning and a weak argument.

Review Video: <u>Appeal to Emotion</u>
Visit mometrix.com/academy and enter code: 163442

Certain *logical fallacies* are frequent in writing. A logical fallacy is a failure of reasoning. As a reader, it is important to recognize logical fallacies, because they diminish the value of the author's message. The four most common logical fallacies in writing are the false analogy, circular reasoning, false dichotomy, and overgeneralization. In a **false analogy**, the author suggests that two things are similar, when in fact they are different. This fallacy is often committed when the author is attempting to convince the reader that something unknown is like something relatively familiar. The author takes advantage of the reader's ignorance to make this false comparison. One example might be the following statement: *Failing to tip a waitress is like stealing money out of somebody's wallet.* Of course, failing to tip is very rude, especially when the service has been good, but people are not arrested for failing to tip as they would for stealing money from a wallet. To compare stingy diners with thieves is a false analogy.

Review Video: <u>False Analogy</u>
Visit mometrix.com/academy and enter code: 865045

Circular reasoning is one of the more difficult logical fallacies to identify, because it is typically hidden behind dense language and complicated sentences. Reasoning is described as circular when it offers no support for assertions other than restating them in different words. Put another way, a circular argument refers to itself as evidence of truth. A simple example of circular argument is when a person uses a word to define itself, such as saying *Niceness is the state of being nice.* If the reader does not know what *nice* means, then this definition will not be very useful. In a text, circular reasoning is usually more complex. For instance, an author might say *Poverty is a problem for society because it creates trouble for people throughout the community.* It is redundant to say that poverty is a problem because it creates trouble. When an author engages in circular reasoning, it is often because he or she has not fully thought out the argument, or cannot come up with any legitimate justifications.

Review Video: <u>Circular Reasoning</u>
Visit mometrix.com/academy and enter code: 398925

One of the most common logical fallacies is the **false dichotomy**, in which the author creates an artificial sense that there are only two possible alternatives in a situation. This fallacy is common when the author has an agenda and wants to give the impression that his view is the only sensible one. A false dichotomy has the effect of limiting the reader's options and imagination.

An example of a false dichotomy is the statement *You need to go to the party with me, otherwise you'll just be bored at home*. The speaker suggests that the only other possibility besides being at the party is being bored at home. But this is not true, as it is perfectly possible to be entertained at home, or even to go somewhere other than the party. Readers should always be wary of the false dichotomy: when an author limits alternatives, it is always wise to ask whether he is being valid.

> **Review Video: False Dichotomy**
> Visit mometrix.com/academy and enter code: 484397

Overgeneralization is a logical fallacy in which the author makes a claim that is so broad it cannot be proved or disproved. In most cases, overgeneralization occurs when the author wants to create an illusion of authority, or when he is using sensational language to sway the opinion of the reader. For instance, in the sentence *Everybody knows that she is a terrible teacher*, the author makes an assumption that cannot really be believed. This kind of statement is made when the author wants to create the illusion of consensus when none actually exists: it may be that most people have a negative view of the teacher, but to say that *everybody* feels that way is an exaggeration. When a reader spots overgeneralization, she should become skeptical about the argument that is being made, because an author will often try to hide a weak or unsupported assertion behind authoritative language.

> **Review Video: Overgeneralization**
> Visit mometrix.com/academy and enter code: 367357

Two other types of logical fallacies are **slippery slope** arguments and **hasty generalizations**. In a slippery slope argument, the author says that if something happens, it automatically means that something else will happen as a result, even though this may not be true. (i.e., just because you study hard does not mean you are going to ace the test). "Hasty generalization" is drawing a conclusion too early, without finishing analyzing the details of the argument. Writers of persuasive texts often use these techniques because they are very effective. In order to **identify logical fallacies**, readers need to read carefully and ask questions as they read. Thinking critically means not taking everything at face value. Readers need to critically evaluate an author's argument to make sure that the logic used is sound.

ORGANIZATION OF THE TEXT

The way a text is organized can help the reader to understand more clearly the author's intent and his conclusions. There are various ways to organize a text, and each one has its own purposes and uses.

Some nonfiction texts are organized to **present a problem** followed by a solution. In this type of text, it is common for the problem to be explained before the solution is offered. In some cases, as when the problem is well known, the solution may be briefly introduced at the beginning. The entire passage may focus on the solution, and the problem will be referenced only occasionally. Some texts will outline multiple solutions to a problem, leaving the reader to choose among them.

If the author has an interest or an allegiance to one solution, he may fail to mention or may describe inaccurately some of the other solutions. Readers should be careful of the author's agenda when

reading a problem-solution text. Only by understanding the author's point of view and interests can one develop a proper judgment of the proposed solution.

Authors need to organize information logically so the reader can follow it and locate information within the text. Two common organizational structures are cause and effect and chronological order. When using **chronological order**, the author presents information in the order that it happened. For example, biographies are written in chronological order; the subject's birth and childhood are presented first, followed by their adult life, and lastly by the events leading up to the person's death.

In **cause and effect**, an author presents one thing that makes something else happen. For example, if one were to go to bed very late, they would be tired. The cause is going to bed late, with the effect of being tired the next day.

It can be tricky to identify the cause-and-effect relationships in a text, but there are a few ways to approach this task. To begin with, these relationships are often signaled with certain terms. When an author uses words like *because, since, in order*, and *so*, she is likely describing a cause-and-effect relationship. Consider the sentence, "He called her because he needed the homework." This is a simple causal relationship, in which the cause was his need for the homework and the effect was his phone call. Not all cause-and-effect relationships are marked in this way, however. Consider the sentences, "He called her. He needed the homework." When the cause-and-effect relationship is not indicated with a keyword, it can be discovered by asking why something happened. He called her: why? The answer is in the next sentence: He needed the homework.

Persuasive essays, in which an author tries to make a convincing argument and change the reader's mind, usually include cause-and-effect relationships. However, these relationships should not always be taken at face value. An author frequently will assume a cause or take an effect for granted. To read a persuasive essay effectively, one needs to judge the cause-and-effect relationships the author is presenting. For instance, imagine an author wrote the following: "The parking deck has been unprofitable because people would prefer to ride their bikes." The relationship is clear: the cause is that people prefer to ride their bikes, and the effect is that the parking deck has been unprofitable. However, a reader should consider whether this argument is conclusive. Perhaps there are other reasons for the failure of the parking deck: a down economy, excessive fees, etc. Too often, authors present causal relationships as if they are fact rather than opinion. Readers should be on the alert for these dubious claims.

Thinking critically about ideas and conclusions can seem like a daunting task. One way to make it easier is to understand the basic elements of ideas and writing techniques. Looking at the way different ideas relate to each other can be a good way for the reader to begin his analysis. For instance, sometimes writers will write about two different ideas that are in opposition to each other. The analysis of these opposing ideas is known as **contrast**. Contrast is often marred by the author's obvious partiality to one of the ideas. A discerning reader will be put off by an author who does not engage in a fair fight. In an analysis of opposing ideas, both ideas should be presented in their clearest and most reasonable terms. If the author does prefer a side, he should avoid indicating this preference with pejorative language. An analysis of opposing ideas should proceed through the major differences point by point, with a full explanation of each side's view. For instance, in an analysis of capitalism and communism, it would be important to outline each side's view on labor, markets, prices, personal responsibility, etc. It would be less effective to describe the

36

theory of communism and then explain how capitalism has thrived in the West. An analysis of opposing views should present each side in the same manner.

Many texts follow the **compare-and-contrast** model, in which the similarities and differences between two ideas or things are explored. Analysis of the similarities between ideas is called comparison. In order for a comparison to work, the author must place the ideas or things in an equivalent structure. That is, the author must present the ideas in the same way. Imagine an author wanted to show the similarities between cricket and baseball. The correct way to do so would be to summarize the equipment and rules for each game. It would be incorrect to summarize the equipment of cricket and then lay out the history of baseball, since this would make it impossible for the reader to see the similarities. It is perhaps too obvious to say that an analysis of similar ideas should emphasize the similarities. Of course, the author should take care to include any differences that must be mentioned. Often, these small differences will only reinforce the more general similarity.

> **Review Video: Compare and Contrast**
> Visit mometrix.com/academy and enter code: 171799

DRAWING CONCLUSIONS

Authors should have a clear purpose in mind while writing. Especially when reading informational texts, it is important to understand the logical conclusion of the author's ideas. **Identifying this logical conclusion** can help the reader understand whether he agrees with the writer or not. Identifying a logical conclusion is much like making an inference: it requires the reader to combine the information given by the text with what he already knows to make a supportable assertion. If a passage is written well, then the conclusion should be obvious even when it is unstated. If the author intends the reader to draw a certain conclusion, then all of his argumentation and detail should be leading toward it. One way to approach the task of drawing conclusions is to make brief notes of all the points made by the author. When these are arranged on paper, they may clarify the logical conclusion. Another way to approach conclusions is to consider whether the reasoning of the author raises any pertinent questions. Sometimes it will be possible to draw several conclusions from a passage, and on occasion these will be conclusions that were never imagined by the author. It is essential, however, that these conclusions be supported directly by the text.

> **Review Video: Identifying Logical Conclusions**
> Visit mometrix.com/academy and enter code: 281653

The term **text evidence** refers to information that supports a main point or points in a story, and can help lead the reader to a conclusion. Information used as *text evidence* is precise, descriptive, and factual. A main point is often followed by supporting details that provide evidence to back-up a claim. For example, a story may include the claim that winter occurs during opposite months in the Northern and Southern hemispheres. *Text evidence* based on this claim may include countries where winter occurs in opposite months, along with reasons that winter occurs at different times of the year in separate hemispheres (due to the tilt of the Earth as it rotates around the sun).

> **Review Video: Text Evidence**
> Visit mometrix.com/academy and enter code: 486236

Readers interpret text and respond to it in a number of ways. Using textual support helps defend your response or interpretation because it roots your thinking in the text. You are interpreting based on information in the text and not simply your own ideas. When crafting a response, look for important quotes and details from the text to help bolster your argument. If you are writing about a character's personality trait, for example, use details from the text to show that the character acted in such a way. You can also include statistics and facts from a nonfiction text to strengthen your response. For example, instead of writing, "A lot of people use cell phones," use statistics to provide the exact number. This strengthens your argument because it is more precise.

The text used to support an argument can be the argument's downfall if it is not credible. A text is **credible**, or believable, when the author is knowledgeable and objective, or unbiased. The author's motivations for writing the text play a critical role in determining the credibility of the text and must be evaluated when assessing that credibility. The author's motives should be for the dissemination of information. The purpose of the text should be to inform or describe, not to persuade. When an author writes a persuasive text, he has the motivation that the reader will do what they want. The extent of the author's knowledge of the topic and their motivation must be evaluated when assessing the credibility of a text. Reports written about the Ozone layer by an environmental scientist and a hairdresser will have a different level of credibility.

> **Review Video: Credible**
> Visit mometrix.com/academy and enter code: 827257

After determining your own opinion and evaluating the credibility of your supporting text, it is sometimes necessary to communicate your ideas and findings to others. When **writing a response to a text**, it is important to use elements of the text to support your assertion or defend your position. Using supporting evidence from the text strengthens the argument because the reader can see how in depth the writer read the original piece and based their response on the details and facts within that text. Elements of text that can be used in a response include: facts, details, statistics, and direct quotations from the text. When writing a response, one must make sure they indicate which information comes from the original text and then base their discussion, argument, or defense around this information.

> **Review Video: Writing a Response to the Text**
> Visit mometrix.com/academy and enter code: 185093

A reader should always be drawing conclusions from the text. Sometimes conclusions are implied from written information, and other times the information is **stated directly** within the passage. It is always more comfortable to draw conclusions from information stated within a passage, rather than to draw them from mere implications. At times an author may provide some information and then describe a counterargument. The reader should be alert for direct statements that are subsequently rejected or weakened by the author. The reader should always read the entire passage before drawing conclusions. Many readers are trained to expect the author's conclusions at either the beginning or the end of the passage, but many texts do not adhere to this format.

> **Review Video: Conclusions that are Stated Directly**
> Visit mometrix.com/academy and enter code: 851825

Drawing conclusions from information implied within a passage requires confidence on the part of the reader. **Implications** are things the author does not state directly, but which can be assumed based on what the author does say. For instance, consider the following simple passage: "I stepped outside and opened my umbrella. By the time I got to work, the cuffs of my pants were soaked." The author never states that it is raining, but this fact is clearly implied. Conclusions based on implication must be well supported by the text. In order to draw a solid conclusion, a reader should have multiple pieces of evidence, or, if he only has one, must be assured that there is no other possible explanation than his conclusion. A good reader will be able to draw many conclusions from information implied by the text, which enriches the reading experience considerably.

As an aid to drawing conclusions, the reader should be adept at **outlining** the information contained in the passage; an effective outline will reveal the structure of the passage, and will lead to solid conclusions. An effective outline will have a title that refers to the basic subject of the text, though it need not recapitulate the main idea. In most outlines, the main idea will be the first major section. It will have each major idea of the passage established as the head of a category. For instance, the most common outline format calls for the main ideas of the passage to be indicated with Roman numerals. In an effective outline of this kind, each of the main ideas will be represented by a Roman numeral and none of the Roman numerals will designate minor details or secondary ideas. Moreover, all supporting ideas and details should be placed in the appropriate place on the outline. An outline does not need to include every detail listed in the text, but it should feature all of those that are central to the argument or message. Each of these details should be listed under the appropriate main idea.

Review Video: Outlining
Visit mometrix.com/academy and enter code: 584445

It is also helpful to **summarize** the information you have read in a paragraph or passage format. This process is similar to creating an effective outline. To begin with, a summary should accurately define the main idea of the passage, though it does not need to explain this main idea in exhaustive detail. It should continue by laying out the most important supporting details or arguments from the passage. All of the significant supporting details should be included, and none of the details included should be irrelevant or insignificant. Also, the summary should accurately report all of these details. Too often, the desire for brevity in a summary leads to the sacrifice of clarity or veracity. Summaries are often difficult to read, because they omit all of graceful language, digressions, and asides that distinguish great writing. However, if the summary is effective, it should contain much the same message as the original text.

Review Video: Summarizing Text
Visit mometrix.com/academy and enter code: 172903

Paraphrasing is another method the reader can use to aid in comprehension. When paraphrasing, one puts what they have read into their own words, rephrasing what the author has written to make it their own, to "translate" all of what the author says to their own words, including as many details as they can.

Writing

The Extended Response portions of the GED will appear in both the Reasoning Through Language Arts section and the Social Studies section. In both cases, a topic will be introduced through one or more reading passages, often presenting two opposing viewpoints or perspectives about the topic. You will be asked to analyze the topic and the arguments presented, and explain and defend your opinion of the topic, using evidence from the presented text. There is no single "correct" answer to the topics; rather, you will be graded based on your ability to articulate and defend your position

BRAINSTORM

Spend the first three to five minutes brainstorming out ideas. Write down any ideas you might have on the topic. The purpose is to extract from the recesses of your memory any relevant information. In this stage, anything goes down. Write down any idea, regardless of how good it may initially seem. You can use either the scratch paper provided to quickly jot down your thoughts and ideas.

STRENGTH THROUGH DIVERSITY

The best papers will contain diversity of examples and reasoning. As you brainstorm consider different perspectives. Not only are there two sides to every topic, but there are also countless perspectives that can be considered. On any topic, different groups are impacted, with many reaching the same conclusion or position, but through vastly different paths. Try to "see" the topic through as many different eyes as you can. Look at it from every angle and from every vantage point. The more diverse the reasoning used, the more balanced the paper will become and the better the score.

Example:

The topic of free trade is not just two sided. It impacts politicians, domestic (US) manufacturers, foreign manufacturers, the US economy, the world economy, strategic alliances, retailers, wholesalers, consumers, unions, workers, and the exchange of more than just goods, but also of ideas, beliefs, and cultures. The more of these angles that you can approach the topic from, the more solid your reasoning and the stronger your position.

Furthermore, don't just use information as to how the topic impacts other people. Draw liberally from your own experience and your own observations. Explain a personal experience that you have had and your own emotions from that moment. Anything that you've seen in your community or observed in society can be expanded upon to further round out your position on the topic.

Once you have finished with your creative flow, stop and review it. Which idea allowed you to come up with the most supporting information? It's extremely important that you pick an angle that will allow you to have a thorough and comprehensive coverage of the topic. This is not about your personal convictions, but about writing a concise rational discussion of an idea.

Every garden of ideas gets weeds in it. The ideas that you brainstormed over are going to be random pieces of information of mixed value. Go through it methodically and pick out the ones that are the best. The best ideas are strong points that it will be easy to write a few sentences or a paragraph about.

Now that you know which ideas you are going to use and focus upon, organize them. Put your writing points in a logical order. You have your main ideas that you will focus on, and must align them in a sequence that will flow in a smooth, sensible path from point to point, so that the reader

will go smoothly from one idea to the next in a logical path. Readers must have a sense of continuity as they read your paper. You don't want to have a paper that rambles back and forth.

START YOUR ENGINES

You have a logical flow of main ideas with which to start writing. Begin expanding on the topics in the sequence that you have set for yourself. Pace yourself. Don't spend too much time on any one of the ideas that you are expanding upon. You want to have time for all of them. Make sure you watch your time. If you have twenty minutes left to write out your ideas and you have ten ideas, then you can only use two minutes per idea. It can be a daunting task to cram a lot of information down in words in a short amount of time, but if you pace yourself, you can get through it all. If you find that you are falling behind, speed up. Move through each idea more quickly, spending less time to expand upon the idea in order to catch back up.

Once you finish expanding on each idea, go back to your brainstorming session up above, where you wrote out your ideas. Go ahead and scratch through the ideas as you write about them. This will let you see what you need to write about next, and also allow you to pace yourself and see what you have left to cover.

Your first paragraph should have several easily identifiable features.

- First, it should have a quick description or paraphrasing of the topic. Use your own words to briefly explain what the topic is about.
- Second, you should explain your opinion of the topic and give an explanation of why you feel that way. What is your decision or conclusion on the topic?
- Third, you should list your "writing points". What are the main ideas that you came up with earlier? This is your opportunity to outline the rest of your paper. Have a sentence explaining each idea that you will go intend further depth in additional paragraphs. If someone was to only read this paragraph, they should be able to get a good summary of the entire paper.

Each of your successive paragraphs should expand upon one of the points listed in the main paragraph. Use your personal experience and knowledge to support each of your points. Examples should back up everything.

Once you have finished expanding upon each of your main points, wrap it up. Summarize what you have said and covered in a conclusion paragraph. Explain once more your opinion of the topic and quickly review why you feel that way. At this stage, you have already backed up your statements, so there is no need to do that again. All you are doing is refreshing in the mind of the reader the main points that you have made.

DON'T PANIC

Panicking will not put down any more words on paper for you. Therefore, it isn't helpful. When you first see the topic, if your mind goes as blank as the page on which you have to write out your paper, take a deep breath. Force yourself to mechanically go through the steps listed above.

Secondly, don't get clock fever. It's easy to be overwhelmed when you're looking at a page that doesn't seem to have much text, there is a lot of blank space further down, your mind is full of random thoughts and feeling confused, and the clock is ticking down faster than you would like. You brainstormed first so that you don't have to keep coming up with ideas. If you're running out of time and you have a lot of ideas that you haven't expanded upon, don't be afraid to make some cuts.

Start picking the best ideas that you have left and expand on those few. Don't feel like you have to write down and expand all of your ideas.

It is more important to have a shorter paper that is well written and well organized, than a longer paper that is poorly written and poorly organized. Don't keep writing about a subject just to add words and sentences, and certainly don't start repeating yourself. The goal is 250 words. That is your target, but don't mess up your paper in an effort to get exactly 250 words. You want to have a natural end to your work, without having to cut it short. If it is a little long, that isn't a problem as long as it flows. Remember to expand on the ideas that you identified in the brainstorming session and make sure that you save yourself a few minutes at the end to go back and check your work.

Leave time at the end, at least three minutes, to go back and check over your work. Reread and make sure that everything you've written makes sense and flows. Clean up any spelling or grammar mistakes that you might have made. Also, go ahead and erase any brainstorming ideas that you weren't able to expand upon and clean up any other extraneous information that you might have written that doesn't fit into your paper.

As you proofread, make sure there aren't any fragments or run-ons. Check for sentences that are too short or too long. If the sentence is too short, look to see if you have an identifiable subject and verb. If it is too long, break it up into two separate sentences. Watch out for any "big words" you may have used. It's good to use difficult vocabulary words, but only if you are positive that you are using them correctly. Your paper has to be correct; it doesn't have to be fancy. You're not trying to impress anyone with your vocabulary, just your ability to develop and express ideas.

FINAL NOTE

Depending on your test taking preferences and personality, the essay writing will probably be your hardest or your easiest section. You are required to go through the entire process of writing a paper in 45 minutes or less, which can be quite a challenge.

Focus upon each of the steps listed above. Go through the process of creative flow first, generating ideas and thoughts about the topic. Then organize those ideas into a smooth logical flow. Pick out the ones that are best from the list you have created. Decide which main idea or angle of the topic you will discuss.

Create a recognizable structure in your paper, with an introductory paragraph explaining what you have decided upon, and what your main points will be. Use the body paragraphs to expand on those main points and have a conclusion that wraps up the topic.

Save a few moments to go back and review what you have written. Clean up any minor mistakes that you might have had and give it those last few critical touches that can make a huge difference. Finally, be proud and confident of what you have written!

Language and Usage

PUNCTUATION

If a section of text has an opening dash, parentheses, or comma at the beginning of a phrase, then you can be sure there should be a matching closing dash, parentheses, or comma at the end of the phrase. If items in a series all have commas between them, then any additional items in that series will also gain commas. Do not alternate punctuation. If a dash is at the beginning of a statement, then do not put a parenthesis at the ending of the statement.

WORD CONFUSION

"Which" should be used to refer to things only.

John's dog, which was called Max, is large and fierce.

"That" may be used to refer to either persons or things.

Is this the only book that Louis L'Amour wrote?

Is Louis L'Amour the author that [or who] wrote Western novels?

"Who" should be used to refer to persons only.

Mozart was the composer who [or that] wrote those operas.

PRONOUN USAGE

To determine the correct pronoun form in a compound subject, try each subject separately with the verb, adapting the form as necessary. Your ear will tell you which form is correct.

Example: Bob and (I, me) will be going.

Restate the sentence twice, using each subject individually. Bob will be going. I will be going. "Me will be going" does not make sense.

When a pronoun is used with a noun immediately following (as in "we boys"), say the sentence without the added noun. Your ear will tell you the correct pronoun form.

Example: (We/Us) boys played football last year.

Restate the sentence twice, without the noun. We played football last year. Us played football last year. Clearly "We played football last year" makes more sense.

> **Review Video: Pronoun Usage**
> Visit mometrix.com/academy and enter code: 666500

COMMAS

FLOW

Commas break the flow of text. To test whether they are necessary, while reading the text to yourself, pause for a moment at each comma. If the pauses seem natural, then the commas are correct. If they are not, then the commas are not correct.

NONESSENTIAL CLAUSES AND PHRASES

A comma should be used to set off nonessential clauses and nonessential participial phrases from the rest of the sentence. To determine if a clause is essential, remove it from the sentence. If the removal of the clause would alter the meaning of the sentence, then it is essential. Otherwise, it is nonessential.

Example: John Smith, who was a disciple of Andrew Collins, was a noted archeologist.

In the example above, the sentence describes John Smith's fame in archeology. The fact that he was a disciple of Andrew Collins is not necessary to that meaning. Therefore, separating it from the rest of the sentence with commas, is correct.

Do not use a comma if the clause or phrase is essential to the meaning of the sentence.

Example: Anyone who appreciates obscure French poetry will enjoy reading the book.

If the phrase "who appreciates obscure French poetry" is removed, the sentence would indicate that anyone would enjoy reading the book, not just those with an appreciation for obscure French poetry. However, the sentence implies that the book's enjoyment may not be for everyone, so the phrase is essential.

Another perhaps easier way to determine if the clause is essential is to see if it has a comma at its beginning or end. Consistent, parallel punctuation must be used, and so if you can determine a comma exists at one side of the clause, then you can be certain that a comma should exist on the opposite side.

INDEPENDENT CLAUSES

Use a comma before the words and, but, or, nor, for, yet when they join independent clauses. To determine if two clauses are independent, remove the word that joins them. If the two clauses are capable of being their own sentence by themselves, then they are independent and need a comma between them.

Example: He ran down the street, and then he ran over the bridge.

He ran down the street. Then he ran over the bridge. These are both clauses capable of being their own sentence. Therefore, a comma must be used along with the word "and" to join the two clauses together.

If one or more of the clauses would be a fragment if left alone, then it must be joined to another clause and does not need a comma between them.

Example: He ran down the street and over the bridge.

He ran down the street. Over the bridge. "Over the bridge" is a sentence fragment and is not capable of existing on its own. No comma is necessary to join it with "He ran down the street". Note that this does not cover the use of "and" when separating items in a series, such as "red, white, and blue". In these cases, a comma is not always necessary between the last two items in the series, but in general it is best to use one.

PARENTHETICAL EXPRESSIONS

Commas should separate parenthetical expressions such as the following: after all, by the way, for example, in fact, on the other hand.

Example: By the way, she is in my biology class.

If the parenthetical expression is in the middle of the sentence, a comma would be both before and after it.

Example: She is, after all, in my biology class.

However, these expressions are not always used parenthetically. In these cases, commas are not used. To determine if an expression is parenthetical, see if it would need a pause if you were reading the text. If it does, then it is parenthetical and needs commas.

Example: You can tell by the way she plays the violin that she enjoys its music.

No pause is necessary in reading that example sentence. Therefore, the phrase "by the way" does not need commas around it.

HYPHENS

Hyphenate a compound adjective that is directly before the noun it describes.

Example 1: He was the best-known kid in the school.

Example 2: The shot came from that grass-covered hill.

Example 3: The well-drained fields were dry soon after the rain.

SEMICOLONS

PERIOD REPLACEMENT

A semicolon is often described as either a weak period or strong comma. Semicolons should separate independent clauses that could stand alone as separate sentences. To test where a semicolon should go, replace it with a period in your mind. If the two independent clauses would seem normal with the period, then the semicolon is in the right place.

Example: The rain had finally stopped; a few rays of sunshine were pushing their way through the clouds.

The rain had finally stopped. A few rays of sunshine were pushing their way through the clouds. These two sentences can exist independently with a period between them. Because they are also closely related in thought, a semicolon is a good choice to combine them.

TRANSITIONS

When a semicolon is next to a transition word, such as "however", it comes before the word.

Example: The man in the red shirt stood next to her; however, he did not know her name.

If these two clauses were separated with a period, the period would go before the word "however" creating the following two sentences: The man in the red shirt stood next to her. However, he did not know her name. The semicolon can function as a weak period and join the two clauses by replacing the period.

SENTENCE CORRECTION

Each question includes a sentence with part or all of it underlined. Your five answer choices will offer different ways to reword or rephrase the underlined portion of the sentence.

45

These questions will test your ability of correct and effective expression. Choose your answer carefully, utilizing the standards of written English, including grammar rules, the proper choice of words and of sentence construction. The correct answer will flow smoothly and be both clear and concise.

USE YOUR EAR

Read each sentence carefully, inserting the answer choices in the blanks. Don't stop at the first answer choice if you think it is right, but read them all. What may seem like the best choice, at first, may not be after you have had time to read all of the choices. Allow your ear to determine what sounds right. Often one or two answer choices can be immediately ruled out because it doesn't make sound logical or make sense.

CONTEXTUAL CLUES

It bears repeating that contextual clues offer a lot of help in determining the best answer. Key words in the sentence will allow you to determine exactly which answer choice is the best replacement text.

Example:

Archeology has shown that some of the ruins of the ancient city of Babylon are approximately 500 years <u>as old as any supposed</u> Mesopotamian predecessors.

1. as old as their supposed
2. older than their supposed

In this example, the key word "supposed" is used. Archaeology would either confirm that the predecessors to Babylon were more ancient or disprove that supposition. Since supposed was used, it would imply that archaeology had disproved the accepted belief, making Babylon actually older, not as old as, and answer choice 2 correct.

Furthermore, because "500 years" is used, answer choice 1 can be ruled out. Years are used to show either absolute or relative age. If two objects are as old as each other, no years are necessary to describe that relationship, and it would be sufficient to say, "The ancient city of Babylon is approximately as old as their supposed Mesopotamian predecessors," without using the term "500 years".

SIMPLICITY IS BLISS

Simplicity cannot be overstated. You should never choose a longer, more complicated, or wordier replacement if a simple one will do. When a point can be made with fewer words, choose that answer. However, never sacrifice the flow of text for simplicity. If an answer is simple, but does not make sense, then it is not correct.

Beware of added phrases that don't add anything of meaning, such as "to be" or "as to them". Often these added phrases will occur just before a colon, which may come before a list of items. However, the colon does not need a lengthy introduction.

The phrases "of which [...] are" in the below examples are wordy and unnecessary. They should be removed and the colon placed directly after the words "sport" and "following".

Example 1: There are many advantages to running as a sport, of which the top advantages are:

Example 2: The school supplies necessary were the following, of which a few are:

Mathematical Reasoning

Number Operations/Number Sense

NUMBERS AND THEIR CLASSIFICATIONS

Numbers are the basic building blocks of mathematics. Specific features of numbers are identified by the following terms:

Integers – The set of positive and negative numbers, including zero. Integers do not include fractions $\left(\frac{1}{3}\right)$, decimals (0.56), or mixed numbers $\left(7\frac{3}{4}\right)$.

Even number – Any integer that can be divided by 2 without leaving a remainder. For example: 2, 4, 6, 8, and so on.

Odd number – Any integer that cannot be divided evenly by 2. For example: 3, 5, 7, 9, and so on.

Decimal number – a number that uses a decimal point to show the part of the number that is less than one. Example: 1.234.

Decimal point – a symbol used to separate the ones place from the tenths place in decimals or dollars from cents in currency.

Decimal place – the position of a number to the right of the decimal point. In the decimal 0.123, the 1 is in the first place to the right of the decimal point, indicating tenths; the 2 is in the second place, indicating hundredths; and the 3 is in the third place, indicating thousandths.

The decimal, or base 10, system is a number system that uses ten different digits (0, 1, 2, 3, 4, 5, 6, 7, 8, 9). An example of a number system that uses something other than ten digits is the binary, or base 2, number system, used by computers, which uses only the numbers 0 and 1. It is thought that the decimal system originated because people had only their 10 fingers for counting.

> **Review Video: Numbers and Their Classifications**
> Visit mometrix.com/academy and enter code: 461071

OPERATIONS

There are four basic mathematical operations:

Addition increases the value of one quantity by the value of another quantity. Example: 2 + 4 = 6; 8 + 9 = 17. The result is called the sum. With addition, the order does not matter. 4 + 2 = 2 + 4.

Subtraction is the opposite operation to addition; it decreases the value of one quantity by the value of another quantity. Example: 6 – 4 = 2; 17 – 8 = 9. The result is called the difference. Note that with subtraction, the order does matter. 6 – 4 ≠ 4 – 6.

Multiplication can be thought of as repeated addition. One number tells how many times to add the other number to itself. Example: 3 × 2 (three times two) = 2 + 2 + 2 = 6. With multiplication, the order does not matter. 2 × 3 (or 3 + 3) = 3 × 2 (or 2 + 2 + 2).

47

Division is the opposite operation to multiplication; one number tells us how many parts to divide the other number into. Example: 20 ÷ 4 = 5; if 20 is split into 4 equal parts, each part is 5. With division, the order of the numbers does matter. 20 ÷ 4 ≠ 4 ÷ 20.

An exponent is a superscript number placed next to another number at the top right. It indicates how many times the base number is to be multiplied by itself. Exponents provide a shorthand way to write what would be a longer mathematical expression. Example: $a^2 = a \times a$; $2^4 = 2 \times 2 \times 2 \times 2$. A number with an exponent of 2 is said to be "squared," while a number with an exponent of 3 is said to be "cubed." The value of a number raised to an exponent is called its power. So, 8^4 is read as "8 to the 4th power," or "8 raised to the power of 4." A negative exponent is the same as the reciprocal of a positive exponent. Example: $a^{-2} = 1/a^2$.

Parentheses are used to designate which operations should be done first when there are multiple operations. Example: 4 − (2 + 1) = 1; the parentheses tell us that we must add 2 and 1, and then subtract the sum from 4, rather than subtracting 2 from 4 and then adding 1 (this would give us an answer of 3).

Order of Operations is a set of rules that dictates the order in which we must perform each operation in an expression so that we will evaluate it accurately. If we have an expression that includes multiple different operations, Order of Operations tells us which operations to do first. The most common mnemonic for Order of Operations is PEMDAS, or "Please Excuse My Dear Aunt Sally." PEMDAS stands for Parentheses, Exponents, Multiplication, Division, Addition, Subtraction. It is important to understand that multiplication and division have equal precedence, as do addition and subtraction, so those pairs of operations are simply worked from left to right in order.

Example: Evaluate the expression $5 + 20 \div 4 \times (2 + 3)^2 - 6$ using the correct order of operations.

P: Perform the operations inside the parentheses, (2 + 3) = 5.

E: Simplify the exponents, $(5)^2 = 25$.

The equation now looks like this: 5 + 20 ÷ 4 × 25 − 6.

MD: Perform multiplication and division from left to right, 20 ÷ 4 = 5; then 5 × 25 = 125.

The equation now looks like this: 5 + 125 − 6.

AS: Perform addition and subtraction from left to right, 5 + 125 = 130; then 130 − 6 = 124.

Review Video: Order of Operations
Visit mometrix.com/academy and enter code: 259675

The laws of exponents are as follows:

1. Any number to the power of 1 is equal to itself: $a^1 = a$.
2. The number 1 raised to any power is equal to 1: $1^n = 1$.
3. Any number raised to the power of 0 is equal to 1: $a^0 = 1$.
4. Add exponents to multiply powers of the same base number: $a^n \times a^m = a^{n+m}$.
5. Subtract exponents to divide powers of the same number; that is $a^n \div a^m = a^{n-m}$.
6. Multiply exponents to raise a power to a power: $(a^n)^m = a^{n \times m}$.

7. If multiplied or divided numbers inside parentheses are collectively raised to a power, this is the same as each individual term being raised to that power: $(a \times b)^n = a^n \times b^n$; $(a \div b)^n = a^n \div b^n$.

Note: Exponents do not have to be integers. Fractional or decimal exponents follow all the rules above as well. Example: $5^{\frac{1}{4}} \times 5^{\frac{3}{4}} = 5^{\frac{1}{4}+\frac{3}{4}} = 5^1 = 5$.

A root, such as a square root, is another way of writing a fractional exponent. Instead of using a superscript, roots use the radical symbol ($\sqrt{}$) to indicate the operation. A radical will have a number underneath the bar, and may sometimes have a number in the upper left: $\sqrt[n]{a}$, read as "the nth root of a." The relationship between radical notation and exponent notation can be described by this equation: $\sqrt[n]{a} = a^{1/n}$. The two special cases of n = 2 and n = 3 are called square roots and cube roots. If there is no number to the upper left, it is understood to be a square root (n = 2). Nearly all of the roots you encounter will be square roots. A square root is the same as a number raised to the one-half power. When we say that a is the square root of b (a = $\sqrt{b}$), we mean that a multiplied by itself equals b: (a × a = b).

A perfect square is a number that has an integer for its square root. There are 10 perfect squares from 1 to 100: 1, 4, 9, 16, 25, 36, 49, 64, 81, 100 (the squares of integers 1 through 10).

Scientific notation is a way of writing large numbers in a shorter form. The form a × 10^n is used in scientific notation, where a is greater than or equal to 1, but less than 10, and n is the number of places the decimal must move to get from the original number to a. Example: The number 230,400,000 is cumbersome to write. To write the value in scientific notation, place a decimal point between the first and second numbers, and include all digits through the last non-zero digit (a = 2.304). To find the appropriate power of 10, count the number of places the decimal point had to move (n = 8). The number is positive if the decimal moved to the left, and negative if it moved to the right. We can then write 230,400,000 as 2.304 × 10^8. If we look instead at the number 0.00002304, we have the same value for a, but this time the decimal moved 5 places to the right (n = -5). Thus, 0.00002304 can be written as 2.304 × 10^{-5}. Using this notation makes it simple to compare very large or very small numbers. By comparing exponents, it is easy to see that 3.28 × 10^4 is smaller than 1.51×10^5, because 4 is less than 5.

FACTORS AND MULTIPLES

Factors are numbers that are multiplied together to obtain a product. For example, in the equation 2 × 3 = 6, the numbers 2 and 3 are factors. A prime number has only two factors (1 and itself), but other numbers can have many factors.

A common factor is a number that divides exactly into two or more other numbers. For example, the factors of 12 are 1, 2, 3, 4, 6, and 12, while the factors of 15 are 1, 3, 5, and 15. The common factors of 12 and 15 are 1 and 3.

A prime factor is also a prime number. Therefore, the prime factors of 12 are 2 and 3. For 15, the prime factors are 3 and 5.

The greatest common factor (GCF) is the largest number that is a factor of two or more numbers. For example, the factors of 15 are 1, 3, 5, and 15; the factors of 35 are 1, 5, 7, and 35. Therefore, the greatest common factor of 15 and 35 is 5.

The least common multiple (LCM) is the smallest number that is a multiple of two or more numbers. For example, the multiples of 3 include 3, 6, 9, 12, 15, etc.; the multiples of 5 include 5, 10, 15, 20, etc. Therefore, the least common multiple of 3 and 5 is 15.

> **Review Video: Multiples**
> Visit mometrix.com/academy and enter code: 626738

FRACTIONS, PERCENTAGES, AND RELATED CONCEPTS

A fraction is a number that is expressed as one integer written above another integer, with a dividing line between them $\left(\frac{x}{y}\right)$. It represents the quotient of the two numbers "x divided by y." It can also be thought of as x out of y equal parts.

The top number of a fraction is called the numerator, and it represents the number of parts under consideration. The 1 in $\frac{1}{4}$ means that 1 part out of the whole is being considered in the calculation. The bottom number of a fraction is called the denominator, and it represents the total number of equal parts. The 4 in $\frac{1}{4}$ means that the whole consists of 4 equal parts. A fraction cannot have a denominator of zero; this is referred to as "undefined."

Fractions can be manipulated by multiplying or dividing (but not adding or subtracting) both the numerator and denominator by the same number, without changing the value of the fraction. If you divide both numbers by a common factor, you are reducing or simplifying the fraction. Two fractions that have the same value, but are expressed differently are known as equivalent fractions. For example, $\frac{2}{10}, \frac{3}{15}, \frac{4}{20}$, and $\frac{5}{25}$ are all equivalent fractions. They can also all be reduced or simplified to $\frac{1}{5}$.

When two fractions are manipulated so that they have the same denominator, this is known as finding a common denominator. The number chosen to be that common denominator should be the least common multiple of the two original denominators. Example: $\frac{3}{4}$ and $\frac{5}{6}$; the least common multiple of 4 and 6 is 12. Manipulating to achieve the common denominator: $\frac{3}{4} = \frac{9}{12}; \frac{5}{6} = \frac{10}{12}$.

If two fractions have a common denominator, they can be added or subtracted simply by adding or subtracting the two numerators and retaining the same denominator. Example: $\frac{1}{2} + \frac{1}{4} = \frac{2}{4} + \frac{1}{4} = \frac{3}{4}$. If the two fractions do not already have the same denominator, one or both of them must be manipulated to achieve a common denominator before they can be added or subtracted.

Two fractions can be multiplied by multiplying the two numerators to find the new numerator and the two denominators to find the new denominator. Example: $\frac{1}{3} \times \frac{2}{3} = \frac{1 \times 2}{3 \times 3} = \frac{2}{9}$.

Two fractions can be divided flipping the numerator and denominator of the second fraction and then proceeding as though it were a multiplication. Example: $\frac{2}{3} \div \frac{3}{4} = \frac{2}{3} \times \frac{4}{3} = \frac{8}{9}$.

50

A fraction whose denominator is greater than its numerator is known as a proper fraction, while a fraction whose numerator is greater than its denominator is known as an improper fraction. Proper fractions have values less than one and improper fractions have values greater than one.

A mixed number is a number that contains both an integer and a fraction. Any improper fraction can be rewritten as a mixed number. Example: $\frac{8}{3} = \frac{6}{3} + \frac{2}{3} = 2 + \frac{2}{3} = 2\frac{2}{3}$. Similarly, any mixed number can be rewritten as an improper fraction. Example: $1\frac{3}{5} = 1 + \frac{3}{5} = \frac{5}{5} + \frac{3}{5} = \frac{8}{5}$.

> **Review Video: Fractions**
> Visit mometrix.com/academy and enter code: 262335

Percentages can be thought of as fractions that are based on a whole of 100; that is, one whole is equal to 100%. The word percent means "per hundred." Fractions can be expressed as percents by finding equivalent fractions with a denomination of 100. Example: $\frac{7}{10} = \frac{70}{100} = 70\%$; $\frac{1}{4} = \frac{25}{100} = 25\%$.

To express a percentage as a fraction, divide the percentage number by 100 and reduce the fraction to its simplest possible terms. Example: $60\% = \frac{60}{100} = \frac{3}{5}$; $96\% = \frac{96}{100} = \frac{24}{25}$.

Converting decimals to percentages and percentages to decimals is as simple as moving the decimal point. To convert from a decimal to a percent, move the decimal point two places to the right. To convert from a percent to a decimal, move it two places to the left. Example: 0.23 = 23%; 5.34 = 534%; 0.007 = 0.7%; 700% = 7.00; 86% = 0.86; 0.15% = 0.0015.

It may be helpful to remember that the percentage number will always be larger than the equivalent decimal number.

A percentage problem can be presented three main ways: (1) Find what percentage of some number another number is. Example: What percentage of 40 is 8? (2) Find what number is some percentage of a given number. Example: What number is 20% of 40? (3) Find what number another number is a given percentage of. Example: What number is 8 20% of? The three components in all of these cases are the same: a whole (W), a part (P), and a percentage (%). These are related by the equation: P = W × %. This is the form of the equation you would use to solve problems of type (2). To solve types (1) and (3), you would use these two forms: % = P/W and W = P/%.

The thing that frequently makes percentage problems difficult is that they are most often also word problems, so a large part of solving them is figuring out which quantities are what. Example: In a school cafeteria, 7 students choose pizza, 9 choose hamburgers, and 4 choose tacos. Find the percentage that chooses tacos. To find the whole, you must first add all of the parts: 7 + 9 + 4 = 20. The percentage can then be found by dividing the part by the whole (% = P/W): $\frac{4}{20} = \frac{20}{100} = 20\%$.

> **Review Video: Percentages**
> Visit mometrix.com/academy and enter code: 141911

A ratio is a comparison of two quantities in a particular order. Example: If there are 14 computers in a lab, and the class has 20 students, there is a student to computer ratio of 20 to 14, commonly written as 20:14.

A proportion is a relationship between two quantities that dictates how one changes when the other changes. A direct proportion describes a relationship in which a quantity increases by a set amount for every increase in the other quantity, or decreases by that same amount for every decrease in the other quantity. Example: For every 1 sheet cake, 18 people can be served cake. The number of sheet cakes, and the number of people that can be served from them is directly proportional.

Inverse proportion is a relationship in which an increase in one quantity is accompanied by a decrease in the other, or vice versa. Example: the time required for a car trip decreases as the speed increases, and increases as the speed decreases, so the time required is inversely proportional to the speed of the car.

Algebra, Functions, and Patterns

CLASSIFYING NUMBERS

There are several different kinds of numbers. When you learn to count as a child, you typical start with *Natural Numbers*. These are sometimes called "counting numbers" and begin with 1, 2, 3 ... etc. *Whole Numbers* include all natural numbers as well as 0. *Integers* include all whole numbers as well as their associated negative values (...-2, -1, 0, 1, 2...). Fractions with an integer in the numerator and a non-zero integer in the denominator are called *Rational Numbers*. Numbers such as π, that are non-terminating and non-repeating and cannot be expressed as a fraction, are considered *Irrational Numbers*. Any number that contains the imaginary number *i*, where $i^2 = -1$ and $i = \sqrt{-1}$, is referred to as a *Complex Number*. All natural numbers, whole numbers, integers, rational numbers, and irrational numbers are *Real Numbers*; complex numbers are not real numbers.

Aside from the number 1, all natural numbers can either be classified as prime or composite. *Prime Numbers* are natural numbers greater than 1 whose only factors are 1 and itself. On the other hand, *Composite Numbers* are natural numbers greater than 1 that are not prime numbers. 1 is a special case in that it is neither a prime number nor composite number. According to the *Fundamental Theorem of Arithmetic*, every composite number can be uniquely written as the product of prime numbers.

Other properties of natural numbers include greatest common factor, greatest common divisor, and least common multiple. *Greatest Common Factor*, or GCF (*m*, *n*) where *m* and *n* are both natural numbers, is the largest number that will divide evenly into each of two or more natural numbers. To find the GCF, factor each number and identify the largest common factor of each natural number. If there are no common factors, the GCF is 1. *Greatest Common Divisor*, signified by GCD (*m*, *n*), is the same as the GCF (*m*, *n*). *Least Common Multiple*, written as LCM (*m*, *n*), is the smallest integer that is divisible by each original natural number.

HANDLING POSITIVE AND NEGATIVE NUMBERS

A precursor to working with negative numbers is understanding what absolute values are. A number's *Absolute Value* is simply the distance away from zero a number is on the number line. The absolute value of a number is always positive and is written |*x*|.

When adding signed numbers, if the signs are the same simply add the absolute values of the addends and apply the original sign to the sum. For example, (+4) + (+8) = +12 and (−4) + (−8) = −12. When the original signs are different, take the absolute values of the addends and subtract the smaller value from the larger value, then apply the original sign of the larger value to the difference. For instance, (+4) + (−8) = −4 and (−4) + (+8) = +4.

For subtracting signed numbers, change the sign of the number after the minus symbol and then follow the same rules used for addition. For example, (+4)− (+8) = (+4) + (−8) = −4.

If the signs are the same the product is positive when multiplying signed numbers. For example, (+4) × (+8) = +32 and (−4) × (−8) = +32. If the signs are opposite, the product is negative. For example, (+4) × (−8) = −32 and (−4) × (+8) = −32. When more than two factors are multiplied together, the sign of the product is determined by how many negative factors are present. If there are an odd number of negative factors then the product is negative, whereas an even number of negative factors indicates a positive product. For instance, (+4) × (−8) × (−2) = +64 and (−4) × (−8) × (−2) = −64.

The rules for dividing signed numbers are similar to multiplying signed numbers. If the dividend and divisor have the same sign, the quotient is positive. If the dividend and divisor have opposite signs, the quotient is negative. For example, $(-4) \div (+8) = -0.5$.

Below is a list of the field properties of number systems for quick reference.

- Subtraction:
  - $a - b = a + (-b)$
- Additive Identity:
  - $a + 0 = a$
  - $0 + a = a$
- Additive Inverse:
  - $a + (-a) = 0$
  - $(-a) + a = 0$
- Associative:
  - $(a + b) + c = a + (b + c)$ for addition
  - $(ab)c = a(bc)$ for multiplication
- Closure:
  - $a + b$ is a real number for addition
  - ab is a real number for multiplication
- Commutative:
  - $a + b = b + a$ for addition
  - $ab = ba$ for multiplication
- Distributive:
  - $a(b + c) = ab + ac$
  - $(a + b)c = ac + bc$
- Multiplicative Identity:
  - $a \cdot 1 = a$
  - $1 \cdot a = a$
- Multiplicative Inverse:
  - $a \cdot a^{-1} = 1$
  - $a^{-1} \cdot a = 1$
- Division:
  - $a \div b = \dfrac{a}{b} = a \cdot b^{-1} = a \cdot \dfrac{1}{b}$

WORKING WITH EXPONENTS

A positive integer exponent indicates the number of times the base is multiplied by itself. Anything raised to the zero power is equal to 1. A negative integer exponent means you must take the reciprocal of the result of the corresponding positive integer exponent. A fractional exponent signifies a root. The following formulas all apply to exponents:

$$x^0 = 1$$

$$x^{-n} = \frac{1}{x^n}$$

$$\left(\frac{a}{b}\right)^{-1} = \frac{b}{a}$$

$$(x^a)^b = x^{ab}$$

$$(xy)^n = x^n y^n$$

$$\left(\frac{x}{y}\right)^n = \frac{x^n}{y^n}$$

0^0 = undefined

A root, or *Square Root*, is a number that when multiplied by itself yields a real number. For example, $\sqrt{4} = +2, -2$ because $(-2) \times (-2) = 4$ and $(2) \times (2) = 4$. Further, $\sqrt{9} = +3, -3$ because $(-3) \times (-3) = 9$ and $(3) \times (3) = 9$. Therefore, +2 and -2 are square roots of 4 while +3 and -3 are square roots of 9.

Another important rule to understand with regard to exponents is called the *Order of Operations*.

1. Solve expressions inside any parentheses using the order below; then return to 2.
2. Solve any exponents.
3. Do all remaining multiplication and division in the order they appear from left to right.
4. Perform any addition and subtraction as it appears from left to right.

IMPORTANT CONCEPTS

Commonly in algebra and other upper-level fields of math you find yourself working with mathematical expressions that do not equal each other. The statement comparing such expressions with symbols such as < (less than) or > (greater than) is called an *Inequality*. An example of an inequality is $7x > 5$. To solve for x, simply divide both sides by 7 and the solution is shown to be $x > \frac{5}{7}$. Graphs of the solution set of inequalities are represented on a number line. Open circles are used to show that an expression approaches a number but is never quite equal to that number.

Conditional Inequalities are those with certain values for the variable that will make the condition true and other values for the variable where the condition will be false. *Absolute Inequalities* can have any real number as the value for the variable to make the condition true, while there is no real number value for the variable that will make the condition false.

Solving inequalities is done by following the same rules as for solving equations with the exception that when multiplying or dividing by a negative number the direction of the inequality sign must be flipped or reversed. *Double Inequalities* are situations where two inequality statements apply to the same variable expression. An example of this is $-c < ax + b < c$.

Two more comparisons used frequently in algebra are ratios and proportions. A *Ratio* is a comparison of two quantities, expressed in a number of different ways. Ratios can be listed as "a to b", "a:b", or "a/b". Examples of ratios are miles per hour (miles/hour), meters per second (meters/second), miles per gallon (miles/gallon), etc.

Review Video: Ratios
Visit mometrix.com/academy and enter code: 996914

A statement of two equal ratios is a *Proportion*, such as $\frac{m}{b} = \frac{w}{z}$. If Fred travels 2 miles in 1 hour and Jane travels 4 miles in 2 hours, their speeds are said to be proportional because $\frac{2}{1} = \frac{4}{2}$. In a proportion, the product of the numerator of the first ratio and the denominator of the second ratio is equal to the product of the denominator of the first ratio and the numerator of the second ratio. Using the previous example, we see that $m \times z = b \times w$, thus $2 \times 2 = 1 \times 4$.

Review Video: Proportions
Visit mometrix.com/academy and enter code: 505355

A *Weighted Mean*, or weighted average, is a mean that uses "weighted" values. The formula is weighted mean $= \frac{w_1x_1+w_2x_2+w_3x_3\ldots+w_nx_n}{w_1+w_2+w_3+\cdots+w_n}$. Weighted values, such as $w_1, w_2, w_3, \ldots w_n$ are assigned to each member of the set $x_1, x_2, x_3, \ldots x_n$. If calculating weighted mean, make sure a weight value for each member of the set is used.

A fraction that contains a fraction in the numerator, denominator, or both is called a *Complex Fraction*. These can be solved in a number of ways; with the simplest being by following the order of operations as stated earlier. For example, $\frac{\left(\frac{4}{7}\right)}{\left(\frac{5}{8}\right)} = \frac{0.571}{0.625} = 0.914$. Another way to solve this problem is to multiply the fraction in the numerator by the reciprical of the fraction in the denominator. For example, $\frac{\left(\frac{4}{7}\right)}{\left(\frac{5}{8}\right)} = \frac{4}{7} \times \frac{8}{5} = \frac{32}{35} = 0.914$.

EQUATIONS AND GRAPHING

When algebraic functions and equations are shown graphically, they are usually shown on a *Cartesian Coordinate Plane*. The Cartesian coordinate plane consists of two number lines placed perpendicular to each other, and intersecting at the zero point, also known as the origin. The horizontal number line is known as the x-axis, with positive values to the right of the origin, and negative values to the left of the origin. The vertical number line is known as the y-axis, with positive values above the origin, and negative values below the origin. Any point on the plane can be identified by an ordered pair in the form (x,y), called coordinates. The x-value of the coordinate is called the abscissa, and the y-value of the coordinate is called the ordinate. The two number lines divide the plane into four quadrants: I, II, III, and IV.

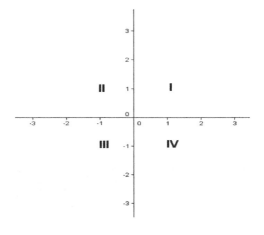

56

Before learning the different forms equations can be written in, it is important to understand some terminology. A ratio of the change in the vertical distance to the change in horizontal distance is called the *Slope*. On a graph with two points, (x_1, y_1) and (x_2, y_2), the slope is represented by the formula $= \frac{y_2 - y_1}{x_2 - x_1}$; $x_1 \neq x_2$. If the value of the slope is positive, the line slopes upward from left to right. If the value of the slope is negative, the line slopes downward from left to right. If the y-coordinates are the same for both points, the slope is 0 and the line is a *Horizontal Line*. If the x-coordinates are the same for both points, there is no slope and the line is a *Vertical Line*. Two or more lines that have equal slopes are *Parallel Lines*. *Perpendicular Lines* have slopes that are negative reciprocals of each other, such as $\frac{a}{b}$ and $\frac{-b}{a}$.

Equations are made up of monomials and polynomials. A *Monomial* is a single variable or product of constants and variables, such as x, $2x$, or $\frac{2}{x}$. There will never be addition or subtraction symbols in a monomial. Like monomials have like variables, but they may have different coefficients. *Polynomials* are algebraic expressions which use addition and subtraction to combine two or more monomials. Two terms make a binomial; three terms make a trinomial; etc. The *Degree of a Monomial* is the sum of the exponents of the variables. The *Degree of a Polynomial* is the highest degree of any individual term.

As mentioned previously, equations can be written many ways. Below is a list of the many forms equations can take.

- Standard Form: $Ax + By = C$; the slope is $\frac{-A}{B}$ and the y-intercept is $\frac{C}{B}$
- *Slope Intercept Form*: $y = mx + b$, where m is the slope and b is the y-intercept
- Point-Slope Form: $y - y_1 = m(x - x_1)$, where m is the slope and (x_1, y_1) is a point on the line
- Two-Point Form: $\frac{y - y_1}{x - x_1} = \frac{y_2 - y_1}{x_2 - x_1}$, where (x_1, y_1) and (x_2, y_2) are two points on the given line
- *Intercept Form*: $\frac{x}{x_1} + \frac{y}{y_1} = 1$, where $(x_1, 0)$ is the point at which a line intersects the x-axis, and $(0, y_1)$ is the point at which the same line intersects the y-axis

Equations can also be written as $ax + b = 0$, where $a \neq 0$. These are referred to as *One Variable Linear Equations*. A solution to an equation is called a *Root*. In the case where we have the equation $5x + 10 = 0$, if we solve for x we get a solution of $x = -2$. In other words, the root of the equation is -2. This is found by first subtracting 10 from both sides, which gives $5x = -10$. Next, simply divide both sides by the coefficient of the variable, in this case 5, to get $x = -2$. This can be checked by plugging -2 back into the original equation $(5)(-2) + 10 = -10 + 10 = 0$.

The *Solution Set* is the set of all solutions of an equation. In our example, the solution set would simply be -2. If there were more solutions (there usually are in multivariable equations) then they would also be included in the solution set. When an equation has no true solutions, this is referred to as an *Empty Set*. Equations with identical solution sets are *Equivalent Equations*. An *Identity* is a term whose value or determinant is equal to 1.

CALCULATIONS USING POINTS

Sometimes you need to perform calculations using only points on a graph as input data. Using points, you can determine what the midpoint and distance are. If you know the equation for a line you can calculate the distance between the line and the point.

To find the *Midpoint* of two points (x_1, y_1) and (x_2, y_2), average the x-coordinates to get the x-coordinate of the midpoint, and average the y-coordinates to get the y-coordinate of the midpoint. The formula is midpoint $= \left(\frac{x_1+x_2}{2}, \frac{y_1+y_2}{2}\right)$.

The *Distance* between two points is the same as the length of the hypotenuse of a right triangle with the two given points as endpoints, and the two sides of the right triangle parallel to the x-axis and y-axis, respectively. The length of the segment parallel to the x-axis is the difference between the x-coordinates of the two points. The length of the segment parallel to the y-axis is the difference between the y-coordinates of the two points. Use the Pythagorean Theorem $a^2 + b^2 = c^2$ or $c = \sqrt{a^2 + b^2}$ to find the distance. The formula is: distance $= \sqrt{(x_2 - x_1)^2 + (y_2 - y_1)^2}$.

When a line is in the format $Ax + By + C = 0$, where A, B, and C are coefficients, you can use a point (x_1, y_1) not on the line and apply the formula $d = \frac{|Ax_1 + By_1 + C|}{\sqrt{A^2 + B^2}}$ to find the distance between the line and the point (x_1, y_1).

> **Review Video: Distance & Midpoint for Points on the Coordinate Plane**
> Visit mometrix.com/academy and enter code: 973653

SYSTEMS OF EQUATIONS

Systems of Equations are a set of simultaneous equations that all use the same variables. A solution to a system of equations must be true for each equation in the system. *Consistent Systems* are those with at least one solution. *Inconsistent Systems* are systems of equations that have no solution. Systems of equations may be solved using one of four methods: substitution, addition, transformation of the augmented matrix and using the trace feature on a graphing calculator. The three most common methods are explained in the following passages.

To solve a system of linear equations by *substitution*, start with the easier equation and solve for one of the variables. Express this variable in terms of the other variable. Substitute this expression in the other equation, and solve for the other variable. The solution should be expressed in the form (x, y). Substitute the values into both of the original equations to check your answer. Consider the following problem.

Solve the system using substitution:

$$x + 6y = 15$$
$$3x - 12y = 18$$
$$x = 15 - 6y$$
$$3(15 - 6y) - 12y = 18$$
$$45 - 18y - 12y = 18$$
$$30y = 27$$
$$y = \frac{27}{30} = \frac{9}{10} = 0.9$$
$$x = 15 - 6(0.9) = 15 - 5.4 = 9.6$$

58

Now check both equations

$$9.6 + 6(0.9) = 9.6 + 5.4 = 15$$

$$3(9.6) - 12(0.9) = 28.8 - 10.8 = 18$$

Therefore, the solution is (9.6, 0.9).

To solve a system of equations using *elimination* or *addition*, begin by rewriting both equations in standard form $Ax + By = C$. Check to see if the coefficients of one pair of like variables add to zero. If not, multiply one or both of the equations by a non-zero number to make one set of like variables add to zero. Add the two equations to solve for one of the variables. Substitute this value into one of the original equations to solve for the other variable. Check your work by substituting into the other equation. Next, we will solve the same problem as above, but using the addition method.

Solve the system using substitution:

$$x + 6y = 15$$

$$3x - 12y = 18$$

For practice we will multiply the first equation by 6 and the second equation by -2 to get rid of the x variables.

$$6x + 36y = 90$$

$$-6x + 24y = -36$$

Add the equations together to get $60y = 54$. Thus, $y = \frac{54}{60} = \frac{9}{10} = 0.9$.

Plug the value for y back in to either of the original equations to get the value for x.

$$x + 6(0.9) = 15$$

$$x = 15 - 5.4 = 9.6$$

Now check both equations

$$9.6 + 6(0.9) = 9.6 + 5.4 = 15$$

$$3(9.6) - 12(0.9) = 28.8 - 10.8 = 18$$

Therefore, the solution is (9.6, 0.9).

Using the *trace feature on a calculator* requires that you rewrite each equation, isolating the y-variable on one side of the equal sign. Enter both equations in the graphing calculator and plot the graphs simultaneously. Use the trace cursor to find where the two lines cross. Use the zoom feature if necessary to obtain more accurate results. Always check your answer by substituting into the original equations. The trace method is likely to be less accurate than other methods due to the resolution of graphing calculators, but is a useful tool to provide an approximate answer.

POLYNOMIAL ALGEBRA

To multiply two binomials, follow the *FOIL* method. FOIL stands for:

- First: Multiply the first term of each binomial
- Outer: Multiply the outer terms of each binomial
- Inner: Multiply the inner terms of each binomial
- Last: Multiply the last term of each binomial

Using FOIL $(Ax + By)(Cx + Dy) = ACx^2 + ADxy + BCxy + BDy^2$.

To divide polynomials, begin by arranging the terms of each polynomial in order of one variable. You may arrange in ascending or descending order, but be consistent with both polynomials. To get the first term of the quotient, divide the first term of the dividend by the first term of the divisor. Multiply the first term of the quotient by the entire divisor and subtract that product from the dividend. Repeat for the second and successive terms until you either get a remainder of zero or a remainder whose degree is less than the degree of the divisor. If the quotient has a remainder, write the answer as a mixed expression in the form: quotient $+ \frac{\text{remainder}}{\text{divisor}}$.

Rational Expressions are fractions with polynomials in both the numerator and the denominator; the value of the polynomial in the denominator cannot be equal to zero. To add or subtract rational expressions, first find the common denominator, then rewrite each fraction as an equivalent fraction with the common denominator. Finally, add or subtract the numerators to get the numerator of the answer, and keep the common denominator as the denominator of the answer. When multiplying rational expressions factor each polynomial and cancel like factors (a factor which appears in both the numerator and the denominator). Then, multiply all remaining factors in the numerator to get the numerator of the product, and multiply the remaining factors in the denominator to get the denominator of the product. Remember – cancel entire factors, not individual terms. To divide rational expressions, take the reciprocal of the divisor (the rational expression you are dividing by) and multiply by the dividend.

Below are patterns of some special products to remember: *perfect trinomial squares*, the *difference between two squares*, the *sum and difference of two cubes*, and *perfect cubes*.

- Perfect Trinomial Squares: $x^2 + 2xy + y^2 = (x + y)^2$ or $x^2 - 2xy + y^2 = (x - y)^2$
- Difference between Two Squares: $x^2 - y^2 = (x + y)(x - y)$
- Sum of Two Cubes: $x^3 + y^3 = (x + y)(x^2 - xy + y^2)$
  Note: the second factor is NOT the same as a perfect trinomial square, so do not try to factor it further.
- Difference between Two Cubes: $x^3 - y^3 = (x - y)(x^2 + xy + y^2)$
  Again, the second factor is NOT the same as a perfect trinomial square.
- Perfect Cubes: $x^3 + 3x^2y + 3xy^2 + y^3 = (x + y)^3$ and $x^3 - 3x^2y + 3xy^2 - y^3 = (x - y)^3$

In order to *factor* a polynomial, first check for a common monomial factor. When the greatest common monomial factor has been factored out, look for patterns of special products: differences of two squares, the sum or difference of two cubes for binomial factors, or perfect trinomial squares for trinomial factors. If the factor is a trinomial but not a perfect trinomial square, look for a factorable form, such as $x^2 + (a + b)x + ab = (x + a)(x + b)$ or $(ac)x^2 + (ad + bc)x + bd = (ax + b)(cx + d)$.

For factors with four terms, look for groups to factor. Once you have found the factors, write the original polynomial as the product of all the factors. Make sure all of the polynomial factors are prime. Monomial factors may be prime or composite. Check your work by multiplying the factors to make sure you get the original polynomial.

> **Review Video: Polynomials**
> Visit mometrix.com/academy and enter code: 305005

SOLVING QUADRATIC EQUATIONS

The *Quadratic Formula* is used to solve quadratic equations when other methods are more difficult. To use the quadratic formula to solve a quadratic equation, begin by rewriting the equation in standard form $ax^2 + bx + c = 0$, where a, b, and c are coefficients. Once you have identified the values of the coefficients, substitute those values into the quadratic formula $= \frac{-b \pm \sqrt{b^2 - 4ac}}{2a}$. Evaluate the equation and simplify the expression. Again, check each root by substituting into the original equation. In the quadratic formula, the portion of the formula under the radical $(b^2 - 4ac)$ is called the *Discriminant*. If the discriminant is zero, there is only one root: zero. If the discriminant is positive, there are two different real roots. If the discriminant is negative, there are no real roots.

To solve a quadratic equation by *Factoring*, begin by rewriting the equation in standard form, if necessary. Factor the side with the variable then set each of the factors equal to zero and solve the resulting linear equations. Check your answers by substituting the roots you found into the original equation. If, when writing the equation in standard form, you have an equation in the form $x^2 + c = 0$ or $x^2 - c = 0$, set $x^2 = -c$ or $x^2 = c$ and take the square root of c. If $c = 0$, the only real root is zero. If c is positive, there are two real roots—the positive and negative square root values. If c is negative, there are no real roots because you cannot take the square root of a negative number.

To solve a quadratic equation by *Completing the Square*, rewrite the equation so that all terms containing the variable are on the left side of the equal sign, and all the constants are on the right side of the equal sign. Make sure the coefficient of the squared term is 1. If there is a coefficient with the squared term, divide each term on both sides of the equal side by that number. Next, work with the coefficient of the single-variable term. Square half of this coefficient, and add that value to both sides. Now you can factor the left side (the side containing the variable) as the square of a binomial. $x^2 + 2ax + a^2 = C \Rightarrow (x + a)^2 = C$, where x is the variable, and a and C are constants. Take the square root of both sides and solve for the variable. Substitute the value of the variable in the original problem to check your work.

In order to solve a *Radical Equation*, begin by isolating the radical term on one side of the equation, and move all other terms to the other side of the equation. Look at the index of the radicand. Remember, if no number is given, the index is 2, meaning square root. Raise both sides of the equation to the power equal to the index of the radical. Solve the resulting equation as you would a

normal polynomial equation. When you have found the roots, you must check them in the original problem to eliminate extraneous roots.

Review Video: <u>Using the Quadratic Formula</u>
Visit mometrix.com/academy and enter code: 163102

Data Analysis, Probability, and Statistics

STATISTICS

Statistics is the branch of mathematics that deals with collecting, recording, interpreting, illustrating, and analyzing large amounts of data. The following terms are often used in the discussion of data and statistics:

Data – the collective name for pieces of information (singular is datum).

Quantitative data – measurements (such as length, mass, and speed) that provide information about quantities in numbers

Qualitative data – information (such as colors, scents, tastes, and shapes) that cannot be measured using numbers

Discrete data – information that can be expressed only by a specific value, such as whole or half numbers; For example, since people can be counted only in whole numbers, a population count would be discrete data.

Continuous data – information (such as time and temperature) that can be expressed by any value within a given range

Primary data – information that has been collected directly from a survey, investigation, or experiment, such as a questionnaire or the recording of daily temperatures; Primary data that has not yet been organized or analyzed is called raw data.

Secondary data – information that has been collected, sorted, and processed by the researcher

Ordinal data – information that can be placed in numerical order, such as age or weight

Nominal data – information that cannot be placed in numerical order, such as names or places

MEASURES OF CENTRAL TENDENCY

The quantities of mean, median, and mode are all referred to as measures of central tendency. They can each give a picture of what the whole set of data looks like with just a single number. Knowing what each of these values represents is vital to making use of the information they provide.

The mean, also known as the arithmetic mean or average, of a data set is calculated by summing all of the values in the set and dividing that sum by the number of values. For example, if a data set has 6 numbers and the sum of those 6 numbers is 30, the mean is calculated as 30/6 = 5.

The median is the middle value of a data set. The median can be found by putting the data set in numerical order, and locating the middle value. In the data set (1, 2, 3, 4, 5), the median is 3. If there is an even number of values in the set, the median is calculated by taking the average of the two middle values. In the data set, (1, 2, 3, 4, 5, 6), the median would be (3 + 4)/2 = 3.5.

The mode is the value that appears most frequently in the data set. In the data set (1, 2, 3, 4, 5, 5, 5), the mode would be 5 since the value 5 appears three times. If multiple values appear the same number of times, there are multiple values for the mode. If the data set were (1, 2, 2, 3, 4, 4, 5, 5), the modes would be 2, 4, and 5. If no value appears more than any other value in the data set, then there is no mode.

MEASURES OF DISPERSION

The standard deviation expresses how spread out the values of a distribution are from the mean. Standard deviation is given in the same units as the original data and is represented by a lower case sigma (σ).

A high standard deviation means that the values are very spread out. A low standard deviation means that the values are close together.

If every value in a distribution is increased or decreased by the same amount, the mean, median, and mode are increased or decreased by that amount, but the standard deviation stays the same.

If every value in a distribution is multiplied or divided by the same number, the mean, median, mode, and standard deviation will all be multiplied or divided by that number.

The range of a distribution is the difference between the highest and lowest values in the distribution. For example, in the data set (1, 3, 5, 7, 9, 11), the highest and lowest values are 11 and 1, respectively. The range then would be calculated as 11 – 1 = 10.

The three quartiles are the three values that divide a data set into four equal parts. Quartiles are generally only calculated for data sets with a large number of values. As a simple example, for the data set consisting of the numbers 1 through 99, the first quartile (Q1) would be 25, the second quartile (Q2), always equal to the median, would be 50, and the third quartile (Q3) would be 75. The difference between Q1 and Q3 is known as the interquartile range.

PROBABILITY

Probability is a branch of statistics that deals with the likelihood of something taking place. One classic example is a coin toss. There are only two possible results: heads or tails. The likelihood, or probability, that the coin will land as heads is 1 out of 2 (1/2, 0.5, 50%). Tails has the same probability. Another common example is a 6-sided die roll. There are six possible results from rolling a single die, each with an equal chance of happening, so the probability of any given number coming up is 1 out of 6.

> **Review Video: Intro to Probability**
> Visit mometrix.com/academy and enter code: 212374

Terms frequently used in probability:

Event – a situation that produces results of some sort (a coin toss)

Compound event – event that involves two or more items (rolling a pair of dice; taking the sum)

Outcome – a possible result in an experiment or event (heads, tails)

Desired outcome (or success) – an outcome that meets a particular set of criteria (a roll of 1 or 2 if we are looking for numbers less than 3)

Independent events – two or more events whose outcomes do not affect one another (two coins tossed at the same time)

Dependent events – two or more events whose outcomes affect one another (two cards drawn consecutively from the same deck)

Certain outcome – probability of outcome is 100% or 1

Impossible outcome – probability of outcome is 0% or 0

Mutually exclusive outcomes – two or more outcomes whose criteria cannot all be satisfied in a single outcome (a coin coming up heads and tails on the same toss)

Theoretical probability is the likelihood of a certain outcome occurring for a given event. It can be determined without actually performing the event. It is calculated as P (probability of success) = (desired outcomes)/(total outcomes).

Example:

There are 20 marbles in a bag and 5 are red. The theoretical probability of randomly selecting a red marble is 5 out of 20, (5/20 = 1/4, 0.25, or 25%).

Most of the time, when we talk about probability, we mean theoretical probability. Experimental probability, or relative frequency, is the number of times an outcome occurs in a particular experiment or a certain number of observed events.

While theoretical probability is based on what *should* happen, experimental probability is based on what *has* happened. Experimental probability is calculated in the same way as theoretical, except that actual outcomes are used instead of possible outcomes.

Theoretical and experimental probability do not always line up with one another. Theoretical probability says that out of 20 coin tosses, 10 should be heads. However, if we were actually to toss 20 coins, we might record just 5 heads. This doesn't mean that our theoretical probability is incorrect; it just means that this particular experiment had results that were different from what was predicted.

> **Review Video: Theoretical and Experimental Probability**
> Visit mometrix.com/academy and enter code: 444349

When trying to calculate the probability of an event using the (desired outcomes)/(total outcomes) formula), you may frequently find that there are too many outcomes to individually count them. Permutation and combination formulas offer a shortcut to counting outcomes. The primary distinction between permutations and combinations is that permutations take into account order, while combinations do not. To calculate the number of possible groupings, there are two necessary parameters: the number of items available for selection and the number to be selected. The number of permutations of r items given a set of n items can be calculated as $_nP_r = \frac{n!}{(n-r)!}$. The number of combinations of r items given a set of n items can be calculated as $_nC_r = \frac{n!}{r!(n-r)!}$ or $_nC_r = \frac{_nP_r}{r!}$.

Example:

Suppose you want to calculate how many different 5-card hands can be drawn from a deck of 52 cards. This is a combination since the order of the cards in a hand does not matter. There are 52 cards available, and 5 to be selected. Thus, the number of different hands is $_{52}C_5 = \frac{52!}{5! \times 47!} = 2,598,960$.

COMMON CHARTS AND GRAPHS

A bar graph is a graph that uses bars to compare data, as if each bar were a ruler being used to measure the data. The graph includes a scale that identifies the units being measured.

A line graph is a graph that connects points to show how data increases or decreases over time. The time line is the horizontal axis. The connecting lines between data points on the graph are a way to more clearly show how the data changes.

A pictograph is a graph that uses pictures or symbols to show data. The pictograph will have a key to identify what each symbol represents. Generally, each symbol stands for one or more objects.

A pie chart or circle graph is a diagram used to compare parts of a whole. The full pie represents the whole, and it is divided into sectors that each represent something that is a part of the whole. Each sector or slice of the pie is either labeled to indicate what it represents, or explained on a key associated with the chart. The size of each slice is determined by the percentage of the whole that the associated quantity represents. Numerically, the angle measurement of each sector can be computed by solving the proportion: x/360 = part/whole.

A histogram is a special type of bar graph where the data are grouped in intervals (for example 20-29, 30-39, 40-49, etc.). The frequency, or number of times a value occurs in each interval, is indicated by the height of the bar. The intervals do not have to be the same amount but usually are (all data in ranges of 10 or all in ranges of 5, for example). The smaller the intervals, the more detailed the information.

A stem-and-leaf plot is a way to organize data visually so that the information is easy to understand. A stem-and-leaf plot is simple to construct because a simple line separates the stem (the part of the plot listing the tens digit, if displaying two-digit data) from the leaf (the part that shows the ones digit). Thus, the number 45 would appear as 4 | 5. The stem-and-leaf plot for test scores of a group of 11 students might look like the following:

```
9 | 5
8 | 1, 3, 8
7 | 0, 2, 4, 6, 7
6 | 2, 8
```

A stem-and-leaf plot is similar to a histogram or other frequency plot, but with a stem-and-leaf plot, all the original data is preserved. In this example, it can be seen at a glance that nearly half the students scored in the 70's, yet all the data has been maintained. These plots can be used for larger numbers as well, but they tend to work better for small sets of data as they can become unwieldy with larger sets.

Measurement and Geometry

LINES AND PLANES

A point is a fixed location in space; has no size or dimensions; commonly represented by a dot.

A line is a set of points that extends infinitely in two opposite directions. It has length, but no width or depth. A line can be defined by any two distinct points that it contains. A line segment is a portion of a line that has definite endpoints. A ray is a portion of a line that extends from a single point on that line in one direction along the line. It has a definite beginning, but no ending.

A plane is a two-dimensional flat surface defined by three non-collinear points. A plane extends an infinite distance in all directions in those two dimensions. It contains an infinite number of points, parallel lines and segments, intersecting lines and segments, as well as parallel or intersecting rays. A plane will never contain a three-dimensional figure or skew lines. Two given planes will either be parallel or they will intersect to form a line. A plane may intersect a circular conic surface, such as a cone, to form conic sections, such as the parabola, hyperbola, circle or ellipse.

Perpendicular lines are lines that intersect at right angles. They are represented by the symbol ⊥. The shortest distance from a line to a point not on the line is a perpendicular segment from the point to the line.

Parallel lines are lines in the same plane that have no points in common and never meet. It is possible for lines to be in different planes, have no points in common, and never meet, but they are not parallel because they are in different planes.

A bisector is a line or line segment that divides another line segment into two equal lengths. A perpendicular bisector of a line segment is composed of points that are equidistant from the endpoints of the segment it is dividing.

Intersecting lines are lines that have exactly one point in common. Concurrent lines are multiple lines that intersect at a single point.

A transversal is a line that intersects at least two other lines, which may or may not be parallel to one another. A transversal that intersects parallel lines is a common occurrence in geometry.

ANGLES

An angle is formed when two lines or line segments meet at a common point. It may be a common starting point for a pair of segments or rays, or it may be the intersection of lines. Angles are represented by the symbol ∠.

The vertex is the point at which two segments or rays meet to form an angle. If the angle is formed by intersecting rays, lines, and/or line segments, the vertex is the point at which four angles are formed. The pairs of angles opposite one another are called vertical angles, and their measures are equal.

An acute angle is an angle with a degree measure less than 90°.

A right angle is an angle with a degree measure of exactly 90°.

An obtuse angle is an angle with a degree measure greater than 90° but less than 180°.

A straight angle is an angle with a degree measure of exactly 180°. This is also a semicircle.

A reflex angle is an angle with a degree measure greater than 180° but less than 360°.

A full angle is an angle with a degree measure of exactly 360°.

Two angles whose sum is exactly 90° are said to be complementary. The two angles may or may not be adjacent. In a right triangle, the two acute angles are complementary.

Two angles whose sum is exactly 180° are said to be supplementary. The two angles may or may not be adjacent. Two intersecting lines always form two pairs of supplementary angles. Adjacent supplementary angles will always form a straight line.

Two angles that have the same vertex and share a side are said to be adjacent. Vertical angles are not adjacent because they share a vertex but no common side.

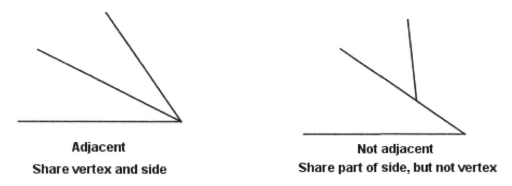

Adjacent
Share vertex and side

Not adjacent
Share part of side, but not vertex

When two parallel lines are cut by a transversal, the angles that are between the two parallel lines are interior angles. In the diagram below, angles 3, 4, 5, and 6 are interior angles.

When two parallel lines are cut by a transversal, the angles that are outside the parallel lines are exterior angles. In the diagram below, angles 1, 2, 7, and 8 are exterior angles.

When two parallel lines are cut by a transversal, the angles that are in the same position relative to the transversal and a parallel line are corresponding angles. The diagram below has four pairs of corresponding angles: angles 1 and 5; angles 2 and 6; angles 3 and 7; and angles 4 and 8. Corresponding angles formed by parallel lines are congruent.

When two parallel lines are cut by a transversal, the two interior angles that are on opposite sides of the transversal are called alternate interior angles. In the diagram below, there are two pairs of alternate interior angles: angles 3 and 6, and angles 4 and 5. Alternate interior angles formed by parallel lines are congruent.

When two parallel lines are cut by a transversal, the two exterior angles that are on opposite sides of the transversal are called alternate exterior angles. In the diagram below, there are two pairs of alternate exterior angles: angles 1 and 8, and angles 2 and 7. Alternate exterior angles formed by parallel lines are congruent.

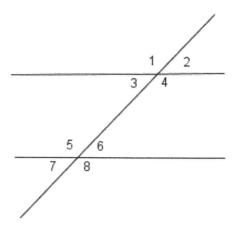

When two lines intersect, four angles are formed. The non-adjacent angles at this vertex are called vertical angles. Vertical angles are congruent. In the diagram, $\angle ABD \cong \angle CBE$ and $\angle ABC \cong \angle DBE$.

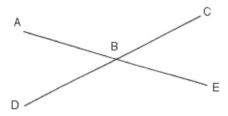

TRIANGLES

An equilateral triangle is a triangle with three congruent sides. An equilateral triangle will also have three congruent angles, each 60°. All equilateral triangles are also acute triangles.

An isosceles triangle is a triangle with two congruent sides. An isosceles triangle will also have two congruent angles opposite the two congruent sides.

A scalene triangle is a triangle with no congruent sides. A scalene triangle will also have three angles of different measures. The angle with the largest measure is opposite the longest side, and the angle with the smallest measure is opposite the shortest side.

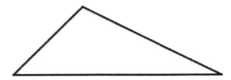

An acute triangle is a triangle whose three angles are all less than 90°. If two of the angles are equal, the acute triangle is also an isosceles triangle. If the three angles are all equal, the acute triangle is also an equilateral triangle.

A right triangle is a triangle with exactly one angle equal to 90°. All right triangles follow the Pythagorean Theorem. A right triangle can never be acute or obtuse.

An obtuse triangle is a triangle with exactly one angle greater than 90°. The other two angles may or may not be equal. If the two remaining angles are equal, the obtuse triangle is also an isosceles triangle.

TERMINOLOGY

Altitude of a Triangle: A line segment drawn from one vertex perpendicular to the opposite side. In the diagram below, $\overline{BE}$, $\overline{AD}$, and $\overline{CF}$ are altitudes. The three altitudes in a triangle are always concurrent.

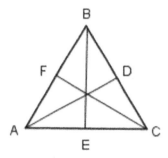

Height of a Triangle: The length of the altitude, although the two terms are often used interchangeably.

Orthocenter of a Triangle: The point of concurrency of the altitudes of a triangle. Note that in an obtuse triangle, the orthocenter will be outside the triangle, and in a right triangle, the orthocenter is the vertex of the right angle.

Median of a Triangle: A line segment drawn from one vertex to the midpoint of the opposite side. This is not the same as the altitude, except the altitude to the base of an isosceles triangle and all three altitudes of an equilateral triangle.

Centroid of a Triangle: The point of concurrency of the medians of a triangle. This is the same point as the orthocenter only in an equilateral triangle. Unlike the orthocenter, the centroid is always inside the triangle. The centroid can also be considered the exact center of the triangle. Any shape triangle can be perfectly balanced on a tip placed at the centroid. The centroid is also the point that is two-thirds the distance from the vertex to the opposite side.

> **Review Video: <u>Incenter, Circumcenter, Orthocenter, and Centroid</u>**
> Visit mometrix.com/academy and enter code: 598260

PYTHAGOREAN THEOREM

The side of a triangle opposite the right angle is called the hypotenuse. The other two sides are called the legs. The Pythagorean Theorem states a relationship among the legs and hypotenuse of a right triangle: $a^2 + b^2 = c^2$, where a and b are the lengths of the legs of a right triangle, and c is the length of the hypotenuse. Note that this formula will only work with right triangles.

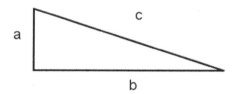

> **Review Video: <u>Pythagorean Theorem</u>**
> Visit mometrix.com/academy and enter code: 906576

GENERAL RULES

The Triangle Inequality Theorem states that the sum of the measures of any two sides of a triangle is always greater than the measure of the third side. If the sum of the measures of two sides were equal to the third side, a triangle would be impossible because the two sides would lie flat across the third side and there would be no vertex. If the sum of the measures of two of the sides was less than the third side, a closed figure would be impossible because the two shortest sides would never meet.

The sum of the measures of the interior angles of a triangle is always 180°. Therefore, a triangle can never have more than one angle greater than or equal to 90°.

In any triangle, the angles opposite congruent sides are congruent, and the sides opposite congruent angles are congruent. The largest angle is always opposite the longest side, and the smallest angle is always opposite the shortest side.

The line segment that joins the midpoints of any two sides of a triangle is always parallel to the third side and exactly half the length of the third side.

SIMILARITY AND CONGRUENCE RULES

Similar triangles are triangles whose corresponding angles are equal and whose corresponding sides are proportional. Represented by AA. Similar triangles whose corresponding sides are congruent are also congruent triangles.

Three sides of one triangle are congruent to the three corresponding sides of the second triangle. Represented as SSS.

Two sides and the included angle (the angle formed by those two sides) of one triangle are congruent to the corresponding two sides and included angle of the second triangle. Represented by SAS.

Two angles and the included side (the side that joins the two angles) of one triangle are congruent to the corresponding two angles and included side of the second triangle. Represented by ASA.

Two angles and a non-included side of one triangle are congruent to the corresponding two angles and non-included side of the second triangle. Represented by AAS.

Note that AAA is not a form for congruent triangles. This would say that the three angles are congruent, but says nothing about the sides. This meets the requirements for similar triangles, but not congruent triangles.

AREA AND PERIMETER FORMULAS

The perimeter of any triangle is found by summing the three side lengths; $P = a + b + c$. For an equilateral triangle, this is the same as $P = 3s$, where s is any side length, since all three sides are the same length.

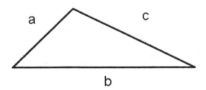

The area of any triangle can be found by taking half the product of one side length (base or b) and the perpendicular distance from that side to the opposite vertex (height or h). In equation form, $A = \frac{1}{2}bh$. For many triangles, it may be difficult to calculate h, so using one of the other formulas given here may be easier.

Review Video: Area and Perimeter of a Triangle
Visit mometrix.com/academy and enter code: 853779

Another formula that works for any triangle is $A = \sqrt{s(s-a)(s-b)(s-c)}$, where A is the area, s is the semiperimeter $s = \frac{a+b+c}{2}$, and a, b, and c are the lengths of the three sides.

The area of an equilateral triangle can be found by the formula $A = \frac{\sqrt{3}}{4}s^2$, where A is the area and s is the length of a side. You could use the $30° - 60° - 90°$ ratios to find the height of the triangle and then use the standard triangle area formula, but this is faster.

The area of an isosceles triangle can be found by the formula, $A = \frac{1}{2}b\sqrt{a^2 - \frac{b^2}{4}}$, where A is the area, b is the base (the unique side), and a is the length of one of the two congruent sides. If you do not

72

remember this formula, you can use the Pythagorean Theorem to find the height so you can use the standard formula for the area of a triangle.

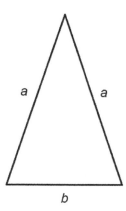

TRIGONOMETRIC FORMULAS

In the diagram below, angle C is the right angle, and side c is the hypotenuse. Side a is the side adjacent to angle B and side b is the side adjacent to angle A. These formulas will work for any acute angle in a right triangle. They will NOT work for any triangle that is not a right triangle. Also, they will not work for the right angle in a right triangle, since there are not distinct adjacent and opposite sides to differentiate from the hypotenuse.

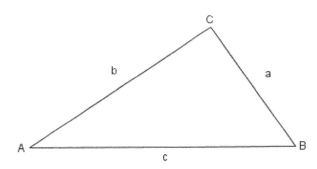

$$\sin A = \frac{\text{opposite side}}{\text{hypotenuse}} = \frac{a}{c}$$

$$\cos A = \frac{\text{adjacent side}}{\text{hypotenuse}} = \frac{b}{c}$$

$$\tan A = \frac{\text{opposite side}}{\text{adjacent side}} = \frac{a}{b}$$

$$\csc A = \frac{1}{\sin A} = \frac{\text{hypotenuse}}{\text{opposite side}} = \frac{c}{a}$$

$$\sec A = \frac{1}{\cos A} = \frac{\text{hypotenuse}}{\text{adjacent side}} = \frac{c}{b}$$

$$\cot A = \frac{1}{\tan A} = \frac{\text{adjacent side}}{\text{opposite side}} = \frac{b}{a}$$

POLYGONS

Each straight line segment of a polygon is called a side.

The point at which two sides of a polygon intersect is called the vertex. In a polygon, the number of sides is always equal to the number of vertices.

A polygon with all sides congruent and all angles equal is called a regular polygon.

A line segment from the center of a polygon perpendicular to a side of the polygon is called the apothem. In a regular polygon, the apothem can be used to find the area of the polygon using the formula $A = \frac{1}{2}ap$, where a is the apothem and p is the perimeter.

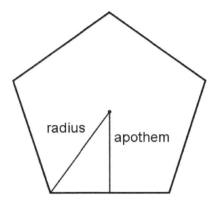

A line segment from the center of a polygon to a vertex of the polygon is called a radius. The radius of a regular polygon is also the radius of a circle that can be circumscribed about the polygon.

$$\begin{aligned}
\text{Triangle} &= 3 \text{ sides} \\
\text{Quadrilateral} &= 4 \text{ sides} \\
\text{Pentagon} &= 5 \text{ sides} \\
\text{Hexagon} &= 6 \text{ sides} \\
\text{Heptagon} &= 7 \text{ sides} \\
\text{Octagon} &= 8 \text{ sides} \\
\text{Nonagon} &= 9 \text{ sides} \\
\text{Decagon} &= 10 \text{ sides} \\
\text{Dodecagon} &= 12 \text{ sides}
\end{aligned}$$

More generally, an n-gon is a polygon that has n angles and n sides.

The sum of the interior angles of an n-sided polygon is $(n-2)180°$. For example, in a triangle n = 3, so the sum of the interior angles is $(3-2)180° = 180°$. In a quadrilateral, n = 4, and the sum of the angles is $(4-2)180° = 360°$. The sum of the interior angles of a polygon is equal to the sum of the interior angles of any other polygon with the same number of sides.

A diagonal is a line segment that joins two non-adjacent vertices of a polygon.

A convex polygon is a polygon whose diagonals all lie within the interior of the polygon.

A concave polygon is a polygon with a least one diagonal that lies outside the polygon. In the diagram below, quadrilateral *ABCD* is concave because diagonal $\overline{AC}$ lies outside the polygon.

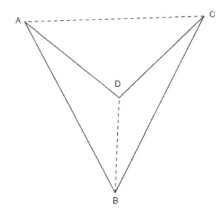

The number of diagonals a polygon has can be found by using the formula: number of diagonals = $\frac{n(n-3)}{2}$, where *n* is the number of sides in the polygon. This formula works for all polygons, not just regular polygons.

Congruent figures are geometric figures that have the same size and shape. All corresponding angles are equal, and all corresponding sides are equal. It is indicated by the symbol ≅.

Congruent polygons

Similar figures are geometric figures that have the same shape, but do not necessarily have the same size. All corresponding angles are equal, and all corresponding sides are proportional, but they do not have to be equal. It is indicated by the symbol ~.

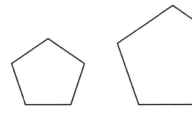

Similar polygons

Note that all congruent figures are also similar, but not all similar figures are congruent.

Line of Symmetry: The line that divides a figure or object into two symmetric parts. Each symmetric half is congruent to the other. An object may have no lines of symmetry, one line of symmetry, or more than one line of symmetry.

Lines of symmetry:

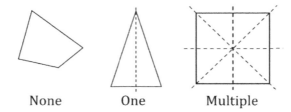

None   One   Multiple

Quadrilateral: A closed two-dimensional geometric figure composed of exactly four straight sides. The sum of the interior angles of any quadrilateral is 360°.

Parallelogram: A quadrilateral that has exactly two pairs of opposite parallel sides. The sides that are parallel are also congruent. The opposite interior angles are always congruent, and the consecutive interior angles are supplementary. The diagonals of a parallelogram bisect each other. Each diagonal divides the parallelogram into two congruent triangles.

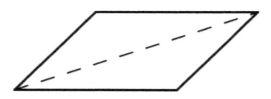

Trapezoid: Traditionally, a quadrilateral that has exactly one pair of parallel sides. Some math texts define trapezoid as a quadrilateral that has at least one pair of parallel sides. Because there are no rules governing the second pair of sides, there are no rules that apply to the properties of the diagonals of a trapezoid.

Rectangles, rhombuses, and squares are all special forms of parallelograms.

Rectangle: A parallelogram with four right angles. All rectangles are parallelograms, but not all parallelograms are rectangles. The diagonals of a rectangle are congruent.

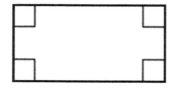

Rhombus: A parallelogram with four congruent sides. All rhombuses are parallelograms, but not all parallelograms are rhombuses. The diagonals of a rhombus are perpendicular to each other.

Square: A parallelogram with four right angles and four congruent sides. All squares are also parallelograms, rhombuses, and rectangles. The diagonals of a square are congruent and perpendicular to each other.

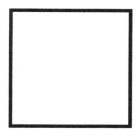

A quadrilateral whose diagonals bisect each other is a parallelogram. A quadrilateral whose opposite sides are parallel (2 pairs of parallel sides) is a parallelogram.

A quadrilateral whose diagonals are perpendicular bisectors of each other is a rhombus. A quadrilateral whose opposite sides (both pairs) are parallel and congruent is a rhombus.

A parallelogram that has a right angle is a rectangle. (Consecutive angles of a parallelogram are supplementary. Therefore, if there is one right angle in a parallelogram, there are four right angles in that parallelogram.)

A rhombus with one right angle is a square. Because the rhombus is a special form of a parallelogram, the rules about the angles of a parallelogram also apply to the rhombus.

AREA AND PERIMETER FORMULAS

The area of a square is found by using the formula $A = s^2$, where and s is the length of one side.

The perimeter of a square is found by using the formula $P = 4s$, where s is the length of one side. Because all four sides are equal in a square, it is faster to multiply the length of one side by 4 than to add the same number four times. You could use the formulas for rectangles and get the same answer.

> **Review Video: Area and Perimeter of a Square**
> Visit mometrix.com/academy and enter code: 620902

The area of a rectangle is found by the formula $A = lw$, where A is the area of the rectangle, l is the length (usually considered to be the longer side) and w is the width (usually considered to be the shorter side). The numbers for l and w are interchangeable.

The perimeter of a rectangle is found by the formula $P = 2l + 2w$ or $P = 2(l + w)$, where l is the length, and w is the width. It may be easier to add the length and width first and then double the result, as in the second formula.

The area of a parallelogram is found by the formula $A = bh$, where b is the length of the base, and h is the height. Note that the base and height correspond to the length and width in a rectangle, so this formula would apply to rectangles as well. Do not confuse the height of a parallelogram with the length of the second side. The two are only the same measure in the case of a rectangle.

The perimeter of a parallelogram is found by the formula $P = 2a + 2b$ or $P = 2(a + b)$, where a and b are the lengths of the two sides.

The area of a trapezoid is found by the formula $A = \frac{1}{2}h(b_1 + b_2)$, where h is the height (segment joining and perpendicular to the parallel bases), and b_1 and b_2 are the two parallel sides (bases). Do not use one of the other two sides as the height unless that side is also perpendicular to the parallel bases.

The perimeter of a trapezoid is found by the formula $P = a + b_1 + c + b_2$, where a, b_1, c, and b_2 are the four sides of the trapezoid.

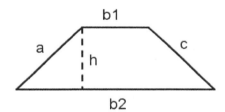

CIRCLES

The center is the single point inside the circle that is equidistant from every point on the circle. (Point O in the diagram below.)

The radius is a line segment that joins the center of the circle and any one point on the circle. All radii of a circle are equal. (Segments OX, OY, and OZ in the diagram below.)

The diameter is a line segment that passes through the center of the circle and has both endpoints on the circle. The length of the diameter is exactly twice the length of the radius. (Segment *XZ* in the diagram below.)

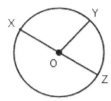

The area of a circle is found by the formula $A = \pi r^2$, where r is the length of the radius. If the diameter of the circle is given, remember to divide it in half to get the length of the radius before proceeding.

The circumference of a circle is found by the formula $C = 2\pi r$, where r is the radius. Again, remember to convert the diameter if you are given that measure rather than the radius.

Review Video: <u>Area and Circumference of a Circle</u>
Visit mometrix.com/academy and enter code: 243015

Concentric circles are circles that have the same center, but not the same length of radii. A bulls-eye target is an example of concentric circles.

An arc is a portion of a circle. Specifically, an arc is the set of points between and including two points on a circle. An arc does not contain any points inside the circle. When a segment is drawn from the endpoints of an arc to the center of the circle, a sector is formed.

A central angle is an angle whose vertex is the center of a circle and whose legs intercept an arc of the circle. Angle *XOY* in the diagram above is a central angle. A minor arc is an arc that has a measure less than 180°. The measure of a central angle is equal to the measure of the minor arc it intercepts. A major arc is an arc having a measure of at least 180°. The measure of the major arc can be found by subtracting the measure of the central angle from 360°.

A semicircle is an arc whose endpoints are the endpoints of the diameter of a circle. A semicircle is exactly half of a circle.

An inscribed angle is an angle whose vertex lies on a circle and whose legs contain chords of that circle. The portion of the circle intercepted by the legs of the angle is called the intercepted arc. The measure of the intercepted arc is exactly twice the measure of the inscribed angle. In the diagram below, angle *ABC* is an inscribed angle. $\overset{\frown}{AC} = 2(m\angle ABC)$.

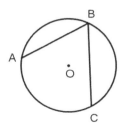

Any angle inscribed in a semicircle is a right angle. The intercepted arc is 180°, making the inscribed angle half that, or 90°. In the diagram below, angle *ABC* is inscribed in semicircle *ABC*, making angle *ABC* equal to 90°.

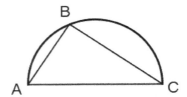

A chord is a line segment that has both endpoints on a circle. In the diagram below, $\overline{EB}$ is a chord.

Secant: A line that passes through a circle and contains a chord of that circle. In the diagram below, $\overleftrightarrow{EB}$ is a secant and contains chord $\overline{EB}$.

A tangent is a line in the same plane as a circle that touches the circle in exactly one point. While a line segment can be tangent to a circle as part of a line that is tangent, it is improper to say a tangent can be simply a line segment that touches the circle in exactly one point. In the diagram below, $\overleftrightarrow{CD}$ is tangent to circle *A*. Notice that $\overline{FB}$ is not tangent to the circle. $\overline{FB}$ is a line segment that touches the circle in exactly one point, but if the segment were extended, it would touch the circle in a second point.

The point at which a tangent touches a circle is called the point of tangency. In the diagram below, point *B* is the point of tangency.

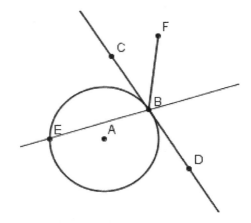

Review Video: Tangent Lines of a Circle
Visit mometrix.com/academy and enter code: 780167

A secant is a line that intersects a circle in two points. Two secants may intersect inside the circle, on the circle, or outside the circle. When the two secants intersect on the circle, an inscribed angle is formed.

When two secants intersect inside a circle, the measure of each of two vertical angles is equal to half the sum of the two intercepted arcs. In the diagram below, m∠$AEB = \frac{1}{2}(\widehat{AB} + \widehat{CD})$ and m∠$BEC = \frac{1}{2}(\widehat{BC} + \widehat{AD})$.

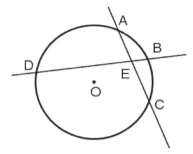

When two secants intersect outside a circle, the measure of the angle formed is equal to half the difference of the two arcs that lie between the two secants. In the diagram below, m∠$AEB = \frac{1}{2}(\widehat{AB} - \widehat{CD})$.

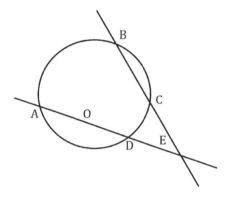

The **arc length** is the length of that portion of the circumference between two points on the circle. The formula for arc length is $s = \frac{\pi r \theta}{180°}$ where s is the arc length, r is the length of the radius, and θ is the angular measure of the arc in degrees, or $s = r\theta$, where θ is the angular measure of the arc in radians (2π radians = 360 degrees).

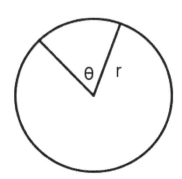

81

A sector is the portion of a circle formed by two radii and their intercepted arc. While the arc length is exclusively the points that are also on the circumference of the circle, the sector is the entire area bounded by the arc and the two radii.

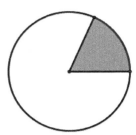

The area of a sector of a circle is found by the formula, $A = \frac{\theta r^2}{2}$, where A is the area, θ is the measure of the central angle in radians, and r is the radius. To find the area when the central angle is in degrees, use the formula, $A = \frac{\theta \pi r^2}{360}$, where θ is the measure of the central angle in degrees and r is the radius.

A circle is inscribed in a polygon if each of the sides of the polygon is tangent to the circle. A polygon is inscribed in a circle if each of the vertices of the polygon lies on the circle.

A circle is circumscribed about a polygon if each of the vertices of the polygon lies on the circle. A polygon is circumscribed about the circle if each of the sides of the polygon is tangent to the circle.

If one figure is inscribed in another, then the other figure is circumscribed about the first figure.

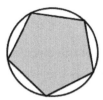

Circle circumscribed about a pentagon
Pentagon inscribed in a circle

OTHER CONIC SECTIONS

An ellipse is the set of all points in a plane, whose total distance from two fixed points called the foci (singular: focus) is constant, and whose center is the midpoint between the foci.

The standard equation of an ellipse that is taller than it is wide is $\frac{(y-k)^2}{a^2} + \frac{(x-h)^2}{b^2} = 1$, where a and b are coefficients. The center is the point (h, k) and the foci are the points $(h, k + c)$ and $(h, k - c)$, where $c^2 = a^2 - b^2$ and $a^2 > b^2$.

The major axis has length $2a$, and the minor axis has length $2b$.

Eccentricity (e) is a measure of how elongated an ellipse is, and is the ratio of the distance between the foci to the length of the major axis. Eccentricity will have a value between 0 and 1. The closer to 1 the eccentricity is, the closer the ellipse is to being a circle. The formula for eccentricity is $= \frac{c}{a}$.

Parabola: The set of all points in a plane that are equidistant from a fixed line, called the directrix, and a fixed point not on the line, called the focus.

Axis: The line perpendicular to the directrix that passes through the focus.

For parabolas that open up or down, the standard equation is $(x - h)^2 = 4c(y - k)$, where h, c, and k are coefficients. If c is positive, the parabola opens up. If c is negative, the parabola opens down. The vertex is the point (h, k). The directrix is the line having the equation $y = -c + k$, and the focus is the point $(h, c + k)$.

For parabolas that open left or right, the standard equation is $(y - k)^2 = 4c(x - h)$, where k, c, and h are coefficients. If c is positive, the parabola opens to the right. If c is negative, the parabola opens to the left. The vertex is the point (h, k). The directrix is the line having the equation $x = -c + h$, and the focus is the point $(c + h, k)$.

A hyperbola is the set of all points in a plane, whose distance from two fixed points, called foci, has a constant difference.

The standard equation of a horizontal hyperbola is $\frac{(x-h)^2}{a^2} - \frac{(y-k)^2}{b^2} = 1$, where a, b, h, and k are real numbers. The center is the point (h, k), the vertices are the points $(h + a, k)$ and $(h - a, k)$, and the foci are the points that every point on one of the parabolic curves is equidistant from and are found using the formulas $(h + c, k)$ and $(h - c, k)$, where $c^2 = a^2 + b^2$. The asymptotes are two lines the graph of the hyperbola approaches but never reaches, and are given by the equations $y = \left(\frac{b}{a}\right)(x - h) + k$ and $y = -\left(\frac{b}{a}\right)(x - h) + k$.

A vertical hyperbola is formed when a plane makes a vertical cut through two cones that are stacked vertex-to-vertex.

The standard equation of a vertical hyperbola is $\frac{(y-k)^2}{a^2} - \frac{(x-h)^2}{b^2} = 1$, where a, b, k, and h are real numbers. The center is the point (h, k), the vertices are the points $(h, k + a)$ and $(h, k - a)$, and the foci are the points that every point on one of the parabolic curves is equidistant from and are found using the formulas $(h, k + c)$ and $(h, k - c)$, where $c^2 = a^2 + b^2$. The asymptotes are two lines the graph of the hyperbola approaches but never reach, and are given by the equations $y = \left(\frac{a}{b}\right)(x - h) + k$ and $y = -\left(\frac{a}{b}\right)(x - h) + k$.

SOLIDS

The surface area of a solid object is the area of all sides or exterior surfaces. For objects such as prisms and pyramids, a further distinction is made between base surface area (B) and lateral surface area (LA). For a prism, the total surface area (SA) is $SA = LA + 2B$. For a pyramid or cone, the total surface area is $SA = LA + B$.

The surface area of a sphere can be found by the formula $A = 4\pi r^2$, where r is the radius. The volume is given by the formula $V = \frac{4}{3}\pi r^3$, where r is the radius. Both quantities are generally given in terms of π.

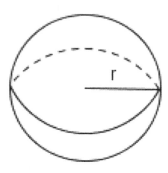

The volume of any prism is found by the formula $V = Bh$, where B is the area of the base, and h is the height (perpendicular distance between the bases). The surface area of any prism is the sum of the areas of both bases and all sides. It can be calculated as $SA = 2B + Ph$, where P is the perimeter of the base.

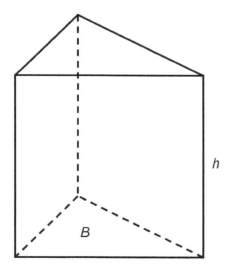

For a rectangular prism, the volume can be found by the formula $V = lwh$, where V is the volume, l is the length, w is the width, and h is the height. The surface area can be calculated as $SA = 2lw + 2hl + 2wh$ or $SA = 2(lw + hl + wh)$.

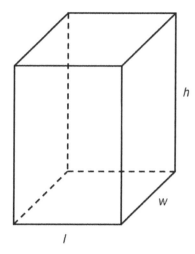

The volume of a cube can be found by the formula $V = s^3$, where s is the length of a side. The surface area of a cube is calculated as $SA = 6s^2$, where SA is the total surface area and s is the length of a side. These formulas are the same as the ones used for the volume and surface area of a rectangular prism, but simplified since all three quantities (length, width, and height) are the same.

Review Video: Volume and Surface Area of a Rectangular Solid
Visit mometrix.com/academy and enter code: 386780

The volume of a cylinder can be calculated by the formula $V = \pi r^2 h$, where r is the radius, and h is the height. The surface area of a cylinder can be found by the formula $SA = 2\pi r^2 + 2\pi rh$. The first term is the base area multiplied by two, and the second term is the perimeter of the base multiplied by the height.

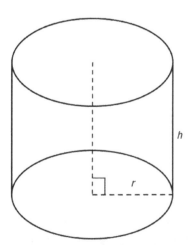

Review Video: Volume and Surface Area of a Right Circular Cylinder
Visit mometrix.com/academy and enter code: 226463

85

The volume of a pyramid is found by the formula $V = \frac{1}{3}Bh$, where B is the area of the base, and h is the height (perpendicular distance from the vertex to the base). Notice this formula is the same as $\frac{1}{3}$ times the volume of a prism. Like a prism, the base of a pyramid can be any shape. Finding the surface area of a pyramid is not as simple as the other shapes we've looked at thus far. If the pyramid is a right pyramid, meaning the base is a regular polygon and the vertex is directly over the center of that polygon, the surface area can be calculated as $SA = B + \frac{1}{2}Ph_s$, where P is the perimeter of the base, and h_s is the slant height (distance from the vertex to the midpoint of one side of the base). If the pyramid is irregular, the area of each triangle side must be calculated individually and then summed, along with the base.

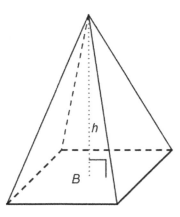

Review Video: <u>Volume and Surface Area of a Pyramid</u>
Visit mometrix.com/academy and enter code: 621932

The volume of a cone is found by the formula $V = \frac{1}{3}\pi r^2 h$, where r is the radius, and h is the height. Notice this is the same as $\frac{1}{3}$ times the volume of a cylinder. The surface area can be calculated as $SA = \pi r^2 + \pi rs$, where s is the slant height. The slant height can be calculated using the Pythagorean Theorem to be $\sqrt{r^2 + h^2}$, so the surface area formula can also be written as $SA = \pi r^2 + \pi r\sqrt{r^2 + h^2}$.

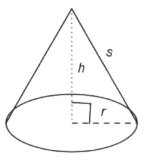

Review Video: <u>Volume and Surface Area of a Right Circular Cone</u>
Visit mometrix.com/academy and enter code: 573574

Science

Physical Science

SCIENTIFIC METHOD

One could argue that scientific knowledge is the sum of all scientific inquiries for truths about the natural world carried out throughout the history of human kind. More simply put, it is thanks to scientific inquiry that we know what we do about the world. Scientists use a number of generally accepted techniques collectively known as the scientific method. The scientific method generally involves carrying out the following steps:

- Identifying a problem or posing a question
- Formulating a hypothesis or an educated guess
- Conducting experiments or tests that will provide a basis to solve the problem or answer the question
- Observing the results of the test
- Drawing conclusions

An important part of the scientific method is using acceptable experimentation techniques to ensure results are not skewed. Objectivity is also important if valid results are to be obtained. Another important part of the scientific method is peer review. It is essential that experiments be performed and data be recorded in such a way that experiments can be reproduced to verify results.

A scientific fact is considered an objective and verifiable observation. A scientific theory is a greater body of accepted knowledge, principles, or relationships that might explain why something happens. A hypothesis is an educated guess that is not yet proven. It is used to predict the outcome of an experiment in an attempt to solve a problem or answer a question. A law is an explanation of events that always lead to the same outcome. It is a fact that an object falls. The law of gravity explains why an object falls. The theory of relativity, although generally accepted, has been neither proven nor disproved. A model is used to explain something on a smaller scale or in simpler terms to provide an example. It is a representation of an idea that can be used to explain events or applied to new situations to predict outcomes or determine results.

> **Review Video: The Scientific Method**
> Visit mometrix.com/academy and enter code: 191386

HISTORY OF SCIENCE

When one examines the history of scientific knowledge, it is clear that it is constantly evolving. The body of facts, models, theories, and laws grows and changes over time. In other words, one scientific discovery leads to the next. Some advances in science and technology have important and long-lasting effects on science and society. Some discoveries were so alien to the accepted beliefs of the time that not only were they rejected as wrong, but were also considered outright blasphemy. Today, however, many beliefs once considered incorrect have become an ingrained part of scientific knowledge, and have also been the basis of new advances. Examples of advances include: Copernicus's heliocentric view of the universe, Newton's laws of motion and planetary orbits, relativity, geologic time scale, plate tectonics, atomic theory, nuclear physics, biological evolution, germ theory, industrial revolution, molecular biology, information and communication, quantum theory, galactic universe, and medical and health technology.

Anton van Leeuwenhoek (d. 1723) used homemade magnifying glasses to become the first person to observe single-celled organisms. He observed bacteria, yeast, plants, and other microscopic organisms. His observations contributed to the field of microbiology. Carl Linnaeus (d. 1778) created a method to classify plants and animals, which became known as the Linnaean taxonomy. This was an important contribution because it offered a way to organize and therefore study large amounts of data. Charles Robert Darwin (d. 1882) is best known for contributing to the survival of the fittest through natural selection theory of evolution by observing different species of birds, specifically finches, in various geographic locations. Although the species Darwin looked at were different, he speculated they had a common ancestor. He reasoned that specific traits persisted because they gave the birds a greater chance of surviving and reproducing. He also discovered fossils, noted stratification, dissected marine animals, and interacted with indigenous peoples. He contributed to the fields of biology, marine biology, anthropology, paleontology, geography, and zoology.

Gregor Johann Mendel (d. 1884) is famous for experimenting with pea plants to observe the occurrence of inherited traits. He eventually became known as the father of genetics. Barbara McClintock (d. 1992) created the first genetic map for maize and was able to demonstrate basic genetic principles, such as how recombination is an exchange of chromosomal information. She also discovered how transposition flips the switch for traits. Her work contributed to the field of genetics, in particular to areas of study concerned with the structure and function of cells and chromosomes. James Watson and Francis Crick (d. 2004) were co-discoverers of the structure of deoxyribonucleic acid (DNA), which has a double helix shape. DNA contains the code for genetic information. The discovery of the double helix shape was important because it helped to explain how DNA replicates.

MATHEMATICS OF SCIENCE

Using the metric system is generally accepted as the preferred method for taking measurements. Having a universal standard allows individuals to interpret measurements more easily, regardless of where they are located. The basic units of measurement are: the meter, which measures length; the liter, which measures volume; and the gram, which measures mass. The metric system starts with a base unit and increases or decreases in units of 10. The prefix and the base unit combined are used to indicate an amount. For example, deka is 10 times the base unit. A dekameter is 10 meters; a dekaliter is 10 liters; and a dekagram is 10 grams. The prefix hecto refers to 100 times the base amount; kilo is 1,000 times the base amount. The prefixes that indicate a fraction of the base unit are deci, which is 1/10 of the base unit; centi, which is 1/100 of the base unit; and milli, which is 1/1000 of the base unit.

The mathematical concept of significant figures or significant digits is often used to determine the accuracy of measurements or the level of confidence one has in a specific measurement. The significant figures of a measurement include all the digits known with certainty plus one estimated or uncertain digit. There are a number of rules for determining which digits are considered "important" or "interesting." They are: all non-zero digits are significant, zeros between digits are significant, and leading and trailing zeros are not significant unless they appear to the right of the non-zero digits in a decimal. For example, in 0.01230 the significant digits are 1230, and this number would be said to be accurate to the hundred-thousandths place. The zero indicates that the amount has actually been measured as 0. Other zeros are considered place holders, and are not

Copyright © Mometrix Media. You have been licensed one copy of this document for personal use only. Any other reproduction or redistribution is strictly prohibited. All rights reserved.

important. A decimal point may be placed after zeros to indicate their importance (in 100. for example).

Scientific notation is used because values in science can be very large or very small, which makes them unwieldy. A number in decimal notation is 93,000,000. In scientific notation, it is 9.3 x 107. The first number, 9.3, is the coefficient. It is always greater than or equal to 1 and less than 10. This number is followed by a multiplication sign. The base is always 10 in scientific notation. If the number is greater than ten, the exponent is positive. If the number is between zero and one, the exponent is negative. The first digit of the number is followed by a decimal point and then the rest of the number. In this case, the number is 9.3. To get that number, the decimal point was moved seven places from the end of the number, 93,000,000. The number of places, seven, is the exponent.

STATISTICS

Data collected during a science lab can be organized and presented in any number of ways. While straight narrative is a suitable method for presenting some lab results, it is not a suitable way to present numbers and quantitative measurements. These types of observations can often be better presented with tables and graphs. Data that is presented in tables and organized in rows and columns may also be used to make graphs quite easily. Other methods of presenting data include illustrations, photographs, video, and even audio formats. In a formal report, tables and figures are labeled and referred to by their labels. For example, a picture of a bubbly solution might be labeled Figure 1, Bubbly Solution. It would be referred to in the text in the following way: "The reaction created bubbles 10 mm in size, as shown in Figure 1, Bubbly Solution." Graphs are also labeled as figures. Tables are labeled in a different way. Examples include: Table 1, Results of Statistical Analysis, or Table 2, Data from Lab 2.

Graphs and charts are effective ways to present scientific data such as observations, statistical analyses, and comparisons between dependent variables and independent variables. On a line chart, the independent variable (the one that is being manipulated for the experiment) is represented on the horizontal axis (the x-axis). Any dependent variables (the ones that may change as the independent variable changes) are represented on the y-axis. The points are charted and a line is drawn to connect the points. An XY or scatter plot is often used to plot many points. A "best fit" line is drawn, which allows outliers to be identified more easily. Charts and their axes should have titles. The x and y interval units should be evenly spaced and labeled. Other types of charts are bar charts and histograms, which can be used to compare differences between the data collected for two variables. A pie chart can graphically show the relation of parts to a whole.

Mean: The mean is the sum of a list of numbers divided by the number of numbers.

Median: The median is the middle number in a list of numbers sorted from least to greatest. If the list has an even number of entries, the median is the smaller of the two in the middle.

Standard deviation: This measures the variability of a data set and determines the amount of confidence one can have in the conclusions.

Mode: This is the value that appears most frequently in a data set.

Range: This is the difference between the highest and lowest numbers, which can be used to determine how spread out data is.

Regression Analysis: This is a method of analyzing sets of data and sets of variables that involves studying how the typical value of the dependent variable changes when any one of the independent variables is varied and the other independent variables remain fixed.

CHEMISTRY

Matter refers to substances that have mass and occupy space (or volume). The traditional definition of matter describes it as having three states: solid, liquid, and gas. These different states are caused by differences in the distances and angles between molecules or atoms, which result in differences in the energy that binds them. Solid structures are rigid or nearly rigid and have strong bonds. Molecules or atoms of liquids move around and have weak bonds, although they are not weak enough to readily break. Molecules or atoms of gases move almost independently of each other, are typically far apart, and do not form bonds. The current definition of matter describes it as having four states. The fourth is plasma, which is an ionized gas that has some electrons that are described as free because they are not bound to an atom or molecule.

All matter consists of atoms. Atoms consist of a nucleus and electrons. The nucleus consists of protons and neutrons. The properties of these are measurable; they have mass and an electrical charge. The nucleus is positively charged due to the presence of protons. Electrons are negatively charged and orbit the nucleus. The nucleus has considerably more mass than the surrounding electrons. Atoms can bond together to make molecules. Atoms that have an equal number of protons and electrons are electrically neutral. If the number of protons and electrons in an atom is not equal, the atom has a positive or negative charge and is an ion.

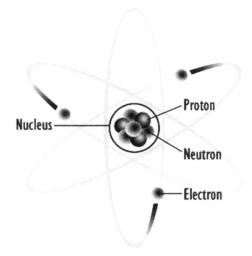

An element is matter with one particular type of atom. It can be identified by its atomic number, or the number of protons in its nucleus. There are approximately 117 elements currently known, 94 of which occur naturally on Earth. Elements from the periodic table include hydrogen, carbon, iron, helium, mercury, and oxygen. Atoms combine to form molecules. For example, two atoms of hydrogen (H) and one atom of oxygen (O) combine to form water (H_2O).

Compounds are substances containing two or more elements. Compounds are formed by chemical reactions and frequently have different properties than the original elements. Compounds are decomposed by a chemical reaction rather than separated by a physical one. Solutions are homogeneous mixtures composed of two or more substances that have become one. Mixtures contain two or more substances that are combined but have not reacted chemically with each other. Mixtures can be separated using physical methods, while compounds cannot.

A solution is a homogeneous mixture. A mixture is two or more different substances that are mixed together, but not combined chemically. Homogeneous mixtures are those that are uniform in their composition. Solutions consist of a solute (the substance that is dissolved) and a solvent (the substance that does the dissolving). An example is sugar water. The solvent is the water and the solute is the sugar. The intermolecular attraction between the solvent and the solute is called solvation. Hydration refers to solutions in which water is the solvent. Solutions are formed when the forces of the molecules of the solute and the solvent are as strong as the individual molecular forces of the solute and the solvent. An example is that salt (NaCl) dissolves in water to create a solution. The Na^+ and the Cl^- ions in salt interact with the molecules of water and vice versa to overcome the individual molecular forces of the solute and the solvent.

Review Video: Solutions
Visit mometrix.com/academy and enter code: 995937

Elements are represented in upper case letters. If there is no subscript, it indicates there is only one atom of the element. Otherwise, the subscript indicates the number of atoms. In molecular formulas, elements are organized according to the Hill system. Carbon is first, hydrogen comes next, and the remaining elements are listed in alphabetical order. If there is no carbon, all elements are listed alphabetically. There are a couple of exceptions to these rules. First, oxygen is usually listed last in oxides. Second, in ionic compounds the positive ion is listed first, followed by the negative ion. In CO_2, for example, C indicates 1 atom of carbon and O_2 indicates 2 atoms of oxygen. The compound is carbon dioxide. The formula for ammonia (an ionic compound) is NH_3, which is one atom of nitrogen and three of hydrogen. H_2O is two atoms of hydrogen and one of oxygen. Sugar is $C_6H_{12}O_6$, which is 6 atoms of carbon, 12 of hydrogen, and 6 of oxygen.

An **atom** is one of the most basic units of matter. An atom consists of a central nucleus surrounded by electrons. The **nucleus** of an atom consists of protons and neutrons. It is positively charged, dense, and heavier than the surrounding electrons. The plural form of nucleus is nuclei. **Neutrons** are the uncharged atomic particles contained within the nucleus. The number of neutrons in a nucleus can be represented as "N." Along with neutrons, **protons** make up the nucleus of an atom. The number of protons in the nucleus determines the atomic number of an element. Carbon atoms, for example, have six protons. The atomic number of carbon is 6. **Nucleon** refers collectively to neutrons and protons. **Electrons** are atomic particles that are negatively charged and orbit the nucleus of an atom. The number of protons minus the number of electrons indicates the charge of an atom.

Review Video: Structure of Atoms
Visit mometrix.com/academy and enter code: 905932

The **atomic number** of an element refers to the number of protons in the nucleus of an atom. It is a unique identifier. It can be represented as Z. Atoms with a neutral charge have an atomic number that is equal to the number of electrons. **Atomic mass** is also known as the mass number. The atomic mass is the total number of protons and neutrons in the nucleus of an atom. It is referred to as "A." The atomic mass (A) is equal to the number of protons (Z) plus the number of neutrons (N). This can be represented by the equation $A = Z + N$. The mass of electrons in an atom is basically insignificant because it is so small. **Atomic weight** may sometimes be referred to as "relative atomic mass," but should not be confused with atomic mass. Atomic weight is the ratio of the average mass per atom of a sample (which can include various isotopes of an element) to 1/12 of the mass of an atom of carbon-12.

Chemical properties are qualities of a substance which can't be determined by simply looking at the substance and must be determined through chemical reactions. Some chemical properties of elements include: atomic number, electron configuration, electrons per shell, electronegativity, atomic radius, and isotopes.

In contrast to chemical properties, **physical properties** can be observed or measured without chemical reactions. These include properties such as color, elasticity, mass, volume, and temperature. **Mass** is a measure of the amount of substance in an object. **Weight** is a measure of the gravitational pull of Earth on an object. **Volume** is a measure of the amount of space occupied. There are many formulas to determine volume. For example, the volume of a cube is the length of one side cubed (a^3) and the volume of a rectangular prism is length times width times height ($l \cdot w \cdot h$). The volume of an irregular shape can be determined by how much water it displaces.

Density is a measure of the amount of mass per unit volume. The formula to find density is mass divided by volume ($D=m/V$). It is expressed in terms of mass per cubic unit, such as grams per cubic centimeter (g/cm^3). **Specific gravity** is a measure of the ratio of a substance's density compared to the density of water.

> **Review Video: Mass, Weight, Volume, Density, and Specific Gravity**
> Visit mometrix.com/academy and enter code: 920570

Both physical changes and chemical reactions are everyday occurrences. Physical changes do not result in different substances. For example, when water becomes ice it has undergone a physical change, but not a chemical change. It has changed its form, but not its composition. It is still H_2O. Chemical properties are concerned with the constituent particles that make up the physicality of a substance. Chemical properties are apparent when chemical changes occur. The chemical properties of a substance are influenced by its electron configuration, which is determined in part by the number of protons in the nucleus (the atomic number). Carbon, for example, has 6 protons and 6 electrons. It is an element's outermost valence electrons that mainly determine its chemical properties. Chemical reactions may release or consume energy.

PERIODIC TABLE

The periodic table groups elements with similar chemical properties together. The grouping of elements is based on atomic structure. It shows periodic trends of physical and chemical properties and identifies families of elements with similar properties. It is a common model for organizing and understanding elements. In the periodic table, each element has its own cell that includes varying amounts of information presented in symbol form about the properties of the element. Cells in the table are arranged in rows (periods) and columns (groups or families). At minimum, a cell includes the symbol for the element and its atomic number. The cell for hydrogen, for example, which appears first in the upper left corner, includes an "H" and a "1" above the letter. Elements are ordered by atomic number, left to right, top to bottom.

In the periodic table, the groups are the columns numbered 1 through 18 that group elements with similar outer electron shell configurations. Since the configuration of the outer electron shell is one of the primary factors affecting an element's chemical properties, elements within the same group have similar chemical properties. Previous naming conventions for groups have included the use of Roman numerals and upper-case letters. Currently, the periodic table groups are: Group 1, alkali metals; Group 2, alkaline earth metals; Groups 3-12, transition metals; Group 13, boron family; Group 14; carbon family; Group 15, pnictogens; Group 16, chalcogens; Group 17, halogens; Group 18, noble gases.

In the periodic table, there are seven periods (rows), and within each period there are blocks that group elements with the same outer electron subshell (more on this in the next section). The number of electrons in that outer shell determines which group an element belongs to within a given block. Each row's number (1, 2, 3, etc.) corresponds to the highest number electron shell that is in use. For example, row 2 uses only electron shells 1 and 2, while row 7 uses all shells from 1-7.

For example, hydrogen is in the s-block as its highest-energy electron is in the s-orbital. The f-block is organized separately from the rest of the periodic table and includes atoms or ions that have valence electrons in f-orbitals.

Atomic radii will decrease from left to right across a period (row) on the periodic table. In a group (column), there is an increase in the atomic radii of elements from top to bottom. Ionic radii will be smaller than the atomic radii for metals, but the opposite is true for non-metals. From left to right, electronegativity, or an atom's likeliness of taking another atom's electrons, increases. In a group, electronegativity decreases from top to bottom. Ionization energy or the amount of energy needed to get rid of an atom's outermost electron, increases across a period and decreases down a group. Electron affinity will become more negative across a period but will not change much within a

93

group. The melting point decreases from top to bottom in the metal groups and increases from top to bottom in the non-metal groups.

Group→	1	2	3	4	5	6	7	8	9	10	11	12	13	14	15	16	17	18
↓Period																		
1	1 H																	2 He
2	3 Li	4 Be											5 B	6 C	7 N	8 O	9 F	10 Ne
3	11 Na	12 Mg											13 Al	14 Si	15 P	16 S	17 Cl	18 Ar
4	19 K	20 Ca	21 Sc	22 Ti	23 V	24 Cr	25 Mn	26 Fe	27 Co	28 Ni	29 Cu	30 Zn	31 Ga	32 Ge	33 As	34 Se	35 Br	36 Kr
5	37 Rb	38 Sr	39 Y	40 Zr	41 Nb	42 Mo	43 Tc	44 Ru	45 Rh	46 Pd	47 Ag	48 Cd	49 In	50 Sn	51 Sb	52 Te	53 I	54 Xe
6	55 Cs	56 Ba	*	72 Hf	73 Ta	74 W	75 Re	76 Os	77 Ir	78 Pt	79 Au	80 Hg	81 Tl	82 Pb	83 Bi	84 Po	85 At	86 Rn
7	87 Fr	88 Ra	**	104 Rf	105 Db	106 Sg	107 Bh	108 Hs	109 Mt	110 Ds	111 Rg	112 Cn	113 Uut	114 Fl	115 Uup	116 Lv	117 Uus	118 Uuo

*	57 La	58 Ce	59 Pr	60 Nd	61 Pm	62 Sm	63 Eu	64 Gd	65 Tb	66 Dy	67 Ho	68 Er	69 Tm	70 Yb	71 Lu
**	89 Ac	90 Th	91 Pa	92 U	93 Np	94 Pu	95 Am	96 Cm	97 Bk	98 Cf	99 Es	100 Fm	101 Md	102 No	103 Lr

Review Video: Periodic Table
Visit mometrix.com/academy and enter code: 154828

ELECTRONS

Electrons are subatomic particles that orbit the nucleus at various levels commonly referred to as layers, shells, or clouds. The orbiting electron or electrons account for only a fraction of the atom's mass. They are much smaller than the nucleus, are negatively charged, and exhibit wave-like characteristics. Electrons are part of the lepton family of elementary particles. Electrons can occupy orbits that are varying distances away from the nucleus, and tend to occupy the lowest energy level they can. If an atom has all its electrons in the lowest available positions, it has a stable electron arrangement. The outermost electron shell of an atom in its uncombined state is known as the valence shell. The electrons there are called valence electrons, and it is their number that determines bonding behavior. Atoms tend to react in a manner that will allow them to fill or empty their valence shells.

There are seven electron shells. One is closest to the nucleus and seven is the farthest away. Electron shells can also be identified with the letters K, L, M, N, O, P, and Q. Traditionally, there were four subshells identified by the first letter of their descriptive name: s (sharp), p (principal), d (diffuse), and f (fundamental). The maximum number of electrons for each subshell is as follows: s is 2, p is 6, d is 10, and f is 14. Every shell has an s subshell; the second shell and those above also have a p subshell; the third shell and those above also have a d subshell; and so on. Each subshell contains atomic orbitals, which describes the wave-like characteristics of an electron or a pair of electrons expressed as two angles and the distance from the nucleus. Atomic orbital is a concept used to express the likelihood of an electron's position in accordance with the idea of wave-particle duality.

Electron configuration: This is a trend whereby electrons fill shells and subshells in an element in a particular order and with a particular number of electrons. The chemical properties of the elements reflect their electron configurations. Energy levels (shells) do not have to be completely filled before the next one begins to be filled. An example of electron configuration notation is $1s^22s^22p^5$, where the first number is the row (period), or shell. The letter refers to the subshell of the shell, and the number in superscript is the number of electrons in the subshell. A common shorthand method for electron configuration notation is to use a noble gas (in a bracket) to abbreviate the shells that elements have in common. For example, the electron configuration for neon is $1s^22s^22p^6$.

The configuration for phosphorus is $1s^22s^22p^63s^23p^3$, which can be written as $[Ne]3s^23p^3$. Subshells are filled in the following manner: 1s, 2s, 2p, 3s, 3p, 4s, 3d, 4p, 5s, 4d, 5p, 6s, 4f, 5d, 6p, 7s, 5f, 6d, and 7p.

Review Video: <u>Order of Electron Filling in the Periodic Table</u>
Visit mometrix.com/academy and enter code: 761477

Most atoms are neutral since the positive charge of the protons in the nucleus is balanced by the negative charge of the surrounding electrons. Electrons are transferred between atoms when they come into contact with each other. This creates a molecule or atom in which the number of electrons does not equal the number of protons, which gives it a positive or negative charge. A negative ion is created when an atom gains electrons, while a positive ion is created when an atom loses electrons. An ionic bond is formed between ions with opposite charges. The resulting compound is neutral. Ionization refers to the process by which neutral particles are ionized into charged particles. Gases and plasmas can be partially or fully ionized through ionization.

Atoms interact by transferring or sharing the electrons furthest from the nucleus. Known as the outer or valence electrons, they are responsible for the chemical properties of an element. Bonds between atoms are created when electrons are paired up by being transferred or shared. If electrons are transferred from one atom to another, the bond is ionic. If electrons are shared, the bond is covalent. Atoms of the same element may bond together to form molecules or crystalline solids. When two or more different types of atoms bind together chemically, a compound is made. The physical properties of compounds reflect the nature of the interactions among their molecules. These interactions are determined by the structure of the molecule, including the atoms they consist of and the distances and angles between them.

ISOTOPES AND MOLECULES

The number of protons in an atom determines the element of that atom. For instance, all helium atoms have exactly two protons, and all oxygen atoms have exactly eight protons. If two atoms have the same number of protons, then they are the same element. However, the number of neutrons in two atoms can be different without the atoms being different elements. Isotope is the term used to distinguish between atoms that have the same number of protons but a different number of neutrons. The names of isotopes have the element name with the mass number. Recall that the mass number is the number of protons plus the number of neutrons. For example, carbon-12 refers to an atom that has 6 protons, which makes it carbon, and 6 neutrons. In other words, 6 protons + 6 neutrons = 12. Carbon-13 has six protons and seven neutrons, and carbon-14 has six protons and eight neutrons. Isotopes can also be written with the mass number in superscript before the element symbol. For example, carbon-12 can be written as ^{12}C.

Review Video: <u>Isotopes</u>
Visit mometrix.com/academy and enter code: 294271

The important properties of water (H_2O) are high polarity, hydrogen bonding, cohesiveness, adhesiveness, high specific heat, high latent heat, and high heat of vaporization. It is essential to life as we know it, as water is one of the main if not the main constituent of many living things. Water is a liquid at room temperature. The high specific heat of water means it resists the breaking of its hydrogen bonds and resists heat and motion, which is why it has a relatively high boiling point and high vaporization point. It also resists temperature change. Water is peculiar in that its solid-state floats in its liquid state. Most substances are denser in their solid forms. Water is cohesive, which means it is attracted to itself. It is also adhesive, which means it readily attracts other molecules. If water tends to adhere to another substance, the substance is said to be hydrophilic. Water makes a good solvent. Substances, particularly those with polar ions and molecules, readily dissolve in water.

Electrons in an atom can orbit different levels around the nucleus. They can absorb or release energy, which can change the location of their orbit or even allow them to break free from the atom. The outermost layer is the valence layer, which contains the valence electrons. The valence layer tends to have or share eight electrons. Molecules are formed by a chemical bond between atoms, a bond which occurs at the valence level. Two basic types of bonds are covalent and ionic. A covalent bond is formed when atoms share electrons. An ionic bond is formed when an atom transfers an electron to another atom. A hydrogen bond is a weak bond between a hydrogen atom of one molecule and an electronegative atom (such as nitrogen, oxygen, or fluorine) of another molecule. The Van der Waals force is a weak force between molecules. This type of force is much weaker than actual chemical bonds between atoms.

Review Video: Molecules
Visit mometrix.com/academy and enter code: 349910

REACTIONS

Chemical reactions measured in human time can take place quickly or slowly. They can take fractions of a second or billions of years. The rates of chemical reactions are determined by how frequently reacting atoms and molecules interact. Rates are also influenced by the temperature and various properties (such as shape) of the reacting materials. Catalysts accelerate chemical reactions, while inhibitors decrease reaction rates. Some types of reactions release energy in the form of heat and light.

Some types of reactions involve the transfer of either electrons or hydrogen ions between reacting ions, molecules, or atoms. In other reactions, chemical bonds are broken down by heat or light to form reactive radicals with electrons that will readily form new bonds. Processes such as the formation of ozone and greenhouse gases in the atmosphere and the burning and processing of fossil fuels are controlled by radical reactions.

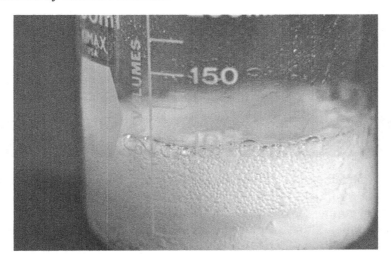

Chemical equations describe chemical reactions. The reactants are on the left side before the arrow and the products are on the right side after the arrow. The arrow indicates the reaction or change. The coefficient, or stoichiometric coefficient, is the number before the element, and indicates the ratio of reactants to products in terms of moles. The equation for the formation of water from hydrogen and oxygen, for example, is $2H_2(g) + O_2(g) \rightarrow 2H_2O(l)$. The 2 preceding hydrogen and water is the coefficient, which means there are 2 moles of hydrogen and 2 of water. There is 1 mole of oxygen, which does not have to be indicated with the number 1. In parentheses, g stands for gas, l stands for liquid, s stands for solid, and aq stands for aqueous solution (a substance dissolved in water). Charges are shown in superscript for individual ions, but not for ionic compounds. Polyatomic ions are separated by parentheses so the ion will not be confused with the number of ions.

Review Video: Reaction Process
Visit mometrix.com/academy and enter code: 808039

An unbalanced equation is one that does not follow the law of conservation of mass, which states that matter can only be changed, not created. If an equation is unbalanced, the numbers of atoms indicated by the stoichiometric coefficients on each side of the arrow will not be equal. Start by writing the formulas for each species in the reaction. Count the atoms on each side and determine if the number is equal. Coefficients must be whole numbers. Fractional amounts, such as half a molecule, are not possible.

Equations can be balanced by multiplying the coefficients by a constant that will produce the smallest possible whole number coefficient. $H_2 + O_2 \rightarrow H_2O$ is an example of an unbalanced equation. The balanced equation is $2H_2 + O_2 \rightarrow 2H_2O$, which indicates that it takes two moles of hydrogen and one of oxygen to produce two moles of water.

Review Video: How to Balance a Chemical Equation
Visit mometrix.com/academy and enter code: 341228

One way to organize chemical reactions is to sort them into two categories: oxidation/reduction reactions (also called redox reactions) and metathesis reactions (which include acid/base reactions). Oxidation/reduction reactions can involve the transfer of one or more electrons, or they can occur as a result of the transfer of oxygen, hydrogen, or halogen atoms. The species that loses electrons is oxidized and is referred to as the reducing agent. The species that gains electrons is reduced and is referred to as the oxidizing agent. The element undergoing oxidation experiences an increase in its oxidation number, while the element undergoing reduction experiences a decrease in its oxidation number. Single replacement reactions are types of oxidation/reduction reactions. In a single replacement reaction, electrons are transferred from one chemical species to another. The transfer of electrons results in changes in the nature and charge of the species.

Review Video: Reduction
Visit mometrix.com/academy and enter code: 317289

Single substitution, displacement, or replacement reactions are when one reactant is displaced by another to form the final product ($A + BC \rightarrow B + AC$). Single substitution reactions can be cationic or anionic. When a piece of copper (Cu) is placed into a solution of silver nitrate ($AgNO_3$), the solution turns blue. The copper appears to be replaced with a silvery-white material. The equation is $2AgNO_3 + Cu \rightarrow Cu(NO_3)2 + 2Ag$. When this reaction takes place, the copper dissolves and the silver in the silver nitrate solution precipitates (becomes a solid), thus resulting in copper nitrate and silver. Copper and silver have switched places in the nitrate.

Review Video: Single-Replacement Reactions
Visit mometrix.com/academy and enter code: 442975

Combination, or synthesis, reactions: In a combination reaction, two or more reactants combine to form a single product ($A + B \rightarrow C$). These reactions are also called synthesis or addition reactions. An example is burning hydrogen in air to produce water. The equation is $2H_2 (g) + O_2 (g) \rightarrow 2H_2O (l)$. Another example is when water and sulfur trioxide react to form sulfuric acid. The equation is $H_2O + SO_3 \rightarrow H_2SO_4$.

Double displacement, double replacement, substitution, metathesis, or ion exchange reactions are when ions or bonds are exchanged by two compounds to form different compounds ($AC + BD \rightarrow AD + BC$). An example of this is that silver nitrate and sodium chloride form two different products (silver chloride and sodium nitrate) when they react. The formula for this reaction is $AgNO_3 + NaCl \rightarrow AgCl + NaNO_3$.

Double replacement reactions are metathesis reactions. In a double replacement reaction, the chemical reactants exchange ions but the oxidation state stays the same. One of the indicators of this is the formation of a solid precipitate. In acid/base reactions, an acid is a compound that can donate a proton, while a base is a compound that can accept a proton. In these types of reactions, the acid and base react to form a salt and water. When the proton is donated, the base becomes water and the remaining ions form a salt. One method of determining whether a reaction is an oxidation/reduction or a metathesis reaction is that the oxidation number of atoms does not change during a metathesis reaction.

A neutralization, acid-base, or proton transfer reaction is when one compound acquires H^+ from another. These types of reactions are also usually double displacement reactions. The acid has an H^+ that is transferred to the base and neutralized to form a salt.

Decomposition (or desynthesis, decombination, or deconstruction) reactions; in a decomposition reaction, a reactant is broken down into two or more products ($A \rightarrow B + C$). These reactions are also called analysis reactions. Thermal decomposition is caused by heat. Electrolytic decomposition is due to electricity. An example of this type of reaction is the decomposition of water into hydrogen and oxygen gas. The equation is $2H_2O \rightarrow 2H_2 + O_2$. Decomposition is considered a chemical reaction whereby a single compound breaks down into component parts or simpler compounds. When a compound or substance separates into these simpler substances, the byproducts are often substances that are different from the original. Decomposition can be viewed as the opposite of combination reactions. Most decomposition reactions are endothermic. Heat needs to be added for the chemical reaction to occur. Separation processes can be mechanical or chemical, and usually involve re-organizing a mixture of substances without changing their chemical nature. The separated products may differ from the original mixture in terms of chemical or physical properties. Types of separation processes include filtration, crystallization, distillation, and chromatography. Basically, decomposition breaks down one compound into two or more compounds or substances that are different from the original; separation sorts the substances from the original mixture into like substances.

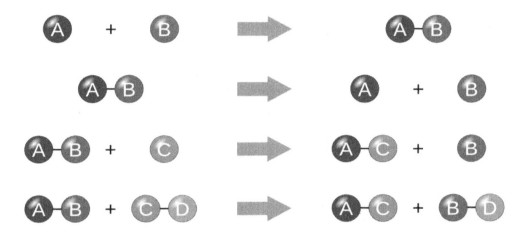

Endothermic reactions are chemical reactions that absorb heat and exothermic reactions are chemical reactions that release heat. Reactants are the substances that are consumed during a reaction, while products are the substances that are produced or formed. A balanced equation is one that uses reactants, products, and coefficients in such a way that the number of each type of atom (law of conservation of mass) and the total charge remains the same. The reactants are on the left side of the arrow and the products are on the right. The heat difference between endothermic and exothermic reactions is caused by bonds forming and breaking. If more energy is needed to break the reactant bonds than is released when they form, the reaction is endothermic. Heat is absorbed and the environmental temperature decreases. If more energy is released when product bonds form than is needed to break the reactant bonds, the reaction is exothermic. Heat is released and the environmental temperature increases.

The collision theory states that for a chemical reaction to occur, atoms or molecules have to collide with each other with a certain amount of energy. A certain amount of energy is required to breach the activation barrier. Heating a mixture will raise the energy levels of the molecules and the rate of reaction (the time it takes for a reaction to complete). Generally, the rate of reaction is doubled for every 10 degrees Celsius temperature increase. However, the increase needed to double a reaction rate increases as the temperature climbs. This is due to the increase in collision frequency that occurs as the temperature increases. Other factors that can affect the rate of reaction are surface area, concentration, pressure, and the presence of a catalyst.

The particles of an atom's nucleus (the protons and neutrons) are bound together by nuclear force, also known as residual strong force. Unlike chemical reactions, which involve electrons, nuclear reactions occur when two nuclei or nuclear particles collide. This results in the release or absorption of energy and products that are different from the initial particles. The energy released in a nuclear reaction can take various forms, including the release of kinetic energy of the product particles and the emission of very high energy photons known as gamma rays. Some energy may also remain in the nucleus. Radioactivity refers to the particles emitted from nuclei as a result of nuclear instability. There are many nuclear isotopes that are unstable and can spontaneously emit some kind of radiation. The most common types of radiation are alpha, beta, and gamma radiation, but there are several other varieties of radioactive decay.

INORGANIC AND ORGANIC

The terms inorganic and organic have become less useful over time as their definitions have changed. Historically, inorganic molecules were defined as those of a mineral nature that were not created by biological processes. Organic molecules were defined as those that were produced biologically by a "life process" or "vital force." It was then discovered that organic compounds could be synthesized without a life process. Currently, molecules containing carbon are considered organic. Carbon is largely responsible for creating biological diversity, and is more capable than all other elements of forming large, complex, and diverse molecules of an organic nature. Carbon often completes its valence shell by sharing electrons with other atoms in four covalent bonds, which is also known as tetravalence.

The main trait of inorganic compounds is that they lack carbon. Inorganic compounds include mineral salts, metals and alloys, non-metallic compounds such as phosphorus, and metal complexes. A metal complex has a central atom (or ion) bonded to surrounding ligands (molecules or anions). The ligands sacrifice the donor atoms (in the form of at least one pair of electrons) to the central atom. Many inorganic compounds are ionic, meaning they form ionic bonds rather than share electrons. They may have high melting points because of this. They may also be colorful, but this is not an absolute identifier of an inorganic compound. Salts, which are inorganic compounds, are an example of inorganic bonding of cations and anions. Some examples of salts are magnesium chloride ($MgCl_2$) and sodium oxide (Na_2O). Oxides, carbonates, sulfates, and halides are classes of inorganic compounds. They are typically poor conductors, are very water soluble, and crystallize easily. Minerals and silicates are also inorganic compounds.

Two of the main characteristics of organic compounds are that they include carbon and are formed by covalent bonds. Carbon can form long chains, double and triple bonds, and rings. While inorganic compounds tend to have high melting points, organic compounds tend to melt at temperatures below 300° C. They also tend to boil, sublimate, and decompose below this temperature. Unlike inorganic compounds, they are not very water soluble. Organic molecules are organized into functional groups based on their specific atoms, which helps determine how they will react chemically. A few groups are alkanes, nitro, alkenes, sulfides, amines, and carbolic acids. The hydroxyl group (-OH) consists of alcohols. These molecules are polar, which increases their solubility. By some estimates, there are more than 16 million organic compounds.

Review Video: Organic Compounds
Visit mometrix.com/academy and enter code: 264922

Nomenclature refers to the manner in which a compound is named. First, it must be determined whether the compound is ionic (formed through electron transfer between cations and anions) or molecular (formed through electron sharing between molecules). When dealing with an ionic compound, the name is determined using the standard naming conventions for ionic compounds. This involves indicating the positive element first (the charge must be defined when there is more than one option for the valency) followed by the negative element plus the appropriate suffix. The rules for naming a molecular compound are as follows: write elements in order of increasing group number and determine the prefix by determining the number of atoms. Exclude mono for the first atom. The name for CO_2, for example, is carbon dioxide. The end of oxygen is dropped and "ide" is added to make oxide, and the prefix "di" is used to indicate there are two atoms of oxygen.

ACIDS AND BASES

The potential of hydrogen (pH) is a measurement of the concentration of hydrogen ions in a substance in terms of the number of moles of H^+ per liter of solution. All substances fall between 0 and 14 on the pH scale. A lower pH indicates a higher H^+ concentration, while a higher pH indicates a lower H^+ concentration. Pure water has a neutral pH, which is 7. Anything with a pH lower than water (0-7) is considered acidic. Anything with a pH higher than water (7-14) is a base. Drain cleaner, soap, baking soda, ammonia, egg whites, and sea water are common bases. Urine, stomach acid, citric acid, vinegar, hydrochloric acid, and battery acid are acids. A pH indicator is a substance that acts as a detector of hydrogen or hydronium ions. It is halochromic, meaning it changes color to indicate that hydrogen or hydronium ions have been detected.

> **Review Video: <u>Strong and Weak Acids and Bases</u>**
> Visit mometrix.com/academy and enter code: 268930

When they are dissolved in aqueous solutions, some properties of acids are that they conduct electricity, change blue litmus paper to red, have a sour taste, react with bases to neutralize them, and react with active metals to free hydrogen. A weak acid is one that does not donate all of its protons or disassociate completely. Strong acids include hydrochloric, hydriodic, hydrobromic, perchloric, nitric, and sulfuric. They ionize completely. Superacids are those that are stronger than 100 percent sulfuric acid. They include fluoroantimonic, magic, and perchloric acids. Acids can be used in pickling, a process used to remove rust and corrosion from metals. They are also used as catalysts in the processing of minerals and the production of salts and fertilizers. Phosphoric acid (H_3PO_4) is added to sodas and other acids are added to foods as preservatives or to add taste.

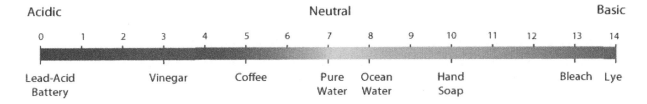

When they are dissolved in aqueous solutions, some properties of bases are that they conduct electricity, change red litmus paper to blue, feel slippery, and react with acids to neutralize their properties. A weak base is one that does not completely ionize in an aqueous solution, and usually has a low pH. Strong bases can free protons in very weak acids. Examples of strong bases are hydroxide compounds such as potassium, barium, and lithium hydroxides. Most are in the first and second groups of the periodic table. A superbase is extremely strong compared to sodium hydroxide and cannot be kept in an aqueous solution. Superbases are organized into organic, organometallic, and inorganic classes. Bases are used as insoluble catalysts in heterogeneous reactions and as catalysts in hydrogenation.

Some properties of salts are that they are formed from acid base reactions, are ionic compounds consisting of metallic and nonmetallic ions, dissociate in water, and are comprised of tightly bonded ions. Some common salts are sodium chloride (NaCl), sodium bisulfate, potassium dichromate ($K_2Cr_2O_7$), and calcium chloride ($CaCl_2$). Calcium chloride is used as a drying agent, and may be used to absorb moisture when freezing mixtures. Potassium nitrate (KNO_3) is used to make fertilizer and in the manufacture of explosives. Sodium nitrate ($NaNO_3$) is also used in the making of fertilizer. Baking soda (sodium bicarbonate) is a salt, as are Epsom salts [magnesium sulfate ($MgSO_4$)]. Salt and water can react to form a base and an acid. This is called a hydrolysis reaction.

A buffer is a solution whose pH remains relatively constant when a small amount of an acid or a base is added. It is usually made of a weak acid and its conjugate base (proton receiver) or one of its soluble salts. It can also be made of a weak base and its conjugate acid (proton donator) or one of its salts. A constant pH is necessary in living cells because some living things can only live within a certain pH range. If that pH changes, the cells could die. Blood is an example of a buffer.

A pKa is a measure of acid dissociation or the acid dissociation constant. Buffer solutions can help keep enzymes at the correct pH. They are also used in the fermentation process, in dyeing fabrics, and in the calibration of pH meters. An example of a buffer is HC_2H_3O (a weak acid) and $NaC_2H_3O_2$ (a salt containing the $C_2H_3O_2^-$ ion).

> **Review Video: Buffer**
> Visit mometrix.com/academy and enter code: 389183

GENERAL CONCEPTS

Lewis formulas: These show the bonding or nonbonding tendency of specific pairs of valence electrons. Lewis dot diagrams use dots to represent valence electrons. Dots are paired around an atom. When an atom forms a covalent bond with another atom, the elements share the dots as they would electrons. Double and triple bonds are indicated with additional adjacent dots. Methane (CH_4), for instance, would be shown as a C with 2 dots above, below, and to the right and left and an H next to each set of dots. In structural formulas, the dots are single lines.

Kekulé diagrams: Like Lewis dot diagrams, these are two-dimensional representations of chemical compounds. Covalent bonds are shown as lines between elements. Double and triple bonds are shown as two or three lines and unbonded valence electrons are shown as dots.

Molar mass: This refers to the mass of one mole of a substance (element or compound), usually measured in grams per mole (g/mol). This differs from molecular mass in that molecular mass is the mass of one molecule of a substance relative to the atomic mass unit (amu).

Atomic mass unit (amu) is the smallest unit of mass, and is equal to 1/12 of the mass of the carbon isotope carbon-12. A mole (mol) is a measurement of molecular weight that is equal to the molecule's amu in grams. For example, carbon has an amu of 12, so a mole of carbon weighs 12 grams. One mole is equal to about 6.0221415×10^{23} elementary entities, which are usually atoms or molecules. This amount is also known as the Avogadro constant or Avogadro's number (NA). Another way to say this is that one mole of a substance is the same as one Avogadro's number of that substance. One mole of chlorine, for example, is 6.0221415×10^{23} chlorine atoms. The charge on one mole of electrons is referred to as a Faraday.

The kinetic theory of gases assumes that gas molecules are small compared to the distances between them and that they are in constant random motion. The attractive and repulsive forces between gas molecules are negligible. Their kinetic energy does not change with time as long as the temperature remains the same. The higher the temperature is, the greater the motion will be. As the temperature of a gas increases, so does the kinetic energy of the molecules. In other words, gas will occupy a greater volume as the temperature is increased and a lesser volume as the temperature is decreased. In addition, the same amount of gas will occupy a greater volume as the temperature increases, but pressure remains constant. At any given temperature, gas molecules have the same average kinetic energy. The ideal gas law is derived from the kinetic theory of gases.

Charles's law: This states that gases expand when they are heated. It is also known as the law of volumes.

Boyle's law: This states that gases contract when pressure is applied to them. It also states that if temperature remains constant, the relationship between absolute pressure and volume is inversely proportional. When one increases, the other decreases. Considered a specialized case of the ideal gas law, Boyle's law is sometimes known as the Boyle-Mariotte law.

> **Review Video: Boyle's Law**
> Visit mometrix.com/academy and enter code: 115757

The ideal gas law is used to explain the properties of a gas under ideal pressure, volume, and temperature conditions. It is best suited for describing monatomic gases (gases in which atoms are not bound together) and gases at high temperatures and low pressures. It is not well-suited for instances in which a gas or its components are close to their condensation point. All collisions are perfectly elastic and there are no intermolecular attractive forces at work. The ideal gas law is a way to explain and measure the macroscopic properties of matter. It can be derived from the kinetic theory of gases, which deals with the microscopic properties of matter. The equation for the ideal gas law is $PV = nRT$, where "P" is absolute pressure, "V" is absolute volume, and "T" is absolute temperature. "R" refers to the universal gas constant, which is 8.3145 J/mol Kelvin, and "n" is the number of moles.

PHYSICS: MOTION AND FORCE

Mechanics is the study of matter and motion, and the topics related to matter and motion, such as force, energy, and work. Discussions of mechanics will often include the concepts of vectors and scalars. Vectors are quantities with both magnitude and direction, while scalars have only magnitude. Scalar quantities include length, area, volume, mass, density, energy, work, and power. Vector quantities include displacement, direction, velocity, acceleration, momentum, and force.

Motion is a change in the location of an object, and is the result of an unbalanced net force acting on the object. Understanding motion requires the understanding of three basic quantities: displacement, velocity, and acceleration.

DISPLACEMENT

When something moves from one place to another, it has undergone *displacement*. Displacement along a straight line is a very simple example of a vector quantity. If an object travels from position x = -5 cm to x = 5 cm, it has undergone a displacement of 10 cm. If it traverses the same path in the

opposite direction, its displacement is -10 cm. A vector that spans the object's displacement in the direction of travel is known as a displacement vector.

Review Video: Displacement
Visit mometrix.com/academy and enter code: 236197

VELOCITY

There are two types of velocity to consider: *average velocity* and *instantaneous velocity*. Unless an object has a constant velocity or we are explicitly given an equation for the velocity, finding the instantaneous velocity of an object requires the use of calculus. If we want to calculate the *average velocity* of an object, we need to know two things: the displacement, or the distance it has covered, and the time it took to cover this distance. The formula for average velocity is simply the distance traveled divided by the time required. In other words, the average velocity is equal to the change in position divided by the change in time. Average velocity is a vector and will always point in the same direction as the displacement vector (since time is a scalar and always positive).

ACCELERATION

Acceleration is the change in the velocity of an object. On most test questions, the acceleration will be a constant value. Like position and velocity, acceleration is a vector quantity and will therefore have both magnitude and direction.

Review Video: Velocity and Acceleration
Visit mometrix.com/academy and enter code: 671849

Most motion can be explained by Newton's three laws of motion:

NEWTON'S FIRST LAW

An object at rest or in motion will remain at rest or in motion unless acted upon by an external force. This phenomenon is commonly referred to as inertia, the tendency of a body to remain in its present state of motion. In order for the body's state of motion to change, it must be acted on by an unbalanced force.

Review Video: Newton's First Law of Motion
Visit mometrix.com/academy and enter code: 590367

NEWTON'S SECOND LAW

An object's acceleration is directly proportional to the net force acting on the object, and inversely proportional to the object's mass. It is generally written in equation form $F = ma$, where F is the net force acting on a body, m is the mass of the body, and a is its acceleration. Note that since the mass is always a positive quantity, the acceleration is always in the same direction as the force.

Review Video: Newton's Second Law of Motion
Visit mometrix.com/academy and enter code: 737975

NEWTON'S THIRD LAW

For every force, there is an equal and opposite force. When a hammer strikes a nail, the nail hits the hammer just as hard. If we consider two objects, A and B, then we may express any contact between these two bodies with the equation $F_{AB} = -F_{BA}$, where the order of the subscripts denotes which body is exerting the force. At first glance, this law might seem to forbid any movement at all

since every force is being countered with an equal opposite force, but these equal opposite forces are acting on different bodies with different masses, so they will not cancel each other out.

ENERGY

The two types of energy most important in mechanics are potential and kinetic energy. Potential energy is the amount of energy an object has stored within itself because of its position or orientation. There are many types of potential energy, but the most common is gravitational potential energy. It is the energy that an object has because of its height (h) above the ground. It can be calculated as $PE = mgh$, where m is the object's mass and g is the acceleration of gravity. Kinetic energy is the energy of an object in motion, and is calculated as $KE = mv^2/2$, where v is the magnitude of its velocity.

When an object is dropped, its potential energy is converted into kinetic energy as it falls. These two equations can be used to calculate the velocity of an object at any point in its fall.

WORK

Work can be thought of as the amount of energy expended in accomplishing some goal. The simplest equation for mechanical work (W) is $W = Fd$, where F is the force exerted and d is the displacement of the object on which the force is exerted. This equation requires that the force be applied in the same direction as the displacement. If this is not the case, then the work may be calculated as $W = Fd \cos(\theta)$, where θ is the angle between the force and displacement vectors. If force and displacement have the same direction, then work is positive; if they are in opposite directions, then work is negative; and if they are perpendicular, the work done by the force is zero.

As an example, if a man pushes a block horizontally across a surface with a constant force of 10 N for a distance of 20 m, the work done by the man is 200 N-m or 200 J. If instead the block is sliding and the man tries to slow its progress by pushing against it, his work done is -200 J, since he is pushing in the direction opposite the motion. If the man pushes vertically downward on the block while it slides, his work done is zero, since his force vector is perpendicular to the displacement vector of the block.

FRICTION

Friction is a force that arises as a resistance to motion where two surfaces are in contact. The maximum magnitude of the frictional force (f) can be calculated as $f = F_c\mu$, where F_c is the contact force between the two objects and μ is a coefficient of friction based on the surfaces' material composition. Two types of friction are static and kinetic. To illustrate these concepts, imagine a book resting on a table. The force of its weight (W) is equal and opposite to the force of the table on the book, or the normal force (N). If we exert a small force (F) on the book, attempting to push it to one side, a frictional force (f) would arise, equal and opposite to our force. At this point, it is a *static frictional force* because the book is not moving. If we increase our force on the book, we will eventually cause it to move. At this point, the frictional force opposing us will be a *kinetic frictional force.* Generally, the kinetic frictional force is lower than static frictional force (because the frictional coefficient for static friction is larger), which means that the amount of force needed to maintain the movement of the book will be less than what was needed to start it moving.

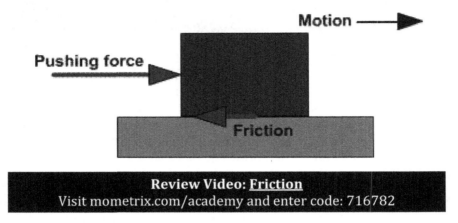

Review Video: Friction
Visit mometrix.com/academy and enter code: 716782

GRAVITATIONAL FORCE

Gravitational force is a universal force that causes every object to exert a force on every other object. The gravitational force between two objects can be described by the formula, $F = Gm_1m_2/r^2$, where m_1 and m_2 are the masses of two objects, r is the distance between them, and G is the gravitational constant, $G = 6.672 \times 10^{-11}$ N-m^2/kg^2. In order for this force to have a noticeable effect, one or both of the objects must be extremely large, so the equation is generally only used in problems involving planetary bodies. For problems involving objects on the earth being affected by earth's gravitational pull, the force of gravity is simply calculated as $F = mg$, where g is 9.81 m/s^2 toward the ground.

ELECTRICAL FORCE

Electrical force is a universal force that exists between any two electrically charged objects. Opposite charges attract one another and like charges repel one another. The magnitude of the force is directly proportional to the magnitude of the charges (q) and inversely proportional to the square of the distance (r) between the two objects: $F = kq_1q_2/r^2$, where $k = 9 \times 10^9$ N-m^2/C^2. Magnetic forces operate on a similar principle.

BUOYANCY

Archimedes's principle states that a buoyant (upward) force on a submerged object is equal to the weight of the liquid displaced by the object. Water has a density of one gram per cubic centimeter. Anything that floats in water has a lower density, and anything that sinks has a higher density. This principle of buoyancy can also be used to calculate the volume of an irregularly shaped object. The mass of the object (m) minus its apparent mass in the water (m_a) divided by the density of water (ρ_w), gives the object's volume: $V = (m-m_a)/\rho_w$.

MACHINES

Simple machines include the inclined plane, lever, wheel and axle, and pulley. These simple machines have no internal source of energy. More complex or compound machines can be formed from them. Simple machines provide a force known as a mechanical advantage and make it easier to accomplish a task. The inclined plane enables a force less than the object's weight to be used to push an object to a greater height. A lever enables a multiplication of force. The wheel and axle allows for movement with less resistance. Single or double pulleys allows for easier direction of force. The wedge and screw are forms of the inclined plane. A wedge turns a smaller force working over a greater distance into a larger force. The screw is similar to an incline that is wrapped around a shaft.

A certain amount of work is required to move an object. The amount cannot be reduced, but by changing the way the work is performed a mechanical advantage can be gained. A certain amount of work is required to raise an object to a given vertical height. By getting to a given height at an angle, the effort required is reduced, but the distance that must be traveled to reach a given height is increased. An example of this is walking up a hill. One may take a direct, shorter, but steeper route, or one may take a more meandering, longer route that requires less effort. Examples of wedges include doorstops, axes, plows, zippers, and can openers.

A lever consists of a bar or plank and a pivot point or fulcrum. Work is performed by the bar, which swings at the pivot point to redirect the force. There are three types of levers: first, second, and third class. Examples of a first-class lever include balances, see-saws, nail extractors, and scissors (which also use wedges). In a second-class lever the fulcrum is placed at one end of the bar and the work is performed at the other end. The weight or load to be moved is in between. The closer to the fulcrum the weight is, the easier it is to move. Force is increased, but the distance it is moved is decreased. Examples include pry bars, bottle openers, nutcrackers, and wheelbarrows. In a third-class lever the fulcrum is at one end and the positions of the weight and the location where the work is performed are reversed. Examples include fishing rods, hammers, and tweezers.

The center of a wheel and axle can be likened to a fulcrum on a rotating lever. As it turns, the wheel moves a greater distance than the axle, but with less force. Obvious examples of the wheel and axle are the wheels of a car, but this type of simple machine can also be used to exert a greater force. For instance, a person can turn the handles of a winch to exert a greater force at the turning axle to move an object. Other examples include steering wheels, wrenches, faucets, waterwheels, windmills, gears, and belts.

Gears work together to change a force. The four basic types of gears are spur, rack and pinion, bevel, and worm gears. The larger gear turns slower than the smaller, but exerts a greater force. Gears at angles can be used to change the direction of forces.

A single pulley consists of a rope or line that is run around a wheel. This allows force to be directed in a downward motion to lift an object. This does not decrease the force required, just changes its direction. The load is moved the same distance as the rope pulling it. When a combination pulley is

used, such as a double pulley, the weight is moved half the distance of the rope pulling it. In this way, the work effort is doubled. Pulleys are never 100% efficient because of friction. Examples of pulleys include cranes, chain hoists, block and tackles, and elevators.

Review Video: <u>Simple Machines</u>
Visit mometrix.com/academy and enter code: 950789

THERMODYNAMICS

Thermodynamics is a branch of physics that studies the conversion of energy into work and heat. It is especially concerned with variables such as temperature, volume, and pressure. Thermodynamic equilibrium refers to objects that have the same temperature because heat is transferred between them to reach equilibrium. Thermodynamics takes places within three different types of systems; open, isolated, and closed systems. Open systems are capable of interacting with a surrounding environment and can exchange heat, work (energy), and matter outside their system boundaries. A closed system can exchange heat and work, but not matter. An isolated system cannot exchange heat, work, or matter with its surroundings. Its total energy and mass stay the same. In physics, surrounding environment refers to everything outside a thermodynamic system (system). The terms "surroundings" and "environment" are also used. The term "boundary" refers to the division between the system and its surroundings.

Review Video: <u>Laws of Thermodynamics</u>
Visit mometrix.com/academy and enter code: 253607

The laws of thermodynamics are generalized principles dealing with energy and heat.

- The zeroth law of thermodynamics states that two objects in thermodynamic equilibrium with a third object are also in equilibrium with each other. Being in thermodynamic equilibrium basically means that different objects are at the same temperature.
- The first law deals with conservation of energy. It states that neither mass nor energy can be destroyed; only converted from one form to another.
- The second law states that the entropy (the amount of energy in a system that is no longer available for work or the amount of disorder in a system) of an isolated system can only increase. The second law also states that heat is not transferred from a lower-temperature system to a higher-temperature one unless additional work is done.
- The third law of thermodynamics states that as temperature approaches absolute zero, entropy approaches a constant minimum. It also states that a system cannot be cooled to absolute zero.

Thermal contact refers to energy transferred to a body by a means other than work. A system in thermal contact with another can exchange energy with it through the process of heat transfer. Thermal contact does not necessarily involve direct physical contact. Heat is energy that can be transferred from one body or system to another without work being done. Everything tends to become less organized and less useful over time (entropy).

In all energy transfers, therefore, the overall result is that the heat is spread out so that objects are in thermodynamic equilibrium and the heat can no longer be transferred without additional work.

The laws of thermodynamics state that energy can be exchanged between physical systems as heat or work, and that systems are affected by their surroundings. It can be said that the total amount of energy in the universe is constant. The first law is mainly concerned with the conservation of

energy and related concepts, which include the statement that energy can only be transferred or converted, not created or destroyed. The formula used to represent the first law is ΔU = Q – W, where ΔU is the change in total internal energy of a system, Q is the heat added to the system, and W is the work done by the system. Energy can be transferred by conduction, convection, radiation, mass transfer, and other processes such as collisions in chemical and nuclear reactions. As transfers occur, the matter involved becomes less ordered and less useful. This tendency towards disorder is also referred to as entropy.

Review Video: First Law of Thermodynamics
Visit mometrix.com/academy and enter code: 340643

The second law of thermodynamics explains how energy can be used. In particular, it states that heat will not transfer spontaneously from a cold object to a hot object. Another way to say this is that heat transfers occur from higher temperatures to lower temperatures. Also covered under this law is the concept that systems not under the influence of external forces tend to become more disordered over time. This type of disorder can be expressed in terms of entropy. Another principle covered under this law is that it is impossible to make a heat engine that can extract heat and convert it all to useful work. A thermal bottleneck occurs in machines that convert energy to heat and then use it to do work. These types of machines are less efficient than ones that are solely mechanical.

Review Video: The Second Law of Thermodynamics
Visit mometrix.com/academy and enter code: 251848

Conduction is a form of heat transfer that occurs at the molecular level. It is the result of molecular agitation that occurs within an object, body, or material while the material stays motionless. An example of this is when a frying pan is placed on a hot burner. At first, the handle is not hot. As the pan becomes hotter due to conduction, the handle eventually gets hot too. In this example, energy is being transferred down the handle toward the colder end because the higher speed particles collide with and transfer energy to the slower ones. When this happens, the original material becomes cooler and the second material becomes hotter until equilibrium is reached. Thermal conduction can also occur between two substances such as a cup of hot coffee and the colder surface it is placed on. Heat is transferred, but matter is not.

Convection refers to heat transfer that occurs through the movement or circulation of fluids (liquids or gases). Some of the fluid becomes or is hotter than the surrounding fluid, and is less dense. Heat is transferred away from the source of the heat to a cooler, denser area. Examples of convection are boiling water and the movement of warm and cold air currents in the atmosphere and the ocean. Forced convection occurs in convection ovens, where a fan helps circulate hot air.

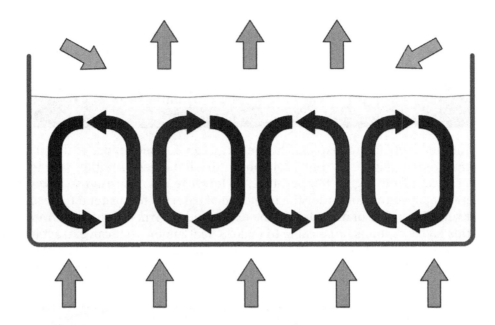

Radiation is heat transfer that occurs through the emission of electromagnetic waves, which carry energy away from the emitting object. All objects with temperatures above absolute zero radiate heat.

Temperature is a measurement of an object's stored heat energy. More specifically, temperature is the average kinetic energy of an object's particles. When the temperature of an object increases and its atoms move faster, kinetic energy also increases. Temperature is not energy since it changes and is not conserved. Thermometers are used to measure temperature.

There are three main scales for measuring temperature. Celsius uses the base reference points of water freezing at 0 degrees and boiling at 100 degrees. Fahrenheit uses the base reference points of water freezing at 32 degrees and boiling at 212 degrees. Celsius and Fahrenheit are both relative temperature scales since they use water as their reference point. The Kelvin temperature scale is an absolute temperature scale. Its zero mark corresponds to absolute zero. Water's freezing and boiling points are 273.15 Kelvin and 373.15 Kelvin, respectively. Where Celsius and Fahrenheit are measured is degrees, Kelvin does not use degree terminology.

Conversion equations:

- Converting Celsius to Fahrenheit: $°F = \frac{9}{5}°C + 32$
- Converting Fahrenheit to Celsius: $°C = \frac{5}{9}(°F - 32)$
- Converting Celsius to Kelvin: $K = °C + 273.15$
- Converting Kelvin to Celsius: $°C = K - 273.15$

Heat capacity, also known as thermal mass, refers to the amount of heat energy required to raise the temperature of an object, and is measured in Joules per Kelvin or Joules per degree Celsius. The equation for relating heat energy to heat capacity is $Q = C\Delta T$, where Q is the heat energy transferred, C is the heat capacity of the body, and ΔT is the change in the object's temperature. Specific heat capacity, also known as specific heat, is the heat capacity per unit mass. Every element and compound has its own specific heat. For example, it takes different amounts of heat energy to raise the temperature of the same amounts of magnesium and lead by one degree. The equation for relating heat energy to specific heat capacity is $Q = mc\Delta T$, where m represents the mass of the object, and c represents its specific heat capacity.

Some discussions of energy consider only two types of energy: kinetic energy (the energy of motion) and potential energy (which depends on relative position or orientation). There are, however, other types of energy. Electromagnetic waves, for example, are a type of energy contained by a field. Another type of potential energy is electrical energy, which is the energy it takes to pull apart positive and negative electrical charges. Chemical energy refers to the manner in which atoms form into molecules, and this energy can be released or absorbed when molecules regroup. Solar energy comes in the form of visible light and non-visible light, such as infrared and ultraviolet rays. Sound energy refers to the energy in sound waves.

Energy is constantly changing forms and being transferred back and forth. An example of a heat to mechanical energy transformation is a steam engine, such as the type used on a steam locomotive. A heat source such as coal is used to boil water. The steam produced turns a shaft, which eventually turns the wheels. A pendulum swinging is an example of both a kinetic to potential and a potential to kinetic energy transformation. When a pendulum is moved from its center point (the point at which it is closest to the ground) to the highest point before it returns, it is an example of a kinetic to potential transformation.

When it swings from its highest point toward the center, it is considered a potential to kinetic transformation. The sum of the potential and kinetic energy is known as the total mechanical energy. Stretching a rubber band gives it potential energy. That potential energy becomes kinetic energy when the rubber band is released.

WAVES
Waves have energy and can transfer energy when they interact with matter. Although waves transfer energy, they do not transport matter. They are a disturbance of matter that transfers energy from one particle to an adjacent particle. There are many types of waves, including sound, seismic, water, light, micro, and radio waves. The two basic categories of waves are mechanical and electromagnetic. Mechanical waves are those that transmit energy through matter. Electromagnetic waves can transmit energy through a vacuum. A transverse wave provides a good illustration of the features of a wave, which include crests, troughs, amplitude, and wavelength. There are a number of important attributes of waves.

Frequency is a measure of how often particles in a medium vibrate when a wave passes through the medium with respect to a certain point or node. Usually measured in Hertz (Hz), frequency might refer to cycles per second, vibrations per second, or waves per second. One Hz is equal to one cycle per second.

Period is a measure of how long it takes to complete a cycle. It is the inverse of frequency; where frequency is measure in cycles per second, period can be thought of as seconds per cycle, though it is measured in units of time only.

Speed refers to how fast or slow a wave travels. It is measured in terms of distance divided by time. While frequency is measured in terms of cycles per second, speed might be measured in terms of meters per second.

Amplitude is the maximum amount of displacement of a particle in a medium from its rest position, and corresponds to the amount of energy carried by the wave. High energy waves have greater amplitudes; low energy waves have lesser amplitudes. Amplitude is a measure of a wave's strength.

Rest position, also called equilibrium, is the point at which there is neither positive nor negative displacement. Crest, also called the peak, is the point at which a wave's positive or upward displacement from the rest position is at its maximum. Trough, also called a valley, is the point at which a wave's negative or downward displacement from the rest position is at its maximum. A wavelength is one complete wave cycle. It could be measured from crest to crest, trough to trough, rest position to rest position, or any point of a wave to the corresponding point on the next wave.

Sound is a pressure disturbance that moves through a medium in the form of mechanical waves, which transfer energy from one particle to the next. Sound requires a medium to travel through, such as air, water, or other matter since it is the vibrations that transfer energy to adjacent particles, not the actual movement of particles over a great distance. Sound is transferred through the movement of atomic particles, which can be atoms or molecules. Waves of sound energy move outward in all directions from the source. Sound waves consist of compressions (particles are forced together) and rarefactions (particles move farther apart and their density decreases). A wavelength consists of one compression and one rarefaction. Different sounds have different wavelengths. Sound is a form of kinetic energy.

> **Review Video: Sound**
> Visit mometrix.com/academy and enter code: 562378

ELECTRICAL CHARGES

A glass rod and a plastic rod can illustrate the concept of static electricity due to friction. Both start with no charge. A glass rod rubbed with silk produces a positive charge, while a plastic rod rubbed with fur produces a negative charge. The electron affinity of a material is a property that helps determine how easily it can be charged by friction. Materials can be sorted by their affinity for electrons into a triboelectric series. Materials with greater affinities include celluloid, sulfur, and rubber. Materials with lower affinities include glass, rabbit fur, and asbestos. In the example of a glass rod and a plastic one, the glass rod rubbed with silk acquires a positive charge because glass has a lower affinity for electrons than silk. The electrons flow to the silk, leaving the rod with fewer electrons and a positive charge. When a plastic rod is rubbed with fur, electrons flow to the rod and result in a negative charge.

The attractive force between the electrons and the nucleus is called the electric force. A positive (+) charge or a negative (-) charge creates a field of sorts in the empty space around it, which is known as an electric field. The direction of a positive charge is away from it and the direction of a negative charge is towards it. An electron within the force of the field is pulled towards a positive charge because an electron has a negative charge. A particle with a positive charge is pushed away, or repelled, by another positive charge. Like charges repel each other and opposite charges attract. Lines of force show the paths of charges. Electric force between two objects is directly proportional to the product of the charge magnitudes and inversely proportional to the square of the distance between the two objects. Electric charge is measured with the unit Coulomb (C). It is the amount of charge moved in one second by a steady current of one ampere ($1C = 1A \times 1s$).

Insulators are materials that prevent the movement of electrical charges, while conductors are materials that allow the movement of electrical charges. This is because conductive materials have free electrons that can move through the entire volume of the conductor. This allows an external charge to change the charge distribution in the material.

In induction, a neutral conductive material, such as a sphere, can become charged by a positively or negatively charged object, such as a rod. The charged object is placed close to the material without touching it. This produces a force on the free electrons, which will either be attracted to or repelled by the rod, polarizing (or separating) the charge. The sphere's electrons will flow into or out of it when touched by a ground. The sphere is now charged. The charge will be opposite that of the charging rod.

Charging by conduction is similar to charging by induction, except that the material transferring the charge actually touches the material receiving the charge. A negatively or positively charged object is touched to an object with a neutral charge. Electrons will either flow into or out of the neutral object and it will become charged. Insulators cannot be used to conduct charges. Charging by conduction can also be called charging by contact. The law of conservation of charge states that the total number of units before and after a charging process remains the same. No electrons have been created. They have just been moved around. The removal of a charge on an object by conduction is called grounding.

CIRCUITS

Electric potential, or electrostatic potential or voltage, is an expression of potential energy per unit of charge. It is measured in volts (V) as a scalar quantity. The formula used is $V = E/Q$, where V is voltage, E is electrical potential energy, and Q is the charge. Voltage is typically discussed in the context of electric potential difference between two points in a circuit. Voltage can also be thought of as a measure of the rate at which energy is drawn from a source in order to produce a flow of electric charge.

Electric current is the sustained flow of electrons that are part of an electric charge moving along a path in a circuit. This differs from a static electric charge, which is a constant non-moving charge rather than a continuous flow. The rate of flow of electric charge is expressed using the ampere (amp or A) and can be measured using an ammeter. A current of 1 ampere means that 1 coulomb of charge passes through a given area every second. Electric charges typically only move from areas of high electric potential to areas of low electric potential. To get charges to flow into a high potential area, you must to connect it to an area of higher potential, by introducing a battery or other voltage source.

Electric currents experience resistance as they travel through a circuit. Different objects have different levels of resistance. The ohm (Ω) is the measurement unit of electric resistance. The symbol is the Greek letter omega. Ohm's Law, which is expressed as $I = V/R$, states that current flow

(I, measured in amps) through an object is equal to the potential difference from one side to the other (V, measured in volts) divided by resistance (R, measured in ohms). An object with a higher resistance will have a lower current flow through it given the same potential difference.

Movement of electric charge along a path between areas of high electric potential and low electric potential, with a resistor or load device between them, is the definition of a simple circuit. It is a closed conducting path between the high and low potential points, such as the positive and negative terminals on a battery. One example of a circuit is the flow from one terminal of a car battery to the other. The electrolyte solution of water and sulfuric acid provides work in chemical form to start the flow. A frequently used classroom example of circuits involves using a D cell (1.5 V) battery, a small light bulb, and a piece of copper wire to create a circuit to light the bulb.

> **Review Video: Electrical Circuits**
> Visit mometrix.com/academy and enter code: 472696

MAGNETS

A magnet is a piece of metal, such as iron, steel, or magnetite (lodestone) that can affect another substance within its field of force that has like characteristics. Magnets can either attract or repel other substances. Magnets have two poles: north and south. Like poles repel and opposite poles (pairs of north and south) attract. The magnetic field is a set of invisible lines representing the paths of attraction and repulsion. Magnetism can occur naturally, or ferromagnetic materials can be magnetized. Certain matter that is magnetized can retain its magnetic properties indefinitely and become a permanent magnet. Other matter can lose its magnetic properties. For example, an iron nail can be temporarily magnetized by stroking it repeatedly in the same direction using one pole of another magnet. Once magnetized, it can attract or repel other magnetically inclined materials, such as paper clips. Dropping the nail repeatedly will cause it to lose its charge.

> **Review Video: Magnets**
> Visit mometrix.com/academy and enter code: 570803

The motions of subatomic structures (nuclei and electrons) produce a magnetic field. It is the direction of the spin and orbit that indicate the direction of the field. The strength of a magnetic field is known as the magnetic moment. As electrons spin and orbit a nucleus, they produce a magnetic field. Pairs of electrons that spin and orbit in opposite directions cancel each other out, creating a net magnetic field of zero. Materials that have an unpaired electron are magnetic.

Those with a weak attractive force are referred to as paramagnetic materials, while ferromagnetic materials have a strong attractive force. A diamagnetic material has electrons that are paired, and therefore does not typically have a magnetic moment. There are, however, some diamagnetic materials that have a weak magnetic field.

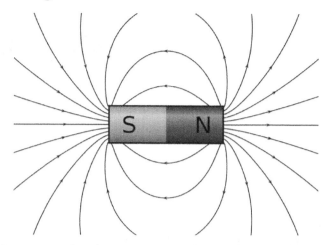

A magnetic field can be formed not only by a magnetic material, but also by electric current flowing through a wire. When a coiled wire is attached to the two ends of a battery, for example, an electromagnet can be formed by inserting a ferromagnetic material such as an iron bar within the coil. When electric current flows through the wire, the bar becomes a magnet. If there is no current, the magnetism is lost. A magnetic domain occurs when the magnetic fields of atoms are grouped and aligned. These groups form what can be thought of as miniature magnets within a material. This is what happens when an object like an iron nail is temporarily magnetized. Prior to magnetization, the organization of atoms and their various polarities are somewhat random with respect to where the north and south poles are pointing. After magnetization, a significant percentage of the poles are lined up in one direction, which is what causes the magnetic force exerted by the material.

ELECTROMAGNETIC WAVES

The electromagnetic spectrum is defined by frequency (f) and wavelength (λ). Frequency is typically measured in hertz and wavelength is usually measured in meters. Because light travels at a fairly constant speed, frequency is inversely proportional to wavelength, a relationship expressed by the formula $f = c/\lambda$, where c is the speed of light (about 300 million meters per second). Frequency multiplied by wavelength equals the speed of the wave; for electromagnetic waves, this is the speed of light, with some variance for the medium in which it is traveling. Electromagnetic waves include (from largest to smallest wavelength) radio waves, microwaves, infrared radiation (radiant heat), visible light, ultraviolet radiation, x-rays, and gamma rays. The energy of electromagnetic waves is carried in packets that have a magnitude inversely proportional to the wavelength. Radio waves have a range of wavelengths, from about 10^{-3} to 10^5 meters, while their frequencies range from 10^3 to about 10^{11} Hz.

Review Video: Electromagnetic Radiation Waves
Visit mometrix.com/academy and enter code: 135307

Atoms and molecules can gain or lose energy only in particular, discrete amounts. Therefore, they can absorb and emit light only at wavelengths that correspond to these amounts. Using a process known as spectroscopy, these characteristic wavelengths can be used to identify substances.

Light is the portion of the electromagnetic spectrum that is visible because of its ability to stimulate the retina. It is absorbed and emitted by electrons, atoms, and molecules that move from one energy level to another. Visible light interacts with matter through molecular electron excitation (which occurs in the human retina) and through plasma oscillations (which occur in metals). Visible light is between ultraviolet and infrared light on the spectrum. The wavelengths of visible light cover a range from 380 nm (violet) to 760 nm (red). Different wavelengths correspond to different colors. The human brain interprets or perceives visible light, which is emitted from the sun and other stars, as color.

For example, when the entire wavelength reaches the retina, the brain perceives the color white. When no part of the wavelength reaches the retina, the brain perceives the color black.

Review Video: Light
Visit mometrix.com/academy and enter code: 900556

When light waves encounter an object, they are either reflected, transmitted, or absorbed. If the light is reflected from the surface of the object, the angle at which it contacts the surface will be the same as the angle at which it leaves, on the other side of the perpendicular. If the ray of light is perpendicular to the surface, it will be reflected back in the direction from which it came. When light is transmitted through the object, its direction may be altered upon entering the object. This is known as refraction. The degree to which the light is refracted depends on the speed at which light travels in the object. Light that is neither reflected nor transmitted will be absorbed by the surface and stored as heat energy. Nearly all instances of light hitting an object will involve a combination of two or even all three of these.

Review Video: Reflection, Transmission, and Absorption of Light
Visit mometrix.com/academy and enter code: 109410

When light waves are refracted, or bent, an image can appear distorted. Sound waves and water waves can also be refracted. Diffraction refers to the bending of waves around small objects and the spreading out of waves past small openings. The narrower the opening, the greater the level of diffraction will be. Larger wavelengths also increase diffraction. A diffraction grating can be created by placing a number of slits close together, and is used more frequently than a prism to separate light. Different wavelengths are diffracted at different angles. The particular color of an object depends upon what is absorbed and what is transmitted or reflected.

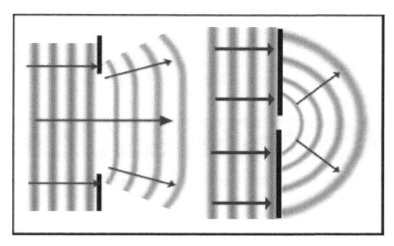

For example, a leaf consists of chlorophyll molecules, the atoms of which absorb all wavelengths of the visible light spectrum except for green, which is why a leaf appears green. Certain wavelengths of visible light can be absorbed when they interact with matter. Wavelengths that are not absorbed can be transmitted by transparent materials or reflected by opaque materials.

Review Video: Diffraction of Light Waves
Visit mometrix.com/academy and enter code: 785494

The various properties of light have numerous real-life applications. For example, polarized sunglasses have lenses that help reduce glare, while non-polarized sunglasses reduce the total amount of light that reaches the eyes. Polarized lenses consist of a chemical film of molecules aligned in parallel. This allows the lenses to block wavelengths of light that are intense, horizontal, and reflected from smooth, flat surfaces. The "fiber" in fiber optics refers to a tube or pipe that channels light. Because of the composition of the fiber, light can be transmitted greater distances before losing the signal. The fiber consists of a core, cladding, and a coating. Fibers are bundled, allowing for the transmission of large amounts of data.

Life Science

CELL STRUCTURE

The basic tenets of cell theory are that all living things are made up of cells and that cell are the basic units of life. Cell theory has evolved over time and is subject to interpretation. The development of cell theory is attributed to Matthias Schleiden and Theodor Schwann, who developed the theory in the early 1800s. Early cell theory was comprised of four statements: all organisms (living things) are made of cells; new cells are formed from pre-existing cells; all cells are similar; and cells are the most basic units of life. Other concepts related to classic and modern cell theory include statements such as: cells provide the basic units of functionality and structure in living things; cells are both distinct stand-alone units and basic building blocks; energy flow occurs within cells; cells contain genetic information in the form of DNA; and all cells consist of mostly the same chemicals.

> **Review Video: Cell Theory**
> Visit mometrix.com/academy and enter code: 736687

The functions of plant and animal cells vary greatly, and the functions of different cells within a single organism can also be vastly different. Animal and plant cells are similar in structure in that they are eukaryotic, which means they contain a nucleus. The nucleus is a round structure that controls the activities of the cell and contains chromosomes. Both types of cells have cell membranes, cytoplasm, vacuoles, and other structures. The main difference between the two is that plant cells have a cell wall made of cellulose that can handle high levels of pressure within the cell, which can occur when liquid enters a plant cell. Plant cells have chloroplasts that are used during the process of photosynthesis, which is the conversion of sunlight into food. Plant cells usually have one large vacuole, whereas animal cells can have many smaller ones. Plant cells have a regular shape, while the shapes of animal cell can vary.

Plant cells can be much larger than animal cells, ranging from 10 to 100 micrometers. Animal cells are 10 to 30 micrometers in size. Plant cells can have much larger vacuoles that occupy a large portion of the cell. They also have cell walls, which are thick barriers consisting of protein and sugars. Animal cells lack cell walls. Chloroplasts in plants that perform photosynthesis absorb sunlight and convert it into energy. Mitochondria produce energy from food in animal cells. Plant and animal cells are both eukaryotic, meaning they contain a nucleus. Both plant and animal cells duplicate genetic material, separate it, and then divide in half to reproduce. Plant cells build a cell plate between the two new cells, while animal cells make a cleavage furrow and pinch in half. Microtubules are components of the cytoskeleton in both plant and animal cells. Microtubule organizing centers (MTOCs) make microtubules in plant cells, while centrioles make microtubules in animal cells.

> **Review Video: Plant and Animal Cells**
> Visit mometrix.com/academy and enter code: 115568

Photosynthesis is the conversion of sunlight into energy in plant cells, and also occurs in some types of bacteria and protists. Carbon dioxide and water are converted into glucose during photosynthesis, and light is required during this process. Cyanobacteria are thought to be the descendants of the first organisms to use photosynthesis about 3.5 billion years ago. Photosynthesis is a form of cellular respiration. It occurs in chloroplasts that use thylakoids, which are structures in the membrane that contain light reaction chemicals. Chlorophyll is a pigment that absorbs light. During the process, water is used and oxygen is released. The equation for the chemical reaction that occurs during photosynthesis is 6H2O + 6CO2 → C6H12O6 + 6O2. During photosynthesis, six molecules of water and six molecules of carbon dioxide react to form one molecule of sugar and six molecules of oxygen.

Cellular respiration refers to a set of metabolic reactions that convert chemical bonds into energy stored in the form of ATP. Respiration includes many oxidation and reduction reactions that occur thanks to the electron transport system within the cell. Oxidation is a loss of electrons and reduction is a gain of electrons. Electrons in C-H (carbon/hydrogen) and C-C (carbon/carbon) bonds are donated to oxygen atoms. Processes involved in cellular respiration include glycolysis, the Krebs cycle, the electron transport chain, and chemiosmosis. The two forms of respiration are aerobic and anaerobic. Aerobic respiration is very common, and oxygen is the final electron acceptor. In anaerobic respiration, the final electron acceptor is not oxygen. Aerobic respiration results in more ATP than anaerobic respiration. Fermentation is another process by which energy is converted.

The main difference between eukaryotic and prokaryotic cells is that eukaryotic cells have a nucleus and prokaryotic cells do not. Eukaryotic cells are considered more complex, while prokaryotic cells are smaller and simpler. Eukaryotic cells have membrane-bound organelles that perform various functions and contribute to the complexity of these types of cells. Prokaryotic cells do not contain membrane-bound organelles. In prokaryotic cells, the genetic material (DNA) is not contained within a membrane-bound nucleus. Instead, it aggregates in the cytoplasm in a nucleoid. In eukaryotic cells, DNA is mostly contained in chromosomes in the nucleus, although there is some DNA in mitochondria and chloroplasts. Prokaryotic cells usually divide by binary fission and are haploid. Eukaryotic cells divide by mitosis and are diploid. Prokaryotic structures include plasmids, ribosomes, cytoplasm, a cytoskeleton, granules of nutritional substances, a plasma membrane, flagella, and a few others. They are single-celled organisms. Bacteria are prokaryotic cells.

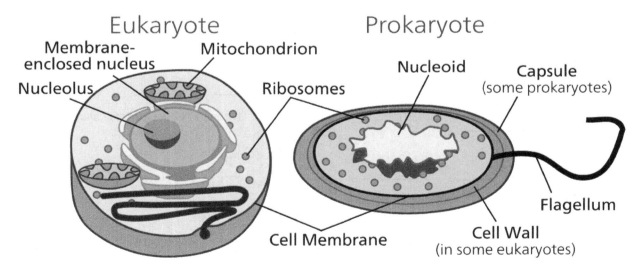

CELL ANATOMY

Cell membrane (plasma membrane): This defines the cell by acting as a barrier. It helps keeps cytoplasm in and substances located outside the cell out. It also determines what is allowed to enter and exit the cell.

Cytoplasm: This is a general term that refers to cytosol and the substructures (organelles) found within the plasma membrane, but not within the nucleus.

Cytoskeleton: This consists of microtubules that help shape and support the cell.

Cytosol: This is the liquid material in the cell. It is mostly water, but also contains some floating molecules.

Ribosomes: Ribosomes are involved in synthesizing proteins from amino acids. They are numerous, making up about one quarter of the cell. Some cells contain thousands of ribosomes. Some are mobile and some are embedded in the rough endoplasmic reticulum.

Vacuoles: These are sacs used for storage, digestion, and waste removal. There is one large vacuole in plant cells. Animal cells have small, sometimes numerous vacuoles.

Vesicle: This is a small organelle within a cell. It has a membrane and performs varying functions, including moving materials within a cell.

Endoplasmic reticulum: The two types of endoplasmic reticulum are rough (has ribosomes on the surface) and smooth (does not have ribosomes on the surface). It is a tubular network that comprises the transport system of a cell. It is fused to the nuclear membrane and extends through the cytoplasm to the cell membrane.

Golgi complex (Golgi apparatus): This is involved in synthesizing materials such as proteins that are transported out of the cell. It is located near the nucleus and consists of layers of membranes.

Microtubules: These are part of the cytoskeleton and help support the cell. They are made of protein.

Mitochondrion (pl. mitochondria): These cell structures vary in terms of size and quantity. Some cells may have one mitochondrion, while others have thousands. This structure performs various functions such as generating ATP, and is also involved in cell growth and death. Mitochondria contain their own DNA that is separate from that contained in the nucleus.

Cell Structure

Cilia

Lysosome

Centrioles

Microtubules

Golgi apparatus

Smooth endoplasmic reticulum

Mitochondrion

Rough endoplasmic reticulum

Cell membrane

Cytoplasm

Nucleolus

Chromatin

Ribosomes

Nuclear membrane

Cell wall: Made of cellulose and composed of numerous layers, the cell wall provides plants with a sturdy barrier that can hold fluid within the cell. The cell wall surrounds the cell membrane.

Chloroplast: This is a specialized organelle that plant cells use for photosynthesis, which is the process plants use to create food energy from sunlight. Chloroplasts contain chlorophyll, which has a green color.

Plasmodesmata (sing. plasmodesma): These are channels between the cell walls of plant cells that allow for transport between cells.

Plastid: This is a membrane-bound organelle found in plant cells that is used to make chemical compounds and store food. It can also contain pigments used during photosynthesis. Plastids can develop into more specialized structures such as chloroplasts, chromoplasts (make and hold yellow and orange pigments), amyloplasts (store starch), and leucoplasts (lack pigments, but can become differentiated).

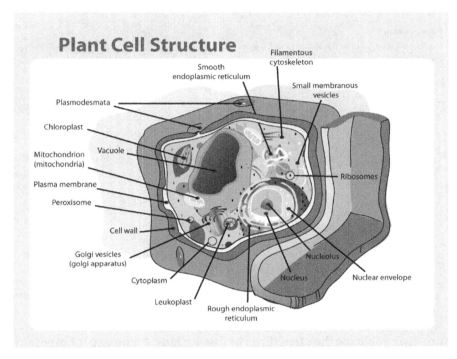

Centrosome: This is comprised of the pair of centrioles located at right angles to each other and surrounded by protein. The centrosome is involved in mitosis and the cell cycle.

Centriole: These are cylinder-shaped structures near the nucleus that are involved in cellular division. Each cylinder consists of nine groups of three microtubules. Centrioles occur in pairs.

Lysosome: This digests proteins, lipids, and carbohydrates, and also transports undigested substances to the cell membrane so they can be removed. The shape of a lysosome depends on the material being transported.

Cilia (singular: cilium): These are appendages extending from the surface of the cell, the movement of which causes the cell to move. They can also result in fluid being moved by the cell.

Flagella: These are tail-like structures on cells that use whip-like movements to help the cell move. They are similar to cilia, but are usually longer and not as numerous. A cell usually only has one or a few flagella.

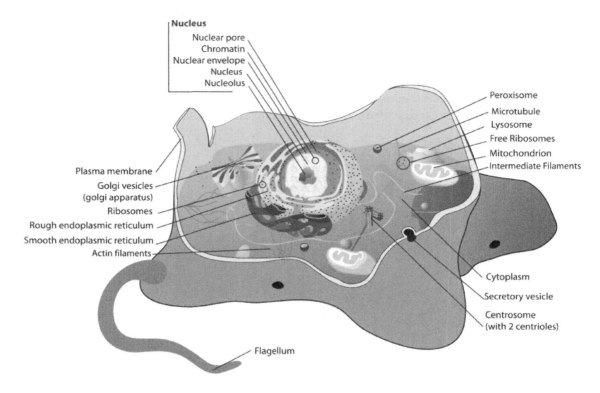

Chromatin: This consists of the DNA and protein that make up chromosomes.

Chromosomes: These are highly condensed, threadlike rods of DNA. Short for deoxyribonucleic acid, DNA is the genetic material that stores information about the plant or animal.

Nuclear envelope: This encloses the structures of the nucleus. It consists of inner and outer membranes made of lipids.

Nuclear pores: These are involved in the exchange of material between the nucleus and the cytoplasm.

Nucleolus (nucleole): This structure contained within the nucleus consists of protein. It is small, round, does not have a membrane, is involved in protein synthesis, and synthesizes and stores RNA (ribonucleic acid).

Nucleoplasm: This is the liquid within the nucleus, and is similar to cytoplasm.

Nucleus (pl. nuclei): This is a small structure that contains the chromosomes and regulates the DNA of a cell. The nucleus is the defining structure of eukaryotic cells, and all eukaryotic cells have a nucleus. The nucleus is responsible for the passing on of genetic traits between generations. The nucleus contains a nuclear envelope, nucleoplasm, a nucleolus, nuclear pores, chromatin, and ribosomes.

122

Size: The size of the nucleus in a eukaryotic cell is about 6 micrometers (μm). It occupies about 10 percent of the cell. A chloroplast is about 1 μm. Plant and animal cell sizes range from about 10 μm to 100 μm, while the sizes of bacteria range from about 1 μm to 10 μm. Atoms have a size of about 0.1 nanometers.

CELL METABOLISM

Metabolism is all of the chemical reactions that take place within a living organism. These chemical changes convert nutrients to energy and macromolecules. Macromolecules are large and complex, and play an important role in cell structure and function. Metabolic pathways refer to a series of reactions in which the product of one reaction is the substrate for the next. These pathways are dependent upon enzymes that act as catalysts. An anabolic reaction is one that builds larger and more complex molecules (macromolecules) from smaller ones. Catabolic reactions are the opposite. Larger molecules are broken down into smaller, simpler molecules. Catabolic reactions release energy, while anabolic ones require energy. The four basic organic macromolecules produced by anabolic reactions are carbohydrates (polysaccharides), nucleic acids, proteins, and lipids. The four basic building blocks involved in catabolic reactions are monosaccharides (glucose), amino acids, fatty acids (glycerol), and nucleotides.

In glycolysis, glucose is converted into pyruvate and energy stored in ATP bonds is released. Glycolysis can involve various pathways. Various intermediates are produced that are used in other processes, and the pyruvic acid produced by glycolysis can be further used for respiration by the Krebs cycle or in fermentation. Glycolysis occurs in both aerobic and anaerobic organisms. Oxidation of molecules produces reduced coenzymes, such as NADH. The coenzymes relocate hydrogens to the electron transport chain. The proton is transported through the cell membrane and the electron is transported down the chain by proteins. At the end of the chain, water is formed when the final acceptor releases two electrons that combine with oxygen. The protons are pumped back into the cell or organelle by the ATP synthase enzyme, which uses energy produced to add a phosphate to ADP to form ATP. The proton motive force is produced by the protons being moved across the membrane.

The Krebs cycle is also called the citric acid cycle or the tricarboxylic acid cycle (TCA). It is a catabolic pathway in which the bonds of glucose and occasionally fats or lipids are broken down and reformed into ATP. It is a respiration process that uses oxygen and produces carbon dioxide, water, and ATP. Cells require energy from ATP to synthesize proteins from amino acids and replicate DNA. The cycle is acetyl CoA, citric acid, isocitric acid, ketoglutaric acid (products are amino acids and CO2), succinyl CoA, succinic acid, fumaric acid, malic acid, and oxaloacetic acid. One of the products of the Krebs cycle is NADH, which is then used in the electron chain transport system to manufacture ATP. From glycolysis, pyruvate is oxidized in a step linking to the Krebs cycle. After the Krebs cycle, NADH and succinate are oxidized in the electron transport chain.

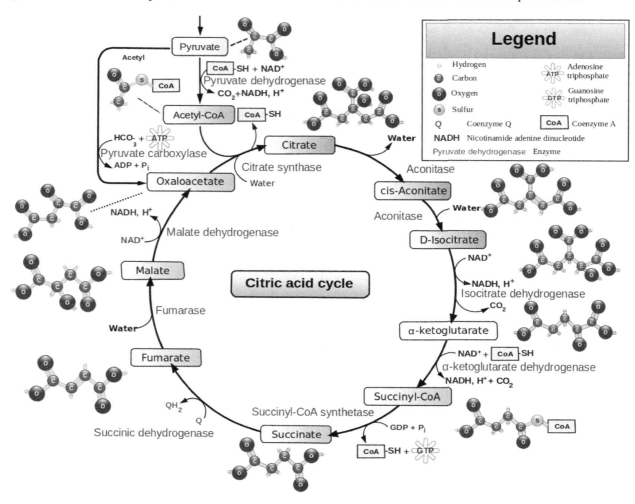

Homeostasis is the ability and tendency of an organism, cell, or body to adjust to environmental changes to maintain equilibrium. One way an organism, such as a human body, can maintain homeostasis is through the release of hormones. Some hormones work in pairs. When a condition reaches an upper limit, a hormone is released to correct the condition. When a condition reaches the other end of the spectrum, another hormone is released. Hormones that work in this way are termed antagonistic. Insulin and glucagon are a pair of antagonistic hormones that help regulate the level of glucose in the blood. Positive feedback loops actually tend to destabilize systems by increasing changes. A negative feedback loop acts to make a system more stable by buffering changes.

The hormones insulin and glucagon (an antagonistic pair of hormones) are involved in negative feedback loops in the liver's control of blood sugar levels. Alpha cells secrete glucagon when the concentration of blood glucose decreases. Glucagon is broken down and fatty acids and amino acids are converted to glucose. Once there is more glucose, glucagon secretion is reduced. Beta cells secrete insulin when the concentration of blood glucose increases. This leads to the liver absorbing glucose. Glucose is converted to glycogen, and fat and the concentration of glucose decrease. Insulin production is then reduced. Hormones work in other ways aside from antagonistically. For example, follicle stimulating hormone (FSH) increases the production of estrogen. Once estrogen

124

reaches a certain level, it suppresses FSH production. In some cases, a single hormone can increase or decrease the level of a substance.

CELL REPRODUCTION

The term cell cycle refers to the process by which a cell reproduces, which involves cell growth, the duplication of genetic material, and cell division. Complex organisms with many cells use the cell cycle to replace cells as they lose their functionality and wear out. The entire cell cycle in animal cells can take 24 hours. The time required varies among different cell types. Human skin cells, for example, are constantly reproducing. Some other cells only divide infrequently. Once neurons are mature, they do not grow or divide. The two ways that cells can reproduce are through meiosis and mitosis. When cells replicate through mitosis, the "daughter cell" is an exact replica of the parent cell. When cells divide through meiosis, the daughter cells have different genetic coding than the parent cell. Meiosis only happens in specialized reproductive cells called gametes.

Cell division is performed in organisms so they can grow and replace cells that are old, worn out, or damaged.

Chromatids: During cell division, the DNA is replicated, and chromatids are the two identical replicated pieces of chromosome that are joined at the centromere to form an "X."

Gametes: These are cells used by organisms to reproduce sexually. Gametes in humans are haploid, meaning they contain only half of the organism's genetic information (23 chromosomes). Other human cells contain all 46 chromosomes.

Haploid/diploid: Haploid means there is one set of chromosomes. Diploid means there are two sets of chromosomes (one set from each parent).

Mitosis is the process of cell reproduction in which a eukaryotic cell splits into two separate, but completely identical, cells. This process is divided into a number of different phases.

Interphase: The cell prepares for division by replicating its genetic and cytoplasmic material. Interphase can be further divided into G1, S, and G2.

Prophase: The chromatin thickens into chromosomes and the nuclear membrane begins to disintegrate. Pairs of centrioles move to opposite sides of the cell and spindle fibers begin to form. The mitotic spindle, formed from cytoskeleton parts, moves chromosomes around within the cell.

Metaphase: The spindle moves to the center of the cell and chromosome pairs align along the center of the spindle structure.

Anaphase: The pairs of chromosomes, called sisters, begin to pull apart, and may bend. When they are separated, they are called daughter chromosomes. Grooves appear in the cell membrane.

Telophase: The spindle disintegrates, the nuclear membranes reform, and the chromosomes revert to chromatin. In animal cells, the membrane is pinched. In plant cells, a new cell wall begins to form.

Cytokinesis: This is the physical splitting of the cell (including the cytoplasm) into two cells. Some believe this occurs following telophase. Others say it occurs from anaphase, as the cell begins to furrow, through telophase, when the cell actually splits into two.

Meiosis is another process by which eukaryotic cells reproduce. However, meiosis is used by more complex life forms such as plants and animals and results in four unique cells rather than two identical cells as in mitosis. Meiosis has the same phases as mitosis, but they happen twice. In addition, different events occur during some phases of meiosis than mitosis. The events that occur during the first phase of meiosis are interphase (I), prophase (I), metaphase (I), anaphase (I), telophase (I), and cytokinesis (I). During this first phase of meiosis, chromosomes cross over, genetic material is exchanged, and tetrads of four chromatids are formed. The nuclear membrane dissolves. Homologous pairs of chromatids are separated and travel to different poles. At this point, there has been one cell division resulting in two cells. Each cell goes through a second cell division, which consists of prophase (II), metaphase (II), anaphase (II), telophase (II), and cytokinesis (II). The result is four daughter cells with different sets of chromosomes. The daughter cells are haploid, which means they contain half the genetic material of the parent cell. The second phase of meiosis is similar to the process of mitosis. Meiosis encourages genetic diversity.

> **Review Video: Mitosis**
> Visit mometrix.com/academy and enter code: 849894

Other cell reproductive concepts:

Cellular differentiation: This is the process by which a less specialized cell becomes a more specialized cell.

Gene expression: This refers to the use of information in a gene, usually during the processes of transcription and translation, that result in a protein product.

Transcription: This refers to the synthesis of RNA. Information is provided by DNA.

Translation: This is the decoding of mRNA (messenger RNA) used in the fabrication of protein. It occurs after transcription.

DNA

Chromosomes consist of genes, which are single units of genetic information. Genes are made up of deoxyribonucleic acid (DNA). DNA is a nucleic acid located in the cell nucleus. There is also DNA in the mitochondria. DNA replicates to pass on genetic information. The DNA in almost all cells is the same. It is also involved in the biosynthesis of proteins. The model or structure of DNA is described as a double helix. A helix is a curve, and a double helix is two congruent curves connected by horizontal members. The model can be likened to a spiral staircase. It is right-handed. The British scientist Rosalind Elsie Franklin is credited with taking the x-ray diffraction image in 1952 that was used by Francis Crick and James Watson to formulate the double-helix model of DNA and speculate about its important role in carrying and transferring genetic information.

DNA has a double helix shape, resembles a twisted ladder, and is compact. It consists of nucleotides. Nucleotides consist of a five-carbon sugar (pentose), a phosphate group, and a nitrogenous base. Two bases pair up to form the rungs of the ladder. The "side rails" or backbone consists of the covalently bonded sugar and phosphate. The bases are attached to each other with hydrogen bonds, which are easily dismantled so replication can occur. Each base is attached to a phosphate and to a sugar. There are four types of nitrogenous bases: adenine (A), guanine (G), cytosine (C), and thymine (T). There are about 3 billion bases in human DNA. The bases are mostly the same in everybody, but their order is different. It is the order of these bases that creates diversity in people. Adenine (A) pairs with thymine (T), and cytosine (C) pairs with guanine (G).

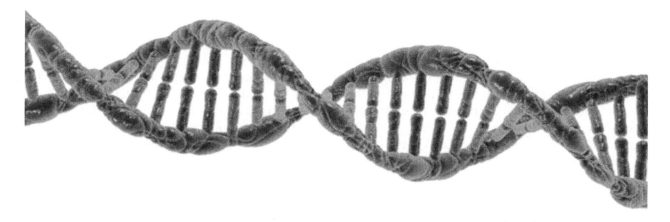

Review Video: DNA
Visit mometrix.com/academy and enter code: 639552

RNA acts as a helper to DNA and carries out a number of other functions. Types of RNA include ribosomal RNA (rRNA), transfer RNA (tRNA), and messenger RNA (mRNA). Viruses can use RNA to carry their genetic material to DNA. Ribosomal RNA is not believed to have changed much over time. For this reason, it can be used to study relationships in organisms. Messenger RNA carries a copy of a strand of DNA and transports it from the nucleus to the cytoplasm. Transcription is the process whereby DNA uses RNA in transcription. DNA unwinds itself and serves as a template while RNA is being assembled. The DNA molecules are copied to RNA. Translation is the process whereby ribosomes use transcribed RNA to put together the needed protein. Transfer RNA is a molecule that helps in the translation process, and is found in the cytoplasm. Ribosomal RNA is in the ribosomes.

RNA and DNA differ in terms of structure and function. RNA has a different sugar than DNA. It has ribose rather than deoxyribose sugar. The RNA nitrogenous bases are adenine (A), guanine (G), cytosine (C), and uracil (U). Uracil is found only in RNA and thymine in found only in DNA. RNA consists of a single strand and DNA has two strands. If straightened out, DNA has two side rails. RNA only has one "backbone," or strand of sugar and phosphate group components. RNA uses the fully hydroxylated sugar pentose, which includes an extra oxygen compared to deoxyribose, which is the sugar used by DNA. RNA supports the functions carried out by DNA. It aids in gene expression, replication, and transportation.

Review Video: RNA
Visit mometrix.com/academy and enter code: 888852

Codons are groups of three nucleotides on the messenger RNA, and can be visualized as three rungs of a ladder. A codon has the code for a single amino acid. There are 64 codons but 20 amino acids. More than one combination, or triplet, can be used to synthesize the necessary amino acids. For example, AAA (adenine-adenine-adenine) or AAG (adenine-adenine-guanine) can serve as codons for lysine. These groups of three occur in strings, and might be thought of as frames. For example, AAAUCUUCGU, if read in groups of three from the beginning, would be AAA, UCU, UCG, which are codons for lysine, serine, and serine, respectively. If the same sequence was read in groups of three starting from the second position, the groups would be AAU (asparagine), CUU (proline), and so on.

The resulting amino acids would be completely different. For this reason, there are start and stop codons that indicate the beginning and ending of a sequence (or frame). AUG (methionine) is the start codon. UAA, UGA, and UAG, also known as ocher, opal, and amber, respectively, are stop codons.

Pairs of chromosomes are composed of DNA, which is tightly wound to conserve space. When replication starts, it unwinds. The steps in DNA replication are controlled by enzymes. The enzyme helicase instigates the deforming of hydrogen bonds between the bases to split the two strands. The splitting starts at the A-T bases (adenine and thymine) as there are only two hydrogen bonds. The cytosine-guanine base pair has three bonds. The term "origin of replication" is used to refer to where the splitting starts. The portion of the DNA that is unwound to be replicated is called the replication fork. Each strand of DNA is transcribed by an mRNA. It copies the DNA onto itself, base by base, in a complementary manner. The exception is that uracil replaces thymine.

Many proteins are involved in the replication of DNA, and each has a specific function. Helicase is a protein that facilitates the unwinding of the double helix structure of DNA. Single strand binding (SSB) proteins attach themselves to each strand to prevent the DNA strands from joining back together. After DNA is unwound, there are leading and lagging strands. The leading strand is synthesized continuously and the lagging strand is synthesized in Okazaki fragments. Primase, an RNA polymerase (catalyzing enzyme), acts as a starting point for replication by forming short strands, or primers, of RNA. The DNA clamp, or sliding clamp, helps prevent DNA polymerase from coming apart from the strand. DNA polymerase helps form the DNA strand by linking nucleotides. As the process progresses, RNase H removes the primers. DNA ligase then links the existing shorter strands into a longer strand.

Gene disorders are the result of DNA mutations. DNA mutations lead to unfavorable gene disorders, but also provide genetic variability. This diversity can lead to increased survivability of a species. Mutations can be neutral, beneficial, or harmful. Mutations can be hereditary, meaning they are passed from parent to child. Polymorphism refers to differences in humans, such as eye and hair color, that may have originally been the result of gene mutations, but are now part of the normal variation of the species. Mutations can be de novo, meaning they happen either only in sex cells or shortly after fertilization. They can also be acquired, or somatic. These are the kinds that happen as a result of DNA changes due to environmental factors or replication errors. Mosaicism is when a mutation happens in a cell during an early embryonic stage. The result is that some cells will have the mutation and some will not.

A DNA mutation occurs when the normal gene sequence is altered. Mutations can happen when DNA is damaged as a result of environmental factors, such as chemicals, radiation, or ultraviolet rays from the sun. It can also happen when errors are made during DNA replication. The phosphate-sugar side rail of DNA can be damaged if the bonds between oxygen and phosphate groups are disassociated. Translocation happens when the broken bonds attempt to bond with others DNA. This repair can cause a mutation. The nucleotide itself can be altered. A C, for example, might look like a T. During replication, the damaged C is replicated as a T and paired with a G, which is incorrect base pairing. Another way mutations can occur is if an error is made by the DNA polymerase while replicating a base. This happens about once for every 100,000,000 bases. A repair protein proofreads the code, however, so the mistake is usually repaired.

Translocation is a genetic mutation in which one piece of a chromosome is transferred to another chromosome. Burkitt's lymphoma, chronic myelogenous leukemia, and Down syndrome are all examples. Trisomy 21, or Down syndrome, occurs when a copy of chromosome 21 attaches to chromosome 14. Most Down syndrome cases are caused by a pair of chromosomes (the 21st) that does not split during meiosis. Both divided cells will have an abnormal number of chromosomes. One will have 22 and the other will have 24. When this egg gets fertilized, it will have three copies of chromosome 21 instead of two. Down syndrome can also be caused by translocation between the 14th and 21st chromosomes. In these instances, genetic material is swapped. There are 200 to 250 genes on the 21st chromosome. The overexpression of the gene results in the following Down syndrome traits: premature aging, decreased immune system function, heart defects, skeletal abnormalities, disruption of DNA synthesis and repair, intellectual disabilities, and cataracts.

GENETICS

A gene is a portion of DNA that identifies how traits are expressed and passed on in an organism. A gene is part of the genetic code. Collectively, all genes form the genotype of an individual. The genotype includes genes that may not be expressed, such as recessive genes. The phenotype is the physical, visual manifestation of genes. It is determined by the basic genetic information and how genes have been affected by their environment. An allele is a variation of a gene. Also known as a trait, it determines the manifestation of a gene. This manifestation results in a specific physical appearance of some facet of an organism, such as eye color or height. For example, the genetic information for eye color is a gene. The gene variations responsible for blue, green, brown, or black eyes are called alleles. Locus (pl. loci) refers to the location of a gene or alleles.

Mendel's laws are the law of segregation (the first law) and the law of independent assortment (the second law). The law of segregation states that there are two alleles and that half of the total number of alleles are contributed by each parent organism. The law of independent assortment states that traits are passed on randomly and are not influenced by other traits. The exception to this is linked traits. A Punnett square can illustrate how alleles combine from the contributing genes to form various phenotypes. One set of a parent's genes are put in columns, while the genes from the other parent are placed in rows. The allele combinations are shown in each cell. When two different alleles are present in a pair, the dominant one is expressed. A Punnett square can be used to predict the outcome of crosses.

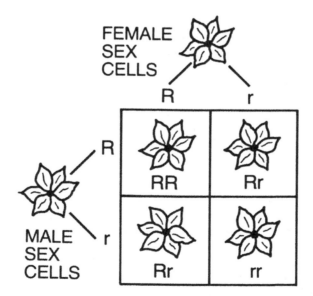

The non-Mendelian concept of polygenetic inheritance takes into account environmental factors on phenotypes. For example, an individual inherits genes that help determine height, but a diet lacking in certain nutrients could limit that individual's ability to reach that height. Another example is the concept of genetic disposition, which is a propensity for a certain disease that is genetically inherited, but not necessarily manifested. For example, individuals with certain skin types are more likely to develop skin cancer. If they limit their exposure to solar radiation, however, this will not necessarily occur.

Gene traits are represented in pairs with an upper-case letter for the dominant trait (A) and a lower-case letter for the recessive trait (a). Genes occur in pairs (AA, Aa, or aa). There is one gene on each chromosome half supplied by each parent organism. Since half the genetic material is from each parent, the offspring's traits are represented as a combination of these. A dominant trait only requires one gene of a gene pair for it to be expressed in a phenotype, whereas a recessive requires both genes in order to be manifested. For example, if the mother's genotype is Dd and the father's is dd, the possible combinations are Dd and dd. The dominant trait will be manifested if the genotype is DD or Dd. The recessive trait will be manifested if the genotype is dd. Both DD and dd are homozygous pairs. Dd is heterozygous.

Genetic crosses are the possible combinations of alleles, and can be represented using Punnett squares. A monohybrid cross refers to a cross involving only one trait. Typically, the ratio is 3:1 (DD, Dd, Dd, dd), which is the ratio of dominant gene manifestation to recessive gene manifestation. This ratio occurs when both parents have a pair of dominant and recessive genes. If one parent has a pair of dominant genes (DD) and the other has a pair of recessive (dd) genes, the recessive trait cannot be expressed in the next generation because the resulting crosses all have the Dd genotype. A dihybrid cross refers to one involving more than one trait, which means more combinations are possible. The ratio of genotypes for a dihybrid cross is 9:3:3:1 when the traits are not linked. The ratio for incomplete dominance is 1:2:1, which corresponds to dominant, mixed, and recessive phenotypes.

There are four possible blood types: A, B, AB, and O. These types are produced by combinations of the three alleles. AA and AO lead to type A blood. BB and BO lead to type B blood. AB leads to type AB blood because the alleles are co-dominant. AB has both A protein and antigens and B protein and antigens. The O allele is recessive. OO leads to blood type O, which lacks proteins and blood-surface antigens. Blood donors with an O blood type are known as universal donors because they do not have the type of antigens that can trigger immune system responses. Blood donors with type AB blood are known as universal recipients because they do not have the antibodies that will attack A and B antigen molecules. If parents have AB and O blood, offspring have a 50% chance of having type A blood and a 0% chance of having type O blood.

Recombinant DNA (rDNA) refers to manipulating sequences of DNA. One portion of DNA is removed and replaced with another. Gene splicing is a way to recombine DNA. In gene splicing, base pairs of DNA are chemically cleaved. Restriction enzymes are used to perform the cutting part of gene splicing. Once base pairs are separated, different additional genetic information can be added by a vector. DNA ligase (an enzyme) is used to put the pieces back together. The process of DNA recombination happens naturally and incrementally as a result of evolution. Use of recombinant DNA produced through genetic engineering has been used in the laboratory in diagnostic, medical forensic and agricultural applications.

Diagnostic and medical applications of genetic engineering include treating diabetes with insulin, producing human proteins, treating hemophilia, anemia, and blood clots, and manufacturing hepatitis B vaccine. Gene therapy has been used to replace defective alleles with normal alleles. For example, if a patient has a condition caused by an enzyme deficiency, replacing the defective allele enables the person to produce that enzyme. Medical forensic applications involving DNA analysis include using it to identify individuals and solve criminal cases. Agricultural applications include crop modification to develop types of wheat, cotton, and soybeans that resist weed controlling herbicides. Plants can be altered to make them grow bigger or vaccinated to make them resistant to plant viruses and insects.

Other genetic concepts:

Epistasis: This refers to the situation in which two or more genes determine a single phenotype.

Karyotype: This is a picture of genes based on a sample of blood or skin.

Lethal allele: This is when a mutation in an essential gene results in the death of the organism. Cystic fibrosis and Tay-Sachs disease are examples of lethal recessive alleles.

Pleiotropy: This refers to a gene that affects more than one trait.

EVOLUTION

One theory of how life originated on Earth is that life developed from nonliving materials. The first stage of this transformation happened when abiotic (nonliving) synthesis took place, which is the formation of monomers like amino acids and nucleotides. Next, monomers joined together to create polymers such as proteins and nucleic acids. These polymers are then believed to have formed into protobionts. The last stage was the development of the process of heredity. Supporters of this theory believe that RNA was the first genetic material. Another theory postulates that hereditary systems came about before the origination of nucleic acids. Another theory is that life, or the precursors for it, were transported to Earth from a meteorite or other object from space. There is no real evidence to support this theory.

Scientific evidence supporting the theory of evolution can be found in biogeography, comparative anatomy and embryology, the fossil record, and molecular evidence. Biogeography studies the geographical distribution of animals and plants. Evidence of evolution related to the area of biogeography includes species that are well suited for extreme environments. The fossil record shows that species lived only for a short time period before becoming extinct. The fossil record can also show the succession of plants and animals. Living fossils are existing species that have not changed much morphologically and are very similar to ancient examples in the fossil record. Examples include the horseshoe crab and ginkgo. Comparative embryology studies how species are similar in the embryonic stage, but become increasingly specialized and diverse as they age. Vestigial organs are those that still exist, but become nonfunctional. Examples include the hind limbs of whales and the wings of birds that can no longer fly, such as ostriches.

Three types of evolution are divergent, convergent, and parallel. Divergent evolution refers to two species that become different over time. This can be caused by one of the species adapting to a different environment. Convergent evolution refers to two species that start out fairly different, but evolve to share many similar traits. Parallel evolution refers to species that are not similar and do not become more or less similar over time. Mechanisms of evolution include descent (the passing on of genetic information), mutation, migration, natural selection, and genetic variation and drift. The biological definition of species refers to a group of individuals that can mate and reproduce. Speciation refers to the evolution of a new biological species. The biological species concept (BSC) basically states that a species is a community of individuals that can reproduce and have a niche in nature.

The rate of evolution is affected by the variability of a population. Variability increases the likelihood of evolution. Variability in a population can be increased by mutations, immigration, sexual reproduction (as opposed to asexual reproduction), and size. Natural selection, emigration, and smaller populations can lead to decreased variability. Sexual selection affects evolution. If fewer genes are available, it will limit the number of genes passed on to subsequent generations. Some animal mating behaviors are not as successful as others. A male that does not attract a female because of a weak mating call or dull feathers, for example, will not pass on its genes. Mechanical isolation, which refers to sex organs that do not fit together very well, can also decrease successful mating.

The gene pool refers to all alleles of a gene and their combinations. The Hardy-Weinberg principle (or Castle-Hardy Weinberg principle) postulates that the allele frequency for dominant and recessive alleles will remain the same in a population through successive generations if certain conditions exist. These conditions are: no mutations, large populations, random mating, no migration, and equal genotypes. This is an ideal and not how most population's function. Changes in the frequency and types of alleles in a gene pool can be caused by gene flow, random mutation, nonrandom mating, and genetic drift. In organisms that reproduce by sexual reproduction, reproduction isolation is defined as something that acts as a barrier to two species reproducing. These barriers are classified as prezygotic and postzygotic.

Gene migration: Also known as gene flow, gene migration is the movement of alleles to another population. This can occur through immigration, when individuals of a species move into an area, or through emigration, when individuals of a species move out of an area.

PREZYGOTIC BARRIERS TO REPRODUCTION

Spatial: This refers to species that are separated by a distance that prevents them from mating.

Geographical: This is when species are physically separated by a barrier. A barrier can divide a population, which is known as vicariance. If a population crosses a barrier to create two species, it is known as dispersal.

Habitat: This refers to species that live in different habitats in the same area.

Temporal: This refers to the fact that species reach sexual maturity at different times. An example is plants that flower at different times of the year.

Behavioral: This refers to the fact that mating rituals distinguish interaction between sexes. For example, many species of crickets are morphologically (structurally) the same, yet a female of one species will only respond to the mating rituals of males within her species.

Mechanical: This refers to physiological structural differences that prevent mating or the transfer of gametes.

Gametic isolation: This refers to the fact that fertilization may not occur when gametes of different species are not compatible.

POSTZYGOTIC BARRIERS TO REPRODUCTION

Hybrid viability: This is when a hybrid zygote does not reach maturity.

Hybrid sterility: This is also known as hybrid infertility. It occurs when two species produce a hybrid offspring that reaches maturity, but is sterile. An example of this is the mule. Mules are the result of a horse and a donkey mating. Mules, however, cannot reproduce.

Hybrid breakdown: This is when the first generation is not only viable, but also reaches maturity and can reproduce. Subsequent generations, however, are neither viable nor fertile.

Hybrid zygote abnormality: This is when two species produce a zygote that does not survive to birth or germination, does not develop normally or reach sexual maturity, and cannot reproduce.

Allopatric speciation: This refers to speciation that occurs because of geographical factors, such as physical barriers or dispersal.

Sympatric speciation: This refers to speciation that happens within parent populations.

Parapatric speciation: This refers to speciation that occurs because of an extreme change in habitat.

MUTATION CONCEPTS

Random mutations: These are genetic changes caused by DNA errors or environmental factors such as chemicals and radiation. Mutations can be beneficial or harmful.

Nonrandom mating: This refers to the fact that the probability of two individuals mating in a population is not the same for all pairs. Nonrandom mating can be caused by geographical isolation, small populations, and other factors. Nonrandom mating can lead to inbreeding (mating with a relative), which can lead to a decline in physical fitness as seen in a phenotype and the reduction of allele frequency and occurrence.

ORGANISM CLASSIFICATION

The groupings in the five kingdom classification system are kingdom, phylum/division, class, order, family, genus, and species. A memory aid for this is: King Phillip Came Over For Good Soup. The five kingdoms are Monera, Protista, Fungi, Plantae, and Animalia. The kingdom is the top-level classification in this system. Below that are the following groupings: phylum, class, order, family, genus, and species. The Monera kingdom includes about 10,000 known species of prokaryotes, such as bacteria and cyanobacteria. Members of this kingdom can be unicellular organisms or colonies. The next four kingdoms consist of eukaryotes. The Protista kingdom includes about 250,000 species of unicellular protozoans and unicellular and multicellular algae. The Fungi kingdom includes about 100,000 species. A recently introduced system of classification includes a three domain grouping above kingdom. The domain groupings are Archaea, Bacteria (which both consist of prokaryotes), and Eukarya, which include eukaryotes. According to the five kingdom classification system, humans are: kingdom Animalia, phylum Chordata, subphylum Vertebrata, class Mammalia, order Primate, family Hominidae, genus Homo, and species Sapiens.

The Monera kingdom consists of unicellular organisms. A unicellular organism is a living thing that has only one cell. Examples of unicellular organisms are bacteria and paramecium. A multicellular organism is one that consists of many cells. Humans are a good example. By some estimates, the human body is made up of billions of cells. Others think the human body has more than 75 trillion cells. The term microbe refers to small organisms that are only visible through a microscope. Examples include viruses, bacteria, fungi, and protozoa. Microbes are also referred to as microorganisms, and it is these that are studied by microbiologists. Bacteria can be rod shaped, round (cocci), or spiral (spirilla). These shapes are used to differentiate among types of bacteria. Bacteria can be identified by staining them. This particular type of stain is called a gram stain. If bacteria are gram-positive, they absorb the stain and become purple. If bacteria are gram-negative, they do not absorb the stain and become a pinkish color.

Viruses are microorganisms that replicate in the cells of other organisms, including plants, animals, bacteria, and other microorganisms. All viruses have a head. Some also have a tail consisting of protein. The tail is used to attach to a host cell and enter it. This is one way in which viruses introduce their genetic material to the host. The head of a virus, also called a protein capsid, contains genetic material in the form of DNA, RNA, or enzymes. The adenovirus and the herpes virus are both DNA viruses. The HIV retrovirus, influenza, and the rotavirus are RNA viruses. The number of virus types is thought to be in the millions. Virology is a branch of microbiology that is devoted to the study of viruses. Viruses can be transmitted to other organisms in a number of ways, such as by insects, by air, and through direct contact.

Organisms in the Protista kingdom are classified according to their methods of locomotion, their methods of reproduction, and how they get their nutrients. Protists can move by the use of a flagellum, cilia, or pseudopod. Flagellates have flagellum, which are long tails or whip-like structures that are rotated to help the protist move. Ciliates use cilia, which are smaller hair-like structures on the exterior of a cell that wiggle to help move the surrounding matter. Amoeboids use pseudopodia to move. Bacteria reproduce either sexually or asexually. Binary fission is a form of asexual reproduction whereby bacteria divide in half to produce two new organisms that are clones of the parent. In sexual reproduction, genetic material is exchanged. When kingdom members are categorized according to how they obtain nutrients, the three types of protists are photosynthetic, consumers, and saprophytes. Photosynthetic protists convert sunlight into energy. Organisms that use photosynthesis are considered producers. Consumers, also known as heterotrophs, eat or consume other organisms. Saprophytes consume dead or decaying substances.

Mycology is the study of fungi. The Fungi kingdom includes about 100,000 species. They are further delineated as mushrooms, yeasts, molds, rusts, mildews, stinkhorns, puffballs, and truffles. Fungi are characterized by cell walls that have chitin, a long chain polymer carbohydrate. Fungi are different from species in the Plant kingdom, which have cell walls consisting of cellulose. Fungi are thought to have evolved from a single ancestor. Although they are often thought of as a type of plant, they are more similar to animals than plants. Fungi are typically small and numerous, and have a diverse morphology among species. They can have bright red cups and be orange jellylike masses, and their shapes can resemble golf balls, bird nests with eggs, starfish, parasols, and male genitalia. Some members of the stinkhorn family emit odors similar to dog scat to attract flies that help transport spores that are involved in reproduction. Fungi of this family are also consumed by humans.

Both vascular and nonvascular plants are part of the Plantae kingdom. Vascular plants have vascular tissue in the form of xylem and phloem. These make up the parts of the plants, such as the roots, stems, and leaves that are involved in transporting minerals and water throughout the plant. This capability enables vascular plants to grow tall. Food/energy that is converted by photosynthesis in the leaves is brought down to the roots, while water is brought to the top of the plant. Nonvascular (or avascular) plants lack true leaves, stems, and roots. Nonvascular plants do not develop vascular tissue, such as xylem and phloem. They tend to be small, and individual cells are adjacent to their environment.

Chlorophyta are green algae. Bryophyta are nonvascular mosses and liverworts. They have root-like parts called rhizoids. Since they do not have the vascular structures to transport water, they live in moist environments. Lycophyta are club mosses. They are vascular plants. They use spores and need water to reproduce. Equisetopsida (sphenophyta) are horsetails. Like lycophyta, they need water to reproduce with spores. They have rhizoids and needle-like leaves. The pteridophytes (filicopsida) are ferns. They have stems (rhizomes). Spermatopsida are the seed plants. Gymnosperms are a conifer, which means they have cones with seeds that are used in reproduction. Plants with seeds require less water. Cycadophyta are cone-bearing and look like palms. Gnetophyta are plants that live in the desert. Coniferophyta are pine trees, and have both cones and needles. Ginkgophyta are gingkos. Anthophyta is the division with the largest number of plant species, and includes flowering plants with true seeds.

Plants are autotrophs, which mean they make their own food. In a sense, they are self-sufficient. Three major processes used by plants are photosynthesis, transpiration, and respiration. Photosynthesis involves using sunlight to make food for plants. Transpiration evaporates water out of plants. Respiration is the utilization of food that was produced during photosynthesis.

Two major systems in plants are the shoot and the root system. The shoot system includes leaves, buds, and stems. It also includes the flowers and fruits in flowering plants. The shoot system is located above the ground. The root system is the component of the plant that is underground, and includes roots, tubers, and rhizomes. Meristems form plant cells by mitosis. Cells then differentiate into cell types to form the three types of plant tissues, which are dermal, ground, and vascular. Dermal refers to tissues that form the covering or outer layer of a plant. Ground tissues consist of parenchyma, collenchyma, and/or sclerenchyma cells.

Plant roots include zones where cell differentiation, elongation and division, and meristem formation occur. Primary meristems include protoderms, ground meristems, procambiums, and apical meristems. There is also a root cap. A tuber is an underground stem that is enlarged and used for food storage. A rhizome is an underground stem of sorts that sends out roots and shoots from its nodes (bulging or swelling points). Vascular tissues include xylem and phloem. Xylem can be scattered throughout a pith or formed into rings. Phloem allows for food transport down a plant. The food travels from where it was produced through photosynthesis to other structures, such as roots, that require the food. Phloem can be made up of bundles of sieve tubes. It is usually located outside the xylem.

Transpiration is the movement of water through a vascular plant. It is also the method by which water is evaporated out of plants. Transpiration mainly happens during the process of photosynthesis, when water and minerals travel up through the xylem and are used and water is released through stomata (flattened oval-shaped openings). During transpiration, water is drawn up a plant. This process also helps cool leaves. Respiration is the process of metabolizing sugars to provide plants with the energy they need for growth and reproduction. The chemical equation is $C_6H_{12}O_6 + 6O_2 \rightarrow 6CO_2 + 6H_2O$ + energy. During the process of respiration, sugars are burned, energy is released, oxygen is used, and water and carbon dioxide are produced. Respiration can occur as a light or dark reaction.

Bryophytes are seedless plants. They include liverworts, hornworts, and mosses. They use spores that form into gametophytes to reproduce. Sperm are flagellated, meaning they require at least some water to swim to the egg. Some bryophytes are plants that are one sex or the other, but other bryophytes have both sexes on the same plant. Ferns also have flagellated sperm and require water for the same reason as bryophytes. Both ferns and bryophytes undergo alternation of generations. These plants spend about half of their reproductive cycles as sporophytes, making haploid spores through meiosis during this stage. The other half of the cycle is spent as a haploid gametophyte. At this point, male and female gametes join to form one zygote. Seed plants use seeds to reproduce. Flowering plants use flowers and seeds.

There are at least 230,000 species of flowering plants. They represent about 90 percent of all plants. Angiosperms have a sexual reproduction phase that includes flowering. When growing plants, one may think they develop in the following order: seeds, growth, flowers, and fruit. The reproductive cycle has the following order: flowers, fruit, and seeds. In other words, seeds are the products of successful reproduction. The colors and scents of flowers serve to attract pollinators.

Flowers and other plants can also be pollinated by wind. When a pollen grain meets the ovule and is successfully fertilized, the ovule develops into a seed. A seed consists of three parts: the embryo, the endosperm, and a seed coat. The embryo is a small plant that has started to develop, but this development is paused. Germination is when the embryo starts to grow again. The endosperm consists of proteins, carbohydrates, or fats. It typically serves as a food source for the embryo. The seed coat provides protection from disease, insects, and water.

Flowering plants can be categorized sexually according to which organs they have. Flowers can be bisexual or unisexual. Species can be dioecious, which means male and female flowers are contained on different individual plants. Monoecious means that both male and female flowers are on one individual. Bisexual flowers are those that have all of the following: sepal, petal, stamen, and pistil. If they have all of these parts, they are considered complete. They have both the male stamen and the female counterpart, the pistil. Unisexual flowers only have a pistil or a stamen, not both. Incomplete flowers do not have all four parts. The flower rests upon a pedicel and is contained with the receptacle. The carpal is made up of the stigma at the tip, a style, and the ovary at the base. The ovary contains the ovules (eggs). Carpels are sometimes formed as a single pistil. The stamen includes the anther and the filament, and produces the male pollen.

The anthers of the stamens (male parts) have microsporangia that form into a pollen grain, which consists of a small germ cell within a larger cell. The pollen grain is released and lands on a stigma (female) portion of the pistil. It grows a pollen tube the length of the style and ends up at the ovule. The pollen grain releases the sperm and fertilization occurs. In double fertilization, one of the sperm joins with the egg to become a diploid zygote. The other sperm becomes the endosperm nucleus. Seeds are formed. One cotyledon (monocot) or two cotyledons (dicot) also form to store food and surround the embryo. Correspondingly, monocots produce one seed leaf, while dicots produce two. The seed matures and becomes dormant, and fruits typically form.

Tropism refers to the fact that plants grow in response to specific stimuli. Seeds are geotropic (or gravitropic), meaning they grow as a response to gravity. Roots are positively geotropic and grow towards gravity. Stems are negatively geotropic and grow away from the force of gravity. A seed planted upside down will still grow roots and stems in the right direction. Plagiotropic refers to the fact that secondary branches and roots grow at right angles to gravity. Phototropism refers to the fact that a plant bends or grows toward a light source. Thigmotropism refers to how plants respond to contact. Plant hormones are organic compounds that usually influence changes in plants. They can cause fruit to ripen or instigate plant growth. Five major groups of hormones are auxins, gibberellins, ethylenes, cytokinins, and abscisic acids. Auxins occur naturally and can be synthesized. They affect plant cell elongation, apical dominance, and rooting. Gibberellins affect plant height. Ethylenes help fruit ripen. Cytokinins are involved in cell division. Abscisic acids inhibit other hormones.

The animal kingdom is comprised of more than one million species in about 30 phyla (the plant kingdom sometimes uses the term division). There about 800,000 species of insects alone, representing half of all animal species. The characteristics that distinguish members of the animal kingdom from members of other kingdoms are that they are multicellular, are heterotrophic, reproduce sexually (there are some exceptions), have cells that do not contain cell walls or photosynthetic pigments, can move at some stage of life, and can rapidly respond to the environment as a result of specialized tissues like nerve and muscle. Heterotrophic refers to the method of getting energy by eating food that has energy releasing substances. Plants, on the other hand, are autotrophs, which mean they make their own energy. During reproduction, animals have a diploid embryo in the blastula stage. This structure is unique to animals. The blastula resembles a fluid-filled ball.

Metazoans are multicellular animals. Food is ingested and enters a mesoderm-lined coelom (body cavity). Phylum porifera and coelenterate are exceptions. The taxonomy of animals involves grouping them into phyla according to body symmetry and plan, as well as the presence of or lack of segmentation. The more complex phyla that have a coelom and a digestive system are further classified as protostomes or deuterostomes according to blastula development. In protostomes, the blastula's blastopore (opening) forms a mouth. In deuterostomes, the blastopore forms an anus. Taxonomy schemes vary, but there are about 36 phyla of animals. The corresponding term for plants at this level is division. The most notable phyla include chordata, mollusca, porifera, cnidaria, platyhelminthes, nematoda, annelida, arthropoda, and echinodermata, which account for about 96 percent of all animal species.

Systems in animals have developed to perform various functions, including providing physical protection and obtaining food. Some animals have internal or external skeletons, shells, or skin that provide protection and support. Skin helps prevent water loss. Muscle systems enable movement. Brains and nervous systems help animals respond to external stimuli by processing incoming and outgoing signals. The main systems in animals are skeletal, muscular, nervous, digestive, respiratory, reproductive, and circulatory. The human stomach, for example, aids in the process of turning consumed food sources into energy. It has many tissue types: smooth muscle tissue, loose connective tissue, nervous tissue, blood, and columnar epithelial tissue. Many animals have a stomach or digestive chamber with two openings. These are known as metazoans.

Extrinsic refers to homeostatic systems that are controlled from outside the body. In higher animals, the nervous system and endocrine system help regulate body functions by responding to stimuli. Hormones in animals regulate many processes, including growth, metabolism, reproduction, and fluid balance. The names of hormones tend to end in "-one." Endocrine hormones are proteins or steroids. Steroid hormones (anabolic steroids) help control the manufacture of protein in muscles and bones.

Invertebrates do not have a backbone, whereas vertebrates do. The great majority of animal species (an estimated 98 percent) are invertebrates, including worms, jellyfish, mollusks, slugs, insects, and spiders. They comprise 30 phyla in all. Vertebrates belong to the phylum chordata. The vertebrate body has two cavities. The thoracic cavity holds the heart and lungs and the abdominal cavity holds the digestive organs. Animals with exoskeletons have skeletons on the outside. Examples are crabs and turtles. Animals with endoskeletons have skeletons on the inside. Examples are humans, tigers, birds, and reptiles.

Animals have four main tissues types: epithelial, connective, muscle, and bone. Epithelial tissue is found on body surfaces (like skin) and lining body cavities (like the stomach). Its function is to form and protect various glands. The three types of epithelial tissue are squamous (flattened), cuboidal (cube-shaped), and columnar (elongated). It can be further classified as simple (a single layer) or stratified (more than one layer). Epithelial cells move substances in, around, and out of the body. They can also have protective and secretory functions. Glands comprised of epithelial tissue can be unicellular or multicellular. Connective tissue is used to bind, support, protect, form blood, store fat, and fill space. The two kinds of connective tissue are loose and fibrous. In the human body, cartilage, bone, tendons, ligaments, blood, and protective layers on muscle, nerve, and blood vessels are types of connective tissue. The three types of muscle tissue are skeletal (striated), smooth, and cardiac.

Skeletal muscle is strong, quick, and capable of voluntary contraction. Skeletal muscle fibers are striated and cylinder shaped. They have about 25 nuclei that are located to the side of the cell. Skeletal muscle consists of myofibrils that contain two types of filaments (myofilaments) made of proteins. The two types of filaments are actin and myosin. These filaments are aligned, giving the appearance of striation. During contraction, they slide against each other and become more overlapped. Smooth muscle is weak, slow, and usually contracts involuntarily.

Examples in humans can be found in the gastrointestinal tract, blood vessels, bladder, uterus, hair follicles, and parts of the eye. Smooth muscle fibers are not striated, but spindle shaped. They are somewhat long and a little wider in the center. Each cell contains one nucleus that is centrally located. Smooth muscle cells also contain myofibrils, but they are not aligned. Cardiac muscle is strong, quick, and continuously contracts involuntarily. It is found in the myocardium of the heart.

ANATOMY

MAJOR ORGAN SYSTEMS

Skeletal: This consists of the bones and joints. The skeletal system provides support for the body through its rigid structure, provides protection for internal organs, and works to make organisms motile. Growth hormone affects the rate of reproduction and the size of body cells, and also helps amino acids move through membranes.

Muscular: This includes the muscles. The muscular system allows the body to move and respond to its environment.

Nervous: This includes the brain, spinal cord, and nerves. The nervous system is a signaling system for intrabody communications among systems, responses to stimuli, and interaction within an environment. Signals are electrochemical. Conscious thoughts and memories and sense interpretation occur in the nervous system. It also controls involuntary muscles and functions, such as breathing and the beating of the heart.

Digestive: This includes the mouth, pharynx, esophagus, stomach, intestines, rectum, anal canal, teeth, salivary glands, tongue, liver, gallbladder, pancreas, and appendix. The system helps change food into a form that the body can process and use for energy and nutrients. Food is eventually eliminated as solid waste. Digestive processes can be mechanical, such as chewing food and churning it in the stomach, and chemical, such as secreting hydrochloric acid to kill bacteria and converting protein to amino acids. The overall system converts large food particles into molecules so the body can use them. The small intestine transports the molecules to the circulatory system. The large intestine absorbs nutrients and prepares the unused portions of food for elimination.

Carbohydrates are the primary source of energy as they can be easily converted to glucose. Fats (oils or lipids) are usually not very water soluble, and vitamins A, D, E, and K are fat soluble. Fats are needed to help process these vitamins and can also store energy. Fats have the highest calorie value per gram (9,000 calories). Dietary fiber, or roughage, helps the excretory system. In humans, fiber can help regulate blood sugar levels, reduce heart disease, help food pass through the digestive system, and add bulk. Dietary minerals are chemical elements that are involved with biochemical functions in the body. Proteins consist of amino acids. Proteins are broken down in the body into amino acids that are used for protein biosynthesis or fuel. Vitamins are compounds that are not made by the body, but obtained through the diet. Water is necessary to prevent dehydration since water is lost through the excretory system and perspiration.

Respiratory: This includes the nose, pharynx, larynx, trachea, bronchi, and lungs. It is involved in gas exchange, which occurs in the alveoli. Fish have gills instead of lungs.

Circulatory: This includes the heart, blood, and blood vessels, such as veins, arteries, and capillaries. Blood transports oxygen and nutrients to cells and carbon dioxide to the lungs.

Skin (integumentary): This includes skin, hair, nails, sense receptors, sweat glands, and oil glands. The skin is a sense organ, provides an exterior barrier against disease, regulates body temperature through perspiration, manufactures chemicals and hormones, and provides a place for nerves from the nervous system and parts of the circulation system to travel through. Skin has three layers: epidermis, dermis, and subcutaneous. The epidermis is the thin, outermost, waterproof layer. Basal cells are located in the epidermis. The dermis contains the sweat glands, oil glands, and hair follicles. The subcutaneous layer has connective tissue, and also contains adipose (fat) tissue, nerves, arteries, and veins.

Excretory: This includes the kidneys, ureters, bladder, and urethra. The excretory system helps maintain the amount of fluids in the body. Wastes from the blood system and excess water are removed in urine. The system also helps remove solid waste.

Immune: This includes the lymphatic system, lymph nodes, lymph vessels, thymus, and spleen. Lymph fluid is moved throughout the body by lymph vessels that provide protection against disease. This system protects the body from external intrusions, such as microscopic organisms and foreign substances. It can also protect against some cancerous cells.

Endocrine: This includes the pituitary gland, pineal gland, hypothalamus, thyroid gland, parathyroids, thymus, adrenals, pancreas, ovaries, and testes. It controls systems and processes by secreting hormones into the blood system. Exocrine glands are those that secrete fluid into ducts. Endocrine glands secrete hormones directly into the blood stream without the use of ducts. Prostaglandin (tissue hormones) diffuses only a short distance from the tissue that created it, and influences nearby cells only. Adrenal glands are located above each kidney. The cortex secretes some sex hormones, as well as mineralocorticoids and glucocorticoids involved in immune suppression and stress response. The medulla secretes epinephrine and norepinephrine. Both elevate blood sugar, increase blood pressure, and accelerate heart rate. Epinephrine also stimulates heart muscle. The islets of Langerhans are clumped within the pancreas and secrete glucagon and insulin, thereby regulating blood sugar levels. The four parathyroid glands at the rear of the thyroid secrete parathyroid hormone.

Reproductive: In the male, this system includes the testes, vas deferens, urethra, prostate, penis, and scrotum. In the female, this system includes the ovaries, fallopian tubes (oviduct and uterine tubes), cervix, uterus, vagina, vulva, and mammary glands. Sexual reproduction helps provide genetic diversity as gametes from each parent contribute half the DNA to the zygote offspring. The system provides a method of transporting the male gametes to the female. It also allows for the growth and development of the embryo. Hormones involved are testosterone, interstitial cell stimulating hormone (ICSH), luteinizing hormone (LH), follicle stimulating hormone (FSH), and estrogen. Estrogens secreted from the ovaries include estradiol, estrone, and estriol. They encourage growth, among other things. Progesterone helps prepare the endometrium for pregnancy.

Based on whether or not and when an organism uses meiosis or mitosis, the three possible cycles of reproduction are haplontic, diplontic, and haplodiplontic. Fungi, green algae, and protozoa are haplontic. Animals and some brown algae and fungi are diplontic. Plants and some fungi are haplodiplontic. Diplontic organisms, like multicelled animals, have a dominant diploid life cycle. The haploid generation is simply the egg and sperm. Monoecious species are bisexual (hermaphroditic). In this case, the individual has both male and female organs: sperm-bearing testicles and egg-bearing ovaries. Hermaphroditic species can self-fertilize. Some worms are hermaphroditic. Cross fertilization is when individuals exchange genetic information. Most animal species are dioecious, meaning individuals are distinctly male or female.

139

BIOLOGICAL RELATIONSHIPS

As heterotrophs, animals can be further classified as carnivores, herbivores, omnivores, and parasites. Predation refers to a predator that feeds on another organism, which results in its death. Detritivory refers to heterotrophs that consume organic dead matter. Carnivores are animals that are meat eaters. Herbivores are plant eaters, and omnivores eat both meat and plants. A parasite's food source is its host. A parasite lives off of a host, which does not benefit from the interaction. Nutrients can be classified as carbohydrates, fats, fiber, minerals, proteins, vitamins, and water. Each supply a specific substance required for various species to survive, grow, and reproduce. A calorie is a measurement of heat energy. It can be used to represent both how much energy a food can provide and how much energy an organism needs to live.

Biochemical cycles are how chemical elements required by living organisms cycle between living and nonliving organisms. Elements that are frequently required are phosphorus, sulfur, oxygen, carbon, gaseous nitrogen, and water. Elements can go through gas cycles, sedimentary cycles, or both. Elements circulate through the air in a gas cycle and from land to water in a sedimentary one.

A food chain is a linking of organisms in a community that is based on how they use each other as food sources. Each link in the chain consumes the link above it and is consumed by the link below it. The exceptions are the organism at the top of the food chain and the organism at the bottom.

Biomagnification (bioamplification): This refers to an increase in concentration of a substance within a food chain. Examples are pesticides or mercury. Mercury is emitted from coal-fired power plants and gets into the water supply, where it is eaten by a fish. A larger fish eats smaller fish, and humans eat fish. The concentration of mercury in humans has now risen. Biomagnification is affected by the persistence of a chemical, whether it can be broken down and negated, food chain energetics, and whether organisms can reduce or negate the substance.

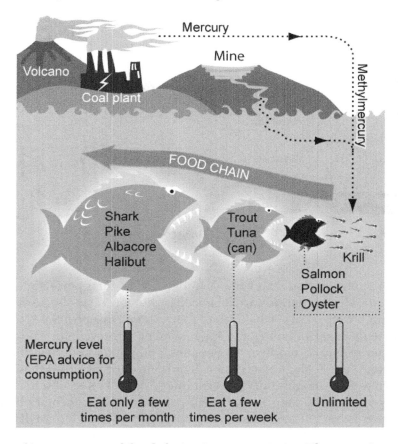

A food web consists of interconnected food chains in a community. The organisms can be linked to show the direction of energy flow. Energy flow in this sense is used to refer to the actual caloric flow through a system from trophic level to trophic level. Trophic level refers to a link in a food chain or a level of nutrition. The 10% rule is that from trophic level to level, about 90% of the energy is lost (in the form of heat, for example). The lowest trophic level consists of primary producers (usually plants), then primary consumers, then secondary consumers, and finally tertiary consumers (large carnivores). The final link is decomposers, which break down the consumers at the top. Food chains usually do not contain more than six links. These links may also be referred to as ecological pyramids.

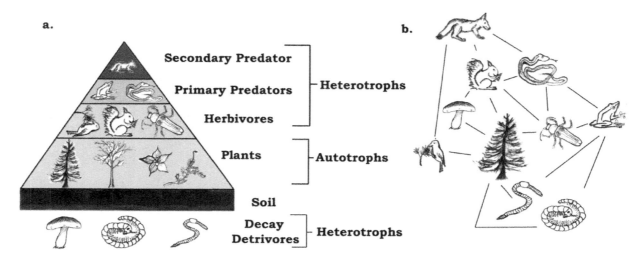

Ecosystem stability is a concept that states that a stable ecosystem is perfectly efficient. Seasonal changes or expected climate fluctuations are balanced by homeostasis. It also states that interspecies interactions are part of the balance of the system. Four principles of ecosystem stability are that waste disposal and nutrient replenishment by recycling is complete, the system uses sunlight as an energy source, biodiversity remains, and populations are stable in that they do not over consume resources. Ecologic succession is the concept that states that there is an orderly progression of change within a community. An example of primary succession is that over hundreds of years bare rock decomposes to sand, which eventually leads to soil formation, which eventually leads to the growth of grasses and trees. Secondary succession occurs after a disturbance or major event that greatly affects a community, such as a wild fire or construction of a dam.

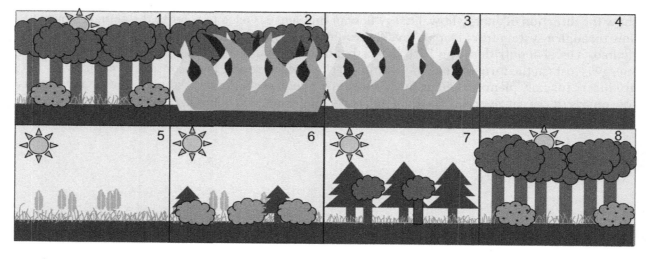

Population is a measure of how many individuals exist in a specific area. It can be used to measure the size of human, plant, or animal groups. Population growth depends on many factors. Factors that can limit the number of individuals in a population include lack of resources such as food and water, space, habitat destruction, competition, disease, and predators. Exponential growth refers to an unlimited rising growth rate. This kind of growth can be plotted on a chart in the shape of a J.

Carrying capacity is the population size that can be sustained. The world's population is about 6.8 billion and growing. The human population has not yet reached its carrying capacity. Population dynamics refers to how a population changes over time and the factors that cause changes. An S-shaped curve shows that population growth has leveled off. Biotic potential refers to the maximum reproductive capacity of a population given ideal environmental conditions.

BIOLOGICAL CONCEPTS

Territoriality: This refers to members of a species protecting areas from other members of their species and from other species. Species members claim specific areas as their own.

Dominance: This refers to the species in a community that is the most populous.

Altruism: This is when a species or individual in a community exhibits behaviors that benefit another individual at a cost to itself. In biology, altruism does not have to be a conscious sacrifice.

Threat display: This refers to behavior by an organism that is intended to intimidate or frighten away members of its own or another species.

The principle of **competitive exclusion** (Gause's Law) states that if there are limited or insufficient resources and species are competing for them, these species will not be able to co-exist. The result is that one of the species will become extinct or be forced to undergo a behavioral or evolutionary change. Another way to say this is that "complete competitors cannot coexist."

A **community** is any number of species interacting within a given area. A **niche** is the role of a species within a community. **Species diversity** refers to the number of species within a community and their populations. A **biome** refers to an area in which species are associated because of climate. The six major biomes in North America are desert, tropical rain forest, grassland, coniferous forest, deciduous forest, and tundra.

Biotic: Biotic factors are the living factors, such as other organisms, that affect a community or population. Abiotic factors are nonliving factors that affect a community or population, such as facets of the environment.

Ecology: Ecology is the study of plants, animals, their environments, and how they interact.

Ecosystem: An ecosystem is a community of species and all of the environment factors that affect them.

Biomass: In ecology, biomass refers to the mass of one or all of the species (species biomass) in an ecosystem or area.

Predation, parasitism, commensalism, and mutualism are all types of species interactions that affect species populations. **Intraspecific relationships** are relationships among members of a species. **Interspecific relationships** are relationships between members of different species.

Predation: This is a relationship in which one individual feeds on another (the prey), causing the prey to die. **Mimicry** is an adaptation developed as a response to predation. It refers to an organism that has a similar appearance to another species, which is meant to fool the predator into thinking the organism is more dangerous than it really is. Two examples are the drone fly and the io moth. The fly looks like a bee, but cannot sting. The io moth has markings on its wings that make it look like an owl. The moth can startle predators and gain time to escape. Predators can also use mimicry to lure their prey.

143

Symbiotic Relationships: A relationship where at least one of the organisms benefits. Mutualism, competition, commensalism, and parasitism are all types of symbiotic relationships.

- **Mutualism**: A relationship where both organisms benefit from having contact.
- **Competition**: A relationship where both organisms are harmed.
- **Commensalism**: A relationship where one organism is benefitted while the other organism is not affected.
- **Parasitism**: A relationship where one organism benefits and the other is harmed.

Review Video: <u>Mutualism, Commensalism, and Parasitism</u>
Visit mometrix.com/academy and enter code: 757249

Earth and Space Science

PREHISTORY

Geologists use the geologic time scale when discussing Earth's chronology and the formation of rocks and minerals. Age is calculated in millions of years before the present time. Units of time are often delineated by geologic or paleontologic events. Smaller units of time such as eras are distinguished by the abundance and/or extinction of certain plant and animal life. For example, the extinction of the dinosaurs marks the end of the Mesozoic era and the beginning of the Cenozoic, the present, era. We are in the Holocene epoch. The supereon encompasses the greatest amount of time. It is composed of eons. Eons are divided into eras, eras into periods, and periods into epochs. Layers of rock also correspond to periods of time in geochronology. Current theory holds that the Earth was formed 4.5 billion years ago.

Earth's early development began after a supernova exploded. This led to the formation of the Sun out of hydrogen gas and interstellar dust. These same elements swirled around the newly-formed Sun and formed the planets, including Earth. Scientists theorize that about 4.5 billion years ago, Earth was a chunk of rock surrounded by a cloud of gas. It is believed it lacked water and the type of atmosphere that exists today. Heat from radioactive materials in the rock and pressure in the Earth's interior melted the interior. This caused the heavier materials, such as iron, to sink. Lighter silicate-type rocks rose to the Earth's surface. These rocks formed the Earth's earliest crust. Other chemicals also rose to the Earth's surface, helping to form the water and atmosphere. There is one material that has been dated by scientists and found to be 4.4 billion years old. The material is zircon, which consists of zirconium, silicon, and oxygen. Zircon is a mineral that has a high resistance to weathering.

The Paleozoic era began about 542 Ma (Millions of years ago) and lasted until 251 Ma. It is further divided into six periods. The Paleozoic era began after the supercontinent Pannotia started to break up and at the end of a global ice age. By the end of the era, the supercontinent Pangaea had formed. The beginning of the Paleozoic era is marked by Cambrian Explosion, a time when there were abundant life forms according to the fossil record. The end of the era is marked by one of the major extinction events, the Permian extinction, during which almost 90 percent of the species living at the time became extinct. Many plant and animal forms appeared on the land and in the sea during this era. It is also when large land plants first appeared in the fossil record. There are many invertebrates found in the fossil record of the Paleozoic era, and fish, amphibians, and reptiles also first appeared in the fossil record during this era. There were also large swamps and forests, some of which were formed into coal deposits that exist today.

The Mesozoic era is known as the Age of the Dinosaurs. It is also the era during which the dinosaurs became extinct. The fossil record also shows the appearance of mammals and birds. Trees that existed included gymnosperms, which have uncovered seeds and are mostly cone bearing, and angiosperms, which have covered seeds and are flowering plants. The angiosperm group is currently the dominant plant group. It was also during this era that the supercontinent Pangaea divided into the continental pieces that exist today. During the Cretaceous period, sea levels rose until one-third of the Earth's present land mass was underwater, and then receded. This period created huge marine deposits and chalk. The extinction of the dinosaurs happened about 65 Ma, and was believed to have been triggered by the impact of an asteroid.

The Cenozoic era began about 65.5 Ma and continues to the present. It is marked by the Cretaceous-Tertiary extinction event (extinction of the dinosaurs as well as many invertebrates and plants). The Cenozoic era is further divided into the Paleogene, Neogene, and Quaternary periods. During

145

the Cenozoic era, Pangaea continued to drift, and the plates eventually moved into their present positions. The Pleistocene Ice Age, also known as Quaternary glaciation or the current ice age began about 2.58 Ma and includes the glaciation occurring today. Mammals continued to evolve and other plants and animals came into existence during this era. The fossil record includes the ancestors of the horse, rhinoceros, and camel. It also includes the first dogs and cats and the first humanlike creatures. The first humans appeared less than 200,000 years ago.

Fossils are preservations of plants, animals, their remains, or their traces that date back to about 10,000 years ago. Fossils and where they are found in rock strata makes up the fossil record. Fossils are formed under a very specific set of conditions. The fossil must not be damaged by predators and scavengers after death, and the fossil must not decompose. Usually, this happens when the organism is quickly covered with sediment. This sediment builds up and molecules in the organism's body are replaced by minerals. Fossils come in an array of sizes, from single-celled organisms to large dinosaurs.

Fossils provide a wealth of information about the past, particularly about the flora and fauna that once occupied the Earth, but also about the geologic history of the Earth itself and how Earth and its inhabitants came to be. Some fossilized remains in the geohistorical record exemplify ongoing processes in the Earth's environment, such as weathering, glaciation, and volcanism. These have all led to evolutionary changes in plants and animals. Other fossils support the theory that catastrophic events caused drastic changes in the Earth and its living creatures. One example of this type of theory is that a meteor struck the Earth and caused dinosaurs to become extinct. Both types of fossils provide scientists with a way to hypothesize whether these types of events will happen again.

GEOLOGY

Minerals are naturally occurring, inorganic solids with a definite chemical composition and an orderly internal crystal structure. A polymorph is two minerals with the same chemical composition, but a different crystal structure. Rocks are aggregates of one or more minerals, and may also contain mineraloids (minerals lacking a crystalline structure) and organic remains. The three types of rocks are sedimentary, igneous, and metamorphic. Rocks are classified based on their formation and the minerals they contain. Minerals are classified by their chemical composition. Geology is the study of the planet Earth as it pertains to the composition, structure, and origin of its rocks. Petrology is the study of rocks, including their composition, texture, structure, occurrence, mode of formation, and history. Mineralogy is the study of minerals.

Minerals are classified by chemical composition and internal crystalline structure. They are organized into classes. Native elements such as gold and silver are not classified in this manner. The eight classes are sulfides, oxides\hydroxides, halides, carbonates, sulfates, phosphates, and silicates. These classes are based on the dominant anion (negatively charged ion) or anionic group. Minerals are classified in this way for three main reasons. First, minerals with the same anion have unmistakable resemblances. Second, minerals with the same anion are often found in the same geologic environment. For example, calcite and dolomite, which belong to the same group, are often found together. Last, this method is similar to the naming convention used to identify inorganic compounds in chemistry. Minerals can be further separated into groups on the basis of internal structure.

The physical properties (as opposed to chemical structures) used to identify minerals are hardness, luster, color, cleavage, streak, form (the external shape), and other special properties. Senses other than sight, such as touch, taste, and smell, may be used to observe physical properties. Hardness is the resistance a mineral has to scratches. The Mohs Hardness Scale is used to rate hardness from 1 to 10. Color can often not be determined definitively as some minerals can be more than one color. Luster is determined by reflected light. Luster can be described as metallic (shiny), sub-metallic (dull), non-metallic (vitreous, like glass), or earthy (like dirt or powder). Streak is the true color of the mineral in powdered form. It can be determined by rubbing the specimen across an unglazed porcelain tile. Fracture or cleavage is how a mineral reacts to stress, such as being struck with a hammer. Other properties that can be used to identify rocks and minerals include magnetism, a salty taste, or a pungent odor in a streak test.

> **Review Video: Rocks vs. Minerals**
> Visit mometrix.com/academy and enter code: 947587

The Earth's core consists of hot iron and forms of nickel. The mantle consists of different materials, including iron, magnesium, and calcium. The crust covers the mantle, consists of a thin layer of much lighter rocks, and is further subdivided into continental and oceanic portions. The continental portion consists mainly of silicates, such as granite. The oceanic portion consists of heavier, volcanic rocks, such as basalt. The upper 10 miles of the lithosphere layer (the crust and part of the mantle) is made up of 95% igneous rock (or its metamorphic equivalent), 4% shale, 0.75% sandstone, and 0.25% limestone. There are over 4,000 known minerals, but only about 20 make up some 95% of all rocks. There are, however, more than 3,000 individual kinds of minerals in the Earth's crust. Silicates are the largest group of minerals.

Sedimentary rocks are formed by the process of lithification, which involves compaction, the expulsion of liquids from pores, and the cementation of the pre-existing rock. It is pressure and temperature that are responsible for this process. Sedimentary rocks are often formed in layers in the presence of water, and may contain organic remains, such as fossils. Sedimentary rocks are organized into three groups: detrital, biogenic, and chemical. Texture refers to the size, shape, and grains of sedimentary rock. Texture can be used to determine how a particular sedimentary rock was created. Composition refers to the types of minerals present in the rock. The origin of sedimentary rock refers to the type of water that was involved in its creation. Marine deposits, for example, likely involved ocean environments, while continental deposits likely involved dry land and lakes.

147

Igneous rock is formed from magma, which is molten material originating from beneath the Earth's surface. Depending upon where magma cools, the resulting igneous rock can be classified as intrusive, plutonic, hypabyssal, extrusive, or volcanic. Magma that solidifies at a depth is intrusive, cools slowly, and has a coarse grain as a result. An example is granite. Magma that solidifies at or near the surface is extrusive, cools quickly, and usually has a fine grain. An example is basalt. Magma that actually flows out of the Earth's surface is called lava. Some extrusive rock cools so quickly that crystals do not have time to form. These rocks have a glassy appearance. An example is obsidian. Hypabyssal rock is igneous rock that is formed at medium depths.

Metamorphic rock is that which has been changed by great heat and pressure. This results in a variety of outcomes, including deformation, compaction, destruction of the characteristics of the original rock, bending, folding, and formation of new minerals because of chemical reactions, and changes in the size and shape of the mineral grain. For example, the igneous rock ferromagnesian can be changed into schist and gneiss. The sedimentary rock carbonaceous can be changed into marble. The texture of metamorphic rocks can be classified as foliated and unfoliated. Foliation, or layering, occurs when rock is compressed along one axis during recrystallization. This can be seen in schist and shale. Unfoliated rock does not include this banding. Rocks that are compressed equally from all sides or lack specific minerals will be unfoliated. An example is marble.

Review Video: Igneous, Sedimentary, and Metamorphic Rocks
Visit mometrix.com/academy and enter code: 689294

There are two basic types of weathering: mechanical and chemical. Weathering is a very prominent process on the Earth's surface. Materials weather at different rates, which are known as differential weathering. Mechanical and chemical weathering is interdependent. For example, chemical weathering can loosen the bonds between molecules and allow mechanical weathering to take place. Mechanical weathering can expose the surfaces of land masses and allow chemical weathering to take place. Impact, abrasion, frost wedging, root wedging, salt wedging, and uploading are types of mechanical weathering. Types of chemical weathering are dissolution, hydration, hydrolysis, oxidation, biological, and carbonation. The primary type of chemical weathering is caused by water dissolving a mineral. The more acidic water is, the more effective it is at weathering. Carbonic and sulfuric acids can enter rain when they are present in the atmosphere. This lowers the pH value of rain, making it more acidic. Normal rain water has a pH value of 5.5. Acid rain has a pH value of 4 or less.

Erosion is the wearing away of rock materials from the Earth's surface. Erosion can be classified as natural geologic erosion and erosion due to human activity. Natural geologic erosion occurs due to weathering and gravity. Factors involved in natural geologic erosion are typically long term forces. Human activity such as development, farming, and deforestation occurs over shorter periods of time. Soil, which supports plant growth, is the topmost layer of organic material. One type of erosion is sheet erosion, which is the gradual and somewhat uniform removal of surface soil. Rills are small rivulets that cut into soil. Gullies are rills that have become enlarged due to extended water run-off. Sand blows are caused by wind blowing away particles. Negative effects of erosion include sedimentation in rivers, which can pollute water and damage ecosystems. Erosion can also result in the removal of topsoil, which destroys crops and prevents plants from growing. This reduces food production and alters ecosystems.

Deposition, or sedimentation, is the geological process in which previously eroded material is transported or added to a land form or land mass. Erosion and sedimentation are complementary geological processes. Running water causes a substantial amount of deposition of transported materials in both fresh water and coastal areas. Examples include gravity transporting material down the slope of a mountain and depositing it at the base of the slope. Another example is when

149

sandstorms deposit particles in other locations. When glaciers melt and retreat, it can result in the deposition of sediments. Evaporation is also considered to cause deposition since dissolved materials are left behind when water evaporates. Deposition can include the buildup of organic materials. For example, chalk is partially made up of the small calcium carbonate skeletons of marine plankton, which helps create more calcium carbonate from chemical processes. Superposition, in geology, and in the field of stratigraphy in particular, the law of superposition is that underground layers closer to the surface were deposited more recently.

Uniformitarianism, also known as gradualism, uniformitarianism is the belief among modern geologists that the forces, processes, and laws that we see today have existed throughout geologic time. It involves the belief that the present is the key to the past, and that relatively slow processes have shaped the geological features of Earth. Catastrophism is the belief that the Earth was shaped by sudden, short-term catastrophic events.

Stratigraphy is a branch of geology that involves the study of rock layers and layering. Sedimentary rocks are the primary focus of stratigraphy. Subfields include lithostratigraphy, which is the study of the vertical layering of rock types, and biostratigraphy, which is the study of fossil evidence in rock layers. Magnetostratigraphy is the study of changes in detrital remnant magnetism (DRM), which is used to measure the polarity of Earth's magnetic field at the time a stratum was deposited. Chronostratigraphy focuses on the relative dating of rock strata based on the time of rock formation. Unconformity refers to missing layers of rock.

A numerical, or "absolute," age is a specific number of years, such as 150 million years ago. A "relative" age refers to a time range, such as the Mesozoic era. It is used to determine whether one rock formation is older or younger than another formation. Radioactive dating is a form of absolute dating and stratigraphy is a form of relative dating. Radioactive dating techniques have provided the most information about the absolute age of rocks and other geological features. Together, geochronologists have created a geologic time scale. Biostratigraphy uses plant and animal fossils within rock to determine its relative age.

The first known observations of stratigraphy were made by Aristotle, who lived before the time of Christ. He observed seashells in ancient rock formations and on the beach, and concluded that the fossilized seashells were similar to current seashells. Avicenna, a Persian scholar from the 11th century, also made early advances in the development of stratigraphy with the concept of superposition. Nicolas Steno, a Danish scientist from the 17th century, expounded upon this with the belief that layers of rock are piled on top of each other. In the 18th century, Abraham Werner categorized rocks from four different periods: the Primary, Secondary, Tertiary, and Quaternary periods. This fell out of use when the belief emerged that rock layers containing the same fossils had been deposited at the same time, and were therefore from the same age. British geologists created the names for many of the time divisions in use today. For example, the Devonian period was named after the county of Devon, and the Permian period was named after Perm, Russia.

PLATE TECTONICS

The Earth is ellipsoid, not perfectly spherical. This means the diameter is different through the poles and at the equator. Through the poles, the Earth is about 12,715 km in diameter. The approximate center of the Earth is at a depth of 6,378 km. The Earth is divided into a crust, mantle, and core. The core consists of a solid inner portion. Moving outward, the molten outer core occupies the space from about a depth of 5,150 km to a depth of 2,890 km. The mantle consists of a lower and upper layer. The lower layer includes the D' (D prime) and D" (D double-prime) layers. The solid portion of the upper mantle and crust together form the lithosphere, or rocky sphere. Below this, but still within the mantle, is the asthenosphere, or weak sphere. These layers are distinguishable because the lithosphere is relatively rigid, while the asthenosphere resembles a thick liquid.

The theory of plate tectonics states that the lithosphere, the solid portion of the mantle and Earth's crust, consists of major and minor plates. These plates are on top of and move with the viscous upper mantle, which is heated because of the convection cycle that occurs in the interior of the Earth. There are different estimates as to the exact number of major and minor plates. The number of major plates is believed to be between 9 and 15, and it is thought that there may be as many as 40 minor plates. The United States is atop the North American plate. The Pacific Ocean is atop the Pacific plate. The point at which these two plates slide horizontally along the San Andreas fault is an example of a transform plate boundary. The other two types of boundaries are divergent (plates that are spreading apart and forming new crust) and convergent (the process of subduction causes one plate to go under another). The movement of plates is what causes other features of the Earth's crust, such as mountains, volcanoes, and earthquakes.

> **Review Video: Plate Tectonic Theory**
> Visit mometrix.com/academy and enter code: 535013

Most earthquakes are caused by tectonic plate movement. They occur along fractures called faults or fault zones. Friction in the faults prevents smooth movement. Tension builds up over time, and the release of that tension results in earthquakes. Faults are grouped based on the type of slippage that occurs. The types of faults are dip-slip, strike-slip, and oblique-slip. A dip-slip fault involves vertical movement along the fault plane. In a normal dip-slip fault, the wall that is above the fault plane moves down. In a reverse dip-slip fault, the wall above the fault plane moves up. A strike-slip fault involves horizontal movement along the fault plane. Oblique-slip faults involve both vertical and horizontal movement. The Richter magnitude scale measures how much seismic energy was released by an earthquake.

Orogeny refers to the formation of mountains, particularly the processes of folding and faulting caused by plate tectonics. Folding is when layers of sedimentary rock are pressed together by continental plate movements. Sections of rock that are folded upward are called anticlines. Sections of rock that are folded downward are called synclines. Examples of folded mountains are the Alps and the Himalayans. Fault-block mountains are created when tectonic plate movement produces tension that results in displacement. Mountains in the Southwest United States are examples of fault-blocking mountains. Mountains can also be caused by volcanic activity and erosion.

Volcanoes can occur along any type of tectonic plate boundary. At a divergent boundary, as plates move apart, magma rises to the surface, cools, and forms a ridge. An example of this is the mid-Atlantic ridge. Convergent boundaries, where one plate slides under another, are often areas with a lot of volcanic activity. The subduction process creates magma. When it rises to the surface, volcanoes can be created. Volcanoes can also be created in the middle of a plate over hot spots. Hot spots are locations where narrow plumes of magma rise through the mantle in a fixed place over a long period of time. The Hawaiian Islands and Midway are examples. The plate shifts and the island moves. Magma continues to rise through the mantle, however, which produces another island. Volcanoes can be active, dormant, or extinct. Active volcanoes are those that are erupting or about to erupt. Dormant volcanoes are those that might erupt in the future and still have internal volcanic activity. Extinct volcanoes are those that will not erupt. The three types of volcanoes are shield, cinder cone, and composite. A shield volcano is created by a long-term, relatively gentle eruption. This type of volcanic mountain is created by each progressive lava flow that occurs over time. A cinder cone volcano is created by explosive eruptions. Lava is spewed out of a vent into the air. As it falls to the ground, the lava cools into cinders and ash, which build up around the volcano in a cone shape. A composite volcano is a combination of the other two types of volcanoes. In this type, there are layers of lava flows and layers of ash and cinder.

OCEANS

The hydrologic, or water, cycle refers to water movement on, above, and in the Earth. Water can be in any one of its three states during different phases of the cycle. The three states of water are liquid water, frozen ice, and water vapor. Processes involved in the hydrologic cycle include precipitation, canopy interception, snow melt, runoff, infiltration, subsurface flow, evaporation, sublimation, advection, condensation, and transpiration. Precipitation is when condensed water vapor falls to Earth. Examples include rain, fog drip, and various forms of snow, hail, and sleet. Canopy interception is when precipitation lands on plant foliage instead of falling to the ground and evaporating. Snow melt is runoff produced by melting snow. Infiltration occurs when water flows from the surface into the ground. Subsurface flow refers to water that flows underground. Evaporation is when water in a liquid state changes to a gas. Sublimation is when water in a solid state (such as snow or ice) changes to water vapor without going through a liquid phase. Advection is the movement of water through the atmosphere. Condensation is when water vapor changes to liquid water. Transpiration is when water vapor is released from plants into the air.

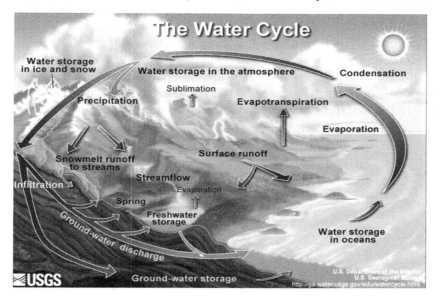

The ocean is the salty body of water that encompasses the Earth. It has a mass of 1.4 x 1024 grams. Geographically, the ocean is divided into three large oceans: the Pacific Ocean, the Atlantic Ocean, and the Indian Ocean. There are also other divisions, such as gulfs, bays, and various types of seas, including Mediterranean and marginal seas. Ocean distances can be measured by latitude, longitude, degrees, meters, miles, and nautical miles. The ocean accounts for 70.8% of the surface of the Earth, amounting to 361,254,000 km2. The ocean's depth is greatest at Challenger Deep in the Mariana Trench. The ocean floor here is 10,924 meters below sea level. The depths of the ocean are mapped by echo sounders and satellite altimeter systems. Echo sounders emit a sound pulse from the surface and record the time it takes to return. Satellite altimeters provide better maps of the ocean floor.

The ocean floor includes features similar to those found on land, such as mountains, ridges, plains, and canyons. The oceanic crust is a thin, dense layer that is about 10 km thick. The greatest volume of water is contained in the basins with lesser volumes that occupy the low-lying areas of the continents, which are known as the continental shelves. The continental slope connects the shelf to the ocean floor of the basin. The continental rise is a slightly sloping area between the slope and the basin. A seamount is an undersea volcanic peak that rises to a height of at least 1,000 meters. A guyot is a seamount with a flat top. A mid-ocean ridge is a continuous undersea mountain chain. Sills are low parts of ridges separating ocean basins or other seas. Trenches are long, narrow troughs. Many isolated peaks and seamounts are scattered throughout the ocean basins, and interrupt ocean currents.

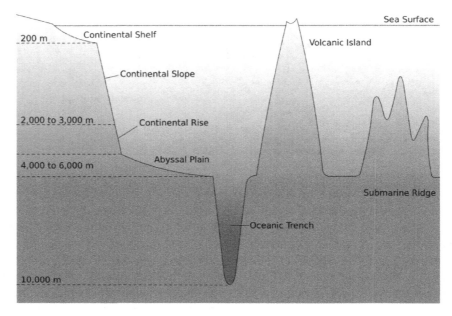

Salinity is a measure of the amount of dissolved salts in ocean water. It is defined in terms of conductivity. Salinity is influenced by the geologic formations in the area, with igneous formations leading to lower salinity and sedimentary formations leading to higher salinity. Dryer areas with greater rates of evaporation also have higher salt concentrations. Areas where fresh water mixes with ocean water have lower salt concentrations. Hydrogen and oxygen make up about 96.5% of sea water. The major constituents of the dissolved solids of sea water at an atomic level are chlorine (55.3%), sodium (30.8%), magnesium (3.7%), sulfur (2.6%), calcium (1.2%), and potassium (1.1%). The salinity of ocean water is fairly constant, ranging from 34.60 to 34.80 parts per thousand, which is 200 parts per million. Measuring variation on this small of a scale requires instruments that are accurate to about one part per million.

The carbon and nutrient cycles of the ocean are processes that are due in part to the deep currents, mixing, and upwelling that occur in the ocean. Carbon dioxide (CO_2) from the atmosphere is dissolved into the ocean at higher latitudes and distributed to the denser deep water. Where upwelling occurs, CO_2 is brought back to the surface and emitted into the tropical air. Phytoplankton are typically single-celled organisms that are nourished by the Sun. They are photosynthetic autotrophs, meaning they convert water, carbon dioxide, and solar energy into food. They drift with the currents, produce oxygen as a byproduct, and serve as a food source. Zooplankton feed on phytoplankton. Zooplankton are heterotrophic organisms, meaning they do not synthesize their own food. Zooplankton can be single-celled creatures or much larger organisms, such as jellyfish, mollusks, and crustaceans.

Surface currents are caused by winds. Subsurface currents, which occur deep beneath the ocean's surface, are caused by land masses and the Earth's rotation. The density of ocean water can also affect currents. Sea water with a higher salinity is denser than sea water with a lower salinity. Water from denser areas flows to areas with water that is less dense. Currents are classified by temperature. Colder polar sea water flows south towards warmer water, forming cold currents. Warm water currents swirl around the basins and equator. In turn, heat lost and gained by the ocean creates winds. Ocean currents play a significant role in transferring this heat toward the poles, which aids in the development of many types of weather phenomena.

Gyres are surface ocean currents that form large circular patterns. In the Northern Hemisphere, they flow clockwise. In the Southern Hemisphere, they flow counterclockwise. These directions are caused by the Coriolis effect. The Coriolis effect occurs due to the fact that the Earth is a rotating object. In the Northern Hemisphere, currents appear to be curving to the right. In the Southern Hemisphere, currents appear to be curving to the left. This is because the Earth is rotating. Gyres tend to flow in the opposite direction near the Earth's poles. In the portion of the Pacific Ocean north of the equator, the major currents are North Pacific, California, North Equatorial, and Kuroshio. In the South Pacific, they are South Equatorial, East Australia, South Pacific, and Peru. In the North Atlantic, they are the North Atlantic Drift, Canary, North Equatorial, and Gulf Stream. In the South Atlantic, they are South Equatorial, Brazil, South Atlantic, and Benguela.

Most waves in the ocean are formed by winds. The stronger the winds are, the larger the waves will be. The highest point of a wave is the crest. The lowest point of a wave is the trough. The wavelength is measured from crest to crest. The wave height is measured from the trailing trough to the peak of the crest. The wave frequency refers to the number of wave crests passing a designated point each second. A wave period is the time it takes for a wave crest to reach the point of the wave crest of the previous wave. The energy in the wave runs into the shallow sea floor. This causes the wave to become steeper and then fall over, or break.

The gravitational pull of the Sun and Moon causes the oceans to rise and fall each day, creating high and low tides. Most areas have two high tides and two low tides per day. Because the Moon is closer to the Earth than the Sun, its gravitational pull is much greater. The water on the side of the Earth that is closest to the Moon and the water on the opposite side experience high tide. The two low tides occur on the other sides. This changes as the Moon revolves around the Earth. Tidal range is the measurement of the height difference between low and high tide. Tidal range also changes with the location of the Sun and Moon throughout the year, creating spring and neap tides. When all these bodies are aligned, the combined gravitational pull is greater and the tidal range is also greater. This is what creates the spring tide. The neap tide is when the tidal range is at its lowest, which occurs when the Sun and Moon are not at right angles.

Review Video: <u>Moon and Sun on Ocean Tides</u>
Visit mometrix.com/academy and enter code: 902956

The area where land meets the sea is called the shoreline. This marks the average position of the ocean. Longshore currents create longshore drift or transport (also called beach drift). This is when ocean waves move toward a beach at an angle, which moves water along the coast. Sediment is eroded from some areas and deposited in others. In this way, it is moved along the beach. Rip currents are strong, fast currents that occur when part of longshore current moves away from the beach. Hard, man-made structures built perpendicular to the beach tend to trap sand on the up-current side. Erosion occurs on the down-current side. Features formed by the sediment deposited by waves include spits, bay-mouth bars, tombolos, barrier islands, and buildups. Sand is composed of weather-resistant, granular materials like quartz and orthoclase. In some locations, it is composed of rock and basalt.

Weathering erodes the parent material of beaches, rock and soil, into sand, which is typically quartz. Other parts of the soil such as clay and silt are deposited in areas of the continental shelf. The larger sand particles get deposited in the form of a beach. This includes a near shore, which is underwater, a fore shore, the area typically considered the beach, and a back shore. The offshore starts about 5 meters from the shoreline and extends to about 20 meters. The beach also includes wet and dry parts and a fore dune and rear dune. Waves typically move sand from the sea to the beach, and gravity and wave action move it back again. Wind gradually pushes sand particles uphill in a jumping motion called saltation. Sand stays deposited in the form of dunes and the dunes appear as if they roll backward. Storms can both erode a beach and provide additional deposition.

ATMOSPHERE

The atmosphere consists of 78% nitrogen, 21% oxygen, and 1% argon. It also includes traces of water vapor, carbon dioxide and other gases, dust particles, and chemicals from Earth. The atmosphere becomes thinner the farther it is from the Earth's surface. It becomes difficult to breathe at about 3 km above sea level. The atmosphere gradually fades into space. The lowest layer of the atmosphere is called the troposphere. Its thickness varies at the poles and the equator, varying from about 7 to 17 km. This is where most weather occurs. The stratosphere is next, and continues to an elevation of about 51 km. The mesosphere extends from the stratosphere to an elevation of about 81 km. It is the coldest layer and is where meteors tend to ablate. The next layer is the thermosphere. It is where the International Space Station orbits. The exosphere is the outermost layer, extends to 10,000 km, and mainly consists of hydrogen and helium.

Earth's atmosphere has five main layers. From lowest to highest, these are the troposphere, the stratosphere, the mesosphere, the thermosphere, and the exosphere. Between each pair of layers is a transition layer called a pause. The troposphere includes the tropopause, which is the transitional layer of the stratosphere. Energy from Earth's surface is transferred to the troposphere. Temperature decreases with altitude in this layer. In the stratosphere, the temperature is inverted, meaning that it increases with altitude. The stratosphere includes the ozone layer, which helps block ultraviolet light from the Sun. The stratopause is the transitional layer to the mesosphere. The temperature of the mesosphere decreases with height. It is considered the coldest place on Earth, and has an average temperature of -85 degrees Celsius. Temperature increases with altitude in the thermosphere, which includes the thermopause. Just past the thermosphere is the exobase, the base layer of the exosphere. Beyond the five main layers are the ionosphere, homosphere, heterosphere, and magnetosphere.

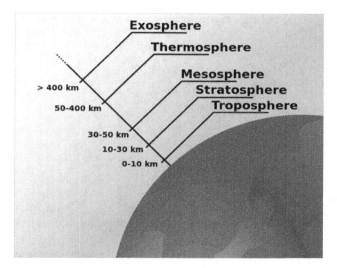

The ozone layer, although contained within the stratosphere, is determined by ozone (O_3) concentrations. It absorbs the majority of ultraviolet light from the Sun. The ionosphere is part of both the exosphere and the thermosphere. It is characterized by the fact that it is a plasma, a partially ionized gas in which free electrons and positive ions are attracted to each other, but are too energetic to remain fixed as a molecule. It starts at about 50 km above Earth's surface and goes to 1,000 km. It affects radio wave transmission and auroras. The ionosphere pushes against the inner edge of the Earth's magnetosphere, which is the highly magnetized, non-spherical region around the Earth. The homosphere encompasses the troposphere, stratosphere, and mesosphere. Gases in the homosphere are considered well mixed. In the heterosphere, the distance that particles can move without colliding is large. As a result, gases are stratified according to their molecular weights. Heavier gases such as oxygen and nitrogen occur near the bottom of the heterosphere, while hydrogen, the lightest element, is found at the top.

Most weather takes place in the troposphere. Air circulates in the atmosphere by convection and in various types of "cells." Air near the equator is warmed by the Sun and rises. Cool air rushes under it, and the higher, warmer air flows toward Earth's poles. At the poles, it cools and descends to the surface. It is now under the hot air, and flows back to the equator. Air currents coupled with ocean currents move heat around the planet, creating winds, weather, and climate. Winds can change direction with the seasons. For example, in Southeast Asia and India, summer monsoons are caused

157

by air being heated by the Sun. This air rises, draws moisture from the ocean, and causes daily rains. In winter, the air cools, sinks, pushes the moist air away, and creates dry weather.

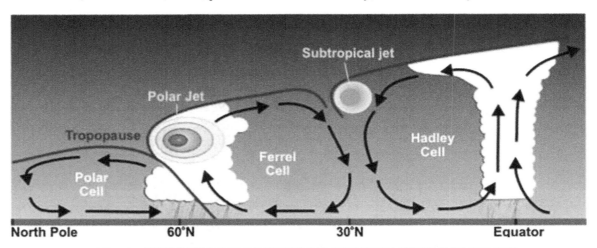

Review Video: Earth's Atmosphere
Visit mometrix.com/academy and enter code: 417614

WEATHER

Meteorology is the study of the atmosphere, particularly as it pertains to forecasting the weather and understanding its processes. Weather is the condition of the atmosphere at any given moment. Most weather occurs in the troposphere. Weather includes changing events such as clouds, storms, and temperature, as well as more extreme events such as tornadoes, hurricanes, and blizzards. Climate refers to the average weather for a particular area over time, typically at least 30 years. Latitude is an indicator of climate. Changes in climate occur over long time periods.

Common atmospheric conditions that are frequently measured are temperature, precipitation, wind, and humidity. These weather conditions are often measured at permanently fixed weather stations so weather data can be collected and compared over time and by region. Measurements may also be taken by ships, buoys, and underwater instruments. Measurements may also be taken under special circumstances. The measurements taken include temperature, barometric pressure, humidity, wind speed, wind direction, and precipitation. Usually, the following instruments are used: A thermometer is used for measuring temperature; a barometer is used for measuring barometric/air pressure; a hygrometer is used for measuring humidity; an anemometer is used for measuring wind speed; a weather vane is used for measuring wind direction; and a rain gauge is used for measuring precipitation.

Winds are the result of air moving by convection. Masses of warm air rise, and cold air sweeps into their place. The warm air also moves, cools, and sinks. The term "prevailing wind" refers to the wind that usually blows in an area in a single direction. Dominant winds are the winds with the highest speeds. Belts or bands that run latitudinally and blow in a specific direction are associated with convection cells. Hadley cells are formed directly north and south of the equator. The Farrell cells occur at about 30° to 60°. The jet stream runs between the Farrell cells and the polar cells. At the higher and lower latitudes, the direction is easterly. At mid latitudes, the direction is westerly. From the North Pole to the south, the surface winds are Polar High Easterlies, Subpolar Low Westerlies, Subtropical High or Horse Latitudes, North-East Trade winds, Equatorial Low or Doldrums, South-East Trades, Subtropical High or Horse Latitudes, Subpolar Low Easterlies, and Polar High.

Terrain affects several local atmospheric conditions, including temperature, wind speed, and wind direction. When there are land forms, heating of the ground can be greater than the heating of the surrounding air than it would be at the same altitude above sea level. This creates a thermal low in the region and amplifies any existing thermal lows. It also changes the wind circulation. Terrain such as hills and valleys increase friction between the air and the land, which disturbs the air flow. This physical block deflects the wind, and the resulting air flow is called a barrier jet. Just as the heating of the land and air affect sea and land breezes along the coast, rugged terrain affects the wind circulation between mountains and valleys.

Humidity refers to water vapor contained in the air. The amount of moisture contained in air depends upon its temperature. The higher the air temperature, the more moisture it can hold. These higher levels of moisture are associated with higher humidity. Absolute humidity refers to the total amount of moisture air is capable of holding at a certain temperature. Relative humidity is the ratio of water vapor in the air compared to the amount the air is capable of holding at its current temperature. As temperature decreases, absolute humidity stays the same and relative humidity increases. A hygrometer is a device used to measure humidity. The dew point is the temperature at which water vapor condenses into water at a particular humidity.

Clouds form when air cools and warm air is forced to give up some of its water vapor because it can no longer hold it. This vapor condenses and forms tiny droplets of water or ice crystals called clouds. Particles, or aerosols, are needed for water vapor to form water droplets. These are called condensation nuclei. Clouds are created by surface heating, mountains and terrain, rising air masses, and weather fronts. Clouds precipitate, returning the water they contain to Earth. Clouds can also create atmospheric optics. They can scatter light, creating colorful phenomena such as rainbows, colorful sunsets, and the green flash phenomenon.

After clouds reach the dew point, precipitation occurs. Precipitation can take the form of a liquid or a solid. It is known by many names, including rain, snow, ice, dew, and frost. Liquid forms of precipitation include rain and drizzle. Rain or drizzle that freezes on contact is known as freezing rain or freezing drizzle. Solid or frozen forms of precipitation include snow, ice needles or diamond dust, sleet or ice pellets, hail, and graupel or snow pellets. Virga is a form of precipitation that evaporates before reaching the ground. It usually looks like sheets or shafts falling from a cloud. The amount of rainfall is measured with a rain gauge. Intensity can be measured according to how fast precipitation is falling or by how severely it limits visibility. Precipitation plays a major role in the water cycle since it is responsible for depositing much of the Earth's fresh water.

Most clouds can be classified according to the altitude of their base above Earth's surface. High clouds occur at altitudes between 5,000 and 13,000 meters. Middle clouds occur at altitudes between 2,000 and 7,000 meters. Low clouds occur from the Earth's surface to altitudes of 2,000 meters. Types of high clouds include cirrus (Ci), thin wispy mare's tails that consist of ice; cirrocumulus (Cc), small, pillow-like puffs that often appear in rows; and cirrostratus (Cs), thin, sheetlike clouds that often cover the entire sky. Types of middle clouds include altocumulus (Ac), gray-white clouds that consist of liquid water; and altostratus (As), grayish or blue-gray clouds that span the sky. Types of low clouds include stratus (St), gray and fog-like clouds consisting of water droplets that take up the whole sky; stratocumulus (Sc), low-lying, lumpy gray clouds; and nimbostratus (Ns), dark gray clouds with uneven bases that indicate rain or snow. Two types of clouds, cumulus (Cu) and cumulonimbus (Cb), are capable of great vertical growth. They can start at a wide range of altitudes, from the Earth's surface to altitudes of 13,000 meters.

Air masses are large volumes of air in the troposphere of the Earth. They are categorized by their temperature and by the amount of water vapor they contain. Arctic and Antarctic air masses are cold, polar air masses are cool, and tropical and equatorial air masses are hot. Other types of air masses include maritime and monsoon, both of which are moist and unstable. There are also continental and superior air masses, which are dry. A weather front separates two masses of air of different densities. It is the principal cause of meteorological phenomena. Air masses are quickly and easily affected by the land they are above. They can have certain characteristics, and then develop new ones when they get blown over a different area.

The Bergeron classification system uses three sets of letters to identify the following characteristics of air masses: moisture content, thermal characteristics from where they originated, and the stability of the atmosphere. The first, moisture content, uses the following letters: "c" represents the dry continental air masses and "m" stands for the moist maritime air masses. The second set of abbreviations are as follows: "T" indicates the air mass is tropical in origin; "P" indicates the air mass is polar in origin; "A" indicates the air mass is Antarctic in origin; "M" stands for monsoon; "E" indicates the air mass is equatorial in origin; and "S" is used to represent superior air, which is dry air formed by a downward motion. The last set of symbols provides an indicator of the stability of the mass. "K" indicates the mass is colder than the ground below it, while "w" indicates the mass is warmer than the ground. For example, cP is a continental polar air mass, while cPk is a polar air mass blowing over the Gulf Stream, which is warmer than the mass.

The concept of atmospheric pressure involves the idea that air exerts a force. An imaginary column of air 1 square inch in size rising through the atmosphere would exert a force of 14.7 pounds per square inch (psi). Both temperature and altitude affect atmospheric pressure. Low- and high-pressure systems tend to want to equalize. Air tends to move from areas of high pressure to areas of low pressure. When air moves into a low-pressure system, the air that was there gets pushed up, creating lower temperatures and pressures. Water vapor condenses and forms clouds and possibly rain and snow. A barometer is used to measure air pressure.

A weather front is the area between two differing masses of air that affects weather. Frontal movements are influenced by the jet stream and other high winds. Movements are determined by the type of front. Cold fronts move up to twice as fast as warm ones. It is in the turbulent frontal area that commonplace and dramatic weather events take place. This area also creates temperature changes. Weather phenomena include rain, thunderstorms, high winds, tornadoes, cloudiness, clear skies, and hurricanes. Different fronts can be plotted on weather maps using a set of designated symbols. Surface weather maps can also include symbols representing clouds, rain, temperature, air pressure, and fair weather.

A cold front is a mass of cold air, usually fast moving and dense, that moves into a warm air front, producing clouds. This often produces a temperature drop and rain, hail (frozen rain), thunder, and lightning. A warm front is pushed up by a fast-moving cold front. It is often associated with high wispy clouds, such as cirrus and cirrostratus clouds. A stationary front forms when a warm and cold front meet, but neither is strong enough to move the other. Winds blowing parallel to the fronts keep the front stationary. The front may remain in the same place for days until the wind direction changes and both fronts become a single warm or cold front. In other cases, the entire front dissipates. An occluded front is when a cold front pushes into a warm front. The warm air rises and the two masses of cool air join. These types of fronts often occur in areas of low atmospheric pressure.

A shearline evolves from a stationary front that has gotten smaller. Wind direction shifts over a short distance. A dry line or dew point line separates two warm air masses of differing moisture content. At lower altitudes, the moist air mass wedges under the drier air. At higher altitudes, the dry air wedges under the moist air. This is a frequent occurrence in the Midwest and Canada, where the dry air of the Southwest and the moister air of the Gulf of Mexico meet. This can lead to extreme weather events, including tornadoes and thunderstorms. A squall line is severe thunderstorms forming at the front of or ahead of a cold front. In some cases, severe thunderstorms can also outrun cold fronts. A squall line can produce extreme weather in the form of heavy rain, hail, lightning, strong winds, tornadoes, and waterspouts. Tropical waves or easterly waves are atmospheric troughs or areas of low air pressure that travel westward in the tropics, causing clouds and thunderstorms.

Cold fronts are represented on weather maps as a blue line. Solid blue triangles are used to indicate the direction of movement. Warm fronts are represented with a red line. Solid red semi-circles are used to indicate the direction of the front. The cold and warm front symbols are merged and alternated to point in opposite directions to indicate a stationary front. An occluded front is represented by a purple line with alternating solid purple triangles and semi-circles. A surface trough is represented by an orange dashed line. A squall or shear line is represented by a red line. Two dots and a dash are alternated to form the line. A dry line is represented by an orange line with semi-circles in outline form. A tropical wave is represented by a straight orange line. An "L" is used to indicate an area of low atmospheric pressure and an "H" is used to indicate an area of high atmospheric pressure.

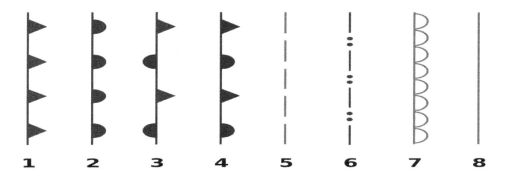

Short and long-term weather forecasting is important because the day-to-day weather greatly affects humans and human activity. Severe weather and natural events can cause devastating harm to humans, property, and sources of livelihood, such as crops. The persistence method of forecasting can be used to create both short and long-term forecasts in areas that change very little or change slowly. It assumes that the weather tomorrow will be similar to the weather today. Barometric pressure is measured because a change in air pressure can indicate the arrival of a cold front that could lead to precipitation. Long-term forecasts based on climate data are useful to help people prepare for seasonal changes and severe events such as hurricanes.

The tilt of the Earth on its axis is 23.5°. This tilt causes the seasons and affects the temperature because it affects the amount of Sun the area receives. When the Northern or Southern Hemispheres are tilted toward the Sun, the hemisphere tilted toward the sun experiences summer and the other hemisphere experiences winter. This reverses as the Earth revolves around the Sun. Fall and spring occur between the two extremes. The equator gets the same amount of sunlight every day of the year, about 12 hours, and doesn't experience seasons. Both poles have days during the winter when they are tilted away from the Sun and receive no daylight. The opposite effect occurs during the summer. There are 24 hours of daylight and no night. The summer solstice, the day with the most amount of sunlight, occurs on June 21st in the Northern Hemisphere and on December 21st in the Southern Hemisphere. The winter solstice, the day with the least amount of sunlight, occurs on December 21st in the Northern Hemisphere and on June 21st in the Southern Hemisphere.

Latitude is a measurement of the distance from the equator. The distance from the equator indicates how much solar radiation a particular area receives. The equator receives more sunlight, while polar areas receive less. The Earth tilts slightly on its rotational axis. This tilt determines the seasons and affects weather. There are eight biomes or ecosystems with particular climates that are associated with latitude. Those in the high latitudes, which get the least sunlight, are tundra and taiga. Those in the mid latitudes are grassland, temperate forest, and chaparral. Those in latitudes closest to the equator are the warmest. The biomes are desert and tropical rain forest. The eighth biome is the ocean, which is unique because it consists of water and spans the entire globe. Insolation refers to incoming solar radiation. Diurnal variations refer to the daily changes in insolation. The greatest insolation occurs at noon.

ASTRONOMY

Astronomy is the scientific study of celestial objects and their positions, movements, and structures. Celestial does not refer to the Earth in particular, but does include its motions as it moves through space. Other objects include the Sun, the Moon, planets, satellites, asteroids, meteors, comets, stars, galaxies, the universe, and other space phenomena. The term astronomy has its roots in the Greek words "astro" and "nomos," which means "laws of the stars."

The universe can be said to consist of everything and nothing. The universe is the source of everything we know about space, matter, energy, and time. There are likely still phenomena that have yet to be discovered. The universe can also be thought of as nothing, since a vast portion of the known universe is empty space. It is believed that the universe is expanding. The Big Bang theory, which is widely accepted among astronomers, was developed to explain the origin of the universe. There are other theories regarding the origin of the universe, such as the Steady-State theory and the Creationist theory. The Big Bang theory states that all the matter in the universe was once in one place. This matter underwent a huge explosion that spread the matter into space. Galaxies formed from this material and the universe is still expanding.

What can be seen of the universe is believed to be at least 93 billion light years across. To put this into perspective, the Milky Way galaxy is about 100,000 light years across. Our view of matter in the universe is that it forms into clumps. Matter is organized into stars, galaxies, clusters of galaxies, superclusters, and the Great Wall of galaxies. Galaxies consist of stars, some with planetary systems. Some estimates state that the universe is about 13 billion years old. It is not considered dense, and is believed to consist of 73 percent dark energy, 23 percent cold dark matter, and 4 percent regular matter. Cosmology is the study of the universe. Interstellar medium (ISM) is the gas and dust in the interstellar space between a galaxy's stars.

Galaxies consist of stars, stellar remnants, and dark matter. Dwarf galaxies contain as few as 10 million stars, while giant galaxies contain as many as 1 trillion stars. Galaxies are gravitationally bound, meaning the stars, star systems, other gases, and dust orbits the galaxy's center. The Earth exists in the Milky Way galaxy and the nearest galaxy to ours is the Andromeda galaxy. Galaxies can be classified by their visual shape into elliptical, spiral, irregular, and starburst galaxies. It is estimated that there are more than 100 billion galaxies in the universe ranging from 1,000 to 100,000 parsecs in diameter. Galaxies can be megaparsecs apart. Intergalactic space consists of a gas with an average density of less than one atom per cubic meter. Galaxies are organized into clusters which form superclusters. Dark matter may account for up to 90% of the mass of galaxies. Dark matter is still not well understood.

A nebula is a cloud of dust and gas that is composed primarily of hydrogen (97%) and helium (3%). Gravity causes parts of the nebula to clump together. This accretion continues adding atoms to the center of an unstable protostar. Equilibrium between gravity pulling atoms and gas pressure

162

pushing heat and light away from the center is achieved. A star dies when it is no longer able to maintain equilibrium. A protostar may never become a star if it does not reach a critical core temperature. It may become a brown dwarf or a gas giant instead. If nuclear fusion of hydrogen into helium begins, a star is born. The "main sequence" of a star's life involves nuclear fusion reactions. During this time, the star contracts over billions of years to compensate for the heat and light energy lost. In the star's core, temperature, density, and pressure increase as the star contracts and the cycle continues.

There are different life cycle possibilities for stars after they initially form and enter into the main sequence stage. Small, relatively cold red dwarfs with relatively low masses burn hydrogen slowly, and will remain in the main sequence for hundreds of billions of years. Massive, hot supergiants will leave the main sequence after just a few million years. The Sun is a mid-sized star that may be in the main sequence for 10 billion years. After the main sequence, the star expands to become a red giant. Depending upon the initial mass of the star, it can become a black dwarf (from a medium-sized star), and then a small, cooling white dwarf. Massive stars become red supergiants (and sometimes blue supergiants), explode in a supernova, and then become neutron stars. The largest stars can become black holes.

A planetary system consists of the various non-stellar objects orbiting a star, such as planets, dwarf planets, moons, asteroids, meteoroids, comets, and cosmic dust. The Sun, together with its planetary system, which includes Earth, is known as the solar system. The theory of how the solar system was created is that it started with the collapse of a cloud of interstellar gas and dust, which formed the solar nebula. This collapse is believed to have occurred because the cloud was disturbed. As it collapsed, it heated up and compressed at the center, forming a flatter protoplanetary disk with a protostar at the center. Planets formed as a result of accretion from the disk. Gas cooled and condensed into tiny particles of rock, metal, and ice. These particles collided and formed into larger particles, and then into object the size of small asteroids. Eventually, some became large enough to have significant gravity.

An astronomical unit, also known as AU, is a widely used measurement in astronomy. One AU is equal to the distance from the Earth to the Sun, which is 150 million km, or 93 million miles. These distances can also be expressed as 149.60×10^9 m or 92.956×10^6 mi. A light year (ly) is the distance that light travels in a vacuum in one year. A light year is equal to about 10 trillion km, or 64,341 AU, and is used to measure large astronomical units. Also used for measuring large distances is the parsec (pc), which is the preferred unit since it is better suited for recording observational data. A parsec is the parallax of one arcsecond, and is about 31 trillion km (about 19 trillion miles), or about 3.26 light years. It is used to calculate distances by triangulation. The AU distance from the Earth to the Sun is used to form the side of a right triangle.

A sidereal day is four minutes shorter than a solar day. A solar day is the time it takes the Earth to complete one revolution and face the Sun again. From noon to noon is 24 hours. A sidereal day is measured against a distant "fixed" star. As the Earth completes one rotation, it has also completed part of its revolution around the Sun, so it completes a sidereal rotation in reference to the fixed star before it completes a solar rotation. The Sun travels along the ecliptic in 365.25 days. This can be tracked day after day before dawn. After one year, the stars appear back in their original positions. As a result, different constellations are viewable at different times of the year. Sidereal years are slightly longer than tropical years. The difference is caused by the precession of the equinoxes. A calendar based on the sidereal year will be out of sync with the seasons at a rate of about one day every 71 years.

SOLAR SYSTEM

The Sun is at the center of the solar system. It is composed of 70% hydrogen (H) and 28% helium (He). The remaining 2% is made up of metals. The Sun is one of 100 billion stars in the Milky Way galaxy. Its diameter is 1,390,000 km, its mass is 1.989 x 1030 kg, its surface temperature is 5,800 K, and its core temperature is 15,600,000 K. The Sun represents more than 99.8% of the total mass of the solar system. At the core, the temperature is 15.6 million K, the pressure is 250 billion atmospheres, and the density is more than 150 times that of water. The surface is called the photosphere. The chromosphere lies above this, and the corona, which extends millions of kilometers into space, is next. Sunspots are relatively cool regions on the surface with a temperature of 3,800 K. Temperatures in the corona are over 1,000,000 K. Its magnetosphere, or heliosphere, extends far beyond Pluto.

The Sun's energy is produced by nuclear fusion reactions. Each second, about 700,000,000 tons of hydrogen are converted (or fused) to about 695,000,000 tons of helium and 5,000,000 tons of energy in the form of gamma rays. In nuclear fusion, four hydrogen nuclei are fused into one helium nucleus, resulting in the release of energy. In the Sun, the energy proceeds towards the surface and is absorbed and re-emitted at lower and lower temperatures. Energy is mostly in the form of visible light when it reaches the surface. It is estimated that the Sun has used up about half of the hydrogen at its core since its birth. It is expected to radiate in this fashion for another 5 billion years. Eventually, it will deplete its hydrogen fuel, grow brighter, expand to about 260 times its diameter, and become a red giant. The outer layers will ablate and become a dense white dwarf the size of the Earth. The solar system is a planetary system of objects that exist in an ecliptic plane. Objects orbit around and are bound by gravity to a star called the Sun. Objects that orbit around the Sun include: planets, dwarf planets, moons, asteroids, meteoroids, cosmic dust, and comets. The definition of planets has changed. At one time, there were nine planets in the solar system. There are now eight. Planetary objects in the solar system include four inner, terrestrial planets: Mercury, Venus, Earth, and Mars. They are relatively small, dense, rocky, lack rings, and have few or no moons. The four outer, or Jovian, planets are Jupiter, Saturn, Uranus, and Neptune, which are large and have low densities, rings, and moons. They are also known as gas giants. Between the inner and outer planets is the asteroid belt. Beyond Neptune is the Kuiper belt. Within these belts are five dwarf planets: Ceres, Pluto, Haumea, Makemake, and Eris.

PLANETS

Mercury: Mercury is the closest to the Sun and is also the smallest planet. It orbits the Sun every 88 days, has no satellites or atmosphere, has a Moon-like surface with craters, appears bright, and is dense and rocky with a large iron core.

Venus: Venus is the second planet from the Sun. It orbits the Sun every 225 days, is very bright, and is similar to Earth in size, gravity, and bulk composition. It has a dense atmosphere composed of carbon dioxide and some sulfur. It is covered with reflective clouds made of sulfuric acid and exhibits signs of volcanism. Lightning and thunder have been recorded on Venus's surface.

Earth: Earth is the third planet from the Sun. It orbits the Sun every 365 days. Approximately 71% of its surface is salt-water oceans. The Earth is rocky, has an atmosphere composed mainly of oxygen and nitrogen, has one moon, and supports millions of species. It contains the only known life in the solar system.

Mars: Mars it the fourth planet from the Sun. It appears reddish due to iron oxide on the surface, has a thin atmosphere, has a rotational period similar to Earth's, and has seasonal cycles. Surface features of Mars include volcanoes, valleys, deserts, and polar ice caps. Mars has impact craters and the tallest mountain, largest canyon, and perhaps the largest impact crater yet discovered.

Jupiter: Jupiter is the fifth planet from the Sun and the largest planet in the solar system. It consists mainly of hydrogen, and 25% of its mass is made up of helium. It has a fast rotation and has clouds in the tropopause composed of ammonia crystals that are arranged into bands sub-divided into lighter-hued zones and darker belts causing storms and turbulence. Jupiter has wind speeds of 100 m/s, a planetary ring, 63 moons, and a Great Red Spot, which is an anticyclonic storm.

Saturn: Saturn is the sixth planet from the Sun and the second largest planet in the solar system. It is composed of hydrogen, some helium, and trace elements. Saturn has a small core of rock and ice, a thick layer of metallic hydrogen, a gaseous outer layer, wind speeds of up to 1,800 km/h, a system of rings, and 61 moons.

Uranus: Uranus is the seventh planet from the Sun. Its atmosphere is composed mainly of hydrogen and helium, and also contains water, ammonia, methane, and traces of hydrocarbons. With a minimum temperature of 49 K, Uranus has the coldest atmosphere. Uranus has a ring system, a magnetosphere, and 13 moons.

Neptune: Neptune is the eighth planet from the Sun and is the planet with the third largest mass. It has 12 moons, an atmosphere similar to Uranus, a Great Dark Spot, and the strongest sustained winds of any planet (wind speeds can be as high as 2,100 km/h). Neptune is cold (about 55 K) and has a fragmented ring system.

The asteroid belt is between Mars and Jupiter. The many objects contained within are composed of rock and metal similar to those found on the terrestrial planets. The Kuiper Belt is beyond Neptune's orbit, but the influence of the gas giants may cause objects from the Kuiper Belt to cross Neptune's orbit. Objects in the Kuiper Belt are still being discovered. They are thought to be composed of the frozen forms of water, ammonia, and methane, and may be the source of short-period comets. It is estimated that there are 35,000 Kuiper Belt objects greater than 100 km in diameter and perhaps 100 million objects about 20 km in diameter. There is also a hypothetical Oort Cloud that may exist far beyond the Kuiper Belt and act as a source for long-period comets.

A comet consists of frozen gases and rocky and metallic materials. Comets are usually small and typically have long tails. A comet's tail is made of ionized gases. It points away from the Sun and follows the comet as it approaches the Sun. The tail precedes the head as the comet moves away from the Sun. It is believed that as many as 100 billion comets exist. About 12 new ones are discovered each year. Their orbits are elliptical, not round. Some scientists theorize that short-period comets originate from the Kuiper Belt and long-period comets originate from the Oort Cloud, which is thought to be 100,000 AU away. Comets orbit the Sun in time periods varying from a few years to hundreds of thousands of years. A well-known comet, Halley's Comet, has an orbit of 76 years. It is 80 percent water, and consists of frozen water, carbon dioxide (dry ice), ammonia, and methane.

A meteoroid is the name for a rock from space before it enters the Earth's atmosphere. Most meteoroids burn up in the atmosphere before reaching altitudes of 80 km. A meteor is the streak of light from a meteoroid in the Earth's atmosphere, and is also known as a shooting star. Meteor showers are associated with comets, happen when the Earth passes through the debris of a comet, and are associated with a higher than normal number of meteors. Meteorites are rocks that reach the Earth's surface from space. Fireballs are very bright meteors with trails that can last as long as 30 minutes. A bolide is a fireball that burns up when it enters Earth's atmosphere. There are many types of meteorites, and they are known to be composed of various materials. Iron meteorites consist of iron and nickel with a criss-cross, or Widmanstatten, internal metallic crystalline structure. Stony iron meteorites are composed of iron, nickel, and silicate materials. Stony meteorites consist mainly of silicate and also contain iron and nickel.

There are about 335 moons, or satellites, that orbit the planets and objects in the solar system. Many of these satellites have been recently discovered, a few are theoretical, some are asteroid moons (moons orbiting asteroids), some are moonlets (small moons), and some are moons of dwarf planets and objects that have not been definitively categorized, such as trans-Neptunian objects. Mercury and Venus do not have any moons. There are several moons larger than the dwarf planet Pluto and two larger than Mercury. Some consider the Earth and Moon a pair of double planets rather than a planet and a satellite. Some satellites may have started out as asteroids. They were eventually captured by a planet's gravity and became moons.

The Earth-Moon-Sun system is responsible for eclipses. From Earth, the Sun and the Moon appear to be about the same size. An eclipse of the Sun occurs during a new Moon, when the side of the Moon facing the Earth is not illuminated. The Moon passes in front of the Sun and blocks its view from Earth. Eclipses do not occur every month because the orbit of the Moon is at about a 5° angle to the plane of Earth's orbit. An eclipse of the Moon happens during the full Moon phase. The Moon passes through the shadow of the Earth and blocks sunlight from reaching it, which temporarily causes darkness. During a lunar eclipse, there are two parts to the shadow. The umbra is the dark, inner region. The sun is completely blocked in this area. The penumbra is a partially lighted area around the umbra. Earth's shadow is four times longer than the Moon's shadow.

It takes about one month for the Moon to go through all its phases. Waxing refers to the two weeks during which the Moon goes from a new moon to a full moon. About two weeks is spent waning, going from a full moon to a new moon. The lit part of the Moon always faces the Sun. The phases of waxing are: new moon, during which the Moon is not illuminated and rises and sets with the Sun; crescent moon, during which a tiny sliver is lit; first quarter, during which half the Moon is lit and the phase of the Moon is due south on the meridian; gibbous, during which more than half of the Moon is lit and has a shape similar to a football; right side, during which the Moon is lit; and full moon, during which the Moon is fully illuminated, rises at sunset, and sets at sunrise. After a full moon, the Moon is waning. The phases of waning are: gibbous, during which the left side is lit and the Moon rises after sunset and sets after sunrise; third quarter, during which the Moon is half lit and rises at midnight and sets at noon; crescent, during which a tiny sliver is lit; and new moon, during which the Moon is not illuminated and rises and sets with the Sun.

Remote sensing refers to the gathering of data about an object or phenomenon without physical or intimate contact with the object being studied. The data can be viewed or recorded and stored in many forms (visually with a camera, audibly, or in the form of data). Gathering weather data from a ship, satellite, or buoy might be thought of as remote sensing. The monitoring of a fetus through the use of ultrasound technology provides a remote image. Listening to the heartbeat of a fetus is another example of remote sensing. Methods for remote sensing can be grouped as radiometric, geodetic, or acoustic. Examples of radiometric remote sensing include radar, laser altimeters, light detection and ranging (LIDAR) used to determine the concentration of chemicals in the air, and radiometers used to detect various frequencies of radiation. Geodetic remote sensing involves measuring the small fluctuations in Earth's gravitational field. Examples of acoustic remote sensing include underwater sonar and seismographs.

For the purposes of tracking time and location, the Earth is divided into sections with imaginary lines. Lines that run vertically around the globe through the poles are lines of longitude, sometimes called meridians. The Prime Meridian is the longitudinal reference point of 0. Longitude is measured in 15-degree increments toward the east or west. Degrees are further divided into 60 minutes, and each minute is divided into 60 seconds. Lines of latitude run horizontally around the Earth parallel to the equator, which is the 0-reference point and the widest point of the Earth.

Latitude is the distance north or south from the equator, and is also measured in degrees, minutes, and seconds.

A geosynchronous orbit around the Earth has an orbital period matching the Earth's sidereal rotation period. Sidereal rotation is based on the position of a fixed star, not the Sun, so a sidereal day is slightly shorter than a 24-hour solar day. A satellite in a geosynchronous orbit appears in the same place in the sky at the same time each day. Technically, any object with an orbit time period equal to the Earth's rotational period is geosynchronous. A geostationary orbit is a geosynchronous orbit that is circular and at zero inclination, which means the object is located directly above the equator. Geostationary orbits are useful for communications satellites because they are fixed in the same spot relative to the Earth. A semisynchronous orbit has an orbital period of half a sidereal day.

The first satellite to orbit the Earth was the Soviet Union's Sputnik 1 in 1957. Its two radio transmitters emitted beeps that were received by radios around the world. Analysis of the radio signals was used to gather information about the electron density of the ionosphere. Soviet success escalated the American space program. In 1958, the U.S. put Explorer 1 into orbit. The Osumi was the first Japanese satellite, which was put into orbit in 1970. The Vanguard 1 is the satellite that has orbited the Earth the longest. It was put into orbit in 1958 and was still in orbit in June, 2009. The Mir Space Station orbited Earth for 11 years, and was assembled in space starting in 1986. It was almost continuously occupied until 1999. The International Space Station began being assembled in orbit in 1998. At 43,000 cubic feet, it is the largest manned object sent into space. It circles the Earth every 90 minutes.

The Soviet space program successfully completed the first space flight by orbiting Yuri Gagarin in 1961 on Vostok 1. His orbit lasted 1 hour, 48 minutes. Later in 1961, the U.S. completed its first piloted space flight by launching Alan Shepard into space in the Mercury-Redstone 3. This space mission was suborbital. The first woman in space was Valentina Tereshkova, who orbited the Earth 48 times aboard Vostok 6 in 1963. The first space flight with more than one person and also the first that didn't involve space suits took place on the Voskhod in 1964. The first person on the Moon was American Neil Armstrong. In 1969, he traveled to the Moon on Apollo 11, which was the 11th manned space flight completed in the Apollo program, which was conducted from 1968 to 1972. In 2003, Yang Liwei became the first person from China to go into space. He traveled onboard the Shenzhou 5. The Space Shuttle Orbiter has included piloted space shuttles from 1981 until the present. The program was suspended after two space shuttle disasters: Challenger in 1986 and Columbia in 2003.

The first artificial object to reach another space object was Luna 2. It crashed on the Moon in 1959. The first automatic landing was by Luna 9. It landed on the Moon in 1966. Mariner 2's flyby of Venus in 1962 was the first successful interplanetary flyby. Venera 7 landing on and transmitting data from Venus was the first interplanetary surface landing, which took place in 1970. The first soft landing on Mars was in 1971. Unpiloted spacecraft have also made successful soft landings on the asteroids Eros and Itokawa, as well as Titan, a moon of Saturn. The first flyby of Jupiter was in 1973 by Pioneer 10. Pioneer 10 was also the first craft of its kind to leave the solar system. The first flyby of Mercury was in 1974 by Mariner. The first flyby of Saturn was in 1979 by Pioneer 11. The first flyby of Uranus was in 1986 by Voyager 2, which also flew by Neptune in 1989.

There are many limitations of space exploration. The main limitation is knowledge. Space exploration is currently time-consuming, dangerous, and costly. Manned and unmanned missions, even within the solar system, take years of planning and years to complete. The associated financial costs are great. Interstellar travel and intergalactic is not yet realistically feasible. Technological advances are needed before these types of missions can be carried out. By some estimates, it would

take more than 70 years to travel to Proxima Centauri (the nearest star) using the fastest rocket technology available. It would take much longer using less advanced technologies. Space travel is dangerous for many reasons. Rocket fuel is highly explosive. Non-Earth environments are uninhabitable for humans. Finally, astronauts are exposed to larger than usual amounts of radiation.

Social Studies

Civics and Government

POLITICAL SCIENCE

Political science focuses on studying different governments and how they compare to each other, general political theory, ways political theory is put into action, how nations and governments interact with each other, and a general study of governmental structure and function. Other elements of political science include the study of elections, governmental administration at various levels, development and action of political parties, and how values such as freedom, power, justice, and equality are expressed in different political cultures. Political science also encompasses elements of other disciplines, including:

- History—how historical events have shaped political thought and process
- Sociology—the effects of various stages of social development on the growth and development of government and politics
- Anthropology—the effects of governmental process on the culture of an individual group and its relationships with other groups
- Economics—how government policies regulate distribution of products and how they can control and/or influence the economy in general

Based on general political theory, there are the four major purposes of any given government.

- Ensuring national security—the government protects against international, domestic and terrorist attack and also ensures ongoing security through negotiating and establishing relationships with other governments.
- Providing public services—government should "promote the general welfare," as stated in the Preamble to the US Constitution, by providing whatever is needed to its citizens.
- Ensure social order—the government supplies means of settling conflicts among citizens as well as making laws to govern the nation, state, or city.
- Make decisions regarding the economy—laws help form the economic policy of the country, regarding both domestic and international trade and related issues. The government also has the ability to distribute goods and wealth among its citizens.

There are the four main theories regarding the origin of the state.

- Evolutionary—the state evolved from the family, with the head of state the equivalent of the family's patriarch or matriarch.
- Force—one person or group of people brought everyone in an area under their control, forming the first government.
- Divine Right—certain people were chosen by the prevailing deity to be the rulers of the nation, which is itself created by the deity or deities.
- Social Contract—there is no natural order. The people allow themselves to be governed to maintain social order, while the state in turn promises to protect the people they govern. If the government fails to protect its people, the people have the right to seek new leaders.

170

There are currently four main political orientations.

- Liberal—believes government should work to increase equality, even at the expense of some freedoms. Government should assist those in need of help. Focus on enforced social justice and free education for everyone.
- Conservative—believes government should be limited in most cases. Government should allow its citizens to help one another and solve their own problems rather than enforcing solutions. Business should not be overregulated, allowing a free market.
- Moderate—incorporates some liberal and some conservative values, generally falling somewhere in between in overall belief.
- Libertarian—believes government's role should be limited to protecting the life and liberty of citizens. Government should not be involved in any citizen's life unless that citizen is encroaching upon the rights of another.

Political theory has developed over the centuries as different thinkers have contributed different and often conflicting ideas. Ancient Greek philosophers Aristotle and Plato believed political science would lead to order in political matters, and that this scientifically organized order would create stable, just societies.

Thomas Aquinas adapted the ideas of Aristotle to a Christian perspective. His ideas stated that individuals should have certain rights, but also certain duties, and that these rights and duties should determine the type and extent of government rule. In stating that laws should limit the role of government, he laid the groundwork for ideas that would eventually become modern constitutionalism.

Niccolò Machiavelli, author of *The Prince*, was a proponent of politics based solely on power.

Thomas Hobbes, author of *Leviathan* (1651), believed that individual's lives were focused solely on a quest for power, and that the state must work to control this urge. Hobbes felt that people were completely unable to live harmoniously without the intervention of government.

John Locke wrote *Two Treatises of Civil Government* in 1690. This work argued against the ideas of Thomas Hobbes. He put forth the theory of *tabula rasa*—that people are born with minds that are a blank slate. Experience molds individual minds, not innate knowledge or intuition. He also believed that all men are essentially good, as well as independent and equal. Many of Locke's ideas found their way into the Constitution of the United States.

Jean-Jacques Rousseau and Montesquieu were two French philosophers who heavily influenced the French Revolution (1789-1815). They believed government policies and ideas should change to alleviate existing problems, an idea referred to as "liberalism." Rousseau in particular directly influenced the Revolution with writings such as *The Social Contract* (1762), *Declaration of the Rights of Man,* and *The Citizen* (1789). Other ideas Rousseau and Montesquieu espoused included:

- Individual freedom and community welfare are of equal importance
- Man's innate goodness leads to natural harmony
- Reason develops with the rise of civilized society
- Individual citizens carry certain obligations to the existing government

Hume and Bentham believed politics should have as its main goal maintaining "the greatest happiness of the greatest number." Hume also believed in empiricism, or that ideas should not be believed until the proof has been observed. He was a natural skeptic, as well, and always sought out the truth of matters himself rather than believing what he was told.

John Stuart Mill, a British philosopher as well as an economist, believed in progressive policies such as women's suffrage, emancipation, and the development of labor organizations and farming cooperatives.

Fichte and Hegel were eighteenth century German philosophers who supported a form of liberalism grounded largely in socialism and a sense of nationalism.

U.S. GOVERNMENT

The six major principles of government as outlined in the United States Constitution:

- Federalism—the power of the government does not belong entirely to the national government, but is divided between national and state governments.
- Popular sovereignty—the government is determined by the people, and gains its authority and power from the people.
- Separation of powers—the government is divided into three branches, executive, legislative and judicial, with each branch having its own set of powers.
- Judicial review—courts at all levels of government can declare laws invalid if they contradict the constitutions of individual states, or the US Constitution, with the Supreme Court serving as the final judicial authority on decisions of this kind.
- Checks and balances—no single branch can act without input from another, and each branch has the power to "check" any other, as well as balance other branches' powers.
- Limited government—governmental powers are limited and certain individual rights are defined as inviolable by the government.

The structure of the US government divides powers between national and state governments. Powers delegated to the national government by the Constitution are:

- Expressed powers—powers directly defined in the Constitution, including power to declare war, regulate commerce, coin money, and collect taxes.
- Implied powers—powers the national government must have in order to carry out the expressed powers.
- Inherent powers—powers inherent to any government. These powers are not expressly defined in the constitution.

Some of these powers, such as collection and levying of taxes, are also granted to the individual state governments.

There are three branches of the US Federal government.

- Legislative Branch—consists of the two Houses of Congress: the House of Representatives and the Senate. All members of the Legislative Branch are elected officials.
- Executive Branch—consists of the President, Vice President, presidential advisors, and other various cabinet members. These advisors are appointed by the President, but must be approved by Congress.
- Judicial Branch—is made up of the federal court system, headed by the Supreme Court.

Each of the three branches of the Federal government has different responsibilities.

The Legislative Branch is largely concerned with law-making. All laws must be approved by Congress before they go into effect. They are also responsible for regulating money and trade, approving presidential appointments, and establishing organizations like the postal service and federal courts. Congress can also propose amendments to the Constitution, and can impeach, or bring charges against, the president. Only Congress can declare war.

The Executive Branch carries out laws, treaties, and war declarations enacted by Congress. The President can also veto bills approved by Congress, and serves as commander-in-chief of the US military. The president appoints cabinet members, ambassadors to foreign countries, and federal judges.

The Judicial Branch makes decisions on challenges as to whether laws passed by Congress meet the requirements of the US Constitution. The Supreme Court may also choose to review decisions made by lower courts to determine their constitutionality.

Debate on how federalism should function in practice has gone on since the period when the Constitution was being written. There were—and still are—two main factions regarding this issue:

- States' rights—those favoring the states' rights position feel that the state governments should take the lead in performing local actions to manage various problems.
- Nationalist—those favoring a nationalist position feel the national government should take the lead to deal with those same matters.

Review Video: Three Branches of Government
Visit mometrix.com/academy and enter code: 718704

The flexibility of the Constitution has allowed US government to shift and adapt as the needs of the country have changed. Power has often shifted from the state governments to the national government and back again, and both levels of government have developed various ways to influence each other.

Federalism has three major effects on public policy in the US.

- Determining whether the local, state or national government originates policy
- Affecting how policies are made
- Ensuring policy-making functions under a set of limitations

Federalism also influences the political balance of power in the US by:

- making it difficult if not impossible for a single political party to seize total power.
- ensuring that individuals can participate in the political system at various levels.
- making it possible for individuals working within the system to be able to affect policy at some level, whether local or more widespread.

The first ten amendments of the US Constitution are known as the Bill of Rights. These amendments prevent the government from infringing upon certain freedoms that the founding fathers felt were natural rights that already belonged to all people. These rights included freedom of speech, freedom of religion, right to bear arms, and freedom of assembly. Many of the rights were formulated in direct response to the way the colonists felt they had been mistreated by the British government.

The first ten amendments were passed by Congress in 1789. Three-fourths of the existing thirteen states had ratified them by December of 1791, making them official additions to the Constitution.

- First Amendment—grants freedom of religion, speech, freedom of the press, and the right to assemble.
- Second Amendment—protects the right to bear arms.
- Third Amendment—Congress cannot force individuals to house troops.
- Fourth Amendment—protection from unreasonable search and seizure.
- Fifth Amendment—no individual is required to testify against himself, and no individual may be tried twice for the same crime.
- Sixth Amendment—right to criminal trial by jury, right to legal counsel.
- Seventh Amendment—right to civil trial by jury.
- Eighth Amendment—no excessive bail, no cruel and unusual punishment.
- Ninth Amendment—prevents the absence of rights not explicitly named in the Constitution from being interpreted as a reason to have them taken away.
- Tenth Amendment—any rights not directly delegated to the national government, or not directly prohibited, belong to the states or to the people

In some cases, the government restricts certain elements of First Amendment rights. Some examples include:

- Freedom of religion—when a religion espouses activities that are otherwise illegal, the government often restricts these forms of religious expression. Examples include polygamy, animal sacrifice, and use of illicit drugs or illegal substances.
- Freedom of speech—can be restricted if exercise of free speech endangers other people.
- Freedom of the press—laws prevent the press from publishing falsehoods.

In emergency situations such as wartime, stricter restrictions are sometimes placed on these rights, especially rights to free speech and assembly, and freedom of the press, in order to protect national security.

The US Constitution makes allowances for the rights of criminals, or anyone who has transgressed established laws. There must be laws to protect citizens from criminals, but those accused of crimes must also be protected and their basic rights as individuals preserved. In addition, the Constitution protects individuals from the power of authorities who act in case of transgressions to prevent police forces and other enforcement organizations from becoming oppressive.

The Fourth, Fifth, Sixth and Eighth amendments specifically address these issues:

- No unreasonable search and seizure (Fourth Amendment)
- No self-incrimination or double jeopardy—being tried for the same crime more than once (Fifth Amendment)
- Right to trial by jury and right to legal counsel (Sixth Amendment)
- No cruel or unusual punishment (Eighth Amendment)

When the Founding Fathers wrote in the Declaration of Independence that "all men are created equal," they meant "men," and, in fact, defined citizens as white men who owned land. However, as the country has developed and changed, the definition has expanded to more wholly include all people.

"Equality" does not mean all people are inherently the same, but it does mean they all should be granted the same rights and should be treated the same by the government. Amendments to the Constitution have granted citizenship and voting rights to all Americans. The Supreme Court evaluates various laws and court decisions to determine if they properly represent the idea of equal protection. One sample case was Brown v. Board of Education, in 1954, which declared separate-but-equal to be unconstitutional.

Anyone born in the US, born abroad to a US citizen, or who has gone through a process of naturalization to become a citizen, is considered a citizen of the United States. It is possible to lose US citizenship as a result of conviction of certain crimes such as treason. Citizenship may also be lost if a citizen pledges an oath to another country or serves in the military of a country engaged in hostilities with the US. A US citizen can also choose to hold dual citizenship, work as an expatriate in another country without losing US citizenship, or even to renounce citizenship if he or she so chooses.

Citizens are granted certain rights under the US government. The most important of these are defined in the Bill of Rights, and include freedom of speech, religion, assembly, and a variety of other rights the government is not allowed to remove.

Duties of a US citizen include:

- Paying taxes
- Loyalty to the government, though the US does not prosecute those who criticize or seek to change the government
- Support and defend the Constitution
- Serve in the Armed Forces as required by law
- Obeying laws as set forth by the various levels of government.

Responsibilities of a US citizen include:

- Voting in elections
- Respecting one another's rights and not infringing upon them
- Staying informed about various political and national issues
- Respecting one another's beliefs

CIVICS

While the terms civil liberties and civil rights are often used synonymously, in actuality their definitions are slightly different. The two concepts work together, however, to define the basics of a free state.

"Civil liberties" defines the role of the state in providing equal rights and opportunities to individuals within that state. An example is non-discrimination policies with regards to granting citizenship.

"Civil rights" defines the limitations of state rights, describing those rights that belong to individuals and which cannot be infringed upon by the government. Examples of these rights include freedom of religion, political freedom, and overall freedom to live how we choose.

The civil rights movements of the 1960s and ongoing struggle for women's rights and rights of other minorities have led to challenges to existing law. In addition, debate has raged over how much information the government should be required to divulge to the public. Major issues in today's political climate include:

- Continued debate over women's rights, especially as regards equal pay for equal work
- Debate over affirmative action to encourage hiring of minorities
- Debate over civil rights of homosexuals, including marriage and military service
- Decisions as to whether any minorities should be compensated for past discriminatory practices
- Balance between the public's right to know and the government's need to maintain national security
- Balance between the public's right to privacy and national security

Suffrage and franchise are both terms referring to the right to vote. Which individuals actually have the right to vote has changed as the US has developed as a nation. In the early years, only white male landowners were granted suffrage. By the nineteenth century, most states had franchised, or granted the right to vote to, all adult white males. The Fifteenth Amendment of 1870 granted suffrage to former slaves. The Nineteenth Amendment gave women the right to vote, and in 1971 the Twenty-sixth Amendment expanded voting rights to include any US citizen over the age of eighteen. However, those who have not been granted full citizenship and citizens who have committed certain crimes do not have voting rights.

The first elections in the US were held by public ballot. However, election abuses soon became common, since public ballot made it easy to intimidate, threaten, or otherwise influence the votes of individuals or groups of individuals. New practices were put into play, including registering voters before elections took place, and using a secret or Australian ballot. In 1892, the introduction of the voting machine further privatized the voting process, since it allowed voters to vote in complete privacy. Even today debate continues about the accuracy of various voting methods, including high-tech voting machines and even low-tech punch cards.

George Washington was adamantly against the establishment of political parties, based on the abuses perpetrated by such parties in Britain. However, political parties developed in US politics almost from the beginning. Major parties throughout US History have included:

- Federalists and Democratic-Republicans—formed in the late 1700s and disagreed on the balance of power between national and state government
- Democrats and Whigs—developed before the Civil War, based on disagreements about various issues such as slavery
- Democrats and Republicans—developed after the Civil War, with issues centering on the treatment of the post-war South.

While third parties sometimes enter the picture in US politics, the government is basically a two-party system, currently dominated by the Democrats and Republicans.

Different types and numbers of political parties can have a significant effect on how a government is run. If there is a single party, or a one-party system, the government is defined by that one party, and all policy is based on that party's beliefs. In a two-party system, two parties with different viewpoints compete for power and influence. The US is basically a two-party system, with checks and balances to make it difficult for one party to gain complete power over the other. There are also multi-party systems, with three or more parties. In multiparty systems, various parties will often come to agreements in order to form a majority and shift the balance of power.

Political parties form organizations at all levels of government. Activities of individual parties include:

- Recruiting and backing candidates for offices
- Discussing various issues with the public, increasing public awareness
- Working toward compromise on difficult issues
- Staffing government offices and providing administrative support
- At the administrative level, parties work to ensure that viable candidates are available for elections and that offices and staff are in place to support candidates as they run for office and afterwards, when they are elected.

Historically, in the quest for political office, a potential candidate has followed one of the following four processes:

- Nominating conventions—an official meeting of the members of a party for the express purpose of nominating candidates for upcoming elections. The Democratic National Convention and the Republican National Convention, convened to announce candidates for presidency, are examples of this kind of gathering.
- Caucuses—a meeting, usually attended by a party's leaders. Some states still use caucuses, but not all.
- Primary elections—the most common method of choosing candidates today, the primary is a publicly held election to choose candidates.
- Petitions—signatures are gathered to place a candidate on the ballot. Petitions can also be used to place legislation on a ballot.

In addition to voting for elected officials, American citizens are able to participate in the political process through several other avenues. These include:

- Participating in local government
- Participating in caucuses for large elections
- Volunteering to help political parties
- Running for election to local, state, or national offices

Individuals can also donate money to political causes, or support political groups that focus on specific causes such as abortion, wildlife conservation or women's rights. These groups often make use of representatives who lobby legislators to act in support of their efforts.

Political campaigns are very expensive ventures. In addition to the basic necessities of a campaign office, including office supplies, office space, etc., a large quantity of the money that funds a political campaign goes toward advertising. Television advertising in particular is quite costly. Money to fund a political campaign can come from several sources including:

- The candidate's personal funds
- Donations by individuals
- Special interest groups

The most significant source of campaign funding is special interest groups. Groups in favor of certain policies will donate money to candidates they believe will support those policies. Special interest groups also do their own advertising in support of candidates they endorse.

The right to free speech guaranteed in the first amendment to the Constitution allows the media to report on government and political activities without fear of retribution. Because the media has access to information about the government, its policies and actions, as well as debates and discussions that occur in Congress, it can ensure that the people are informed about the inner workings of the government. The media can also draw attention to injustices, imbalances of power, and other transgressions the government or government officials might commit. However, media outlets may, like special interest groups, align themselves with certain political viewpoints and skew their reports to fit that viewpoint. The rise of the Internet has made media reporting even more complex, as news can be found from an infinite variety of sources, both reliable and unreliable.

FORMS OF GOVERNMENT

Over the course of human history many different forms of government have been developed. These governments often have functioned very differently in how much the citizens are involved in selecting the leaders, how repressive they are, how much power the government has, how often leadership changes occur and the process by which that happens, and many other issues.

Anarchists believe that all government should be eliminated and that individuals should rule themselves. Historically, anarchists have used violence and assassination to further their beliefs. Communism is based on class conflict, revolution and a one-party state. Ideally, a communist government would involve a single government for the entire world. Communist government controls the production and flow of goods and services rather than leaving this to companies or individuals. Dictatorship involves rule by a single individual. If rule is enforced by a small group, this is referred to as an oligarchy. Few malevolent dictatorships have existed. Dictators tend to rule with a violent hand, using a highly repressive police force to ensure control over the populace.

A totalitarian system believes everything should be under the control of the government, from resource production to the press to religion and other social institutions. All aspects of life under a totalitarian system must conform to the ideals of the government. Authoritarian governments practices widespread state authority, but do not necessarily dismantle all public institutions. If a church, for example, exists as an organization but poses no threat to the authority of the state, an authoritarian government might leave it as it is. While all totalitarian governments are by definition authoritarian, a government can be authoritarian without becoming totalitarian.

Fascism centers on a single leader and is, ideologically, an oppositional belief to Communism. Fascism includes a single party state and centralized control. The power of the fascist leader lies in the "cult of personality," and the fascist state often focuses on expansion and conquering of other nations. Monarchy was the major form of government for Europe through most of its history. A monarchy is led by a king or a queen. This position is hereditary, and the rulers are not elected. In modern times, constitutional monarchy has developed, where the king and queen still exist but most of the governmental decisions are made by democratic institutions such as a parliament.

A Presidential System, like a parliamentary system, has a legislature and political parties, but there is no difference between the head of state and the head of government. Instead of separating these functions, an elected president performs both. Election of the president can be direct or indirect, and the president may not necessarily belong to the largest political party. In Socialism, the state controls production of goods, though it does not necessarily own all means of production. The state also provides a variety of social services to citizens and helps guide the economy. A democratic form of government often exists in socialist countries.

In a parliamentary system, government involves a legislature and a variety of political parties. The head of government, usually a Prime Minister, is typically the head of the dominant party. A head of state can be elected, or this position can be taken by a monarch, such as in Great Britain's constitutional monarchy system. In a democratic system of government, the people elect their government representatives. The term democracy is a Greek term that means "for the rule of the people." There are two forms of democracy—direct and indirect. In a direct democracy, each issue or election is decided by a vote where each individual is counted separately. An indirect democracy employs a legislature that votes on issues that affect large number of people whom the legislative members represent. Democracy can exist as a Parliamentary system or a Presidential system. The US is a presidential, indirect democracy.

INTERNATIONAL RELATIONS

Foreign policy is a set of goals, policies and strategies that determine how an individual nation will interact with other countries. These strategies shift, sometimes quickly and drastically, according to actions or changes occurring in the other countries. However, a nation's foreign policy is often based on a certain set of ideals and national needs.

There are three schools of thought when it comes to foreign policy. The theory of realism states that nations are by nature aggressive, and work in their own self-interest. Relations between nations are determined by military and economic strength. The nation is seen as the highest authority. Liberalism believes states can cooperate, and that they act based on capabilities rather than power. This term was originally coined to describe Woodrow Wilson's theories on international cooperation.

In institutionalism, institutions provide structure and incentive for cooperation among nations. Institutions are defined as a set of rules used to make international decisions. These institutions also help distribute power and determine how nations will interact. Constructivism, like liberalism, is based on international cooperation, but recognizes that perceptions countries have of each other can affect their relations.

Examples of US foreign policy include isolationism versus internationalism. In the 1800s, the US leaned more toward isolationism, exhibiting a reluctance to become involved in foreign affairs. The World Wars led to a period of internationalism, as the US entered these wars in support of other countries and joined the United Nations. Today's foreign policy tends more toward interdependence, or globalism, recognizing the widespread effects of issues like economic health.

US foreign policy is largely determined by Congress and the president, influenced by the secretary of state, secretary of defense, and the national security adviser. Executive officials actually carry out policies. The main departments in charge of these day-to-day issues are the US Department of State, also referred to as the State Department. The Department of State carries out policy, negotiates treaties, maintains diplomatic relations, assists citizens traveling in foreign countries, and ensures that the president is properly informed of any international issues. The Department of Defense, the largest executive department in the US, supervises the armed forces and provides assistance to the president in his role as commander in chief.

Diplomats are individuals who reside in foreign countries in order to maintain communications between that country and their home country. They help negotiate trade agreements, environmental policies, and convey official information to foreign governments. They also help resolve conflicts between the countries, often working to sort out issues without making the conflicts official in any way. Diplomats, or ambassadors, are appointed in America by the president. Appointments must be approved by Congress.

Intergovernmental organizations (IGOs). These organizations are made up of members from various national governments. The UN is an example of an intergovernmental organization. Treaties among the member nations determine the functions and powers of these groups.

Nongovernmental organizations (NGOs). An NGO lies outside the scope of any government and are usually supported through private donations. An example of an NGO is the International Red Cross, which works with governments all over the world when their countries are in crisis, but is formally affiliated with no particular country or government.

The United Nations (UN) helps form international policies by hosting representatives of various countries who then provide input into policy decisions. Countries who are members of the UN must agree to abide by all final UN resolutions, but this is not always the case in practice, as dissent is not uncommon. If countries do not follow UN resolutions, the UN can decide on sanctions against those countries, often economic sanctions, such as trade restriction. The UN can also send military forces to problem areas, with "peace keeping" troops brought in from member nations. An example of this function is the Korean War, the first war in which an international organization played a major role.

United States History

EXPLORATION

The Age of Exploration is also called the Age of Discovery. It is generally considered to have begun in the early fifteenth century, and continued into the seventeenth century. Major developments of the Age of Exploration included technological advances in navigation, mapmaking, and shipbuilding. These advances led to expanded European exploration of the rest of the world. Explorers set out from several European countries, including Portuguese, Spain, France, and England, seeking new routes to Asia. These efforts led to the discovery of new lands, as well as colonization in India, Asia, Africa, and North America.

> **Review Video: Age of Exploration**
> Visit mometrix.com/academy and enter code: 612972

For long ocean journeys, it was important for sailors to be able to find their way home even when their vessels sailed far out to sea, well out of sight of land. A variety of navigational tools enabled them to launch ambitious journeys over long distances. The compass and astrolabe were particularly important advancements. The magnetic compass had been used by Chinese navigators for some time, and knowledge of the astrolabe came to Europe from Arab navigators and traders who had refined designs developed by the ancient Greeks. The Portuguese developed a ship called a caravel in the 1400s that incorporated navigational advancements with the ability to make long sea journeys. Equipped with this advanced vessel, the Portuguese achieved a major goal of the Age of Exploration by discovering a sea route from Europe to Asia in 1498.

In 1492, Columbus, a Genoan explorer, obtained financial backing from King Ferdinand and Queen Isabella of Spain to seek a sea route to Asia. He sought a trade route with the Asian Indies to the west. With three ships, the *Niña*, the *Pinta*, and the *Santa Maria*, he eventually landed in the West Indies. While Columbus failed in his effort to discover a western route to Asia, he is credited with the discovery of the Americas. This discover sparked waves of European exploration, conquest, and colonization.

> **Review Video: Christopher Columbus**
> Visit mometrix.com/academy and enter code: 496598

North America was already inhabited by a number of native tribes when Europeans discovered the continent. The Algonquians in the eastern part of the United States lived in wigwams. The northern tribes subsisted on hunting and gathering, while those who were farther south grew crops such as corn. The Iroquois, also an east coast tribe, spoke a different language from the Algonquians, and lived in rectangular longhouses. The Plains tribes lived between the Mississippi River and the Rocky Mountains. Nomadic tribes, they lived in teepees and followed the buffalo herds. Plains tribes included the Sioux, Cheyenne, Comanche and Blackfoot. Pueblo tribes included the Zuni, Hope, and Acoma. They lived in the Southwest deserts in homes made of stone or adobe. They domesticated animals and cultivated corn and beans. On the Pacific coast, tribes such as the Tlingit, Chinook and Salish lived on fish as well as deer, native berries and roots. Their rectangular homes housed large family groups, and they used totem poles. In the far north, the Aleuts and Inuit lived in skin tents or igloos. Talented fishermen, they built kayaks and umiaks and also hunted caribou, seals, whales and walrus.

Initial French colonies were focused on expanding the fur trade. Later, French colonization led to the growth of plantations in Louisiana which brought numerous African slaves to the New World.

Spanish colonists came to look for wealth, and to converting the natives to Christianity. For some, the desire for gold led to mining in the New World, while others established large ranches. The Dutch were also involved in the fur trade, and also imported slaves as the need for laborers increased. British colonists arrived with various goals. Some were simply looking for additional income, while others were fleeing Britain to escape religious persecution. Squanto, an Algonquian, helped early English settlers survive the hard winter by teaching them the native methods of planting corn, squash, and pumpkins. Pocahontas, also Algonquian, became famous as a liaison with John Smith's Jamestown colony in 1607.

AMERICAN COLONIES

The New England colonies were: New Hampshire, Connecticut, Rhode Island and Massachusetts.

The colonies in New England were founded largely to escape religious persecution in England. The beliefs of the Puritans, who migrated to America in the 1600s, significantly influenced the development of these colonies. Situated in the northeast coastal areas of America, the New England colonies featured numerous harbors as well as dense forest. The soil, however, is rocky and, with a very short growing season, was not well suited for agriculture. The economy of New England during the colonial period centered around fishing, shipbuilding and trade along with some small farms and lumber mills. Although some groups congregated in small farms, life centered largely on towns and cities where merchants largely controlled the trade economy. Coastal cities such as Boston grew and thrived.

The Middle or Middle Atlantic Colonies were: New York, New Jersey, Pennsylvania and Delaware.

Unlike the New England colonies, where most colonists were from England and Scotland, the Middle Colonies founders were from various countries including the Netherlands, Holland and Sweden. Various factors led these colonists to America. More fertile than New England, the Middle Colonies became major producers of crops included rye, oats, potatoes, wheat, and barley. Some particularly wealthy inhabitants owned large farms and/or businesses. Farmers in general were able to produce enough to have a surplus to sell. Tenant farmers also rented land from larger land owners.

The Southern Colonies were Maryland, Virginia, North Carolina, South Carolina and Georgia.

Of the Southern Colonies, Virginia was the first permanent English colony and Georgia the last. The warm climate and rich soil of the south encouraged agriculture, and the growing season was long. As a result, economy in the south was based largely on labor-intensive plantations. Crops included tobacco, rice and indigo, all of which became valuable cash crops. Most land in the south was controlled by wealthy plantation owners and farmers. Labor on the farms came in the form of indentured servants and African slaves. The first of these African slaves arrived in Virginia in 1619, starting a long, unpleasant history of slavery in the American colonies.

Enacted in 1651, the Navigation Acts were an attempt by Britain to dominate international trade. Aimed largely at the Dutch, the Acts banned foreign ships from transporting goods to the British colonies, and from transporting goods to Britain from elsewhere in Europe. While the restrictions on trade angered some colonists, these Acts were helpful to other American colonists who, as members of the British Empire, were legally able to provide ships for Britain's growing trade interests and use the ships for their own trading ventures. By the time the French and Indian War had ended, one-third of British merchant ships were built in the American colonies. Many colonists amassed fortunes in the shipbuilding trade.

Triangular trade began in the Colonies with ships setting off for Africa carrying rum. In Africa, the rum was traded for gold or slaves. Ships then went from Africa to the West Indies, trading slaves for sugar, molasses, or money. To complete the triangle, the ships returned to the colonies with sugar or molasses to make more rum, as well as stores of gold and silver. This trade triangle violated the Molasses Act of 1733, which required the colonists to pay high duties to Britain on molasses acquired from French, Dutch, and Spanish colonies. The colonists ignored these duties, and the British government adopted a policy of salutary neglect by not enforcing them.

Review Video: Triangular Trade
Visit mometrix.com/academy and enter code: 415470

The British defeat of the Spanish Armada in 1588 led to the decline of Spanish power in Europe. This in turn led the British and French into battle over several wars between 1689 and 1748. These wars were:

- King William's War, or the Nine Years War, 1689-1697. This war was fought largely in Flanders.
- The War of Spanish Succession, or Queen Anne's War, 1702-1713
- War of Austrian Succession, or King George's War, 1740-1748

The fourth and final, the French and Indian War begun in 1754, was fought largely in the North American territory, and resulted in the end of France's reign as a colonial power in North America. Although the French held many advantages, including more cooperative colonists and numerous Indian allies, the strong leadership of William Pitt eventually led the British to victory. Costs incurred during the wars eventually led to discontent in the colonies. This helped spark the American Revolution.

Review Video: French and Indian War
Visit mometrix.com/academy and enter code: 502183

The French and Indian War created circumstances for which the British desperately needed more revenue. These included:

- The need to pay off the war debt.
- The need for funds to defend the expanding empire
- The need for funds to govern Britain's thirty-three far-flung colonies, including the American colonies

These needs led the British to pass additional laws to increase revenues from the colonies. Because they had spent so much money to defend the American colonies, the British felt it was appropriate to collect considerably higher taxes from them. The colonists felt this was unfair, and many were led to protest the increasing taxes. Eventually, protest led to violence.

While earlier revenue-generating acts such as the Navigation Acts brought money to the colonists, the new laws after 1763 required colonists to pay money back to Britain. The British felt this was fair since the colonists were British subjects and since they had incurred debt protecting the Colonies. The colonists felt it was not only unfair, but illegal. The development of local government in America had given the colonists a different view of the structure and role of government. This made it difficult for the British to understand colonist's protests against what the British felt was a fair and reasonable solution to the mother country's financial problems.

More and more colonists had been born on American soil, decreasing any sense of kinship with the far away British rulers. Their new environment had led to new ideas of government and a strong view of the colonies as a separate entity from Britain. Colonists were allowed to self-govern in domestic issues, but Britain controlled international issues. In fact, the American colonies were largely left to form their own local government bodies, giving them more freedom than any other colonial territory. This gave the colonists a sense of independence which led them to resent control from Britain. Threats during the French and Indian War led the colonists to call for unification in order to protect themselves.

AMERICAN REVOLUTION

As new towns and other legislative districts developed in America, the colonists began to practice direct representative government. Colonial legislative bodies were made up of elected representatives chosen by male property owners in the districts. These individuals represented interests of the districts from which they had been elected.

By contrast, in Britain the Parliament represented the entire country. Parliament was not elected to represent individual districts. Instead, they represented specific classes. Because of this drastically different approach to government, the British did not understand the colonists' statement that they had no representation in the British Parliament.

In the mid1760s, the British government passed a series of extremely unpopular laws directed at the American colonies. The Sugar Act, 1764: This act not only required taxes to be collected on molasses brought into the colonies, but gave British officials the right to search the homes of anyone suspected of violating it. The Quartering Act, 1765: This act required colonists to provide accommodations and supplies for British troops. In addition, colonists were prohibited from settling west of the Appalachians until given permission by Britain. The Stamp Act, 1765: The Stamp Act taxed printed materials such as newspapers and legal documents. Protests led the Stamp Act to be repealed in 1766, but the repeal also included the Declaratory Act, which stated that Parliament had the right to govern the colonies. The Townshend Acts, 1767: These acts taxed paper, paint, lead and tea that came into the colonies. Colonists led boycotts in protest, and in Massachusetts leaders like Samuel and John Adams began to organize resistance against British rule.

With the passage of the Stamp Act, nine colonies met in New York to demand its repeal. Elsewhere, protests arose in New York City, Philadelphia, Boston and other cities. These protests sometimes escalated into violence, often targeting ruling British officials. The passage of the Townshend Acts in 1767 led to additional tension in the colonies. The British sent troops to New York City and Boston. On March 5, 1770, protesters began to taunt the British troops, throwing snowballs. The soldiers responded by firing into the crowd. This clash between protesters and soldiers led to five deaths and eight injuries, and was christened the Boston Massacre. Shortly thereafter, Britain repealed the majority of the Townshend Acts.

The majority of the Townshend Acts were repealed after the Boston Massacre in 1770, but Britain kept the tax on tea. In 1773, the Tea Act was passed. This allowed the East India Company to sell tea for much lower prices, and also allowed them to bypass American distributors, selling directly to shopkeepers instead. Colonial tea merchants saw this as a direct assault on their business. In December of 1773, 150 merchants boarded ships in Boston Harbor and dumped 342 chests of tea into the sea in protest of the new laws. This act of protest came to be known as the Boston Tea Party.

The Coercive Acts passed by Britain in 1774 were meant to punish Massachusetts for defying British authority. The four Coercive Acts:

- Shut down ports in Boston until the city paid back the value of the tea destroyed during the Boston Tea Party.
- Required that local government officials in Massachusetts be appointed by the governor rather than being elected by the people.
- Allowed trials of British soldiers to be transferred to Britain rather than being held in Massachusetts.
- Required locals to provide lodging for British soldiers any time there was a disturbance, even if lodging required them to stay in private homes.

These Acts led to the assembly of the First Continental Congress in Philadelphia on September 5, 1774. Fifty-five delegates met, representing 12 of the American colonies. They sought compromise with England over England's increasingly harsh efforts to control the colonies.

The First Continental Congress met in Philadelphia on September 5, 1774. Their goal was to achieve a peaceful agreement with Britain. Made up of delegates from 12 of the 13 colonies, the Congress affirmed loyalty to Britain and the power of Parliament to dictate foreign affairs in the colonies. However, they demanded that the Intolerable Acts be repealed, and instituted a trade embargo with Britain until this came to pass.

In response, George III of Britain declared that the American colonies must submit or face military action. The British sought to end assemblies opposing their policies. These assemblies gathered weapons and began to form militias. On April 19, 1775, the British military was ordered to disperse a meeting of the Massachusetts Assembly. A battle ensued on Lexington Common as the armed colonists resisted. The resulting battles became the Battle of Lexington and Concord—the first battles of the American Revolution.

The Second Continental Congress met in Philadelphia on May 10, 1775, a month after Lexington and Concord. Their discussions centered on defense of the American colonies and how to conduct the growing war, as well as local government. The delegates also discussed declaring independence from Britain, with many members in favor of this drastic move. They established an army, and on June 15, named George Washington as its commander in chief. By 1776, it was obvious that there was no turning back from full-scale war with Britain. The colonial delegates of the Continental Congress drafted the Declaration of Independence on July 4, 1776.

Review Video: The First and Second Continental Congress
Visit mometrix.com/academy and enter code: 835211

Penned by Thomas Jefferson and signed on July 4, 1776, the Declaration of Independence stated that King George III had violated the rights of the colonists and was establishing a tyrannical reign over them.

Review Video: Declaration of Independence
Visit mometrix.com/academy and enter code: 256838

Many of Jefferson's ideas of natural rights and property rights were shaped by seventeenth century philosopher John Locke. Jefferson focused on natural rights, as demonstrated by the assertion of people's rights to "life, liberty and the pursuit of happiness." Locke's comparable idea asserted "life, liberty, and private property." Both felt that the purpose of government was to protect the rights of the people, and that individual rights were more important than individuals' obligations to the state.

Major events during the American Revolution include:

The Battle of Lexington and Concord (April, 1775) is considered the first engagement of the Revolutionary War.

The Battle of Bunker Hill, in June of 1775, was one of the bloodiest of the entire war. Although American troops withdrew, about half the British army was lost. The colonists proved they could stand against professional British soldiers. In August, Britain declared that the American colonies were officially in a state of rebellion.

The first colonial victory occurred in Trenton, New Jersey, when Washington and his troops crossed the Delaware River on Christmas Day, 1776 for a December 26, surprise attack on British and Hessian troops.

The Battle of Saratoga effectively ended a plan to separate the New England colonies from their Southern counterparts. The surrender of British general John Burgoyne led to France joining the war as allies of the Americans, and is generally considered a turning point of the war.

On October 19, 1781, General Cornwallis surrendered after a defeat in the Battle of Yorktown, Virginia, ending the Revolutionary War.

The Treaty of Paris was signed on September 3, 1783, bringing an official end to the Revolutionary War. In this document, Britain officially recognized the United States of America as an independent nation. The treaty established the Mississippi River as the country's western border. The treaty also restored Florida to Spain, while France reclaimed African and Caribbean colonies seized by the British in 1763. On November 24, 1783, the last British troops departed from the newly born United States of America.

Review Video: The Revolutionary War
Visit mometrix.com/academy and enter code: 935282

U.S. CONSTITUTION

A precursor to the Constitution, the Articles of Confederation represented the first attempt of the newly independent colonies to establish the basics of independent government. The Continental Congress passed the Articles on November 15, 1777. They went into effect on March 1, 1781, following ratification by the thirteen states. The Articles prevented a central government from gaining too much power, instead giving power to a Congressional body made up of delegates from all thirteen states. However, the individual states retained final authority. Without a strong central executive, though, this weak alliance among the new states proved ineffective in settling disputes or enforcing laws. The idea of a weak central government needed to be revised. Recognition of these weaknesses eventually led to the drafting of a new document, the Constitution.

Review Video: Articles of Confederation
Visit mometrix.com/academy and enter code: 927401

Delegates from twelve of the thirteen states (Rhode Island was not represented) met in Philadelphia in May of 1787, initially intending to revise the Articles of Confederation. However, it quickly became apparent that a simple revision would not provide the workable governmental

country needed. After vowing to keep all the proceedings secret until
...pleted, the delegates set out to draft what would eventually become the
...States of America. By keeping the negotiations secret, the delegates were
...d document to the country for ratification, rather than having every small
...he general public.

...the new nation required a strong central government, but that its overall
...the various branches of the government should have balanced power, so
...ntrol the others. Final power belonged with the citizens who voted
...who would provide the best representation. Disagreement
...en delegates from large states and those from smaller states. The
...l Randolph, felt that representation in Congress should be based on
...Virginia Plan.

...d by William Paterson, from New Jersey, proposed each state have
...oger Sherman from Connecticut formulated the Connecticut
...at Compromise. The result was the familiar structure we have
...presentation of two Senators in the Senate, with the number of
...epresentatives based on population. This is called a bicameral
...ills, but financial matters must originate in the House of

...ution, a disagreement arose between the Northern and Southern
...ould be counted when determining a state's quota of representatives.
...of slaves were commonly used to run plantations. Delegates wanted
...etermine the number of representatives, but not counted to determine the
...tes would pay. The Northern states wanted exactly the opposite
...al decision was to count three-fifths of the slave population both for tax
...etermine representation. This was called the three-fifths compromise.

...ce Compromise also resulted from a North/South disagreement. In the North the
...vas centered on industry and trade. The Southern economy was largely agricultural. The
...n states wanted to give the new government the ability to regulate exports as well as trade
...een the states. The South opposed this plan. Another compromise was in order. In the end,
...ngress received regulatory power over all trade, including the ability to collect tariffs on
exported goods. In the South, this raised another red flag regarding the slave trade, as they were
concerned about the effect on their economy if tariffs were levied on slaves. The final agreement
allowed importing slaves to continue for twenty years without government intervention. Import
taxes on slaves were limited, and after the year 1808, Congress could decide whether to allow
continued imports of slaves.

Once the Constitution was drafted, it was presented for approval by the states. Nine states needed
to approve the document for it to become official. However, debate and discussion continued. Major
concerns included:

- The lack of a bill of rights to protect individual freedoms.
- States felt too much power was being handed over to the central government.
- Voters wanted more control over their elected representatives.

187

- Discussion about necessary changes to the Constitution divided
  Federalists and Anti-Federalists. Federalists wanted a strong cer
  Federalists wanted to prevent a tyrannical government from dev
  government held too much power.

Major Federalist leaders included Alexander Hamilton, John Jay and James
series of letters, called the Federalist Papers, aimed at convincing the states
Constitution. These were published in New York papers. Anti-Federalists inc
Jefferson and Patrick Henry. They argued against the Constitution as it was or
arguments called the Anti-Federalist Papers. The final compromise produced a
government controlled by checks and balances. A Bill of Rights was also added,
ten amendments to the Constitution. These amendments protected rights such as
speech, freedom of religion, and other basic rights. Aside from various amendmen
throughout the years, the United States Constitution has remained unchanged.

> **Review Video: <u>Drafting the Constitution</u>**
> Visit mometrix.com/academy and enter code: 662451

FEDERALISTS AND JEFFERSONIAN REPUBLICANS

George Washington was elected as the first President of the United States in 1789. John A
who finished second in the election, became the first Vice President. Thomas Jefferson was
appointed by Washington as Secretary of State and Alexander Hamilton was appointed Secr
the Treasury.

Many in the U.S. were against political parties after seeing the way parties, or factions, function
Britain. The factions in Britain were more interested in personal profit than the overall good of
country, and they did not want this to happen in the U.S. However, the differences of opinion
between Thomas Jefferson and Alexander Hamilton led to formation of political parties. Hamilton
favored a stronger central government, while Jefferson felt more power should remain with the
states. Jefferson was in favor of strict Constitutional interpretation, while Hamilton believed in a
more flexible approach. As various others joined the separate camps, Hamilton backers began to
term themselves Federalists while those supporting Jefferson became identified as Democratic-
Republicans.

When John Adams became president in 1796, a war was raging between Britain and France. While
Adams and the Federalists backed the British, Thomas Jefferson and the Republican Party
supported the French. The United States nearly went to war with France during this time period,
while France worked to spread its international standing and influence under the leadership of
Napoleon Bonaparte. The Alien and Sedition Acts grew out of this conflict, and made it illegal to
speak in a hostile fashion against the existing government. They also allowed the president to
deport anyone in the U.S. who was not a citizen and who was suspected of treason or treasonous
activity. When Jefferson became the third president in 1800, he repealed these four laws and
pardoned anyone who had been convicted under them.

The main duty of the Supreme Court today is judicial review. This power was largely established by
Marbury v. Madison. When John Adams was voted out of office in 1800, he worked, during his final
days in office, to appoint Federalist judges to Supreme Court positions, knowing Jefferson, his
replacement, held opposing views. As late as March 3, the day before Jefferson was to take office,
Adams made last-minute appointments referred to as "Midnight Judges." One of the late
appointments was William Marbury. The next day, March 4, Jefferson ordered his Secretary of State,

James Madison, not to deliver Marbury's commission. This decision was backed by Chief Justice Marshall, who determined that the Judiciary Act of 1789, which granted the power to deliver commissions, was illegal in that it gave the Judicial Branch powers not granted in the Constitution. This case set precedent for the Supreme Court to nullify laws it found to be unconstitutional.

Judicial review was further exercised by the Supreme Court in McCulloch v Maryland. When Congress chartered a national bank, the Second Bank of the United States, Maryland voted to tax any bank business dealing with banks chartered outside the state, including the federally chartered bank. Andrew McCulloch, an employee of the Second Bank of the US in Baltimore, refused to pay this tax. The resulting lawsuit from the State of Maryland went to the Supreme Court for judgment. John Marshall, Chief Justice of the Supreme Court, stated that Congress was within its rights to charter a national bank. In addition, the State of Maryland did not have the power to levy a tax on the federal bank or on the federal government in general. In cases where state and federal government collided, precedent was set for the federal government to prevail.

After the Revolutionary War, the Treaty of Paris, which outlined the terms of surrender of the British to the Americans, granted large parcels of land to the U.S. that were occupied by Native Americans. The new government attempted to claim the land, treating the natives as a conquered people. This approached proved unenforceable. Next, the government tried purchasing the land from the Indians via a series of treaties as the country expanded westward. In practice, however, these treaties were not honored, and Native Americans were simply dislocated and forced to move farther and farther west as American expansion continued, often with military action.

In the Northeast, the economy mostly depended on manufacturing, industry and industrial development. This led to a dichotomy between rich business owners and industrial leaders and the much poorer workers who supported their businesses. The South continued to depend on agriculture, especially large-scale farms or plantations worked mostly by slaves and indentured servants. In the West, where new settlement had begun to develop, the land was largely wild. Growing communities were essentially agricultural; growing crops and raising livestock. The differences between regions led each to support different interests both politically and economically.

With tension still high between France and Britain, Napoleon was in need of money to support his continuing war efforts. To secure necessary funds, he decided to sell the Louisiana Territory to the U.S. At the same time President Thomas Jefferson wanted to buy New Orleans, feeling U.S. trade was made vulnerable to both Spain and France at that port. Instead, Napoleon sold him the entire territory for the bargain price of fifteen million dollars. The Louisiana Territory was larger than all the rest of the United States put together, and it eventually became fifteen additional states. Federalists in Congress were opposed to the purchase. They feared that the Louisiana Purchase would extend slavery, and that further western growth would weaken the power of the northern states.

The purchase of the Louisiana Territory from France in 1803 more than doubled the size of the United States. President Thomas Jefferson wanted to have the area mapped and explored, since much of the territory was wilderness. He chose Meriwether Lewis and William Clark to head an expedition into the Louisiana Territory. After two years, Lewis and Clark returned, having traveled all the way to the Pacific Ocean. They brought maps, detailed journals, and various types of knowledge and information about the wide expanse of land they had traversed. The Lewis and

Clark Expedition opened up the west in the Louisiana Territory and beyond for further exploration and settlement.

> **Review Video: The Louisiana Purchase**
> Visit mometrix.com/academy and enter code: 920513

Three major planks supported the United States early growth:

- Isolationism – the early US government did not intend to establish colonies, though they did plan to grow larger within the bounds of North America.
- No entangling alliances – both George Washington and Thomas Jefferson were opposed to forming any permanent alliances with other countries or becoming involved in other countries' internal issues.
- Nationalism – a positive patriotic feeling about the United States blossomed quickly among its citizens, particularly after the War of 1812, when the U.S. once again defeated Britain. The Industrial Revolution also sparked increased nationalism by allowing even the most far-flung areas of the U.S. to communicate with each other via telegraph and the expanding railroad.

WAR OF 1812 AND ERA OF GOOD FEELINGS

The War of 1812 grew out of the continuing tension between France and Great Britain. Napoleon continued to strive to conquer Britain, while the U.S. continued trade with both countries, but favoring France and the French colonies. Because of what Britain saw as an alliance between America and France, they determined to bring an end to trade between the two nations. The British had two major objections to America's continued trade with France. First, they saw the US as helping France's war effort by providing supplies and goods. Second, the United States had grown into a competitor, taking trade and money away from British ships and tradesmen. In its attempts to end American trade with France, the British put into effect the Orders in Council, which made any and all French-owned ports off-limits to American ships. They also began to seize American ships and conscript their crews, a practice greatly offensive to the U.S.

With the British preventing U.S. trade with the French and the French preventing trade with the British, James Madison's presidency introduced acts to regulate international trade. If either Britain or France removed their restrictions, America would not trade with the other. Napoleon acted first, and Madison prohibited trade with England. England saw this as the U.S. formally siding with the French, and war ensued in 1812. The War of 1812 has been called the Second American Revolution. It established the superiority of the U.S. naval forces and reestablished U.S. independence from Britain and Europe.

Two major naval battles, at Lake Erie and Lake Champlain, kept the British from invading the U.S. via Canada. American attempts to conquer Canadian lands were not successful. In another memorable British attack, the British invaded Washington DC and burned the White House. Legend has it that Dolly Madison, the First Lady, salvaged the American flag from the fire. On Christmas Eve, 1814, the Treaty of Ghent officially ended the war. However, Andrew Jackson, unaware that the war was over, managed another victory at New Orleans on January 8, 1815. This victory upped American morale and led to a new wave of nationalism and national pride known as the "Era of Good Feelings."

Spurred by the trade conflicts of the War of 1812, and supported by Henry Clay and others, the American System set up tariffs to help protect American interests from competition with products from overseas. Reducing competition led to growth in employment and an overall increase in

American industry. The higher tariffs also provided funds for the government to pay for various improvements. Congress passed high tariffs in 1816 and also chartered a federal bank. The Second Bank of the United States was given the job of regulating America's money supply.

On December 2, 1823, President Monroe delivered a message to Congress in which he introduced the Monroe Doctrine. In this address, he stated that any attempts by European powers to establish new colonies on the North American continent would be considered interference in American politics. The U.S. would stay out of European matters, and expected Europe to offer America the same courtesy. This approach to foreign policy stated in no uncertain terms that America would not tolerate any new European colonies in the New World, and that events occurring in Europe would no longer influence the policies and doctrines of the U.S.

JACKSONIAN ERA

Thomas Jefferson was elected president in 1800 and again in 1804. The Federalist Party began a decline, and its major figure, Alexander Hamilton, died in a duel with Aaron Burr in 1804. By 1816, the Federalist Party virtually disappeared. New parties sprang up to take its place. After 1824, the Democratic-Republican Party suffered a split. The Whigs arose, backing John Quincy Adams and industrial growth. The new Democratic Party formed, in opposition to the Whigs, and their candidate, Andrew Jackson, was elected as president in 1828. By the 1850s, issues regarding slavery led to the formation of the Republican Party, which was anti-slavery, while the Democratic Party of the time, with a larger interest in the South, favored slavery. This Republican/Democrat division formed the basis of today's two-party system.

Jacksonian Democracy is largely seen as a shift from politics favoring the wealthy to politics favoring the common man. All free white males were given the right to vote, not just property owners, as had been the case previously. Jackson's approach favored the patronage system, Laissez faire economics, and relocation of the Indian tribes from the Southeast portion of the country. Jackson opposed the formation of a federal bank, and allowed the Second Band of the United States to collapse by vetoing a bill to renew the charter. Jackson also faced the challenge of the "null and void" or nullification theory when South Carolina claimed that it could ignore or nullify any federal law it considered unconstitutional. Jackson sent troops to the state to enforce the protested tariff laws, and a compromise engineered by Henry Clay in 1833 settled the matter for the time being.

The Indian Removal Act of 1830 gave the new American government power to form treaties with Native Americans. In theory, America would claim land east of the Mississippi in exchange for land west of the Mississippi, to which the natives would relocate voluntarily. In practice, many tribal leaders were forced into signing the treaties, and relocation at times occurred by force. The Treaty of New Echota was supposedly a treaty between the US government and Cherokee tribes in Georgia. However, the treaty was not signed by tribal leaders, but rather by a small portion of the represented people. The leaders protested by refusing to be removed, but the President, Martin Van Buren, enforced the treaty by sending soldiers. During their forced relocation, more than 4,000 Cherokee Indians died on what became known as the Trail of Tears.

MANIFEST DESTINY AND MEXICAN WAR

In the 1800's, many believed America was destined by God to expand west, bringing as much of the North American continent as possible under the umbrella of U.S. government. With the Northwest Ordinance and the Louisiana Purchase, over half of the continent became American. However, the rapid and relentless expansion brought conflict with the Native Americans, Great Britain, Mexico and Spain. One result of "Manifest Destiny" was the Mexican-American War, which occurred in 1846-1848. By the end of the war, Texas, California and a large portion of what is now the American

Southwest joined the growing nation. Conflict also arose over the Oregon country, shared by the US and Britain. In 1846, President James Polk resolved this problem by compromising with Britain, establishing a U.S. boundary south of the 49th parallel.

Spain had held colonial interests in America since the 1540s—earlier even than Great Britain. In 1821, Mexico revolted against Spain and became a free nation. Likewise, this was followed by Texas, who after an 1836 revolution declared its independence. In 1844, the Democrats pressed President Tyler to annex Texas. Unlike his predecessor, Andrew Jackson, Tyler agreed to admit Texas into the Union. In 1845, Texas became a state. During Mexico's war for independence, they had incurred $4.5 million in war debts to the U.S. Polk offered to forgive the debts in return for New Mexico and Upper California, but Mexico refused. In 1846, war was declared in response to a Mexican attack on American troops along the southern border of Texas. Additional conflict arose in Congress over the Wilmot Proviso, which stated that slavery was prohibited in any territory the U.S. acquired from Mexico as a result of the Mexican-American war. The war ended in 1848.

After the Mexican-American war, a second treaty in 1853 determined hundreds of miles of America's southwest borders. In 1854, the Gadsden Purchase was finalized, providing even more territory to aid in the building of the transcontinental railroad. This purchase added what would eventually become the southernmost regions of Arizona and New Mexico to the growing nation. The modern outline of the United States was by this time nearly complete.

19TH CENTURY DEVELOPMENTS

As America expanded its borders, it also developed new technology to travel the rapidly growing country. Roads and railroads traversed the nation, with the Transcontinental Railroad eventually allowing travel from one coast to the other. Canals and steamboats simplified water travel and made shipping easier and less expensive. The Erie Canal (1825) connected the Great Lakes with the Hudson River. Other canals connected other major water ways, further facilitating transportation and the shipment of goods. With growing numbers of settlers moving into the West, wagon trails developed, including the Oregon Trail, California Trail and the Santa Fe Trail. The most common vehicles seen along these westbound trails were covered wagons, also known as prairie schooners.

During the eighteenth century, goods were often manufactured in houses or small shops. With increased technology allowing for the use of machines, factories began to develop. In factories a large volume of salable goods could be produced in a much shorter amount of time. Many Americans, including increasing numbers of immigrants, found jobs in these factories, which were in constant need of labor. Another major invention was the cotton gin, which significantly decreased the processing time of cotton, and was a major factor in the rapid expansion of cotton production in the South.

In 1751, a group of bakers held a protest in which they stopped baking bread. This was technically the first American labor strike. In the 1830s and 1840s, labor movements began in earnest. Boston's masons, carpenters and stoneworkers protested the length of the workday, fighting to reduce it to ten hours. In 1844, a group of women in the textile industry also fought to reduce their workday to ten hours, forming the Lowell Female Labor Reform Association. Many other protests occurred and organizations developed through this time period with the same goal in mind.

Led by Protestant evangelical leaders, the Second Great Awakening occurred between 1800 and 1830. Several missionary groups grew out of the movement, including the American Home Missionary Society, which formed in 1826. The ideas behind the Second Great Awakening focused on personal responsibility, both as an individual and in response to injustice and suffering. The American Bible Society and the American Tract Society provided literature, while various traveling preachers spread the word. New denominations arose, including the Latter-Day Saints and Seventh-Day Adventists. Another movement associated with the Second Great Awakening was the temperance movement, focused on ending the production and use of alcohol. One major organization behind the temperance movement was the Society for the Promotion of Temperance, formed in 1826 in Boston, Massachusetts.

The women's rights movement began in the 1840s with leaders including Elizabeth Cady Stanton, Ernestine Rose and Lucretia Mott. Later, in 1869, the National Woman Suffrage Association, fighting for women's right to vote, came into being. It was led by Susan B. Anthony, Ernestine Rose and Elizabeth Cady Stanton. In 1848 in Seneca Falls, the first women's rights convention was held, with about three hundred attendees. The Seneca Falls Convention brought to the floor the issue that women could not vote or run for office. The convention produced a "Declaration of Sentiments" which outlined a plan for women to attain the rights they deserved. Frederick Douglass supported the women's rights movement, as well as the abolition movement. In fact, women's rights and abolition movements often went hand-in-hand through this time period.

Horace Mann, among others, felt that public schooling could help children become better citizens, keep them away from crime, prevent poverty, and help American society become more unified. His *Common School Journal* brought his ideas of the importance of education into the public consciousness. Increased literacy led to increased awareness of current events, Western expansion, and other major developments of the time period. Public interest and participation in the arts and literature also increased. By the end of the 19th century, all children had access to a free public elementary education.

SECTIONAL CRISIS AND CIVIL WAR

The conflict between North and South coalesced around the issue of slavery, but other elements contributed to the growing disagreement. Though most farmers in the South worked small farms with little or no slave labor, the huge plantations run by the South's rich depended on slaves or indentured servants to remain profitable. They had also become more dependent on cotton, with slave populations growing in concert with the rapid increase in cotton production. In the North, a more diverse agricultural economy and the growth of industry made slaves rarer. The abolitionist movement grew steadily, with Harriet Beecher Stowe's *Uncle Tom's Cabin* giving many an idea to rally around. A collection of anti-slavery organizations formed, with many actively working to free slaves in the South, often bringing them North.

Prominent Abolitionist groups included:

- American Colonization Society—protestant churches formed this group, aimed at returning black slaves to Africa. Former slaves subsequently formed Liberia, but the colony did not do well, as the region was not well-suited for agriculture.
- American Anti-Slavery Society—William Lloyd Garrison, a Quaker, was the major force behind this group and its newspaper, *The Liberator*.

- Female Anti-Slavery Society—a women-only group formed by Margaretta Forten because women were not allowed to join the Anti-Slavery Society formed by her father.
- Anti-Slavery Convention of American Women—This group continued meeting even after pro-slavery factions burned down their original meeting place.
- Female Vigilant Society—an organization that raised funds to help the Underground Railroad, as well as slave refugees.

By 1819, the United States had developed a tenuous balance between slave and free states, with exactly twenty-two senators in Congress from each faction. However, Missouri was ready to join the union as a state. As a slave state, it would tip the balance in Congress. To prevent this imbalance, the Missouri Compromise brought the northern part of Massachusetts into the union as Maine, established as a free state. Maine's admission balanced the admission of Missouri as a slave state, maintaining the status quo. In addition, the remaining portion of the Louisiana Purchase was to remain free north of latitude 36° 30'. Since cotton did not grow well this far north, this limitation was acceptable to congressmen representing the slave states. However, the proposed Missouri constitution presented a problem, as it outlawed immigration of free blacks into the state. Another compromise was in order, this time proposed by Henry Clay. Clay earned his title of the Great Compromiser by stating that the U.S. Constitution overruled Missouri's.

In addition to the pro-slavery and anti-slavery factions, a third group rose who felt that each individual state should decide whether to allow or permit slavery within its borders. This idea was referred to as popular sovereignty. When California applied to join the union in 1849, the balance of congressional power was again threatened. The Compromise of 1850 introduced a group of laws meant to bring an end to the conflict.

These laws included:

- California being admitted as a free state
- Slave trade in Washington, D.C. being outlawed
- An increase in efforts to capture escaped slaves
- New Mexico and Utah territories would decide individually whether or not to allow slavery

In spite of these measures, debate raged each time a new state prepared to enter the union.

With the creation of the Kansas and Nebraska territories in 1854, another debate began. Congress allowed popular sovereignty in these territories, but slavery opponents argued that the Missouri Compromise had already made slavery illegal in this region. In Kansas, two separate governments arose, one pro- and one anti-slavery. Conflict between the two factions rose to violence, leading Kansas to gain the nickname of "Bleeding Kansas."

Abolitionist factions coalesced around the case of Dred Scott, using his case to test the country's laws regarding slavery. Scott, a slave, had been taken by his owner from Missouri, which was a slave state. He then traveled to Illinois, a free state, then on to the Minnesota Territory, also free based on the Missouri Compromise. Then, he returned to Missouri. The owner subsequently died. Abolitionists took Scott's case to court, stating that Scott was no longer a slave but free, since he had lived in free territory. The case went to the Supreme Court. The Supreme Court stated that, because Scott, as a slave, was not a U.S. citizen, his time in free states did not change his status. He also did not have the right to sue. In addition, the Court determined that the Missouri Compromise was unconstitutional, saying Congress had overstepped its bounds by outlawing slavery in the territories.

John Brown, an abolitionist, had participated in several anti-slavery actions, including killing five pro-slavery men in retaliation, after Lawrence, Kansas, an anti-slavery town, was sacked. He and other abolitionists also banded together to pool their funds and build a runaway slave colony.

In 1859, Brown seized a federal arsenal in Harper's Ferry, located in what is now West Virginia. Brown intended to seize guns and ammunition and lead a slave rebellion. Robert E. Lee captured Brown and 22 followers, who were subsequently tried and hanged. While Northerners took the executions as an indication that the government supported slavery, Southerners were of the opinion that most of the North supported Brown and were, in general, anti-slavery.

The 1860 Presidential candidates represented four different parties, each with a different opinion on slavery:

- John Breckenridge, representing the Southern Democrats, was pro-slavery.
- Abraham Lincoln, of the Republican Party, was anti-slavery.
- Stephen Douglas, of the Northern Democrats, felt that the issue should be determined locally, on a state-by-state basis.
- John Bell, of the Constitutional Union Party, focused primarily on keeping the Union intact.

In the end, Abraham Lincoln won both the popular and electoral election. Southern states, who had sworn to secede from the Union if Lincoln was elected did so, led by South Carolina. Shortly thereafter, the Civil War began when shots were fired on Fort Sumter in Charleston.

The Northern states had significant advantages, including:

- Larger population. The North consisted of 24 states to the South's 11.
- Better transportation and finances. With railroads primarily in the North, supply chains were much more dependable, as was trade coming from overseas.
- More raw materials. The North held the majority of America's gold, as well as iron, copper and other minerals vital to wartime.

The South's advantages included:

- Better-trained military officers. Many of the Southern officers were West Point trained and had commanded in the Mexican and Indian wars.
- More familiar with weapons. The climate and lifestyle of the South meant most of the people were well versed in both guns and horses. The industrial North had less extensive experience
- Defensive position. The South felt victory was guaranteed, since they were protecting their own lands, while the North would be invading.
- Well-defined goals. The South was fighting a war to be allowed to govern themselves and preserve their way of life.

The First Battle of Bull Run, July 21, 1861, was the first major land battle of the war. Observers, expecting to enjoy an entertaining skirmish, set up picnics nearby. Instead, they found themselves witness to a bloodbath. Union forces were defeated, and the battle set the course of the Civil War as long, bloody and costly. The Capture of Fort Henry by Ulysses S. Grant in February of 1862 marked the Union's first major victory.

The Emancipation Proclamation, issued by President Lincoln in 1863 after the Battle of Antietam, freed all slaves in Confederate States that did not return to the Union by the beginning of the year.

While the original proclamation did not free any slaves actually under Union control, it did set a precedent for the emancipation of slaves as the war progressed. The Emancipation Proclamation worked in the Union's favor as many freed slaves and other black troops joined the Union Army. Almost 200,000 blacks fought in the Union army, and over 10,000 served in the navy. By the end of the war, over 4 million slaves had been freed, and in 1865 slavery was banned by Constitutional amendment.

> **Review Video: Emancipation Proclamation**
> Visit mometrix.com/academy and enter code: 181778

The Battle of Gettysburg, July 1-3, 1863, is often seen as the turning point of the war, Gettysburg also saw the largest number of casualties of the war, with over 50,000 dead. Robert E. Lee was defeated, and the Confederate army, significantly crippled, withdrew. The Overland Campaign, 1864, Grant, now in command of all the Union armies, led this high casualty campaign that eventually positioned the Union for victory.

Sherman's March to the Sea, in May of 1864, led to the Union conquering of Atlanta. He then continued to Savannah, destroying indiscriminately as he went. Following Lee's defeat at the Appomattox Courthouse, General Grant accepted Lee's surrender in the home of Wilmer McLean, Appomattox, Virginia on April 9, 1865.

The Civil War ended with the surrender of the South on April 9, 1865. Five days later, Lincoln and his wife, Mary, attended the play *Our American Cousin* at the Ford Theater. John Wilkes Booth, unaware that the war was over, performed his part in a conspiracy to aid the Confederacy by shooting Lincoln in the back of the head. Booth was tracked down and killed by Union soldiers 12 days later. Lincoln, carried from the theater to a nearby house, died the next morning.

> **Review Video: Civil War**
> Visit mometrix.com/academy and enter code: 239557

RECONSTRUCTION

Three new amendments to the US Constitution were passed in the wake of the Civil War. The Thirteenth Amendment was passed on December 18, 1865. This amendment prohibited slavery in the United States. The Fourteenth Amendment overturned the Dred Scott decision, and was ratified July 9, 1868. American citizenship was redefined, with all citizens guaranteed equal legal protection by all states. It also guaranteed citizens the right to file a lawsuit or serve on a jury. The Fifteenth Amendment was ratified February 3, 1870. It states that no citizen of the United States can be denied the right to vote based on race, color, or previous status as a slave.

In the aftermath of the Civil War, the South was left in chaos. From 1865 to 1877, government on all levels worked to help restore order to the South, ensure civil rights to the freed slaves, and bring the Confederate states back into the Union. In 1866, Congress passed the Reconstruction Acts, putting former Confederate states under military rule. The Freedmen's Bureau was formed to help freedmen and give assistance to whites in the South who needed basic necessities like food and clothing. Many in the South felt the Freedmen's Bureau worked to set freed slaves against their former owners. The Bureau was intended to help former slaves become self-sufficient, and to keep them from falling prey to those who would take advantage of them.

The chaos in the south attracted a number of people seeking to fill the power vacuums and take advantage of the economic disruption. Scalawags were southern Whites who aligned with

Freedmen to take over local governments. Many in the South who could have filled political offices refused to take the necessary oath required to grant them the right to vote, leaving many opportunities for Scalawags and others. Carpetbaggers were northerners who traveled to the South for various reasons. Some provided assistance, while others sought to make money or to acquire political power during this chaotic period.

The Radical Republicans wished to treat the South quite harshly after the war. Thaddeus Stephens, the House Leader, suggested that the Confederate States be treated as if they were territories again, with ten years of military rule and territorial government before they would be readmitted. They also wanted to give all black men the right to vote. Former Confederate soldiers would be required to swear they had not fought against the Union in order to be granted full rights as American citizens. By contrast, the moderate Republicans wanted only black men who were literate or who had served as Union troops to be able to vote. All Confederate soldiers except troop leaders would also be able to vote. Before his death, Lincoln had favored a more moderate approach to Reconstruction, hoping this approach might bring some states back into the Union before the end of the war.

The Black Codes were proposed to control freed slaves. They would not be allowed to bear arms, assemble, serve on juries, or testify against whites. Schools would be segregated, and unemployed blacks could be arrested and forced to work. The Civil Rights bill countered these codes, providing much wider rights for the freed slaves. Andrew Johnson, who became president after Lincoln's death, supported the Black Codes, and vetoed the Civil Rights bill. Congress overrode his veto and impeached Johnson, the culmination of tensions between Congress and the president. He came within a single vote of being convicted.

Thus there were three phrases to Reconstruction. Presidential Reconstruction – largely driven by President Andrew Johnson's policies, the Presidential phase of Reconstruction was lenient on the South and allowed continued discrimination against and control over blacks. Congressional Reconstruction – Congress, controlled largely by Radical Republicans, took a different stance, providing a wider range of civil rights for blacks and greater control over Southern government. Congressional Reconstruction is marked by military control of the former Confederate States. Redemption – Gradually, the Confederate states were readmitted into the union. During this time, white Democrats took over the government of most of the South. Troops finally departed the South in 1877.

> **Review Video: Reconstruction Era**
> Visit mometrix.com/academy and enter code: 790561

SECOND INDUSTRIAL REVOLUTION

The second industrial revolution in the wake of the Civil War saw many important inventions and discovers being made:

- Alexander Graham Bell—the telephone
- Orville and Wilbur Wright—the airplane
- Richard Gatling—the machine gun
- Walter Hunt, Elias Howe and Isaac Singer—the sewing machine
- Nikola Tesla—alternating current
- George Eastman—the camera
- Thomas Edison—light bulbs, motion pictures, the phonograph
- Samuel Morse—the telegraph

- Charles Goodyear—vulcanized rubber
- Cyrus McCormick—the reaper
- George Westinghouse—the transformer, the air brake

This was an active period for invention, with about 700,000 patents registered between 1860 and 1900.

In 1869, the Union Pacific Railroad completed the first section of a planned transcontinental railroad. This section went from Omaha, Nebraska to Sacramento, California. With the rise of the railroad, products were much more easily transported across country. While this was positive overall for industry throughout the country, it was often damaging to family farmers, who found themselves paying high shipping costs for smaller supply orders while larger companies received major discounts. Ninety percent of the workers constructing the railroad were Chinese, working in very dangerous conditions for very low pay.

During the mid-1800s, irrigation techniques improved significantly. Advances occurred in cultivation and breeding, as well as fertilizer use and crop rotation. In the Great Plains, also known as the Great American Desert, the dense soil was finally cultivated with steel plows. In 1892, gasoline-powered tractors arrived, and were widely used by 1900. Other advancements in agriculture's tool set included barbed wire fences, combines, silos, deep-water wells, and the cream separator.

The government also took major actions that helped improve agriculture for the U.S. in the nineteenth century:

- The Department of Agriculture came into being in 1862, working for the interests of farmers and ranchers across the country.
- The Morrill Land-Grant Acts were passed in 1862, allowing land-grant colleges.
- In conjunction with land-grant colleges, the Hatch Act of 1887 brought agriculture experimental stations into the picture, helping discover new farming techniques.
- In 1914, the Smith-Lever Act provided cooperative programs to help educate people about food, home economics, community development and agriculture. Related agriculture extension programs helped farmers increase crop production to feed the rapidly growing nation.

In 1870, the Naturalization Act put limits on U.S. citizenship, allowing full citizenship only to whites and those of African descent. The Chinese Exclusion Act of 1882 put limits on Chinese immigration. The Immigration Act of 1882 taxed immigrants, charging fifty cents per person. These funds helped pay administrative costs for regulating immigration. Ellis Island opened in 1892 as a processing center those arriving in New York. 1921 saw the Emergency Quota Act passed, also known as the Johnson Quota Act, which severely limited the number of immigrants allowed into the country.

The time period from the end of the Civil War to the beginning of the First World War is often referred to as the Gilded Age, or the Second Industrial Revolution. The U.S. was changing from an agriculturally based economy to an industrial economy, with rapid growth accompanying the shift. In addition, the country itself was expanding, spreading into the seemingly unlimited West. This time period saw the beginning of banks, department stores, chain stores, and trusts—all familiar

features of our modern-day landscape. Cities also grew rapidly, and large numbers of immigrants arrived in the country, swelling the urban ranks.

> **Review Video: <u>Second Industrial Revolution</u>**
> Visit mometrix.com/academy and enter code: 608455

PROGRESSIVE ERA

From the 1890s to the end of the First World War, Progressives set forth an ideology that drove many levels of society and politics. The Progressives were in favor of workers' rights and safety, and wanted measures taken against waste and corruption. They felt science could help improve society, and that the government could—and should—provide answers to a variety of social problems. Progressives came from a wide variety of backgrounds, but were united in their desire to improve society.

The first large, well-organized strike occurred in 1892. Called the Homestead Strike, it occurred when the Amalgamated Association of Iron and Steel Works struck against the Carnegie Steel Company. Gunfire ensued, and Carnegie was able to eliminate the plant's union. In 1894, workers, led by Eugene Debs, initiated the Pullman Strike after the Pullman Palace Car Co. cut their wages by 28 percent. President Grover Cleveland called in troops to break up the strike on the grounds that it interfered with mail delivery. Mary Harris Jones, also known as Mother Jones, organized the Children's Crusade to protest child labor. A protest march proceeded to the home of President Theodore Roosevelt in 1902. Jones also worked with the United Mine Workers of America, and helped found the Industrial Workers of the World.

A major recession struck the United States during the 1890s, with crop prices falling dramatically. Drought compounded the problems, leaving many American farmers in crippling debt. The Farmers Alliance formed, drawing the rural poor into a single political entity. Recession also affected the more industrial parts of the country. The Knights of Labor, formed in 1869 by Uriah Stephens, was able to unite workers into a union to protect their rights. Dissatisfied by views espoused by industrialists, these two groups, the Farmers Alliance and the Knights of Labor, joined to form the Populist Party. Some of the elements of the party's platform included:

- National currency
- Income tax
- Government ownership of railroads, telegraph and telephone systems
- Secret ballot for voting
- Immigration restriction
- Term limits for President and Vice-President

The Populist Party was in favor of decreasing elitism and making the voice of the common man more easily heard in the political process.

The early twentieth century saw several amendments made to the U.S. Constitution. These included:

- Sixteenth Amendment, 1913 established a graduated income tax.
- Seventeenth Amendment, 1913 allowed direct election of Senators.
- Eighteenth Amendment, 1919 prohibited the sale, production and importation of alcohol. This amendment was later repealed by the Twenty-first Amendment.
- Nineteenth Amendment, 1920 gave women the right to vote.

These amendments largely grew out of the Progressive Era, as many citizens worked to improve American society.

"Muckrakers" was a term used to identify aggressive investigative journalists who brought to light scandals, corruption, and many other wrongs being perpetrated in late nineteenth century society. Among these intrepid writers were:

- Ida Tarbell—he exposed the Standard Oil Trust.
- Jacob Riis—a photographer, he helped improve the lot of the poor in New York.
- Lincoln Steffens—he worked to expose political corruption.
- Upton Sinclair—his book *The Jungle* led to reforms in the meat packing industry.

Through the work of these journalists, many new policies came into being, including workmen's compensation, child labor laws, and trust-busting.

Muckrakers such as Ida Tarbell and Lincoln Steffens brought to light the damaging trend of trusts—huge corporations working to monopolize areas of commerce and so control prices and distribution. The Sherman Act and the Clayton Antitrust Act set out guidelines for competition among corporations and set out to eliminate these trusts. The Federal Trade Commission was formed in order to enforce antitrust measures and ensure companies were operated fairly and did not create controlling monopolies.

Far from a U.S.-centric event, the Panic of 1893 was an economic crisis that affected most of the globe. As a response to the Panic, President Grover Cleveland repealed the Sherman Silver Purchase Act, afraid it had caused the downturn rather than boosting the economy as intended. The Panic led to bankruptcies, with railroads going under and factory unemployment rising as high as 25 percent. In the end, the Republican Party regained power due to the economic crisis.

> **Review Video: The Progressive Era**
> Visit mometrix.com/academy and enter code: 722394

AMERICAN IMPERIALISM

America's westward expansion led to conflict and violent confrontations with Native Americans such as the Battle of Little Bighorn. In 1876, the American government ordered all Indians to relocate to reservations. Lack of compliance led to the Dawes Act in 1887, which ordered assimilation rather than separation. This act remained in effect until 1934. Reformers also forced Indian children to attend Indian Boarding Schools, where they were not allowed to speak their native language and were forced to accept Christianity. Children were often abused in these schools, and were indoctrinated to abandon their identity as Native Americans. In 1890, the massacre at Wounded Knee, accompanied by Geronimo's surrender, led the Native Americans to work to preserve their culture rather than fight for their lands.

The Spanish-American war, 1898-1902, saw a number of Native Americans serving with Teddy Roosevelt in the Rough Riders. Apache scouts accompanied General John J. Pershing to Mexico, hoping to find Pancho Villa. More than 17,000 Native Americans were drafted into service for World War I, though at the time they were not considered as legal citizens. In 1924, Indians were finally granted official citizenship by the Indian Citizenship Act. After decades of relocation, forced assimilation and outright genocide the number of Native Americans in the U.S. has greatly declined. Though many Native Americans have chosen—or have been forced—to assimilate, about 300 reservations exist today, with most of their inhabitants living in abject poverty.

Spain had controlled Cuba since the fifteenth century. Over the centuries, the Spanish had quashed a variety of revolts. In 1886, slavery ended in Cuba, and another revolt was rising. In the meantime, the US had expressed interest in Cuba, offering Spain $130 million for the island in 1853, during Franklin Pierce's presidency. In 1898, the Cuban revolt was underway. In spite of various factions supporting the Cubans, the US President, William McKinley, refused to recognize the rebellion, preferring negotiation over involvement in war. Then The Maine, a US battleship in Havana Harbor, was blown up, costing nearly 300 lives. The US declared war two months later, and the war ended four months later with a Spanish surrender.

Initial work began on the Panama Canal in 1880, though the idea had been discussed since the 1500s. The Canal greatly reduces the length and time needed to sail from one ocean to the other by connecting the Atlantic to the Pacific through the Isthmus of Panama, which joins South America to North America. Before the Canal was built, travelers had to sail all the way around South America to reach the West Coast of the US. The French began the work in 1880, after successfully completing the Suez Canal, connecting the Mediterranean Sea to the Red Sea. However, their efforts quickly fell apart. The US moved in to take over, completing the complex canal in 1914. The Panama Canal was constructed as a lock-and-lake canal, with ships actually lifted on locks to travel from one lake to another over the rugged, mountainous terrain. In order to maintain control of the Canal Zone, the US assisted Panama in its battle for independence from Columbia.

Theodore Roosevelt's famous quote, "Speak softly and carry a big stick," is supposedly of African origins, at least according to Roosevelt. He used this proverb to justify expanded involvement in foreign affairs during his tenure as President. The US military was deployed to protect American interests in Latin America. Roosevelt also worked to maintain an equal or greater influence in Latin America than those held by European interests. As a result, the US Navy grew larger, and the US generally became more involved in foreign affairs. Roosevelt felt that if any country was left vulnerable to control by Europe, due to economic issues or political instability, the US had not only a right to intervene, but was obligated to do so. This led to US involvement in Cuba, Nicaragua, Haiti and the Dominican Republic over several decades leading into the First and Second World Wars.

During William Howard Taft's presidency, Taft instituted "Dollar Diplomacy." This approach was used as a description of American efforts to influence Latin America and East Asia through economic rather than military means. Taft saw past efforts in these areas to be political and warlike, while his efforts focused on peaceful economic goals. His justification of the policy was to protect the Panama Canal, which was vital to US trade interests. In spite of Taft's assurance that Dollar Diplomacy was a peaceful approach, many interventions proved violent. During Latin American revolts, such as those in Nicaragua, the US sent troops to settle the revolutions. Afterwards, bankers moved in to help support the new leaders through loans. Dollar Diplomacy continued until 1913, when Woodrow Wilson was elected President.

Turning away from Taft's "Dollar Diplomacy", Wilson instituted a foreign policy he referred to as "moral diplomacy." This approach still influences American foreign policy today. Wilson felt that representative government and democracy in all countries would lead to worldwide stability. Democratic governments, he felt, would be less likely to threaten American interests. He also saw the US and Great Britain as the great role models in this area, as well as champions of world peace and self-government. Free trade and international commerce would allow the US to speak out regarding world events.

Main elements of Wilson's policies included:

- Maintaining a strong military
- Promoting democracy throughout the world
- Expanding international trade to boost the American economy

WORLD WAR I

The First World War occurred from 1914 to 1918 and was fought largely in Europe. Triggered by the assassination of Austrian Archduke Francis Ferdinand, the war rapidly escalated. At the beginning of the conflict, Woodrow Wilson declared the US neutral. Major events influencing US involvement included:

Sinking of the Lusitania. The British passenger liner RMS Lusitania was sunk by a German U-boat in 1915. Among the 1,000 civilian victims were 100 Americans. Outraged by this act, many Americans began to push for US involvement in the war, using the Lusitania as a rallying cry. Wilson continued to keep the US out of the war, with his 1916 reelection slogan, "He kept us out of war." While he continued to work toward an end of the war, German U-boats began to indiscriminately attack American and Canadian merchant ships carrying supplies to Germany's enemies in Europe. The final event that brought the US into World War I was the interception of the Zimmerman Note. In this telegram, Germany communicated with the Mexican government its intentions to invade the US with Mexico's assistance.

American railroads came under government control in December 1917. The widespread system was consolidated into a single system, with each region assigned a director. This greatly increased the efficiency of the railroad system, allowing the railroads to supply both domestic and military needs. Control returned to private ownership in 1920. In 1918, telegraph, telephone and cable services also came under Federal control, to be returned to private management the next year. The American Red Cross supported the war effort by knitting clothes for Army and Navy troops. They also helped supply hospital and refugee clothing and surgical dressings. Over eight million people participated in this effort.

To generate wartime funds, the US government sold Liberty Bonds. In four issues, they sold nearly $25 billion—more than one fifth of Americans purchased them. After the war, Liberty Bonds were replaced with Victory Bonds.

President Woodrow Wilson proposed Fourteen Points as the basis for a peace settlement to end the war. Presented to the US Congress in January 1918, the Fourteen Points included:

- Five points outlining general ideals
- Eight points to resolve immediate problems of political and territorial nature
- One point proposing an organization of nations with the intent of maintaining world peace

In November of that same year, Germany agreed to an armistice, assuming the final treaty would be based on the Fourteen Points. However, during the peace conference in Paris 1919, there was much disagreement, leading to a final agreement that punished Germany and the other Central Powers much more than originally intended. Henry Cabot Lodge, who had become the Foreign Relations Committee chairman in 1918, wanted an unconditional surrender from Germany. A League of Nations was included in the Treaty of Versailles at Wilson's insistence. The Senate rejected the

Treaty of Versailles, and in the end Wilson refused to concede to Lodge's demands. As a result, the US did not join the League of Nations.

Review Video: WWI Overview
Visit mometrix.com/academy and enter code: 659767

1920s

The post-war '20s saw many Americans moving from the farm to the city, with growing prosperity in the US. The Roaring Twenties, or the Jazz Age, was driven largely by growth in the automobile and entertainment industries. Individuals like Charles Lindbergh, the first aviator to make a solo flight cross the Atlantic Ocean, added to the American admiration of individual accomplishment. Telephone lines, distribution of electricity, highways, the radio, and other inventions brought great changes to everyday life.

World War I created many jobs, but after the war ended these jobs disappeared, leaving many unemployed. In the wake of these employment changes the International Workers of the World and the Socialist Party, headed by Eugene Debs, became more and more visible. Workers initiated strikes in an attempt to regain the favorable working conditions that had been put into place before the war. Unfortunately, many of these strikes became violent, and the actions were blamed on "Reds," or Communists, for trying to spread their views into America. With the Bolshevik Revolution being recent news in Russia, many Americans feared a similar revolution might occur here. The Red Scare ensued, with many individuals jailed for supposedly holding communist, anarchist or socialist beliefs.

The American Civil Liberties Union (ACLU), founded in 1920, grew from the American Union Against Militarism. This former organization helped conscientious objectors avoid going to war during WWI, and also helped those being prosecuted under the Espionage Act (1917) and the Sedition Act (1918), many of whom were immigrants. Their major goals were to protect immigrants and other citizens who were threatened with prosecution for their political beliefs, and to support labor unions, which were also under threat by the government during the Red Scare.

In 1866, Confederate Army veterans came together to fight against Reconstruction in the South, forming a group called the Ku Klux Klan (KKK). With white supremacist beliefs, including anti-Semitism, nativism, anti-Catholicism, and overt racism, this organization relied heavily on violence to get its message across. In 1915, they grew again in power, using a film called *The Birth of a Nation*, by D.W. Griffith, to spread their ideas. In the 1920s, the reach of the KKK spread far into the North and Midwest, and members controlled a number of state governments. Its membership and power began to decline during the Great Depression, but experienced a major resurgence later.

In 1913, the Anti-Defamation League was formed to prevent anti-Semitic behavior and practices. Its actions also worked to prevent all forms of racism, and to prevent individuals from being discriminated against for any reason involving their race. They spoke against the Ku Klux Klan, as well as other racist or anti-Semitic organizations. This organization still exists, and still works to fight discrimination against minorities of all kinds. Marcus Garvey founded the Universal Negro Improvement Association, which became a large and active organization focused on building black nationalism. In 1911, the National Association for the Advancement of Colored People (NAACP) came into being, working to defeat Jim Crow laws. The NAACP also helped prevent racial segregation from becoming federal law, fought against lynchings, helped black soldiers in WWI become officers, and helped defend the Scottsboro Boys, who were unjustly accused of rape.

The Harlem Renaissance saw a number of African American artists settling in Harlem, New York City. This community produced a number of well-known artists and writers, including Langston Hughes, Nella Larson, Zora Neale Hurston, Claude McKay, Countee Cullen and Jean Toomer. The growth of jazz, also largely driven by African Americans, defined the Jazz Age. Its unconventional, improvisational style matched the growing sense of optimism and exploration of the decade. Originating as an offshoot of the blues, jazz began in New Orleans. Some significant jazz musicians were Duke Ellington, Louis Armstrong and Jelly Roll Morton. Big Band and Swing Jazz also developed in the 1920s. Well-known musicians of this movement included Bing Crosby, Frank Sinatra, Count Basie, Benny Goodman, Billie Holiday, Ella Fitzgerald and The Dorsey Brothers.

The National Origins Act (Johnson-Reed Act) placed limitations on immigration. The number of immigrants allowed into the US was based on the population of each nationality of immigrants who were living in the country in 1890. Only two percent of each nationality's 1890 population numbers were allowed to immigrate. This led to great disparities between immigrants from various nations, and Asian immigration was not allowed at all. Some of the impetus behind the Johnson-Reed Act came as a result of paranoia following the Russian Revolution. Fear of communist influences in the US led to a general fear of immigrants.

Review Video: 1920's
Visit mometrix.com/academy and enter code: 124996

GREAT DEPRESSION AND NEW DEAL

The Great Depression, which began in 1929 with the Stock Market Crash, grew out of several factors that had developed over the previous years including:

- Growing economic disparity between the rich and middle-class, with the rich amassing wealth much more quickly than the lower classes
- Disparity in economic distribution in industries
- Growing use of credit, leading to an inflated demand for some goods
- Government support of new industries rather than providing additional support for agriculture
- Risky stock market investments, leading to the stock market crash

Review Video: The Great Depression
Visit mometrix.com/academy and enter code: 635912

Additional factors contributing to the Depression also included the Labor Day Hurricane in the Florida Keys (1935) and the Great Hurricane of 1938, in Long Island, along with the Dust Bowl in the Great Plains, which destroyed crops and resulted in the displacement of as many as 2.5 million people.

Franklin D. Roosevelt was elected president in 1932 with his promise of a "New Deal" for Americans. His goals were to provide government work programs to provide jobs, wages and relief to numerous workers throughout the beleaguered US. Congress gave Roosevelt almost free rein to produce relief legislation. The goals of this legislation were:

- Relief: Accomplished largely by creating jobs
- Recovery: Stimulate the economy through the National Recovery Administration
- Reform: Pass legislation to prevent future similar economic crashes

204

Copyright © Mometrix Media. You have been licensed one copy of this document for personal use only. Any other reproduction or redistribution is strictly prohibited. All rights reserved.

The Roosevelt Administration also passed legislation regarding ecological issues, including the Soil Conservation Service, aimed at preventing another Dust Bowl.

The Roosevelt administration passed several laws and established several institutions to initiate the "reform" portion of the New Deal, including:

- Glass-Steagall Act—separated investment from the business of banking
- Securities Exchange Commission (SEC)—helped regulate Wall Street investment practices, making them less dangerous to the overall economy
- Wagner Act—provided worker and union rights to improve relations between employees and employers. This act was later amended by the Taft-Hartley Act of 1947 and the Landrum Griffin Act of 1959, which further clarified certain elements.
- Social Security Act of 1935—provided pensions as well as unemployment insurance
- Davis-Bacon Act (1931)—provided fair compensation for contractors and subcontractors.
- Walsh-Healey Act (1936)—established a minimum wage, child labor laws, safety standards, and overtime pay.

Other actions focused on insuring bank deposits and adjusting the value of American currency. Most of these regulatory agencies and government policies and programs still exist today.

So-called alphabet organizations set up during Roosevelt's administration included:

- Civilian Conservation Corps (CCC)—provided jobs in the forestry service
- Agricultural Adjustment Administration (AAA)—increased agricultural income by adjusting both production and prices.
- Tennessee Valley Authority (TVA)—organized projects to build dams in the Tennessee River for flood control and production of electricity, resulting in increased productivity for industries in the area, and easier navigation of the Tennessee River
- Public Works Administration (PWA) and Civil Works Administration (CWA)—initiated over 34,000 projects, providing employment
- Works Progress Administration (WPA)—helped unemployed persons to secure employment on government work projects or elsewhere

WORLD WAR II

When war broke out in Europe in 1939, President Roosevelt stated that the US would remain neutral. However, his overall approach was considered "interventionist," as he was willing to provide any necessary aid to the Allies short of actually entering the conflict. Thus, the US supplied a wide variety of war materials to the Allied nations. Isolationists believed the US should not provide any aid to the Allies, including supplies. They felt Roosevelt, by assisting the Allies, was leading the US into a war for which it was not prepared. Led by Charles A. Lindbergh, the Isolationists believed any involvement in the European conflict endangered the US by weakening its national defense.

In 1937, Japan invaded China, prompting the US to halt all exports to Japan. Roosevelt also did not allow Japanese interests to withdraw money held in US banks. In 1941, General Tojo rose to power as the Japanese Premier. Recognizing America's ability to bring a halt to Japan's expansion, he authorized the bombing of Pearl Harbor on December 7, of that year. The US responded by declaring war on Japan. Because of the Tipartite Pact among the Axis Powers, Germany and Italy then declared war on the US, followed by Bulgaria and Hungary.

In 1941, Hitler violated the non-aggression pact he had signed with Stalin in 1939 by invading the USSR. Stalin then joined the Allies. Stalin, Roosevelt and Winston Churchill planned to defeat Germany first, then Japan, bringing the war to an end. Starting in 1942 through 1943, the Allies drove Axis forces out of Africa. In addition, the Germans were soundly defeated at Stalingrad. Between July 1943 and May 1945, Allied troops liberated Italy. June 6, 1944, known as D-Day, the Allies invaded France at Normandy. Soviet troops moved on the eastern front at the same time, driving German forces back. April 25, 1945, Berlin was surrounded by Soviet troops. On May 7, Germany surrendered.

War continued with Japan after Germany's surrender. Japanese forces had taken a large portion of Southeast Asia and the Western Pacific, all the way to the Aleutian Islands in Alaska. General Doolittle bombed several Japanese cities while American troops scored a victory at Midway. Additional fighting in the Battle of the Coral Sea further weakened Japan's position. As a final blow, the US dropped two atomic bombs, one on Hiroshima and the other on Nagasaki, Japan. This was the first time atomic bombs had ever been used in warfare, and the devastation was horrific and demoralizing. Japan surrendered on September 2, 1945.

In 1940, the US passed the Alien Registration Act, which required all aliens older than fourteen to be fingerprinted and registered. They were also required to report changes of address within five days.

Tension between whites and Japanese immigrants in California, which had been building since the beginning of the century, came to a head with the bombing of Pearl Harbor in 1941. Believing that even those Japanese living in the US were likely to be loyal to their native country, the president ordered numerous Japanese to be arrested on suspicion of subversive action isolated in exclusion zones known as War Relocation Camps. Over 120,000 Japanese Americans, two thirds of them citizens of the US, were sent to these camps during the war.

The atomic bomb, developed during WWII, was the most powerful bomb ever invented. A single bomb, carried by a single plane, held enough power to destroy an entire city. This devastating effect was demonstrated with the bombing of Hiroshima and Nagasaki in 1945 in what later became a controversial move, but ended the war. The bombings resulted in as many as 200,000 immediate deaths and many more as time passed after the bombings, mostly due to radiation poisoning. Whatever the arguments against the use of "The Bomb", the post WWII era saw many countries develop similar weapons to match the newly expanded military power of the US. The impact of those developments and use of nuclear weapons continues to haunt international relations today.

Minorities made contributions to the war effort:

- The 442nd Regimental Combat Team consisted of Japanese Americans fighting in Europe for the US. The most highly decorated unit per member in US history, they suffered a 93 percent casualty rate during the war.
- The Tuskegee Airmen were African American aviators, the first black Americans allowed to fly for the military. In spite of not being eligible to become official navy pilots, they flew over 15,000 missions and were highly decorated.
- The Navajo Code Talkers were native Navajo who used their traditional language to transmit information among Allied forces. Because Navajo is a language and not simply a code, the Axis powers were never able to translate it. Use of Navajo Code Talkers to transmit information was instrumental in the taking of Iwo Jima and other major victories of the war.

Women served widely in the military during WWII, working in numerous positions, including the Flight Nurses Corps. Women also moved into the workforce while men were overseas, leading to over 19 million women in the US workforce by 1944. Rosie the Riveter stood as a symbol of these women and a means of recruiting others to take needed positions. Women, as well as their families left behind during wartime, also grew Victory Gardens to help provide food.

In February 1945, Joseph Stalin, Franklin D. Roosevelt and Winston Churchill met in Yalta to discuss the post-war treatment of Europe, particularly Germany. Though Germany had not yet surrendered, its defeat was imminent. After Germany's official surrender, Clement Attlee, Harry Truman and Joseph Stalin met to formalize those plans. This meeting was called the Potsdam Conference.

Basic provisions of these agreements included:

- Dividing Germany and Berlin into four zones of occupation
- Demilitarization of Germany
- Poland remaining under Soviet control
- Outlawing the Nazi Party
- Trials for Nazi leaders
- Relocation of numerous German citizens
- The USSR joined the United Nations, established in 1945
- Establishment of the United Nations Security Council, consisting of the US, the UK, the USSR, China and France

General Douglas MacArthur directed the American military occupation of Japan after the country surrendered. The goals the US occupation included removing Japan's military and making the country a democracy. A 1947 constitution removed power from the emperor and gave it to the people, as well as granting voting rights to women. Japan was no longer allowed to declare war, and a group of 25 government officials were tried for war crimes. In 1951, the US finally signed a peace treaty with Japan. This treaty allowed Japan to rearm itself for purposes of self-defense, but stripped the country of the empire it had built overseas.

Following WWII, the US became the strongest political power in the world, becoming a major player in world affairs and foreign policies. The US determined to stop the spread of Communism, naming itself the "arsenal of democracy." In addition, America had emerged with a greater sense of itself as a single, integrated nation, with many regional and economic differences diminished. The government worked for greater equality and the growth of communications increased contact among different areas of the country.

Both the aftermath of the Great Depression and the necessities of WWII had given the government greater control over various institutions as well as the economy. This also meant the American government took on greater responsibility for the well-being of its citizens, both in the domestic arena, such as providing basic needs, and in protecting them from foreign threats. This increased role of providing basic necessities for all Americans has been criticized by some as "the welfare state."

> **Review Video: World War II**
> Visit mometrix.com/academy and enter code: 759402

COLD WAR AND 1960S

Harry S. Truman took over the presidency from Franklin D. Roosevelt near the end of WW II. He made the final decision to drop atomic bombs on Japan, and he played a major role in the final decisions regarding treatment of post-war Germany. On the domestic front, Truman initiated a 21-point plan known as the Fair Deal. This plan expanded Social Security, provided public housing, and made the Fair Employment Practices Act permanent. Truman helped support Greece and Turkey, under threat from the USSR, supported South Korea against communist North Korea, and helped with recovery in Western Europe. He also participated in the formation of NATO, the North Atlantic Treaty Organization.

After the war, major nations, particularly the US and USSR, rushed to develop the atomic bomb, and later the hydrogen bomb, as well as many other highly advanced weapons systems. These countries seemed determined to outpace each other with the development of numerous, deadly weapons. These weapons were expensive and extremely dangerous, and it is possible that the war between US and Soviet interests remained "cold" due to the fear that one side or the other would use these terrifyingly powerful weapons.

The US made a number of foreign policy acts in the wake of World War II:

- Marshall Plan—sent aid to war-torn Europe after WW II, largely focusing on preventing the spread of communism.
- Containment—proposed by George F. Kennan, Containment focused on containing the spread of Soviet communism.
- Truman Doctrine—Harry S. Truman stated that the US would provide both economic and military support to any country threatened by Soviet takeover.
- National Security Act—passed in 1947, this act created the Department of Defense, the Central Intelligence Agency, and the National Security Council.

The combination of these acts led to the cold war, with Soviet communists attempting to spread their influence and the US and other countries trying to contain or stop this spread.

The lines of East versus West were tightened through military alliances and border restrictions:

- NATO, the North Atlantic Treaty Organization, came into being in 1949. It essentially amounted to an agreement among the US and Western European countries that an attack on any one of these countries was to be considered an attack against the entire group.
- Under the influence of the Soviet Union, the Eastern European countries of USSR, Bulgaria, East Germany, Poland, Romania, Albania, Poland and Czechoslovakia responded with the Warsaw Pact, which created a similar agreement among those nations.
- In 1961, a wall was built to separate Communist East Berlin from democratic West Berlin. A similar, though metaphorical, wall lay between east and west, as well, and was referred to as the Iron Curtain.

The Korean War began in 1950 and ended in 1953. For the first time in history, a world organization—the United Nations—played a military role in a war. North Korea sent Communist troops into South Korea, seeking to bring the entire country under Communist control. The UN sent out a call to member nations, asking them to support South Korea. Truman sent troops, as did many other UN member nations. The war ended three years later with a truce rather than a peace treaty, and Korea remains divided at 38 degrees North Latitude, with Communist rule remaining in the North and a democratic government ruling the South.

Eisenhower carried out a middle-of-the-road foreign policy and brought about several steps forward in equal rights. He worked to minimize tensions during the Cold War, and negotiated a peace treaty with Russia after the death of Stalin. He enforced desegregation by sending troops to

Little Rock, Arkansas when the schools there were desegregated, and also ordered the desegregation of the military. Organizations formed during his administration included the Department of Health, Education and Welfare, and the National Aeronautics and Space Administration (NASA).

Numerous technological advances after the Second World War led to more effective treatment of diseases, more efficient communication and transportation, and new means of generating power. Advances in medicine increased the lifespan of people in developed countries, and near-instantaneous communication began to make the world a much smaller place.

- Discovery of penicillin (1928)
- Supersonic air travel (1947)
- First commercial airline flight (1948)
- Nuclear power (1951)
- Orbital leading to manned space flight (Sputnik—1957)
- First man on the moon (1969)

Although cut short by his assassination, during his term JFK instituted economic programs that led to a period of continuous expansion in the US unmatched since before WW II. He formed the Alliance for Progress and the Peace Corps, organizations intended to help developing nations. He also oversaw the passage of new civil rights legislation, and drafted plans to attack poverty and its causes, along with support of the arts. Kennedy's presidency ended when he was assassinated by Lee Harvey Oswald in 1963.

The Cuban Missile Crisis occurred in 1962, during John F. Kennedy's presidency. Russian Premier Nikita Khrushchev decided to place nuclear missiles in Cuba to protect the island from invasion by the US. American U-2 planes flying over the island photographed the missile bases as they were being built. Tensions rose, with the US concerned about nuclear missiles so close to its shores, and the USSR concerned about American missiles that had been placed in Turkey. Eventually, the missile sites were removed, and a US naval blockade turned back Soviet ships carrying missiles to Cuba. During negotiations, the US agreed to remove their missiles from Turkey and agreed to sell surplus wheat to the USSR. A telephone hot line between Moscow and Washington was set up to allow instant communication between the two heads of state to prevent similar incidents in the future.

Kennedy's Vice President, Lyndon Johnson, assumed the presidency after Kennedy's assassination. He supported civil rights bills, tax cuts, and other wide-reaching legislation that Kennedy had also supported. Johnson saw America as a "Great Society," and enacted legislation to fight disease and poverty, renew urban areas, support education and environmental conservation. Medicare was instituted under his administration. He continued Kennedy's supported of space exploration, and he is also known, although less positively, for his handling of the Vietnam War.

Prior to WW II, the US had been limiting immigration for several decades. After WW II, policy shifted slightly to accommodate political refugees from Europe and elsewhere. So many people were displaced by the war that in 1946, The UN formed the International Refugee Organization to deal with the problem.

In 1948, the US Congress passed the Displaced Persons Act, which allowed over 400,000 European refugees to enter the US, most of them concentration camp survivors and refugees from Eastern Europe. In 1952, the President's Escapee Program allowed refugees from Communist Europe to enter the US, as did the Refugee Relief Act, passed in 1953. At the same time, however, the Internal

Security Act of 1950 allowed deportation of declared Communists, and Asians were subjected to a quota based on race, rather than country of origin. Later changes included:

- 1962—Migration and Refugee Assistance Act—helped assist refugees in need.
- 1965—Immigration Act—ended quotas based on nation of origin.
- 1986—Immigration Reform and Control Act—prohibited the hiring of illegal immigrants, but also granted amnesty to about three million illegals already in the country.

In the 1950s, post-war America was experiencing a rapid growth in prosperity. However, African Americans found themselves left behind. Following the lead of Mahatma Gandhi, who lead similar class struggles in India; African Americans began to demand equal rights. Major figures in this struggle included:

- Rosa Parks—often called the "mother of the Civil Rights Movement," her refusal to give up her seat on the bus to a white man served as a seed from which the movement grew.
- Martin Luther King, Jr.—the best-known leader of the movement, King drew on Gandhi's beliefs and encouraged non-violent opposition. He led a march on Washington in 1963, received the Nobel Peace Prize in 1968, and was assassinated in 1968.
- Malcolm X—espousing less peaceful means of change, Malcolm X became a Black Muslim, and supported black nationalism.
- Stokely Carmichael—Carmichael invented the term "Black Power" and served as head of the Student Nonviolent Coordinating Committee. He believed in black pride and black culture, and felt separate political and social institutions should be developed for blacks.
- Adam Clayton Powell—chairman of the Coordinating Committee for Employment, he led rent strikes and other actions, as well as a bus boycott, to increase the hiring of blacks.
- Jesse Jackson—Jackson was selected to head the Chicago Operation Breadbasket in 1966 by Martin Luther King, Jr., and went on to organize boycotts and other actions. He also had an unsuccessful run for President.

Major events from the Civil Rights Movement include:

- Montgomery Bus Boycott—in 1955, Rosa Parks refused to give her seat on the bus to a white man. As a result, she was tried and convicted of disorderly conduct and of violating local ordinances. A 381-day boycott ensued, protesting segregation on public buses.
- Desegregation of Little Rock—In 1957, after the Supreme Court decision on Brown vs. Board of Education, which declared "separate but equal" unconstitutional, the Arkansas school board voted to desegregate their schools. Even though Arkansas was considered progressive, its governor brought in the National Guard to prevent nine black students from entering Central High School in Little Rock. President Eisenhower responded by federalizing the National Guard and ordering them to stand down.
- Birmingham Campaign—Protestors organized a variety of actions such as sit-ins and an organized march to launch a voting campaign. When the City of Birmingham declared the protests illegal, the protestors, including Martin Luther King, Jr., persisted and were arrested and jailed.

These led to major pieces of legislation:

- Brown vs. Board of Education (1954)—the Supreme Court declared that "separate but equal" accommodations and services were unconstitutional.
- Civil Rights Act of 1964—declared discrimination illegal in employment, education, or public accommodation.

- Voting Rights Act of 1965—ended various activities practiced, mostly in the South, to bar blacks from exercising their voting rights. These included poll taxes and literacy tests.

Several major acts have been passed, particularly since WW II, to protect the rights of minorities in America. In addition to the Civil Rights Act (1964) and the Voting Rights Act (1965) these pieces of legislation were also passed:

- Age Discrimination Act—1978
- Americans with Disabilities Act—1990

Other important movements for civil rights included a prisoner's rights movement, movements for immigrant rights, and the women's rights movement. The National Organization for Women (NOW) was established in 1966 and worked to pass the Equal Rights Amendment. The amendment was passed, but not enough states ratified it for it to become part of the Constitution.

After World War II, the US pledged, as part of its foreign policy, to come to the assistance of any country threatened by Communism. When Vietnam was divided into a Communist North and democratic South, much like Korea before it, the eventual attempts by the North to unify the country under Communist rule led to intervention by the US. On the home front, the Vietnam War became more and more unpopular politically, with Americans growing increasingly discontent with the inability of the US to achieve the goals it had set for the Asian country. When President Richard Nixon took office in 1969, his escalation of the war led to protests at Kent State in Ohio, during which several students were killed by National Guard troops. Protests continued, eventually resulting in the end of the compulsory draft in 1973. In that same year, the US departed Vietnam. In 1975, the south surrendered, and Vietnam became a unified country under Communist rule.

Richard Nixon is best known for illegal activities during his presidency, but other important events marked his tenure as president, including:

- Vietnam War comes to an end
- Improved diplomatic relations between the US and China, and the US and the USSR
- National Environmental Policy Act passed, providing for environmental protection
- Compulsory draft ended
- Supreme Court legalizes abortion in Roe v Wade
- Watergate

The Watergate scandal of 1972 ended Nixon's presidency, when he resigned rather than face impeachment and removal from office.

Gerald Ford was appointed to the vice presidency after Nixon's vice president Spiro Agnew resigned under charges of tax evasion. With Nixon's resignation, Ford became president. Ford's presidency saw negotiations with Russia to limit nuclear arms, as well as struggles to deal with inflation, economic downturn, and energy shortages. Ford's policies sought to reduce governmental control of various businesses and reduce the role of government overall. He also worked to prevent escalation of conflicts in the Middle East.

Jimmy Carter was elected president in 1976. Faced with a budget deficit, high unemployment, and continued inflation, Carter also dealt with numerous matters of international diplomacy including:

- Panama Canal Treaties
- Camp David Accords—negotiations between Anwar el-Sadat, the president of Egypt, and Menachem Begin, the Israeli Prime Minister, leading to a peace treaty between the two nations.
- Strategic Arms Limitation Talks (SALT) and resulting agreements and treaties
- Iran Hostage Crisis—when the Shah of Iran was deposed, an Islamic cleric, the Ayatollah Ruholla Khomeini, came into power. Fifty-three American hostages were taken and held for 444 days in the US Embassy.

Ronald Reagan, at 69, became the oldest American president. The two terms of his administration included notable events such as:

- Reaganomics, also known as supply-side or trickle-down economics, involving major tax cuts in the upper income brackets
- Economic Recovery Tax Act of 1981
- First female justice appointed to the Supreme Court, Sandra Day O'Connor
- Massive increase in the national debt—increased from $600 billion to $3 trillion
- Reduction of nuclear weapons via negotiations with Mikhail Gorbachev
- Loss of the space shuttle Challenger
- Iran-Contra scandal—cover-up of US involvement in revolutions in El Salvador and Nicaragua
- Deregulation of savings and loan industry

In the late 1980s, Mikhail Gorbachev ruled the Soviet Union. He introduced a series of reform programs. Also, during this period, the Berlin Wall came down, ending the separation of East and West Germany. The Soviet Union relinquished its power over the various republics in Eastern Europe, and they became independent nations with their own individual governments. With the end of the USSR, the cold war also came to an end.

RECENT HISTORY

Reagan's presidency was followed by a term under his former Vice President, George H. W. Bush. His run for president included the famous "thousand points of light" speech, which was instrumental in increasing his standing in the election polls.

During Bush's presidency, numerous major international events took place, including:

- Fall of the Berlin wall and Germany's unification
- Panamanian dictator Manuel Noriega captured and tried on drug and racketeering charges
- Dissolution of the Soviet Union
- Gulf War, or Operation Desert Storm, triggered by Iraq's invasion of Kuwait
- Tiananmen Square Massacre in Beijing, China
- Ruby Ridge
- The arrival of the World Wide Web

William Jefferson Clinton was the second president in US history to be impeached, but he was not convicted, and maintained high approval ratings in spite of the impeachment. Major events during his presidency included:

- Family and Medical Leave Act
- Don't Ask Don't Tell, a compromise position regarding homosexuals serving in the military
- North American Free Trade Agreement, or NAFTA
- Defense of Marriage Act
- Oslo Accords
- Siege at Waco, Texas, involving the Branch Davidians led by David Koresh
- Bombing of the Murrah Federal Building in Oklahoma City, Oklahoma
- Troops sent to Haiti, Bosnia and Somalia to assist with domestic problems in those areas

Amidst controversy, George W. Bush, son of George Herbert Walker Bush, became president after William Clinton. The election was tightly contested, and though he did not win the popular vote, he won the electoral vote. In the end a Supreme Court ruling was necessary to resolve the issue. His second term was also tightly contested. However, in the election for his second term, Bush won both the popular and the electoral vote. On 9/11/2001, during his first year in office, Bush's presidency was challenged by the first terrorist attack on American soil when al-Qaeda terrorists flew planes into the World Trade Center, destroying it, and into the Pentagon, causing major damage. This event led to major changes in security in the US, especially regarding airline travel. It also led to US troops being deployed in Afghanistan. Later, Bush initiated war in Iraq with the claim that the country held weapons of mass destruction. On March 20, 2003, the US, along with troops from more than 20 other countries, invaded Iraq. The last months of Bush's administration saw a serious economic meltdown in the US and worldwide. Dramatic increases in oil prices resulted in extreme increases of gasoline prices. This, along with the meltdown of the mortgage industry, created serious and overwhelming economic issues for the Bush administration.

In 2008, Barack Obama, a US Senator from Illinois, became the first African-American president of the United States. He ran an emotional energizing campaign, presenting himself as the stark opposite of his predecessor, a candidate of change who would return the country to economic prosperity while ushering in a new era of government accountability and responsibility. Once elected though, Obama chose to continue many of the same policies begun by Bush, including reinforcement of the wars in Iraq and Afghanistan, use of combat and surveillance drones both domestically and abroad, continued operation of the Guantanamo Bay prison facility, and economic stimulus and bailout packages. During his first term, Obama and his congressional allies managed to pass his signature piece of legislation, the controversial Affordable Care Act, popularly known as Obamacare. Obama was reelected to a second term in 2012.

Economics

BASICS OF ECONOMICS

Economics is the study of the ways specific societies allocate resources to individuals and groups within that society. Also important are the choices society makes regarding what efforts or initiatives are funded and which are not. Since resources in any society are finite, allocation becomes a vivid reflection of that society's values. In general, the economic system that drives an individual society is based on:

- What goods are produced
- How those goods are produced
- Who acquires the goods or benefits from them

Economics consists of two main categories, macroeconomics, which studies larger systems, and microeconomics, which studies smaller systems.

A market economy is based on supply and demand. Demand has to do with what customers want and need, as well as how quantity those consumers are able to purchase based on other economic factors. Supply refers to how much can be produced to meet demand, or how much suppliers are willing and able to sell. Where the needs of consumers meet the needs of suppliers is referred to as a market equilibrium price. This price varies depending on many factors, including the overall health of a society's economy, overall beliefs and considerations of individuals in society, and other factors.

Elasticity—based on how the quantity of a particular product responds to the price demanded for that product. If quantity responds quickly to changes in price, the supply/demand for that product is said to be elastic. If they do not respond quickly, then it is inelastic. Market efficiency—when a market is capable of producing output high enough to meet consumer demand, that market is efficient. Comparative advantage—in the field of international trade, this refers to a country focusing on a specific product that it can produce more efficiently and more cheaply, or at a lower opportunity cost, than another country, thus giving it a comparative advantage in production of that product.

In a market economy, supply and demand are determined by consumers. In a planned economy, a public entity or planning authority makes the decisions about what resources will be produced, how they will be produced, and who will be able to benefit from them. The means of production, such as factories, are also owned by a public entity rather than by private interests. In market socialism, the economic structure falls somewhere between the market economy and the planned economy. Planning authorities determine allocation of resources at higher economic levels, while consumer goods are driven by a market economy.

MICROECONOMICS

While economics generally studies how resources are allocated, microeconomics focuses on economic factors such as the way consumers behave, how income is distributed, and output and input markets. Studies are limited to the industry or firm level, rather than an entire country or society. Among the elements studied in microeconomics are factors of production, costs of production, and factor income. These factors determine production decisions of individual firms, based on resources and costs.

The conditions prevailing in a given market are used to classify markets. Conditions considered include:

- Existence of competition
- Number and size of suppliers
- Influence of suppliers over price
- Variety of available products
- Ease of entering the market

Once these questions are answered, an economist can classify a certain market according to its structure and the nature of competition within the market.

When any of the elements for a successfully competitive market are missing, this can lead to a market failure. Certain elements are necessary to create what economists call "perfect competition." If one of these factors is weak or lacking, the market is classified as having "imperfect competition." Worse than imperfect competition, though, is a market failure. There are five major types of market failure:

1. Competition is inadequate
2. Information is inadequate
3. Resources are not mobile
4. Negative externalities, or side effects
5. Failure to provide public goods

Externalities are side effects of a market that affect third parties. These effects can be either negative or positive.

Every good and service requires certain resources, or inputs. These inputs are referred to as factors of production. Every good and service requires four factors of production:

1. Labor
2. Land
3. Capital
4. Entrepreneurship

These factors can be fixed or variable, and can produce fixed or variable costs. Examples of fixed costs include land and equipment. Variable costs include labor. The total of fixed and variable costs makes up the costs of production.

Factors of production all have an associated factor income. Factors that earn income include:

- Labor—earns wages
- Capital—earns interest
- Land—earns rent
- Entrepreneurs—earn profit

Each factor's income is determined by its contribution. In a market economy, this income is not guaranteed to be equal. How scarce the factor is and the weight of its contribution to the overall production process determines the final factor income.

There are four kinds of market structures in an output market.

- Perfect competition—all existing firms sell an identical product. The firms are not able to control the final price. In addition, there is nothing that makes it difficult to become involved in or leave the industry. Anything that would prevent entering or leaving an industry is called a barrier to entry. An example of this market structure is agriculture.
- Monopoly—a single seller controls the product and its price. Barriers to entry, such as prohibitively high fixed cost structures, prevent other sellers from entering the market.
- Monopolistic competition—a number of firms sell similar products, but they are not identical, such as different brands of clothes or food. Barriers to entry are low.
- Oligopoly—only a few firms control the production and distribution of products, such as automobiles. Barriers to entry are high, preventing large numbers of firms from entering the market.

There are four types of monopolies.

- Natural monopoly—occurs when a single supplier has a distinct advantage over the others
- Geographic monopoly—only one business offers the product in a certain area
- Technological monopoly—a single company controls the technology necessary to supply the product
- Government monopoly—a government agency is the only provider of a specific good or service

The US government has passed several acts to regulate businesses, including:

- Sherman Antitrust Act (1890) — prohibited trusts, monopolies, and any other situations that eliminated competition.
- Clayton Antitrust Act (1914) — prohibited price discrimination.
- Robinson-Patman Act (1936) — strengthened provisions of the Clayton Antitrust Act.

The government has also taken other actions to ensure competition, including requirements for public disclosure. The Securities and Exchange Commission (SEC) requires companies that provide public stock to provide financial reports on a regular basis. Because of the nature of their business, banks are further regulated and required to provide various types of information to the government.

Marketing consists of all of the activity necessary to convince consumers to acquire goods. One major way to move products into the hands of consumers is to convince them that any single product will satisfy a need. The ability of a product or service to satisfy the need of a consumer is called utility.

There are four types of utility:

- Form utility—a product's desirability lies in its physical characteristics.
- Place utility—a product's desirability is connected to its location and convenience.
- Time utility—a product's desirability is determined by its availability at a certain time.
- Ownership utility—a product's desirability is increased because ownership of the product passes to the consumer.

Marketing behavior will stress any or all of the types of utility to the consumer to which the product is being marketed.

Successful marketing depends not only on convincing customers they need the product, but also on focusing the marketing towards those who have a need or desire for the product. Before releasing a product into the general marketplace, many producers will test markets to determine which will be the most receptive to the product.

There are three steps usually taken to evaluate a product's market:

- Market research—researching a market to determine if the market will be receptive to the product.
- Market surveys—a part of market research, market surveys ask specific questions of consumers to help determine the marketability of a product to a specific group.
- Test marketing—releasing the product into a small geographical area to see how it sells. Often test marketing is followed by wider marketing if the product does well.

There are four major elements to any marketing plan.

- Product—any elements pertaining directly to the product, including packaging, presentation, or services to include along with it.
- Price—calculates cost of production, distribution, advertising, etc. as well as the desired profit to determine the final price.
- Place—what outlets will be used to sell the product, whether traditional outlets such as brick and mortar stores or through direct mail or Internet marketing.
- Promotion—ways to let consumers know the product is available, through advertising and other means.

Once these elements have all been determined, the producer can proceed with production and distribution of his product.

Distribution channels determine the route a product takes on its journey from producer to consumer, and can also influenced the final price and availability of the product. There are two major forms of distributions: wholesale and retail. A wholesale distributor buys in large quantities and then resells smaller amounts to other businesses. Retailers sell directly to the consumers rather than to businesses.

In the modern marketplace, additional distribution channels have grown up with the rise of markets such as club warehouse stores as well as purchasing through catalogs or over the Internet. Most of these newer distribution channels bring products more directly to the consumer, eliminating the need for middlemen.

Distribution of income in any society lies in a range from poorest to richest. In most societies, income is not distributed evenly. To determine income distribution, family incomes are ranked, lowest to highest. These rankings are divided into sections called quintiles, which are compared to each other.

The uneven distribution of income is often linked to higher levels of education and ability in the upper classes, but can also be due to other factors such as discrimination and existing monopolies. The income gap in America continues to grow, largely due to growth in the service industry, changes in the American family unit and reduced influence of labor unions. Poverty is defined by comparing incomes to poverty guidelines. Poverty guidelines determine the level of income necessary for a family to function. Those below the poverty line are often eligible for assistance from government agencies.

MACROECONOMICS

Macroeconomics examines economies on a much larger level than microeconomics. While microeconomics studies economics on a firm or industry level, macroeconomics looks at economic trends and structures on a national level. Variables studied in macroeconomics include:

- Output
- Consumption
- Investment
- Government spending
- Net exports

The overall economic condition of a nation is defined as the Gross Domestic Product, or GDP. GDP measures a nation's economic output over a limited time period, such as a year.

Marginal propensity to consume defines the tendency of consumers to increase spending in conjunction with increases in income. In general, individuals with greater income will buy more. As individuals increase their income through job changes or growth of experience, they will also increase spending.

Utility is a term that describes the satisfaction experienced by a consumer in relation to acquiring and using a good or service. Providers of goods and services will stress utility to convince consumers they want the products being presented.

There are two major ways to measure the Gross Domestic Product of a country.

- The expenditures approach calculates the GDP based on how much money is spent in each individual sector.
- The income approach calculates based on how much money is earned in each sector.

Both methods yield the same results and both of these calculation methods are based on four economic sectors that make up a country's macro economy:

- Consumers
- Business
- Government
- Foreign sector

Several factors must be considered in order to accurately calculate the GDP using the incomes approach. Income factors are:

- Wages paid to laborers, or Compensation of Employees
- Rental income derived from land
- Interest income derived from invested capital
- Entrepreneurial income

Entrepreneurial income consists of two forms. Proprietor's Income is income that comes back to the entrepreneur himself. Corporate Profit is income that goes back into the corporation as a whole. Corporate profit is divided by the corporation into corporate profits taxes, dividends, and retained earnings.   Two other figures must be subtracted in the incomes approach. These are indirect business taxes, including property and sales taxes, and depreciation.

Changes in population can affect the calculation of a nation's GDP, particularly since GDP and GNP are generally measure per capita. If a country's economic production is low, but the population is high, the income per individual will be lower than if the income is high and the population is lower.

Also, if the population grows quickly and the income grows slowly, individual income will remain low or even drop drastically. Population growth can also affect overall economic growth. Economic growth requires both consumers to purchase goods and workers to produce them. A population that does not grow quickly enough will not supply enough workers to support rapid economic growth.

Ideally, an economy functions efficiently, with the aggregate supply, or the amount of national output, equal to the aggregate demand, or the amount of the output that is purchased. In these cases, the economy is stable and prosperous. However, economies more typically go through phases.

These phases are:

- Boom—GDP is high and the economy prospers
- Recession—GDP falls, unemployment rises
- Trough—the recession reaches its lowest point
- Recovery—Unemployment lessens, prices rise, and the economy begins to stabilize again

These phases happen often, in cycles that are not necessarily predictable or regular.

When demand outstrips supply, prices are driven artificially high, or inflated. This occurs when too much spending causes an imbalance in the economy. In general, inflation occurs because an economy is growing too quickly. When there is too little spending and supply has moved far beyond demand, a surplus of product results. Companies cut back on production, reduce the number of workers they employ, and unemployment rises as people lose their jobs. This imbalance occurs when an economy becomes sluggish. In general, both these economic instability situations are caused by an imbalance between supply and demand. Government intervention is often necessary to stabilize an economy when either inflation or unemployment becomes too serious.

There are five different forms of unemployment.

- Frictional—when workers change jobs and are unemployed while waiting for a new job.
- Structural—when economical shifts reduce the need for workers.
- Cyclical—when natural business cycles bring about loss of jobs.
- Seasonal—when seasonal cycles reduce the need for certain jobs.
- Technological—when advances in technology result in elimination of certain jobs.

Any of these factors can increase unemployment in certain sectors.

Inflation is classified by the overall rate at which it occurs.

- Creeping inflation—an inflation rate of about one to three percent annually.
- Galloping inflation—a high inflation rate of 100 to 300 percent annually.
- Hyperinflation—an inflation rate over 500 percent annually. Hyperinflation usually leads to complete monetary collapse in a society, as individuals become unable to generate sufficient income to purchase necessary goods.

When an economy becomes too imbalanced, either due to excessive spending or not enough spending, government intervention often becomes necessary to put the economy back on track. Government Fiscal Policy can take several forms, including:

- Monetary policy
- Contractionary policies
- Expansionary policies

Contractionary policies help counteract inflation. These include increasing taxes and decreasing government spending to slow spending in the overall economy. Expansionary policies increase government spending and lower taxes in order to reduce unemployment and increase the level of spending in the economy overall. Monetary policy can take several forms, and affects the amount of funds available to banks for making loans.

Money is used in three major ways:

- As an accounting unit
- As a store of value
- As an exchange medium

In general, money must be acceptable throughout a society in exchange for debts or to purchase goods and services. Money should be relatively scarce, its value should remain stable, and it should be easily carried, durable, and easy to divide up. There are three basic types of money: commodity, representative and fiat. Commodity money includes gems or precious metals. Representative money can be exchanged for items such as gold or silver which have inherent value. Fiat money, or legal tender, has no inherent value but has been declared to function as money by the government. It is often backed by gold or silver, but not necessarily on a one-to-one ratio.

Money in the US is not just currency. When economists calculate the amount of money available, they must take into account other factors such as deposits that have been placed in checking accounts, debit cards and "near moneys" such as savings accounts, that can be quickly converted into cash. Currency, checkable deposits and traveler's checks, referred to as M1, are added up, and then M2 is calculated by adding savings deposits, CDs and various other monetary deposits. The final result is the total quantity of available money.

The Federal Reserve System, also known as the Fed, implements all monetary policy in the US. Monetary policy regulates the amount of money available in the American banking system. The Fed can decrease or increase the amount of available money for loans, thus helping regulate the national economy.

Monetary policies implemented by the Fed are part of expansionary or contractionary monetary policies that help counteract inflation or unemployment. The Discount Rate is an interest rate charged by the Fed when banks borrow money from them. A lower discount rate leads banks to borrow more money, leading to increased spending. A higher discount rate has the opposite effect.

Banks earn their income by loaning out money and charging interest on those loans. If less money is available, fewer loans can be made, which affects the amount of spending in the overall economy.

While banks function by making loans, they are not allowed to loan out all the money they hold in deposit. The amount of money they must maintain in reserve is known as the reserve ratio. If the reserve ratio is raised, less money is available for loans and spending decreases. A lower reserve ratio increases available funds and increases spending. This ratio is determined by the Federal Reserve System.

The Federal Reserve System can also expand or contract the overall money supply through Open Market Operations. In this case, the Fed can buy or sell bonds it has purchased from banks, or from individuals. When they buy bonds, more money is put into circulation, creating an expansionary situation to stimulate the economy. When the Fed sells bonds, money is withdrawn from the system, creating a contractionary situation to slow an economy suffering from inflation. Because of international financial markets, however, American banks often borrow and lend money in markets outside the US. By shifting their attention to international markets, domestic banks and other businesses can circumvent whatever contractionary policies the Fed may have put into place in order to help a struggling economy.

International trade can take advantage of broader markets, bringing a wider variety of products within easy reach. By contrast, it can also allow individual countries to specialize in particular products that they can produce easily, such as those for which they have easy access to raw materials. Other products, more difficult to make domestically, can be acquired through trade with other nations. International trade requires efficient use of native resources as well as sufficient disposable income to purchase native products and imported products. Many countries in the world engage extensively in international trade, but others still face major economic challenges.

Populations are studied by size, rates of growth due to immigration, the overall fertility rate, and life expectancy. For example, though the population of the United States is considerably larger than it was two hundred years ago, the rate of population growth has decreased greatly, from about three percent per year to less than one percent per year. In the US, the fertility rate is fairly low, with most women choosing not to have large families, and life expectancy is high, creating a projected imbalance between older and younger people in the near future. In addition, immigration and the mixing of racially diverse cultures is projected to increase the percentages of Asian, Hispanic and African Americans.

There are five major characteristics of a developing nation.

- Low GDP
- Rapid growth of population
- Economy that depends on subsistence agriculture
- Poor conditions, including high infant mortality rates, high disease rates, poor sanitation, and insufficient housing
- Low literacy rate

Developing nations often function under oppressive governments that do not provide private property rights and withhold education and other rights from women. They also often feature an extreme disparity between upper and lower classes, with little opportunity for lower classes to improve their position.

Economic development occurs in three stages that are defined by the activities that drive the economy:

- Agricultural stage
- Manufacturing stage
- Service sector stage

In developing countries, it is often difficult to acquire the necessary funding to provide equipment and training to move into the advanced stages of economic development. Some can receive help from developed countries via foreign aid and investment or international organizations such as the International Monetary Fund or the World Bank. Having developed countries provide monetary, technical, or military assistance can help developing countries move forward to the next stage in their development.

Developing nations typically struggle to overcome obstacles that prevent or slow economic development. Major obstacles can include:

- Rapid, uncontrolled population growth
- Trade restrictions
- Misused resources, often perpetrated by the nation's government
- Traditional beliefs that can slow or reject change.

Corrupt, oppressive governments often hamper the economic growth of developing nations, creating huge economic disparities and making it impossible for individuals to advance, in turn preventing overall growth. Governments sometimes export currency, called capital flight, which is detrimental to a country's economic development. In general, countries are more likely to experience economic growth if their governments encourage entrepreneurship and provide private property rights.

Rapid growth throughout the world leaves some nations behind, and sometimes spurs their governments to move forward too quickly into industrialization and artificially rapid economic growth.

While slow or nonexistent economic growth causes problems in a country, overly rapid industrialization carries its own issues. Four major problems encountered due to rapid industrialization are:

- Use of technology not suited to the products or services being supplied
- Poor investment of capital
- Lack of time for the population to adapt to new paradigms
- Lack of time to experience all stages of development and adjust to each stage

The knowledge economy is a growing sector in the economy of developed countries, and includes the trade and development of:

- Data
- Intellectual property
- Technology, especially in the area of communications

Knowledge as a resource is steadily becoming more and more important. What is now being called the Information Age may prove to bring about changes in life and culture as significant as those brought on by the Agricultural and Industrial Revolutions.

The growth of the Internet has brought many changes to our society, not the least of which is the ways we do business. Where supply channels used to have to move in certain ways, many of these channels are now bypassed as e-commerce makes it possible for nearly any individual to set up a direct market to consumers, as well as direct interaction with suppliers. Competition is fierce. In many instances e-commerce can provide nearly instantaneous gratification, with a wide variety of products. Whoever provides the best product most quickly often rises to the top of a marketplace. How this added element to the marketplace will affect the economy in the near and not-so-near future remains to be seen. Many industries are still struggling with the best ways to adapt to the rapid, continuous changes.

Related to the knowledge economy is what has been dubbed "cybernomics," or economics driven by e-commerce and other computer-based markets and products. Marketing has changed drastically with the growth of cyber communication, allowing suppliers to connect one-on-one with their customers. Other issues coming to the fore regarding cybernomics include:

- Secure online trade
- Intellectual property rights
- Rights to privacy
- Bringing developing nations into the fold

Review Video: Microeconomics and Macroeconomics
Visit mometrix.com/academy and enter code: 538837

As these issues are debated and new laws and policies developed, the face of many industries continues to undergo drastic change. Many of the old ways of doing business no longer work, leaving industries scrambling to function profitably within the new system.

Geography and the World

BASICS OF GEOGRAPHY

Geography literally means the study of the earth. Geographers study physical characteristics of the earth as well as man-made borders and boundaries. They also study the distribution of life on the planet, such as where certain species of animals can be found, as well as how different forms of life interact.

Major elements of the study of geography include:

- Locations
- Regional characteristics
- Spatial relations
- Natural and manmade forces that change elements of the earth

These elements are studied from regional, topical, physical and human perspectives. Geography also focuses on the origins of the earth as well as the history and backgrounds of different human populations. The study of geography is quite old. Eratosthenes lived in the 3rd century BC in ancient Greece, and mathematically calculated the circumference of the earth. In the 1st century AD, the Greek geographer Strabo wrote a description of the ancient world called *Geographica*. The work consisted of seventeen volumes. The 2nd century AD scientist Ptolemy, primarily an astronomer, was also an experienced mapmaker. His skills also contributed to overall knowledge of the earth's geography through his book *Geographia*.

There are four divisions of geographical study.

- Topical—the study of a single feature of the earth or one specific human activity that occurs world-wide.
- Physical—the various physical features of the earth, how they are created, the forces that change them, and how they are related to each other and to various human activities.
- Regional—specific characteristics of individual places and regions.
- Human—how human activity affects the environment. This includes study of political, historical, social, and cultural activities.

Tools used in geographical study include special research methods like mapping, field studies, statistics, interviews, mathematics, and use of various scientific instruments.

Physical geography is the study of the physical characteristics of the earth, how they relate to each other, how they were formed, and how they develop. These characteristics include climate, land, and water, and also how they affect human populations in various areas. Different landforms in combination with various climates and other conditions determine characteristics of various cultures.

Cultural geography is the study of how the various aspects of physical geography affect individual cultures. Cultural geography also compares various cultures, how their lifestyles and customs are affected by their geographical location, climate, and other factors, and how they interact with their environment.

In cities, towns, or other areas where many people have settled, geographers focus on distribution of populations, neighborhoods, industrial areas, transportation, and other elements important to the society in question. For example, they would map out the locations of hospitals, airports, factories, police stations, schools, and housing groups. They would also make note of how these facilities are distributed in relation to the areas of habitation, such as the number of schools a certain neighborhood, or how many grocery stores are located in a specific suburban area. Another area of study and discussion is the distribution of towns themselves, from widely spaced rural towns to large cities that merge into each other to form a megalopolis.

> **Review Video: Physical vs. Cultural Geography**
> Visit mometrix.com/academy and enter code: 912136

CARTOGRAPHY

A cartographer is a mapmaker. Mapmakers produce detailed illustrations of geographic areas to record where various features are located within that area. These illustrations can be compiled into maps, charts, graphs, and even globes.

There are five main elements of any map.

- Title—tells basic information about the map, such as the area represented.
- Legend—also known as the key, the legend explains what symbols used on a particular map represent, such as symbols for major landmarks.
- Grid—most commonly represents the Geographic Grid System, or latitude and longitude marks used to precisely locate specific locations.
- Directions—a compass rose or other symbol used to indicate the cardinal directions.
- Scale—shows the relation between a certain distance on the map and the actual distance. For example, one inch might represent one mile, or ten miles, or even more depending on the size of the map.

A thematic map is constructed to show very specific information about a chosen theme. For example, a thematic map might represent political information, such as how votes were distributed in an election, or show population distribution or climactic features.

A relief map is constructed to show details of various elevations across the area of the map. Higher elevations are represented by different colors than lower elevations. Relief maps often also show additional details, such as the overall ruggedness or smoothness of an area. Mountains would be represented as ridged and rugged, while deserts would be shown as smooth. Elevation in relief maps can also be represented by contour lines, or lines that connect points of the same elevation. Some relief maps even feature textures, reconstructing details in a sort of miniature model.

When constructing maps, cartographers must take into account the phenomenon of distortion. Because the earth is round, a flat map does not accurately represent the correct proportions, especially if a very large geographical area is being depicted. Maps must be designed in such a way as to minimize this distortion and maximize accuracy. Accurately representing the earth's features on a flat surface is achieved through projection.

An equal area map is designed such that the proportional sizes of various areas are accurate. For example, if one land mass is one-fifth the size of another, the lines on the map will be shifted to accommodate for distortion so that the proportional size is accurate. In many maps, areas farther from the equator are greatly distorted; this type of map compensates for this phenomenon.

A conformal map focuses on representing the correct shape of geographical areas, with less concern for comparative size.

With a consistent scale map, the same scale, such as one inch=ten miles, is used throughout the entire map. This is most often used for maps of smaller areas, as maps that cover larger areas, such as the full globe, must make allowances for distortion. Maps of very large areas often make use of more than one scale, with scales closer to the center representing a larger area than those at the edges.

Types of commonly used map projections:

- Cylindrical projection—created by wrapping the globe of the Earth in a cylindrical piece of paper, then using a light to project the globe onto the paper. The largest distortion occurs at the outermost edges.
- Conical projection—the paper is shaped like a cone and contacts the globe only at the cone's base. This type of projection is most useful for middle latitudes.
- Flat-Plane projections—also known as a Gnomonic projection, this type of map is projected onto a flat piece of paper that only touches the globe at a single point. Flat-plane projections make it possible to map out Great-Circle Routes, or the shortest route between one point and another on the globe, as a straight line.
- Winkel tripel projection—the most common projection used for world maps, since it was accepted in 1998 by the National Geographic Society as a standard. The Winkel tripel projection balances size and shape, greatly reducing distortion.
- Robinson projection—east and west sections of the map are less distorted, but continental shapes are somewhat inaccurate.
- Goode's interrupted equal-area projection—Sizes and shapes are accurate, but distances are not. This projection basically represents a globe that has been cut in a way that allows it to lie flat.
- Mercator projection—though distortion is high, particularly in areas farther from the equator, this cylindrical projection is commonly used by seafarers.

> **Review Video: Cartography and Technology**
> Visit mometrix.com/academy and enter code: 642071

GEOGRAPHICAL FEATURES

There are a number of different ways to categorize geographical features. One way of categorize is by elevation above sea level. Mountains are elevated areas that measure 2,000 feet or more above sea level. Often steep and rugged, they usually occur in groups called chains or ranges. Six of the seven continents on Earth contain at least one range. Hills are of lower elevation than mountains, at about 500-2,000 feet. Hills are usually more rounded, and are found everywhere on Earth. Foothills are the transition area between the plains and the mountains, usually consisting of hills that gradually increase in size as they approach the mountain range. Mesas are flat, steep-sided mountains or hills. The term is sometimes used to refer to plateaus. Plateaus are elevated, but flat on top. Some plateaus are extremely dry, such as the Kenya Plateau, because surrounding mountains prevent them from receiving moisture. Valleys lie between hills and mountains. Depending on where they are located, their specific features can vary greatly, from fertile and habitable to rugged and inhospitable. Plains are large, flat areas and are usually very fertile. The majority of Earth's population is supported by crops grown on the Earth's vast plains. Basins are areas of low elevation where rivers drain.

Another method of categorization is through how much water is present. Deserts receive less than ten inches of rain per year. They are usually large areas, such as the Sahara Desert in Africa or the Australian Outback. Marshes and swamps are also lowlands, but they are very wet and largely covered in vegetation such as reeds and rushes. Deltas occur at river mouths. Because the rivers carry sediment to the deltas, these areas are often very fertile.

There are also different categories for bodies of water. Oceans are the largest bodies of water on Earth. They are salt water, and cover about two-thirds of the earth's surface. The five major oceans are the Atlantic, Pacific, Indian, Arctic, and Southern. Seas are generally also salt water, but are smaller than oceans and surrounded by land.

Examples include the Mediterranean Sea, the Caribbean Sea, and the Caspian Sea. Lakes are bodies of freshwater found inland. Sixty percent of all lakes are located in Canada. Rivers are moving bodies of water that flow from higher elevations to lower. They usually start as rivulets or streams, and grow until they finally empty into a sea or an ocean. Canals, such as the Panama Canal and the Suez Canal, are manmade waterways connecting two large bodies of water.

NATURAL PROCESSES

According to the geological theory of plate tectonics, the earth's crust is made up of ten major and several minor tectonic plates. These plates are the solid areas of the crust. They float on top of the earth's mantle, which is made up of molten rock. Because the plates float on this liquid component of the earth's crust, they move, creating major changes in the earth's surface. These changes can happen very slowly, over time, such as in continental drift, or can happen rapidly, such as when earthquakes occur. Interaction between the different continental plates can create mountain ranges, volcanic activity, major earthquakes, and deep rifts.

Plate tectonics defines three types of plate boundaries, determined by the way in which the edges of the plates interact. These plate boundaries are:

- Convergent boundaries—the bordering plates move toward one another. When they collide directly, this is known as continental collision, which can create very large, high mountain ranges such as the Himalayas and the Andes. If one plate slides under the other, this is called subduction. Subduction can lead to intense volcanic activity. One example is the Ring of Fire that lies along the northern Pacific coastlines.
- Divergent boundaries—plates move away from each other. This movement leads to rifts such as the Mid-Atlantic Ridge and east Africa's Great Rift Valley.
- Transform boundaries—plate boundaries slide in opposite directions against each other. Intense pressure builds up along transform boundaries as the plates grind along each other's edges, leading to earthquakes. Many major fault lines, including the San Andreas Fault, lie along transform boundaries.

Plate tectonics isn't the only natural process which modifies geographical features:

- Erosion involves movement of any loose material on the earth's surface. This can include soil, sand, or rock fragments. These loose fragments can be displaced by natural forces such as wind, water, ice, plant cover, and human factors. Mechanical erosion occurs due to natural forces. Chemical erosion occurs as a result of human intervention and activities.
- Weathering occurs when atmospheric elements affect the earth's surface. Water, heat, ice, and pressure all lead to weathering.

- Transportation refers to loose material being moved by wind, water or ice. Glacial movement, for example, carries everything from pebbles to boulders, sometimes over long distances.
- Deposition is the result of transportation. When material is transported, it is eventually deposited, and builds up to form formations like moraines and sand dunes.

CLIMATES

Weather and climate are physical systems that affect geography. Though they deal with similar information, the way this information is measured and compiled is different. Weather involves daily conditions in the atmosphere that affect temperature, precipitation (rain, snow, hail or sleet), wind speed, air pressure, and other factors. Weather focuses on the short-term—for example what the conditions will be today, tomorrow, or over the next few days. By contrast, climate aggregates information about daily and seasonal weather conditions in a region over a long period of time. The climate takes into account average monthly and yearly temperatures, average precipitation over long periods of time, and the growing season of an area.

Because the earth is tilted, its rotation brings about the changes in seasons. Regions closer to the equator, and those nearest the poles, experience very little change in seasonal temperatures. Mid-range latitudes are most likely to experience distinct seasons. Large bodies of water also affect climate. Ocean currents and wind patterns can change the climate for an area that lies in typically cold latitude, such as England, to a much more temperate climate. Mountains can affect both short-term weather and long-term climates. Some deserts occur because precipitation is stopped by the wall of a mountain range. Over time, established climate patterns can shift and change. While the issue is hotly debated, it has been theorized that human activity has also led to climate change.

Climates are classified according to latitude, or how close they lie to the Earth's equator. The three major divisions are:

- Low Latitudes, lying from 0 to 23.5 degrees latitude
- Middle Latitudes, found from 23.5 to 66.5 degrees
- High Latitudes, found from 66.5 degrees to the poles

Desert, savanna and rainforest climates occur in low latitudes. Rainforest climates, near the equator, experience high average temperatures and humidity, as well as relatively high rainfall. Savannas are found to either side of the rainforest region. Mostly grasslands, they typically experience dry winters and wet summers. Beyond the savannas lie the desert regions, with hot, dry climates, sparse rainfall (less than ten inches per year on average) and temperature fluctuations of up to fifty degrees from day into night.

The climate regions found in the middle latitudes are:

- Mediterranean
- Humid-subtropical
- Humid-continental
- Marine
- Steppe
- Desert

The Mediterranean climate occurs between 30- and 40-degrees latitude, both north and south, and on the western coasts. Characteristics include a year-long growing season, hot, dry summers followed by mild winters, and sparse rainfall that occurs mostly during the winter months. Humid-subtropical regions are located on southeastern coastal areas. Winds that blow in over warm ocean currents produce long summers, mild winters, and a long growing season. These areas are highly productive, and support a larger part of the Earth's population than any other climate. The humid continental climate produces the familiar four seasons typical of a good portion of the US. Some of the most productive farmlands in the world lie in these climates. Winters are cold, summers are hot and humid. Marine climates are found near water or on islands. Ocean winds help make these areas mild and rainy. Summers are cooler than humid-subtropical summers, but winters also bring milder temperatures due to the warmth of the ocean winds. Steppe climates, or prairie climates, are found far inland in large continents. Summers are hot and winters are cold, but rainfall is sparser than in continental climates. Desert climates occur where steppe climates receive even less rainfall. Examples include the Gobi Desert in Asia as well as desert areas of Australia and the southwestern US.

The high latitudes consist of two major climate areas, the tundra and taiga. Tundra means marshy plain. Ground is frozen throughout long, cold winters, but there is little snowfall. During the short summers, it becomes wet and marshy. Tundras are not amenable to crops, but many plants and animals have adapted to the conditions. Taigas lie south of tundra regions, and include the largest forest areas in the world, as well as swamps and marshes. Large mineral deposits exist here, as well as many animals valued for their fur. In the winter, taiga regions are colder than the tundra, and summers are hotter. The growing season is short.

A vertical climate exists in high mountain ranges. Increasing elevation leads to varying temperatures, growing conditions, types of vegetation and animals, and occurrence of human habitation, often encompassing elements of various other climate regions.

> **Review Video: Climates**
> Visit mometrix.com/academy and enter code: 991320

ENVIRONMENTAL GEOGRAPHY

Ecology is the study of the way living creatures interact with their environment. Biogeography explores the way physical features of the earth affect living creatures. Ecology bases its studies on three different levels of the environment. These are:

- Ecosystem—a specific physical environment and all the organisms that live there.
- Biomes—a group of ecosystems, usually consisting of a large area with similar flora and fauna as well as similar climate and soil. Examples of biomes include deserts, tropical rain forests, taigas, and tundra.
- Habitat—an area in which a specific species usually lives. The habitat includes the necessary soil, water, and resources for that particular species, as well as predators and other species that compete for the same resources.

Biodiversity refers to the variety of habitats that exist on the planet, as well as the variety of organisms that can exist within these habitats. A greater level of biodiversity makes it more likely that an individual habitat will flourish along with the species that depend upon it. Changes in habitat, including climate change, human intervention, or other factors, can reduce biodiversity by causing the extinction of certain species.

Different interactions occur among species and members of single species within a habitat. These interactions fall into three categories:

- Competition
- Predation
- Symbiosis

Competition occurs when different animals, either of the same species or of different species, compete for the same resources. Robins can compete with other robins for available food, but other insectivores also compete for these same resources.

Predation occurs when one species depends on the other species for food, such as a fox who subsists on small mammals.

Symbiosis occurs when two different species exist in the same environment without affecting the other. Some symbiotic relationships are beneficial to one or both organisms without harm occurring to either.

If a species is relocated from one habitat to another, it must adapt in order to survive. Some species are more capable of adapting than others. Those that cannot adapt will not survive. There are different ways a creature can adapt, including behavior modification as well as structure or physiological changes. Adaptation is also vital if an organism's environment changes around it. Although the creature has not been relocated, it finds itself in a new environment that requires changes in order to survive. The more readily an organism can adapt, the more likely it is to survive. The almost infinite ability of humans to adapt is a major reason why they are able to survive in almost any habitat in any area of the world.

The agricultural revolution led human societies to begin changing their surroundings in order to accommodate their needs for shelter and room to cultivate food and to provide for domestic animals. Clearing ground for crops, redirecting waterways for irrigation purposes, and building permanent settlements all create major changes in the environment. Large-scale agriculture can lead to loose topsoil and damaging erosion. Building large cities leads to degraded air quality, water pollution from energy consumption, and many other side effects that can severely damage the environment. Recently, many countries have taken action by passing laws to reduce human impact on the environment and reduce the potentially damaging side effects. This is called environmental policy.

HUMAN GEOGRAPHY

The agricultural revolution began six thousand years ago when the plow was invented in Mesopotamia. Using a plow drawn by animals, people were able to cultivate crops in large quantities rather than gathering available seeds and grains and planting them by hand. Because large-scale agriculture was labor intensive, this led to the development of stable communities where people gathered to make farming possible. As stable farming communities replaced groups of nomadic hunter-gatherers, human society underwent profound changes. Societies became dependent on limited numbers of crops as well as subject to the vagaries of weather. Trading livestock and surplus agricultural output led to the growth of large-scale commerce and trade routes.

Communities, or groups of people who settle together in a specific area, typically gather where certain conditions exist. These conditions include:

- Easy access to resources such as food, water, and raw materials
- Ability to easily transport raw materials and goods, such as access to a waterway
- Room to house a sufficient work force

People also tend to form groups with others who are similar to them. In a typical community, people can be found who share values, a common language, and common or similar cultural characteristics and religious beliefs. These factors will determine the overall composition of a community as it develops.

Cities develop and grow as an area develops. Modern statistics show over half of the world's people living in cities. That percentage is even higher in developed areas of the globe. Cities are currently growing more quickly in developing regions, and even established cities continue to experience growth throughout the world.

In developing or developed areas, cities often are surrounded by a metropolitan area made up of both urban and suburban sections. In some places, cities have merged into each other and become a megalopolis, or a single, huge city.

Cities develop differently in different areas of the world. The area available for cities to grow, as well as cultural and economic forces, drives how cities develop. For example, North American cities tend to cover wider areas. European cities tend to have better developed transportation systems. In Latin America, the richest inhabitants can be found in the city centers, while in North America wealthier inhabitants tend to live in suburban areas.

In other parts of the world, transportation and communication between cities is less developed. Recent technological innovations such as the cell phone have increased communication even in these areas. Urban areas must also maintain communication with rural areas in order to procure food, resources and raw materials that cannot be produced within the city limits.

Human societies and their interaction have led to divisions of territories into countries and various other subdivisions. While these divisions are at their root artificial, they are important to geographers in the discussion of interactions of various populations.

Geographical divisions often occur through conflict between different human populations. The reasons behind these divisions include:

- Control of resources
- Control of important trade routes
- Control of populations

Conflict often occurs due to religious or political differences, language differences, or race differences. Natural resources are finite and so often lead to conflict over how they are distributed among populations.

State sovereignty recognizes the division of geographical areas into areas controlled by various governments or groups of people. These groups control not only the territory, but also all its natural resources and the inhabitants of the area. The entire planet Earth is divided into political or administratively sovereign areas recognized to be controlled by a particular government with the exception of the continent of Antarctica.

Alliances form between different countries based on similar interests, political goals, cultural values, or military issues. Six existing international alliances include:

- North Atlantic Treaty Organization (NATO)
- Common Market
- European Union (EU)
- United Nations (UN)
- Caribbean Community
- Council of Arab Economic Unity

In addition, very large companies and multi-national corporations can create alliances and various kinds of competition based on the need to control resources, production, and the overall marketplace.

HUMAN SYSTEMS

Geography also studies the way people interact with, use and change their environment. The effects, reasons and consequences of these changes are studied, as are the ways the environment limits or influences human behavior. This kind of study can help determine the best course of action when a nation or group of people are considering making changes to the environment, such as building a dam or removing natural landscape to build or expand roads. Study of the consequences can help determine if these actions are manageable and how long-term detrimental results can be mitigated.

Human systems affect geography in the way in which they settle, form groups that grow into large-scale habitations, and even create permanent changes in the landscape. Geographers study movements of people, how they distribute goods among each other and to other settlements or cultures, and how ideas grow and spread. Migrations, wars, forced relocations, and trade all can spread cultural ideas, language, goods and other practices to wide-spread areas. Some major migrations or the conquering of one people by another have significantly changed cultures throughout history. In addition, human systems can lead to various conflicts or alliances to control access to and the use of natural resources.

North America consists of 23 countries, including (in decreasing population order) the United States of America, Mexico, Canada, Guatemala, Cuba, Dominican Republic, and Haiti. The USA and Canada support similarly diverse cultures, as both were formed from groups of native races as well as large numbers of immigrants. Many North American cultures come from a mixture of indigenous and colonial European influences. Agriculture is important to North American countries, while service industries and technology also play a large part in the economy. On average, North America supports a high standard of living and a high level of development and supports trade with countries throughout the world.

Including Brazil (largest in area and population), Columbia, Argentina, Venezuala, Peru, and 10 more countries or territories, South America is largely defined by its prevailing languages. The majority of countries in South America speak Spanish or Portuguese. Most of South America has experienced a similar history, having been originally dominated by Native cultures, conquered by European nations. The countries of South America have since gained independence, but there is a wide disparity between various countries' economic and political factors. Most South American countries rely on only one or two exports, usually agricultural, with suitable lands often controlled by rich families. Most societies in South America feature major separations between classes, both economically and socially. Challenges faced by developing South American countries include geographical limitations, economic issues, and sustainable development, including the need to preserve the existing rainforests.

Europe contains a wide variety of cultures, ethnic groups, physical geographical features, climates, and resources, all of which have influenced the distribution of its varied population. Europe in general is industrialized and developed, with cultural differences giving each individual country its own unique characteristics. Greek and Roman influences played a major role in European culture, as did Christian beliefs. European countries spread their beliefs and cultural elements throughout the world by means of migration and colonization. They have had a significant influence on nearly every other continent in the world. While Western Europe has been largely democratic, Eastern Europe functioned under Communist rule for many years. The recent formation of the European Union (EU) has increased stability and positive diplomatic relations among European nations. Like other industrialized regions, Europe is now focusing on various environmental issues.

After numerous conflicts, Russia became a Communist state, known as the USSR. With the collapse of the USSR in 1991, the country has struggled in its transition to a market driven economy. Attempts to build a workable system have led to the destruction of natural resources as well as problems with nuclear power, including accidents such as Chernobyl. To complete the transition to a market economy, Russia needs to improve its transportation and communication systems, and find a way to more efficiently use its natural resources. The population of Russia is not distributed evenly, with three quarters of the population living west of the Ural Mountains. The people of Russia encompass over a hundred different ethnic groups. Over eighty percent of the population is ethnically Russian, and Russian is the official language of the country.

The largely desert climate of North Africa, Southwest Asia, and Central Asia has led most population centers to arise around sources of water, such as the Nile River. This area is the home of the earliest known civilizations and the place of origin for Christianity, Judaism, and Islam. After serving as the site of huge, independent civilizations in ancient times, North Africa and Southwest and Central Asia were largely parceled out as European Colonies during the eighteenth and nineteenth centuries. The beginning of the twentieth century saw many of these countries gain their independence. Islam has served as a unifying force for large portions of these areas, and many of the inhabitants speak Arabic. In spite of the arid climate, agriculture is a large business, but the most valuable resource is oil. Centuries of conflict throughout this area has led to ongoing political problems. These political problems have also contributed to environmental issues.

South of the Sahara Desert, Africa is divided into a number of culturally diverse nations. The inhabitants are unevenly distributed due to geographical limitations that prevent settlement in vast areas. AIDS has become a major plague throughout this part of Africa, killing millions, largely due to restrictive beliefs that prevent education about the disease, as well as abject poverty and unsettled political situations that make it impossible to manage the pandemic. The population of this area of Africa is widely diverse due to extensive migration. Many of the people still rely on subsistence farming for their welfare. Starvation and poverty are rampant due to drought and political instability. Some areas are far more stable than others due to greater availability of resources. These have been able to begin the process of industrialization.

South Asia is home to one of the first human civilizations, which grew up in the Indus River Valley. With a great deal of disparity between rural and urban life, South Asia has much to do to improve the quality of life for its lower classes. Two major religions, Hinduism and Buddhism, have their origins in this region. Parts of South Asia, most notably India, were subject to British rule for several centuries, and are still working to improve independent governments and social systems. Overall, South Asia is very culturally diverse, with a wide mix of religions and languages throughout. Many individuals are farmers, but a growing number have found prosperity in the spread of high-tech industries. Industrialization is growing in South Asia, but continues to face environmental, social, religious and economic challenges.

Governments in East Asia are varied, ranging from communist to democratic governments, with some governments that mix both approaches. Isolationism throughout the area limited the countries' contact with other nations until the early twentieth century. The unevenly distributed population of East Asia consists of over one and a half billion people with widely diverse ethnic backgrounds, religions and languages. More residents live in urban areas than in rural areas, creating shortages of farm workers for some. Japan, Taiwan and South Korea are overall more urban, while China and Mongolia are more rural. Japan stands as the most industrial country of East Asia. Some areas of East Asia are suffering from major environmental issues. Japan has dealt with many of these problems and now has some of the strictest environmental laws in the world.

Much of Southeast Asia was colonized by European countries during the eighteenth and nineteenth centuries, with the exception of Siam, now known as Thailand. All the countries of the area are now independent, but the twentieth century saw numerous conflicts between communist and democratic forces. Southeast Asia has been heavily influenced by both Buddhist and Muslim religions. Industrialization is growing, with the population moving in large numbers from rural to urban areas. Some have moved to avoid conflict, oppression, and poverty. Natural disasters, including volcanoes, typhoons and flash flooding, are fairly common in Southeast Asia, creating extensive economic damage and societal disruption.

South Pacific cultures originally migrated from Southeast Asia, creating hunter-gatherer or sometimes settled agricultural communities. European countries moved in during later centuries, seeking the plentiful natural resources of the area. Today, some South Pacific islands remain under the control of foreign governments, and culture in these areas mix modern, industrialized society and indigenous culture. Population is unevenly distributed, largely due to the inhabitability of many parts of the South Pacific, such as the extremely hot desert areas of Australia. Agriculture still drives much of the economy, with tourism growing. Antarctica remains the only continent not claimed by a single country. There are no permanent human habitations in Antarctica, but scientists and explorers visit the area on a temporary basis.

REGIONAL GEOGRAPHY

The largest amount of North America is the USA and Canada, which have a similar distribution of geographical features, mountain ranges in both east and west, stretches of fertile plains through the center, and lakes and waterways. Both areas were shaped by glaciers, which also deposited highly fertile soil. Because they are so large, Canada and the USA experience several varieties of climate, including continental climates with four seasons in median areas, tropical climates in the southern part of the USA, and arctic climes in the far north. The remaining area of North America is comprised primarily of many Islands, including the Caribbean Isles and Greenland.

South America contains a wide variety of geographical features including high mountains such as the Andes, wide plains, and high-altitude plateaus. The region contains numerous natural resources, but many of them have remained unused due to various obstacles, including political issues, geographic barriers, and lack of sufficient economic power. Climate zones in South America are largely tropical, with rainforests and savannahs, but vertical climate zones and grasslands are also included.

Europe spans a wide area with a variety of climate zones. In the east and south are mountain ranges, while the north is dominated by a plains region. The long coastline and the island nature of some countries, such as Britain, mean the climate is often warmer than other lands at similar latitudes, as the area is warmed by ocean currents. Many areas of western Europe have a moderate climate, while areas of the south are dominated by the classic Mediterranean climate. Europe carries a high level of natural resources. Numerous waterways help connect the inner regions with the coastal areas. Much of Europe is industrialized, and agriculture has existed in the area for thousands of years.

Russia's area encompasses part of Asia and Europe. From the standpoint of square footage alone, Russia is the largest country in the world. Due to its size Russia encompasses a wide variety of climatic regions, including plains, plateaus, mountains and tundra. Russia's climate can be quite harsh, with rivers that are frozen through most of the year making transportation of the country's rich natural resources more difficult. Siberia, in the north of Russia, is dominated by permafrost. Native peoples in this area still live hunting and gathering existence, live in portable yurts and subsisting largely on herds of reindeer or caribou. Other areas include taiga with extensive, dense woods in north central Russia and more temperate steppes and grasslands in the southwest.

North Africa, Southwest Asia, and Central Asia is complex in its geographical structure and climate, incorporating seas, peninsulas, rivers, mountains, and numerous other features. Earthquakes remain common, with tectonic plates in the area remaining active. Much of the world's oil lies in this area. The tendency of the large rivers of North Africa, especially the Nile, to follow a set pattern of drought and extreme fertility, led people to settle there from prehistoric times. As technology has advanced, people have tamed this river, making its activity more predictable and the land around it more productive. The extremely arid nature of many other parts of this area has also led to human intervention such as irrigation to increase agricultural production.

South of the Sahara Desert, the high elevations and other geographical characteristics have made it very difficult for human travel or settlement to occur. The geography of the area is dominated by a series of plateaus. There are also mountain ranges and a large rift valley in the eastern part of the continent. Contrasting the wide desert areas, Sub-Saharan Africa contains numerous lakes, rivers, and world-famous waterfalls. The area contains tropical climates, including rain forests, as well as savannahs, steppes, and desert areas. The main natural resources are minerals, including gems, and water.

The longest alluvial plain, a plain caused by shifting floodplains of major rivers and river systems over time, exists in South Asia. South Asia boasts three major river systems in the Ganges, Indus and Brahmaputra. It also has large deposits of minerals, including iron ore that are in great demand internationally. South Asia holds mountains, plains, plateaus, and numerous islands. The climates range from tropical to highlands and desert areas. South Asia also experiences monsoon winds that cause a long rainy season. Variations in climate, elevation and human activity influence agricultural production.

East Asia includes North and South Korea, Mongolia, China, Japan and Taiwan. Mineral resources are plentiful but not evenly distributed throughout. The coastlines are long, and while the population is large, farmlands are sparse. As a result, the surrounding oceans have become a major source of sustenance. East Asia is large enough to also encompass several climate regions. Ocean currents provide milder climates to coastal areas, while monsoons provide the majority of the rainfall for the region. Typhoons are somewhat common, as are earthquakes, volcanoes and tsunamis. The latter occur because of the tectonic plates that meet beneath the continent, and remain somewhat active.

Southeast Asia lies largely on the equator, and roughly half of the countries of the region are island nations. These countries include Indonesia, Philippines, Vietnam, Thailand, Myanmar, and Malaysia. Malaysia is partially on the mainland and partially an island country. The island nations of Southeast Asia feature mountains that are considered part of the Ring of Fire, an area where tectonic plates remain quite active, leading to extensive volcanic activity as well as earthquakes and tsunamis. Southeast Asia boasts many rivers as well as abundant natural resources, including gems, fossil fuels and minerals. There are basically two seasons—wet and dry. The wet season arrives with the monsoons. In general, Southeast Asia consists of tropical rainforest climates, but there are some mountain areas and tropical savannas.

In the far southern hemisphere of the globe, Australia and Oceania present their own climatic combinations. Australia, the only island on earth that is also a continent, has extensive deserts as well as mountains and lowlands. The economy is driven by agriculture, including ranches and farms, and minerals. While the steppes bordering extremely arid inland areas are suitable for livestock, only the coastal areas receive sufficient rainfall for crops without using irrigation. Oceania refers to literally thousands of Pacific islands, created by volcanic activity. Most of these have tropical climates with wet and dry seasons. New Zealand, Australia's nearest neighbor, boasts rich forests as well as mountain ranges and relatively moderate temperatures, including rainfall throughout the year. Antarctica is covered with ice. Its major resource consists of scientific information. It supports some wildlife, such as penguins, and little vegetation, mostly mosses or lichens.

> **Review Video: Regional Geography**
> Visit mometrix.com/academy and enter code: 350378

ANTHROPOLOGY AND ARCHEOLOGY

Anthropology is the study of human culture. Anthropologists study groups of humans, how they relate to each other, and the similarities and differences between these different groups and cultures. Anthropological research takes two approaches: cross-cultural research and comparative research. Most anthropologists work by living among different cultures and participating in those cultures in order to learn about them.

There are three major divisions within anthropology:

- Biological and cultural anthropology
- Archaeology
- Linguistics

Archeology studies past human cultures by evaluating what they leave behind. This can include bones, buildings, art, tools, pottery, graves, and even trash. Archeologists maintain detailed notes and records of their findings and use special tools to evaluate what they find. Photographs, notes, maps, artifacts, and surveys of the area can all contribute to evaluation of an archeological site. By studying all these elements of numerous archeological sites, scientists have been able to theorize that humans or near-humans have existed for about 600,000 years. Before that, more primitive humans are believed to have appeared about one million years ago. These humans eventually developed into Cro-Magnon man, and then Homo sapiens, or modern man.

Prehistory is the period of human history before writing was developed. The three major periods of prehistory are:

- Lower Paleolithic—Humans used crude tools.
- Upper Paleolithic—Humans began to develop a wider variety of tools. These tools were better made and more specialized. They also began to wear clothes, organize in groups with definite social structures, and to practice art. Most lived in caves during this time period.
- Neolithic—Social structures became even more complex, including growth of a sense of family and the ideas of religion and government. Humans learned to domesticate animals and produce crops, build houses, start fires with friction tools, and to knit, spin and weave.

Early human development has been divided into several phases:

- Lower Paleolithic or Old Stone Age, about one million years ago—early humans used tools like needles, hatchets, awls, and cutting tools.
- Upper Paleolithic or New Stone Age, 6,000-8,000 BCE—also known as the Neolithic, textiles and pottery are developed. Humans of this era discovered the wheel, began to practice agriculture, made polished tools, and had some domesticated animals.
- Bronze Age, 3,000 BCE—metals are discovered and the first civilizations emerge as humans become more technologically advanced.
- Iron Age, 1,200-1,000 BCE—metal tools replace stone tools as humans develop knowledge of smelting.

EARLY CIVILIZATIONS

The earliest civilizations are also referred to as fluvial civilizations because they were founded near rivers. Rivers and the water they provide were vital to these early groupings, offering:

- Water for drinking and cultivating crops
- A gathering place for wild animals that could be hunted
- Easily available water for domesticated animals
- Rich soil deposits as a result of regular flooding

Irrigation techniques helped direct water where it was most needed, to sustain herds of domestic animals and to nourish crops of increasing size and quality.

Civilizations are defined as having the following characteristics:

- Use of metal to make weapons and tools
- Written language
- A defined territorial state
- A calendar

The earliest civilizations developed in river valleys where reliable, fertile land was easily found, including:

- Nile River valley in Egypt
- Mesopotamia
- Indus River
- Hwang Ho in China

The very earliest civilizations developed in the Tigris-Euphrates valley in Mesopotamia, which is now part of Iraq, and in Egypt's Nile valley. These civilizations arose between 4,000 and 3,000 BCE. The area where these civilizations grew is known as the Fertile Crescent. There, geography and the availability of water made large-scale human habitation possible.

James Breasted, an archeologist from the University of Chicago, coined the term Fertile Crescent to describe the area in the Near East where the earliest civilizations arose. The region includes modern day Iraq, Syria, Lebanon, Israel/Palestine and Jordan. It is bordered on the south by the Arabian Desert, the west by the Mediterranean Sea, and to the north and east by the Taurus and Zagros Mountains respectively. This area not only provided the raw materials for the development of increasingly advanced civilizations, but also saw waves of migration and invasion, leading to the earliest wars and genocides as groups conquered and absorbed each other's cultures and inhabitants.

The major civilizations of Mesopotamia (Fertile Crescent), in what is now called the Middle East, were:

- Sumerians
- Amorites
- Hittites
- Assyrians
- Chaldeans
- Persians

These cultures controlled different areas of Mesopotamia during various time periods, but were similar in that they were autocratic. This meant a single ruler served as the head of the government and often, the main religious ruler, as well. These, often tyrannical, militaristic leaders, controlled all aspects of life, including law, trade, and religious activity. Portions of the legacies of these civilizations remain in cultures today. These include mythologies, religious systems, mathematical innovations and even elements of various languages.

Sumer, located in the southern part of Mesopotamia, consisted of a dozen city-states. Each city-state had its own gods, and the leader of each city-state also served as the high priest. Cultural legacies of Sumer include:

- The invention of writing
- Invention of the wheel
- The first library—established in Assyria by Ashurbanipal
- The Hanging Gardens of Babylon—one of the Seven Wonders of the Ancient World
- First written laws—Ur-Nammu's Codes and the Codes of Hammurabi
- The *Epic of Gilgamesh*—the first epic story in history

The Egyptians were one of the most advanced ancient cultures, having developed construction methods to build the great pyramids, as well as a form of writing known as hieroglyphics. Their religion was highly developed and complex, and included advanced techniques for the preservation of bodies after death. They also made paper by processing papyrus, a plant commonly found along the Nile, invented the decimal system, devised a solar calendar, and advanced overall knowledge of arithmetic and geometry.

Review Video: Egyptians
Visit mometrix.com/academy and enter code: 398041

The Sumerians were the first to invent the wheel, and also brought irrigation systems into use. Their cuneiform writing was simpler than Egyptian hieroglyphs, and they developed the timekeeping system we still use today. The Babylonians are best known for the Code of Hammurabi, an advanced law code.

The Assyrians developed horse-drawn chariots and an organized military.

Review Video: Early Mesopotamia: The Sumerians
Visit mometrix.com/academy and enter code: 939880

The Hittites were centered in what is now Turkey, but their empire extended into Palestine and Syria. They conquered the Babylonian civilization, but adopted their religion and their system of laws. Overall, the Hittites tended to tolerate other religions, unlike many other contemporary cultures, and absorbed foreign gods into their own belief systems rather than forcing their religion onto peoples they conquered. The Hittite Empire reached its peak in 1600-1200 BCE. After a war with Egypt, which weakened them severely, they were eventually conquered by the Assyrians in 700 BCE.

A whole range of religions were practiced throughout the region and time period. The Hebrew or ancient Israelite culture developed the monotheistic religion that eventually developed into modern Judaism and Christianity. The Persians were conquerors, but those they conquered were allowed to keep their own laws, customs, and religious traditions rather than being forced to accept those of their conquerors. They also developed an alphabet and practicing Zoroastrianism, Mithraism and Gnosticism, religions that have influenced modern religious practice. The Minoans used a syllabic writing system and built large, colorful palaces. These ornate buildings included sewage systems, running water, bathtubs, and even flush toilets. Their script, known as Linear Script A, has yet to be deciphered. The Mycenaeans practiced a religion that grew into the Greek pantheon, worshipping Zeus and other Olympian gods. They developed Linear Script B, a writing system used to write an ancient form of classical Greek.

The Minoans lived on the island of Crete, just off the coast of Greece. This civilization reigned from 2700 to 1450 BCE. The Minoans developed writing systems known to linguists as Linear A and Linear B. Linear A has not yet been translated; Linear B evolved into classical Greek script. "Minoans" is not the name they used for themselves, but is instead a variation on the name of King Minos, a king in Greek mythology believed by some to have been a denizen of Crete. The Minoan civilization subsisted on trade, and their way of life was often disrupted by earthquakes and volcanoes. Much is still unknown about the Minoans, and archeologists continue to study their architecture and archeological remains. The Minoan culture eventually fell to Greek invaders and was supplanted by the Mycenaean civilization.

The Mycenaean civilization was the first major civilization in Europe. In contrast to the Minoans, whom they displaced, the Mycenaeans relied more on conquest than on trade. Mycenaean states included Sparta, Metropolis and Corinth. The history of this civilization, including the Trojan War, was recorded by the Greek poet, Homer. His work was largely considered mythical until archeologists discovered evidence of the city of Troy in Hisarlik, Turkey. Archeologists continue to add to the body of information about this ancient culture, translating documents written in Linear B, a script derived from the Minoan Linear A. It is theorized that the Mycenaean civilization was eventually destroyed in either a Dorian invasion or an attack by Greek invaders from the north. This theory has not been proven, nor is it certain who the invaders might have been.

A Dorian invasion does not refer to an invasion by a particular group of people, but rather is a hypothetical theory to explain the end of the Mycenaean civilization and the growth of classical Greece. Ancient tradition refers to these events as "the return of the Heracleidae," or the sons (descendents) of Hercules. Archeologists and historians still do not know exactly who conquered the Mycenaean, but it is believed to have occurred around 1200 BCE, contemporaneous with the destruction of the Hittite civilization in what is now modern Turkey. The Hittites speak of an attack by people of the Aegean Sea, or the "Sea People." Only Athens was left intact.

Skilled seafarers and navigators, the Phoenicians used the stars to navigate their ships at night. They developed a purple dye that was in great demand in the ancient world, and worked with glass and metals. They also devised their own phonetic alphabet, using symbols to represent individual sounds rather than whole words or syllables.

In ancient China, human civilization developed along the Yangtze and Yellow Rivers., starting as long as 500,000 years ago. These people produced silk, grew millet, and made pottery, including Longshan black pottery. Many historians believe Chinese civilization is the oldest uninterrupted civilization in the world. The Neolithic age in China goes back 10,000 years, with agriculture in China beginning as early as 7,000 years ago. Their system of writing dates to 1,500 BCE. The Yellow River served as the center for the earliest Chinese settlements. In Ningxia, in northwest China, there are carvings on cliffs that date back to the Paleolithic Period, at least 6,000 years ago, indicating the extreme antiquity of Chinese culture. Literature from ancient China includes works by Confucius, *Analects*, the *Tao Te Ching*, and a variety of poetry.

In the Indus Valley, an urban civilization arose in what is now India. These ancient humans developed the concept of zero in mathematics, practiced an early form of the Hindu religion, and developed a caste system which is still prevalent in India today. Archeologists are still uncovering information about this highly developed ancient civilization.

The civilizations of ancient India gave rise to both Hinduism and Buddhism, major world religions that have found their way to countries far away from their place of origin. Practices such as yoga, increasingly popular in the West, can trace their roots to these earliest Indian civilizations. Literature from ancient India includes the *Mahabharata* containing the *Bhagavad Gita,* the *Ramayana, Arthashastra,* and the *Vedas*, a collection of sacred texts. Indo-European languages, including English, find their beginnings in these ancient cultures. Ancient Indo-Aryan languages such as Sanskrit are still used in some formal Hindu practices. Yoga poses are still formally referred to by Sanskrit names.

Kush, or Cush, was located south of ancient Egypt, and the earliest existing records of this civilization were found in Egyptian texts. At one time, Kush was the largest empire on the Nile River, surpassing even Egypt. In Neolithic times, Kushites lived in villages, with buildings made of mud bricks. They were settled rather than nomadic, and practiced hunting and fishing, cultivated grain, and also herded cattle. Kerma, the capitol, was a major center of trade. Kush determined leadership through matrilineal descent of their kings, as did Egypt. Their heads of state, the Kandake or Kentake, were female. Their polytheistic religion included the primary Egyptian gods as well as regional gods, including a lion god, which is commonly found in African cultures. Archeological evidence indicates the Kushites were a mix of Mediterranean and Negroid peoples. Kush was conquered by Nubia in 800 BCE.

Less is known of ancient American civilizations since less was left behind. Those we know something of include:

- The Norte Chico civilization in Peru, an agricultural society of 20 individual communities, that existed over 5,000 years ago. This culture is also known as Caral-Supe, and is the oldest known civilization in the Americas.
- The Anasazi, or Ancient Pueblo People, in what is now the southwestern United States. Emerging about 1200 BCE, the Anasazi built complex adobe dwellings, and were the forerunners of later Pueblo Indian cultures.
- The Maya emerged in southern Mexico and northern Central America as early as 2,600 BCE. They developed a written language and a complex calendar.

HELLENISTIC AGE

Ancient Greece made numerous major contributions to cultural development, including:

- Theater—Aristophanes and other Greek playwrights laid the groundwork for modern theatrical performance.
- Alphabet—the Greek alphabet, derived from the Phoenician alphabet, developed into the Roman alphabet, and then into our modern-day alphabet.
- Geometry—Pythagoras and Euclid pioneered much of the system of geometry still taught today. Archimedes made various mathematical discoveries, including the value of pi.
- Historical writing—much of ancient history doubles as mythology or religious texts. Herodotus and Thucydides made use of research and interpretation to record historical events.
- Philosophy—Socrates, Plato, and Aristotle served as the fathers of Western philosophy. Their work is still required reading for philosophy students.

Both powerful city-states, the Spartans and the Athenians nurtured contrasting cultures.

- The Spartans, located in Peloponnesus, were ruled by an oligarchic military state. They practiced farming, disallowed trade for Spartan citizens, and valued military arts and strict discipline. They emerged as the strongest military force in the area, and maintained this status for many years. In one memorable encounter, a small group of Spartans held off a huge army of Persians at Thermopylae.
- The Athenians were centered in Attica, where there was little land available for farming. Like the Spartans, they descended from invaders who spoke Greek. Their government was very different from Sparta's; it was in Athens that democracy was created by Cleisthenes of Athens in 510 BCE. Athenians excelled in art, theater, architecture, and philosophy.

Athens and Sparta fought each other in the Peloponnesian War, 431-404 BCE.

The Persian Empire, ruled by Cyrus the Great, encompassed an area from the Black Sea to Afghanistan, and beyond into Central Asia. After the death of Cyrus, Darius became king in 522 BCE. The empire reached its zenith during his reign. From 499-448 BCE, the Greeks and Persians fought in the Persian Wars. Battles of the Persian Wars included:

- The Battle of Marathon, in which heavily outnumbered Greek forces managed to achieve victory.
- The Battle of Thermopylae, in which a small band of Spartans held off a throng of Persian troops for several days.

- The Battle of Salamis, a naval battle that again saw outnumbered Greeks achieving victory.
- The Battle of Plataea, another Greek victory, but one in which they outnumbered the Persians.

The Persian Wars did not see the end of the Persian Empire, but discouraged additional attempts to invade Greece.

Born to Philip II of Macedon and tutored by Aristotle, Alexander the Great is considered one of the greatest conquerors in history. He conquered Egypt, the Achaemenid/Persian Empire, a powerful empire founded by Cyrus the Great that spanned three continents, and he traveled as far as India and the Iberian Peninsula. Though Alexander died at the early age of 32, his conquering efforts spread Greek culture into the east. This cultural diffusion left a greater mark on history than did his empire, which fell apart due to internal conflict not long after his death. Trade between the East and West increased, as did an exchange of ideas and beliefs that influenced both regions greatly. The Hellenistic traditions his conquest spread were prevalent in Byzantine culture until as late as the 15th century.

The Maurya Empire was a large, powerful empire established in India. It was one of the largest ever to rule in the Indian subcontinent, and existed from 322 to 185 BCE, ruled by Chandragupta after the withdrawal from India of Alexander the Great. The Maurya Empire was highly developed, including a standardized economic system, waterworks, and private corporations. Trade to the Greeks and others became common, with goods including silk, exotic foods, and spices. Religious development included the rise of Buddhism and Jainism. The laws of the Maurya Empire protected not only civil and social rights of the citizens, but also protected animals, establishing protected zones for economically important creatures such as elephants, lions and tigers. This period of time in Indian history was largely peaceful due to the strong Buddhist beliefs of many of its leaders. The empire finally fell after a succession of weak leaders, and was taken over by Demetrius, a Greco-Bactrian king who took advantage of this lapse in leadership to conquer southern Afghanistan and Pakistan around 180 BCE.

In China, history was divided into a series of dynasties. The most famous of these, the Han Dynasty, existed from 206 BCE to 220 CE. Accomplishments of the Chinese Empires included:

- Building the Great Wall of China
- Numerous inventions, including paper, paper money, printing, and gunpowder
- High level of artistic development
- Silk production

The Chinese Empires were comparable to Rome as far as their artistic and intellectual accomplishments, as well as the size and scope of their influence.

ROMAN EMPIRE

Rome began humbly, in a single town that grew out of Etruscan settlements and traditions, founded, according to legend, by twin brothers Romulus and Remus, who were raised by wolves. Romulus killed Remus, and from his legacy grew Rome. A thousand years later, the Roman Empire covered a significant portion of the known world, from what is now Scotland, across Europe, and into the Middle East. Hellenization, or the spread of Greek culture throughout the world, served as an inspiration and a model for the spread of Roman culture. Rome brought in belief systems of conquered peoples as well as their technological and scientific accomplishments, melding the disparate parts into a Roman core.

Rome's overall government was autocratic, but local officials came from the provinces where they lived. This limited administrative system was probably a major factor in the long life of the empire.

In the early fourth century, the Roman Empire split, with the eastern portion becoming the Eastern Empire, or the Byzantine Empire. In 330 CE, Constantine founded the city of Constantinople, which became the center of the Byzantine Empire. Its major influences came from Mesopotamia and Persia, in contrast to the Western Empire, which maintained traditions more closely linked to Greece and Carthage. Byzantium's position gave it an advantage over invaders from the west and the east, as well as control over trade from both regions. It protected the Western empire from invasion from the Persians and the Ottomans, and practiced a more centralized rule than in the West. The Byzantines were famous for lavish art and architecture, as well as the Code of Justinian, which collected Roman law into a clear system.

The Byzantine Empire was Christian-based but incorporated Greek language, philosophy and literature and drew its law and government policies from Rome. However, there was as yet no unified doctrine of Christianity, as it was a relatively new religion that had spread rapidly and without a great deal of organization. In 325, the First Council of Nicaea addressed this issue. From this conference came the Nicene Creed, addressing the Trinity and other basic Christian beliefs. The Council of Chalcedon in 451 stated that any rejection of the Trinity was blasphemy. Germanic tribes, including the Visigoths, Ostrogoths, Vandals, Saxons and Franks, controlled most of Europe. The Roman Empire faced major opposition on that front. The increasing size of the empire also made it harder to manage, leading to dissatisfaction throughout the empire as Roman government became less efficient. Germanic tribes refused to adhere to the Nicene Creed, instead following Arianism, which led the Roman Catholic Church to declare them heretics. The Franks proved a powerful military force in their defeat of the Muslims in 732. In 768, Charlemagne became king of the Franks. These tribes waged several wars against Rome, including the invasion of Britannia by the Angles and Saxons. Far-flung Rome lost control over this area of its Empire, and eventually Rome itself was invaded.

MIDDLE AGES

The Roman Catholic Church extended significant influence both politically and economically throughout medieval society. The church supplied education, as there were no established schools or universities. To a large extent, the church had filled a power void left by various invasions throughout the former Roman Empire, leading it to exercise a role that was far more political than religious. Kings were heavily influenced by the Pope and other church officials, and churches controlled large amounts of land throughout Europe.

Review Video: The Middle Ages: The Holy Roman Empire
Visit mometrix.com/academy and enter code: 137655

Emperor Leo III ordered the destruction of all icons throughout the Byzantine Empire. Images of Jesus were replaced with a cross, and images of Jesus, Mary or other religious figures were considered blasphemy on grounds of idolatry. The current Pope, Gregory II, called a synod to discuss the issue. The synod declared that destroying these images was heretical, and that strong disciplinary measures would result for anyone who took this step. Leo's response was an attempt to kidnap Pope Gregory, but this plan ended in failure when his ships were destroyed by a storm.

A major element of the social and economic life of Europe, feudalism developed as a way to ensure European rulers would have the wherewithal to quickly raise an army when necessary. Vassals swore loyalty and promised to provide military service for lords, who in return offered a fief, or a parcel of land, for them to use to generate their livelihood. Vassals could work the land themselves, have it worked by peasants or serfs—workers who had few rights and were little more than slaves—or grant the fief to someone else. The king legally owned all the land, but in return promised to protect the vassals from invasion and war. Vassals returned a certain percentage of their income to the lords, who in turn passed a portion of their income on to the king. A similar practice was manorialism, in which the feudal system was applied to a self-contained manor. These manors were often owned by the lords who ran them, but were usually included in the same system of loyalty and promises of military service that drove feudalism.

Review Video: The Middle Ages: Feudalism
Visit mometrix.com/academy and enter code: 165907

Born in 570 CE, Mohammed became prominent in 610, leading his followers in a new religion called Islam, which means submission to God's will. Before this time, the Arabian Peninsula was inhabited largely by Bedouins, nomads who battled amongst each other and lived in tribal organizations. But by the time Mohammed died in 632, most of Arabia had become Muslim to some extent. Mohammed conquered Mecca, where a temple called the Kaaba had long served as a center of the nomadic religions. He declared this temple the most sacred of Islam, and Mecca as the holy city. His writings became the Koran, or Qur'an, divine revelations he said had been delivered to him by the angel Gabriel. Mohammed's teachings gave the formerly tribal Arabian people a sense of unity that had not existed in the area before. After his death, the converted Muslims of Arabia conquered a vast territory, creating an empire and bringing advances in literature, technology, science and art just as Europe was declining under the scourge of the Black Death. Literature from this period includes the *Arabian Nights* and the *Rubaiyat* of Omar Khayyam. Later in its development, Islam split into two factions, the Shiite and the Sunni Muslims. Conflict continues today between these groups.

Vikings invaded Northern France in the tenth century, eventually becoming the Normans. Originating in Scandinavia, the Vikings were accomplished seafarers with advanced knowledge of trade routes. With overpopulation plaguing their native lands, they began to travel. From the eighth to the eleventh centuries, they spread throughout Europe, conquering and colonizing. Vikings invaded and colonized England through several waves, including the Anglo-Saxon invasions that displaced Roman control. Their influence remained significant in England, affecting everything from the language of the country to place names and even the government and social structure. By 900, Vikings had settled in Iceland. They proceeded then to Greenland and eventually to North America, arriving in the New World even before the Spanish and British who claimed the lands several centuries later. They also traded with the Byzantine Empire until the eleventh century when their significant level of activity came to an end. In Europe, the tenth century is largely known as the Dark Ages, as numerous Viking invasions disrupted societies that had been more settled under Roman rule. Vikings settled in Northern France, eventually becoming the Normans. By the eleventh century, Europe would rise again into the High Middle Ages with the beginning of the Crusades.

The Crusades began in the eleventh century and progressed well into the twelfth. The major goal of these various military ventures was to slow the progression of Muslim forces into Europe and to expel them from the Holy Land, where they had taken control of Jerusalem and Palestine. Alexius I, the Eastern emperor, called for helped from Pope Urban II when Palestine was taken. In 1095, the Pope, hoping to reunite Eastern and Western Christian influences, encouraged all Christians to help the cause. Amidst great bloodshed, this Crusade recaptured Jerusalem, but over the next centuries, Jerusalem and other areas of the Holy Land changed hands numerous times. The Second Crusade, in 1145, consisted of an unsuccessful attempt to retake Damascus. The Third Crusade, under Pope

Gregory VIII, attempted to recapture Jerusalem, but failed. The Fourth Crusade, under Pope Innocent III, attempted to come into the Holy Land via Egypt. The Crusades led to greater power for the Pope and the Catholic Church in general and also opened numerous trading and cultural routes between Europe and the East.

In China, wars also raged. This led the Chinese to make use of gunpowder for the first time in warfare.

In the Americas, the Mayan Empire was winding down while the Toltec became more prominent. Pueblo Indian culture was also at its zenith. In the East, the Muslims and the Byzantine Empire were experiencing a significant period of growth and development.

After the Mauryan dynasty, the Guptas ruled India, maintaining a long period of peace and prosperity in the area. During this time, the Indian people invented the decimal system as well as the concept of zero. They produced cotton and calico, as well as other products in high demand in Europe and Asia, and developed a complex system of medicine. The Gupta Dynasty ended in the eleventh century with a Muslim invasion of the region. These sultans ruled for several centuries. Tamerlane, one of the most famous, expanded India's borders and founded the Mogul Dynasty. His grandson Akbar promoted freedom of religion and built a wide-spread number of mosques, forts, and other buildings throughout the country.

After the Mongols, led by Genghis Khan and his grandson Kublai Khan, unified the Mongol Empire, China was led by the Ming and Manchu Dynasties. Both these Dynasties were isolationist, ending China's interaction with other countries until the eighteenth century. The Ming Dynasty was known for its porcelain, while the Manchus focused on farming and road construction as the population grew.

Japan developed independent of China, but borrowed the Buddhist religion, the Chinese writing system, and other elements of Chinese society. Ruled by the divine emperor, Japan basically functioned on a feudal system led by Daimyos, or lords, and soldiers known as samurai. Japan remained isolationist, not interacting significantly with the rest of the world until the 1800s.

Only a few areas of Africa were amenable to habitation, due to the large amount of desert and other inhospitable terrain. Egypt remained important, though most of the northern coast became Muslim as their armies spread through the area. Ghana rose as a trade center in the ninth century, lasting into the twelfth century, primarily trading in gold, which it exchanges for Saharan salt. Mali rose somewhat later, with the trade center Timbuktu becoming an important exporter of goods such as iron, leather and tin. Mali also dealt in agricultural trade, becoming one of the most significant trading centers in West Africa. The Muslim religion dominated, and technological advancement was sparse. African culture was largely defined through migration, as Arab merchants and others settled on the continent, particularly along the east coast. Scholars from the Muslim nations gravitated to Timbuktu, which in addition to its importance in trade, had also become a magnet for those seeking knowledge and education.

The Black Death, believed to be bubonic plague, came to Europe probably brought by fleas carried on rats that were regular passengers on sailing vessels. It killed in excess of a third of the entire population of Europe and effectively ended feudalism as a political system. Many who had formerly served as peasants or serfs found different work, as a demand for skilled labor grew. Nation-states grew in power, and in the face of the pandemic, many began to turn away from faith in God and toward the ideals of ancient Greece and Rome for government and other beliefs.

By 1400, the Ottomans had grown in power in Anatolia and had begun attempts to take Constantinople. In 1453 they finally conquered the Byzantine capital and renamed it Istanbul. The Ottoman Empire's major strength, much like Rome before it, lay in its ability to unite widely disparate people through religious tolerance. This tolerance, which stemmed from the idea that Muslims, Christians, and Jews were fundamentally related and could coexist, enabled the Ottomans to develop a widely varied culture. They also believed in just laws and just government, with government centered in a monarch, known as the sultan.

> **Review Video: The Middle Ages**
> Visit mometrix.com/academy and enter code: 413133

RENAISSANCE AND REFORMATION

Renaissance literally means "rebirth." After the darkness of the Dark Ages and the Black Plague, interest rose again in the beliefs and politics of ancient Greece and Rome. Art, literature, music, science, and philosophy all burgeoned during the Renaissance. Many of the ideas of the Renaissance began in Florence, Italy, spurred by the Medici family. Education for the upper classes expanded to include law, math, reading, writing, and classical Greek and Roman works. As the Renaissance progressed, the world was presented through art and literature in a realistic way that had never been explored before. This realism drove culture to new heights.

Artists of the Renaissance included Leonardo da Vinci, also an inventor, Michelangelo, also an architect, and others who focused on realism in their work. In literature, major contributions came from the humanist, authors like Petrarch, Erasmus, Sir Thomas More, and Boccaccio, who believed man should focus on reality rather than on the ethereal. Shakespeare, Cervantes and Dante followed in their footsteps, and their works found a wide audience thanks to Gutenberg's development of the printing press. Scientific developments of the Renaissance included the work of Copernicus, Galileo and Kepler, who challenged the geocentric philosophies of the church by proving the earth was not the center of the solar system.

The Reformation consisted of the Protestant Revolution and the Catholic Reformation. The Protestant Revolution rose in Germany when Martin Luther protested abuses of the Catholic Church. John Calvin led the movement in Switzerland, while in England King Henry VIII made use of the Revolution's ideas to further his own political goals.

> **Review Video: The Reformation: Martin Luther**
> Visit mometrix.com/academy and enter code: 691828
>
> **Review Video: The Reformation: The Protestants**
> Visit mometrix.com/academy and enter code: 583582

The Catholic Reformation occurred in response to the Protestant Revolution, leading to various changes in the Catholic Church. Some provided wider tolerance of different religious viewpoints, but others actually increased the persecution of those deemed to be heretics.

> **Review Video: The Counter Reformation**
> Visit mometrix.com/academy and enter code: 950498

From a religious standpoint, the Reformation occurred due to abuses by the Catholic Church such as indulgences and dispensations, religious offices being offered up for sale, and an increasingly dissolute clergy. Politically, the Reformation was driven by increased power of various ruling

monarchs, who wished to take all power to themselves rather than allowing power to remain with the church. They also had begun to chafe at papal taxes and the church's increasing wealth. The ideas of the Protestant Revolution removed power from the Catholic Church and the Pope himself, playing nicely into the hands of those monarchs, such as Henry VIII, who wanted out from under the church's control.

ENLIGHTENMENT

In addition to holding power in the political realm, church doctrine also governed scientific belief. During the Scientific Revolution, astronomers and other scientists began to amass evidence that challenged the church's scientific doctrines. Major figures of the Scientific Revolution included:

- Nicolaus Copernicus—wrote *Revolutions of the Celestial Spheres*, arguing that the Earth revolved around the sun.
- Tycho Brahe—catalogued astronomical observations.
- Johannes Kepler—developed Laws of Planetary Motions.
- Galileo Galilei—defended the heliocentric theories of Copernicus and Kepler, discovered four moons of Jupiter, and died under house arrest by the Church, charged with heresy.
- Isaac Newton—discovered gravity, studied optics, calculus and physics, and believed the workings of nature could be observed, studied, and proven through observation.

During the Enlightenment, philosophers and scientists began to rely more and more on observation to support their ideas, rather than building on past beliefs, particularly those held by the church. A focus on ethics and logic drove their work. Major philosophers of the Enlightenment included:

- Rene Descartes—"I think, therefore I am." He believed strongly in logic and rules of observation.
- David Hume—pioneered empiricism and skepticism, believing that truth could only be found through direct experience, and that what others said to be true was always suspect.
- Immanuel Kant—believed in self-examination and observation, and that the root of morality lay within human beings.
- Jean-Jacques Rousseau—developed the idea of the social contract, that government existed by the agreement of the people, and that the government was obligated to protect the people and their basic rights. His ideas influenced John Locke and Thomas Jefferson.

> **Review Video: Age of Enlightenment**
> Visit mometrix.com/academy and enter code: 143022

Both the American and French Revolution came about as a protest against the excesses and overly controlling nature of their respective monarchs. In America, the British colonies had been left mostly self-governing until the British monarchs began to increase control, leading the colonies to revolt.

In France, the nobility's excesses had led to increasingly difficult economic conditions, with inflation, heavy taxation and food shortages creating horrible burdens on the people. Both revolutions led to the development of republics to replace the monarchies that were displaced. However, the French Revolution eventually led to the rise of the dictator Napoleon Bonaparte, while the American Revolution produced a working republic from the beginning.

In 1789, King Louis XVI, faced with a huge national debt, convened parliament. The Third Estate, or Commons, a division of the French parliament, then claimed power, and the king's resistance led to the storming of the Bastille, the royal prison. The people established a constitutional monarchy. When King Louis XVI and Marie Antoinette attempted to leave the country, they were executed on the guillotine.

From 1793 to 1794, Robespierre and extreme radicals, the Jacobins, instituted a Reign of Terror, executing thousands of nobles as well as anyone considered an enemy of the Revolution. Robespierre was then executed, as well, and the Directory came into power. This governing body proved incompetent and corrupt, allowing Napoleon Bonaparte to come to power in 1799, first as a dictator, then as emperor. While the French Revolution threw off the power of a corrupt monarchy, its immediate results were likely not what the original perpetrators of the revolt had intended.

INDUSTRIAL REVOLUTION

The Industrial Revolution began in Great Britain, bringing coal- and steam-powered machinery into widespread use. Industry began a period of rapid growth with these developments. Goods that had previously been produced in small workshops or even in homes were produced more efficiently and in much larger quantities in factories. Where society had been largely agrarian based, the focus swiftly shifted to an industrial outlook. As electricity and internal combustion engines replaced coal and steam as energy sources, even more drastic and rapid changes occurred. Western European countries in particular turned to colonialism, taking control of portions of Africa and Asia to assure access to the raw materials needed to produce factory goods. Specialized labor became very much in demand, and businesses grew rapidly, creating monopolies, increasing world trade, and creating large urban centers. Even agriculture changed fundamentally as the Industrial Revolution led to a second Agricultural Revolution as the addition of the new technologies advanced agricultural production.

The first phase of the Industrial Revolution took place from roughly 1750 to 1830. The textile industry experienced major changes as more and more elements of the process became mechanized. Mining benefited from the steam engine. Transportation became easier and more widely available as waterways were improved and the railroad came into prominence. In the second phase, from 1830 to 1910, industries further improved in efficiency and new industries were introduced as photography, various chemical processes, and electricity became more widely available to produce new goods or new, improved versions of old goods. Petroleum and hydroelectric became major sources of power. During this time, the Industrial Revolution spread out of Western Europe and into the US and Japan.

The Industrial Revolution led to widespread education, a wider franchise, and the development of mass communication in the political arena. Economically, conflicts arose between companies and their employees, as struggles for fair treatment and fair wages increased. Unions gained power and became more active. Government regulation over industries increased, but at the same time, growing businesses fought for the right to free enterprise. In the social sphere, populations increased and began to concentrate around centers of industry. Cities became larger and more densely populated. Scientific advancements led to more efficient agriculture, greater supply of goods, and increased knowledge of medicine and sanitation, leading to better overall health.

Nationalism, put simply, is a strong belief in, identification with, and allegiance to a particular nation and people. Nationalistic belief unified various areas that had previously seen themselves as fragmented which led to patriotism and, in some cases, imperialism. As nationalism grew, individual nations sought to grow, bringing in other, smaller states that shared similar characteristics such as language and cultural beliefs. Unfortunately, a major side effect of these growing nationalistic beliefs was often conflict and outright war. In Europe, imperialism led countries to spread their influence into Africa and Asia. Africa was eventually divided among several European countries that needed the raw materials to be found there. Asia also came under European control, with the exception of China, Japan and Siam (now Thailand). In the US, Manifest Destiny became the rallying cry as the country expanded west. Italy and Germany formed larger nations from a variety of smaller states.

At their roots, socialism and communism both focus on public ownership and distribution of goods and services. However, communism works toward revolution by drawing on what it sees to be inevitable class antagonism, eventually overthrowing the upper classes and the systems of capitalism. Socialism makes use of democratic procedures, building on the existing order. This was particularly true of the Utopian-Socialists, who saw industrial capitalism as oppressive, not allowing workers to prosper. While socialism struggled between the World Wars, communism took hold, especially in Eastern Europe. After WW II, democratic socialism became more common. Later, capitalism took a stronger hold again, and today most industrialized countries in the world function under an economy that mixes elements of capitalism and socialism.

In Russia, rule lay in the hands of the Czars, and the overall structure was feudalistic. Beneath the Czars was a group of rich nobles, landowners whose lands were worked by peasants and serfs. The Russo-Japanese War (1904-1905) made conditions much worse for the lower classes. When peasants demonstrated outside the Czar's Winter Palace, the palace guard fired upon the crowd. The demonstration had been organized by a trade union leader, and after the violent response, many unions as well as political parties blossomed and began to lead numerous strikes. When the economy ground to a halt, Czar Nicholas II signed a document known as the October Manifesto, which established a constitutional monarchy and gave legislative power to parliament. However, he violated the Manifesto shortly thereafter, disbanding parliament and ignoring the civil liberties granted by the Manifesto. This eventually led to the Bolshevik Revolution of 1917.

> **Review Video: The Industrial Revolution**
> Visit mometrix.com/academy and enter code: 372796

WORLD WARS

WWI began in 1914 with the assassination of Archduke Franz Ferdinand, heir to the throne of Austria-Hungary, by a Serbian national. This led to a conflict between Austria-Hungary and Serbia that quickly escalated into the First World War. Europe split into the Allies—Britain, France and Russia, and later Italy, Japan and the US, against the Central Powers—Austria-Hungary, Germany and Turkey. As the war spread, countries beyond Europe became involved.

Fighting during WW I took place largely in a series of trenches built along the Eastern and Western Fronts. These trenches added up to about 24,000 miles, each side having dug at least 12,000 miles' worth during the course of the war. This produced fronts that stretched nearly 400 miles, from the coast of Belgium to the border of Switzerland. The Allies made use of straightforward open-air trenches with a front line, supporting lines, and communications lines. By contrast, the German trenches sometimes included well-equipped underground living quarters.

The war left Europe deeply in debt, and particularly devastated the German economy. The ensuing Great Depression made matters worse, and economic devastation opened the door for Communist, Fascist and Socialist governments to gain power.

Throughout its modern history, Russia had lagged behind other countries in development. The continued existence of a feudal system, combined with harsh conditions and the overall size of the country, led to massive food shortages and increasingly harsh conditions for the majority of the population. The tyrannical rule favored by the Czars only made this worse, as did repeated losses in various military conflicts. Increasing poverty, decreasing supplies, and the Czar's violation of the October Manifesto which had given some political power and civil rights to the people finally came to a head with the Bolshevik Revolution.

A workers' strike in Petrograd in 1917 set the revolutionary wheels in motion when the army sided with the workers. While parliament set up a provisional government made up of nobles, the workers and military joined to form their own governmental system known as soviets, which consisted of local councils elected by the people. The ensuing chaos opened the doors for formerly exiled leaders Vladimir Lenin, Joseph Stalin and Leon Trotsky to move in and gain popular support as well as the support of the Red Guard. Overthrowing parliament, they took power, creating a communist state in Russia. This development led to the spread of Communism throughout Eastern Europe and elsewhere, greatly affecting diplomatic policies throughout the world for several decades.

The Great Depression had a particularly devastating effect on Germany's economy, especially after the US was no longer able to supply reconstruction loans to help the country regain its footing. With unemployment rising rapidly, dissatisfaction with the government grew. Fascist and Communist parties rose, promising change and improvement. Led by Adolf Hitler, the Fascist, Nazi Party eventually gained power in Parliament based on these promises and the votes of desperate German workers. When Hitler became Chancellor, he launched numerous expansionist policies, violating the peace treaties that had ended WW I. His military buildup and conquering of neighboring countries sparked the aggression that soon led to WW II.

As Germany sank deeper and deeper into dire economic straits, the tendency was to look for a person or group of people to blame for the problems of the country. With distrust of the Jewish people already ingrained, it was easy for German authorities to set up the Jews as scapegoats for Germany's problems.

Under the rule of Hitler and the Nazi party, the "Final Solution" for the supposed Jewish problem was devised. Millions of Jews, as well as Gypsies, homosexuals, Communists, Catholics, the mentally ill and others, simply named as criminals, were transported to concentration camps during the course of the war. At least six million were slaughtered in death camps such as Auschwitz, where horrible conditions and torture of prisoners were commonplace. The Allies were aware of rumors of mass slaughter throughout the war, but many discounted the reports. Only when troops went in to liberate the prisoners was the true horror of the concentration camps brought to light.

The blitzkrieg, or "lightning war," consisted of fast, powerful surprise attacks that disrupted communications, made it difficult if not impossible for the victims to retaliate, and demoralized Germany's foes. The "blitz," or the aerial bombing of England in 1940, was one example, with bombings occurring in London and other cities 57 nights in a row. The Battle of Britain, from 1940 to 1941, also brought intense raids by Germany's air force, the Luftwaffe, mostly targeting ports and British air force bases. Eventually, Britain's Royal Air Force blocked the Luftwaffe, ending Germany's hopes for conquering Britain.

Following the D-Day Invasion, Allied forces gained considerable ground, and began a major campaign to push through Europe. In December of 1944, Hitler launched a counteroffensive, attempting to retake Antwerp, an important port. The ensuing battle became the largest land battle on the war's Western Front, and was known as the Battle of the Ardennes, or the Battle of the Bulge. The battle lasted from December 16, 1944 to January 28, 1945. The Germans pushed forward, making inroads into Allied lines, but in the end the Allies brought the advance to a halt. The

Germans were pushed back, with massive losses on both sides. However, those losses proved crippling to the German army.

The Holocaust resulted in massive loss of human life, but also in the loss and destruction of cultures. Because the genocide focused on specific ethnic groups, many traditions, histories, knowledge, and other cultural elements were lost, particularly among the Jewish and Gypsy populations. After World War II, the United Nations recognized genocide as a "crime against humanity." The UN passed the Universal Declaration of Human Rights in order to further specify what rights the organization protected. Nazi war criminals faced justice during the Nuremberg Trials. There individuals, rather than their governments, were held accountable for war crimes.

> **Review Video: The Holocaust**
> Visit mometrix.com/academy and enter code: 350695

POST-WORLD WAR II

With millions of military and civilian deaths and over 12 million persons displaced, WW II left large regions of Europe and Asia in disarray. Communist governments moved in with promises of renewed prosperity and economic stability. The Soviet Union backed Communist regimes in much of Eastern Europe. In China, Mao Zedong led communist forces in the overthrow of the Chinese Nationalist Party and instituted a Communist government in 1949. While the new Communist governments restored a measure of stability to much of Eastern Europe, it brought its own problems, with dictatorial governments and an oppressive police force. The spread of Communism also led to several years of tension between Communist countries and the democratic west, as the west fought to slow the spread of oppressive regimes throughout the world. With both sides in possession of nuclear weapons, tensions rose. Each side feared the other would resort to nuclear attack. This standoff lasted until 1989, when the Berlin Wall fell. The Soviet Union was dissolved two years later.

The United Nations (UN) came into being toward the end of World War II. A successor to the less-than-successful League of Nations, formed after World War I, the UN built and improved on those ideas. Since its inception, the UN has worked to bring the countries of the world together for diplomatic solutions to international problems, including sanctions and other restrictions. It has also initiated military action, calling for peacekeeping troops from member countries to move against countries violating UN policies.

One example of UN involvement in an international conflict is the Korean War, the first war in which an international alliance of this kind was actively involved.

Unfortunately, the Holocaust is not the only occurrence of a major genocide in the 20th Century.

- Armenian genocide—occurred in the 1900s when the Young Turks, heirs to the Ottoman Empire, slaughtered over a million Armenians between 1915 and 1917. This constituted nearly half the Armenian population at the time.
- Russian purges under Stalin—Scholars have attributed deaths between 3 and 60 million, both directly and indirectly, to the policies and edicts of Joseph Stalin's regime. The deaths took place from 1921 to 1953, when Stalin died. In recent years, many scholars have settled on a number of deaths near 20 million but this is still disputed today.
- Rwandan Genocide—in 1994, hundreds of thousands of Tutsi and Hutu sympathizers were slaughtered during the Rwandan Civil War. The UN did not act or authorize intervention during these atrocities.

In 1910, Japan took control of Korea, and maintained this control until 1945, when Soviet and US troops occupied the country. The Soviet Union controlled North Korea, while the US controlled South Korea. In 1947, the UN ordered elections in Korea to unify the country but the Soviet Union refused to allow them to take place, instead setting up a communist government in North Korea. In 1950, the US withdrew troops, and the North Korean troops moved to invade South Korea. The Korean War was the first war in which the UN—or any international organization—played a major role. The US, Australia, Canada, France, Netherlands, Great Britain, Turkey, China, USSR and other countries sent troops at various times, for both sides, throughout the war. In 1953, the war ended in a truce, but no peace agreement was ever achieved, and Korea remains divided.

A rise of nationalism among European colonies led to many of them declaring independence. India and Pakistan became independent of Britain at this time, and numerous African and Asian colonies declared independence, as well. This period of decolonization lasted into the 1960s. Some colonies moved successfully into independence but many, especially in Africa and Asia, struggled to create stable governments and economies, and suffered from ethnic and religious conflicts. Some of those countries still struggle today.

Vietnam had previously been part of a French colony called French Indochina. The Vietnam War began with the French Indochina War from 1946-1954, in which France battled with the Democratic Republic of Vietnam, ruled by Ho Chi Minh. In 1954, a siege at Dien Bien Phu ended in a Vietnamese victory. Vietnam was then divided into North and South, much like Korea. Communist forces controlled the North and the South was controlled by South Vietnamese forces, supported by the US. Conflict ensued, leading to a war. US troops eventually lead the fight, in support of South Vietnam. The war became a major political issue in the US, with many citizens protesting American involvement. In 1976, South Vietnam surrendered, and Vietnam became the Socialist Republic of Vietnam.

Its location on the globe, with ease of access to Europe and Asia, and its preponderance of oil deposits, makes the middle eastern countries a crucial factor in many international issues both diplomatic and economic. Because of its central location, the Middle East has been a hotbed for violence since before the beginning of recorded history. Conflicts over land, resources, religious and political power continue in the area today, spurred by conflict over control of the area's vast oil fields as well as over territories that have been disputed for literally hundreds—and even thousands—of years.

In the modern era, globalism has emerged as a popular political ideology. Globalism is based in the idea that all people and all nations are interdependent. Each nation is dependent on one or more other nations for production of and markets for goods, and for income generation. Today's ease of international travel and communication, including technological advances such as the airplane, has heightened this sense of interdependence. The global economy, and the general idea of globalism, has shaped many economic and political choices since the beginning of the twentieth century. Many of today's issues, including environmental awareness, economic struggles, and continued warfare, often require the cooperation of many countries if they are to be dealt with effectively.

With countries worldwide often seeking the same resources, some, particularly nonrenewable resources, have experienced high demand. At times this has resulted in wild price fluctuations. One major example is the demand for petroleum products such as oil and natural gas. Increased travel and communication make it possible to deal with diseases in remote locations; however, it also allows diseases to be spread via travelers, as well. A major factor contributing to increased globalization over the past few decades has been the Internet. By allowing instantaneous communication with anyone nearly anywhere on the globe, the Internet has led to interaction

between far-flung individuals and countries, and an ever increasing awareness of happenings all over the world.

GED Practice Test

Reasoning Through Language Arts

READING

Questions 1-6 refer to the following passage:

History of England

by Charles Dickens

If you look at a Map of the World, you will see, in the left-hand upper corner of the Eastern Hemisphere, two Islands lying in the sea. They are England and Scotland, and Ireland. England and Scotland form the greater part of these Islands. Ireland is the next in size. The little neighbouring islands, which are so small upon the Map as to be mere dots, are chiefly little bits of Scotland,—broken off, I dare say, in the course of a great length of time, by the power of the restless water.

In the old days, a long, long while ago..., these Islands were in the same place, and the stormy sea roared round them, just as it roars now. But the sea was not alive, then, with great ships and brave sailors, sailing to and from all parts of the world. It was very lonely. The Islands lay solitary, in the great expanse of water. The foaming waves dashed against their cliffs, and the bleak winds blew over their forests; but the winds and waves brought no adventurers to land upon the Islands, and the savage Islanders knew nothing of the rest of the world, and the rest of the world knew nothing of them.

It is supposed that the Phoenicians, who were an ancient people, famous for carrying on trade, came in ships to these Islands, and found that they produced tin and lead; both very useful things, as you know, and both produced to this very hour upon the sea-coast. The most celebrated tin mines in Cornwall are, still, close to the sea. One of them, which I have seen, is so close to it that it is hollowed out underneath the ocean; and the miners say, that in stormy weather, when they are at work down in that deep place, they can hear the noise of the waves thundering above their heads. So, the Phoenicians, coasting about the Islands, would come, without much difficulty, to where the tin and lead were.

The Phoenicians traded with the Islanders for these metals, and gave the Islanders some other useful things in exchange. The Islanders were, at first, poor savages, going almost naked, or only dressed in the rough skins of beasts, and staining their bodies, as other savages do, with coloured earths and the juices of plants. But the Phoenicians, sailing over to the opposite coasts of France and Belgium, and saying to the people there, 'We have been to those white cliffs across the water, which you can see in fine weather, and from that country, which is called Britain, we bring this tin and lead,' tempted some of the French and Belgians to come over also. These people settled themselves on the south coast of England, which is now called Kent; and, although they were a rough people too, they taught the savage Britons some useful arts, and improved that part of the Islands. It is probable that other people came over from Spain to Ireland, and settled there.

Thus, by little and little, strangers became mixed with the Islanders, and the savage Britons grew into a wild, bold people; almost savage, still, especially in the interior of the country away from the sea where the foreign settlers seldom went; but hardy, brave, and strong.

The whole country was covered with forests, and swamps. The greater part of it was very misty and cold. There were no roads, no bridges, no streets, no houses that you would think deserving of the name. A town was nothing but a collection of straw-covered huts, hidden in a thick wood, with a ditch all round, and a low wall, made of mud, or the trunks of trees placed one upon another. The people planted little or no corn, but lived upon the flesh of their flocks and cattle. They made no coins, but used metal rings for money. They were clever in basket-work, as savage people often are; and they could make a coarse kind of cloth, and some very bad earthenware. But in building fortresses they were much more clever.

They made boats of basket-work, covered with the skins of animals, but seldom, if ever, ventured far from the shore. They made swords, of copper mixed with tin; but these swords were of an awkward shape, and so soft that a heavy blow would bend one. They made light shields, short pointed daggers, and spears—which they jerked back after they had thrown them at an enemy, by a long strip of leather fastened to the stem. The butt-end was a rattle, to frighten an enemy's horse. The ancient Britons, being divided into as many as thirty or forty tribes, each commanded by its own little king, were constantly fighting with one another, as savage people usually do; and they always fought with these weapons.

1. According to the author, why did the ancient Britons regularly fight with each other?

a. They had many weapons.
b. They disliked the Phoenicians.
c. There were no roads or bridges.
d. They were divided into many tribes.

2. Which sentence or phrase best shows the impact that the Phoenicians had on the ancient Britons?

a. "The Phoenicians traded with the Islanders…"
b. "But the Phœnicians, sailing over to the opposite coasts of France and Belgium…"
c. "These people settled themselves on the south coast of England…"
d. "…the savage Britons grew into a wild, bold people…"

3. Which sentence or phrase best expresses the isolation of the islands of England and Scotland and Ireland?

a. "…which are so small upon the Map as to be mere dots"
b. "The Islands lay solitary, in the great expanse of water."
c. "they can hear the noise of the waves thundering above their heads."
d. "Thus, by little and little, strangers became mixed with the Islanders…"

255

4. Read this phrase from paragraph 7:

But seldom, if ever, ventured far from the shore.

Why does the author include this phrase?

a. To show the ways in which the people used boats
b. To highlight the irony of making boats
c. To show where the people used weapons
d. To explain why the people built fortresses

5. Why does the author begin the passage by describing a map?

a. To explain the location of the islands
b. To show the roads that run through England, Scotland, and Ireland
c. To show how the little bits of Scotland broke away from the main island
d. To show the size of the islands in relation to France and Belgium

6. What sentence or phrase best describes the lands in the interior of the islands? In other words, these lands are the parts away from the coast.

a. "These people settled themselves on the south coast of England, which is now called Kent..."
b. "Especially in the interior of the country away from the sea where the foreign settlers seldom went..."
c. The whole country was covered with forests and swamps.
d. "The ancient Britons, being divided into as many as thirty or forty tribes, each commanded by its own little king..."

Questions 7–12 are for the following passage:

"The Gift of the Magi"

by O. Henry

[Jim and Della are a young husband and wife. They are very poor, and it is Christmas Eve. Della has been able to save $1.87 for a Christmas present. To buy a better gift for her husband, she decides to sell her beautiful hair to buy a fob for Jim. The fob will be for Jim's watch which is his most prized possession.]

When Della reached home her intoxication gave way a little to prudence and reason. She got out her curling irons and lighted the gas and went to work repairing the ravages made by generosity added to love. Which is always a tremendous task, dear friends--a mammoth task.

Within forty minutes her head was covered with tiny, close-lying curls that made her look wonderfully like a truant schoolboy. She looked at her reflection in the mirror long, carefully, and critically.

"If Jim doesn't kill me," she said to herself, "before he takes a second look at me, he'll say I look like a Coney Island chorus girl. But what could I do—oh! What could I do with a dollar and eighty-seven cents?"

At seven o'clock the coffee was made and the frying pan was on the back of the stove hot and ready to cook the chops.

Jim was never late. Della doubled the fob chain in her hand and sat on the corner of the table near the door that he always entered. Then she heard his step on the stairway down on the first flight, and she turned white for just a moment. She had a habit of saying little silent prayers about the simplest everyday things and now she whispered: "Please God, make him think I am still pretty."

*　　*　　*

Jim stopped inside the door, as immovable as a setter at the scent of quail. His eyes were fixed upon Della, and there was an expression in them that she could not read, and it terrified her. It was not anger, nor surprise, nor disapproval, nor horror, nor any of the sentiments that she had been prepared for. He simply stared at her fixedly with that peculiar expression on his face.

Della wriggled off the table and went for him.

"Jim, darling," she cried, "don't look at me that way. I had my hair cut off and sold it because I couldn't have lived through Christmas without giving you a present. It'll grow out again—you won't mind, will you? I just had to do it. My hair grows awfully fast. Say 'Merry Christmas!' Jim, and let's be happy. You don't know what a nice— what a beautiful, nice gift I've got for you."

"You've cut off your hair?" asked Jim, laboriously, as if he had not arrived at that patent fact yet even after the hardest mental labor.

"Cut it off and sold it," said Della. "Don't you like me just as well, anyhow? I'm me without my hair, ain't I?"

Jim looked about the room curiously.

"You say your hair is gone?" he said, with an air almost of idiocy.

"You needn't look for it," said Della. "It's sold, I tell you—sold and gone, too. It's Christmas Eve, boy. Be good to me, for it went for you. Maybe the hairs of my head were numbered," she went on with a sudden serious sweetness, "but nobody could ever count my love for you. Shall I put the chops on, Jim?"

Out of his trance Jim seemed quickly to wake. He enfolded his Della.

*　　*　　*

Jim drew a package from his overcoat pocket and threw it upon the table.

"Don't make any mistake, Dell," he said, "about me. I don't think there's anything in the way of a haircut or a shave or a shampoo that could make me like my girl any less. But if you'll unwrap that package you may see why you had me going a while at first." White fingers and nimble tore at the string and paper. And then an ecstatic scream of joy; and then, alas! a quick, feminine change to hysterical tears and wails, necessitating the immediate employment of all the comforting powers of the lord of the flat.

For there lay the Combs—the set of combs, side and back, that Della had worshipped for long in a Broadway window. Beautiful combs, pure tortoise shell, with jeweled rims—just the shade to wear in the beautiful vanished hair. They were expensive combs, she knew, and her heart had simply craved and yearned over them without the least hope of possession. And now, they were hers, but the tresses that should have adorned the coveted adornments were gone. But she hugged them to her bosom, and at length she was able to look up with dim eyes and a smile and say: "My hair grows so fast, Jim!"

And then Della leaped up like a little singed cat and cried, "Oh, oh!"

Jim had not yet seen his beautiful present. She held it out to him eagerly upon her open palm. The dull precious metal seemed to flash with a reflection of her bright and ardent spirit.

"Isn't it a dandy, Jim? I hunted all over town to find it. You'll have to look at the time a hundred times a day now. Give me your watch. I want to see how it looks on it."

Instead of obeying, Jim tumbled down on the couch and put his hands under the back of his head and smiled.

"Della," said he, "let's put our Christmas presents away and keep 'em a while. They're too nice to use just at present. I sold the watch to get the money to buy your combs. And now suppose you put the chops on."

7. What is the meaning of the word *ardent*?

    a. procrastinate
    b. passionate
    c. lukewarm
    d. uncaring

8. What is the chronological order of these events: ?

(1) Jim gives Della's present to her | (2) Della prepares dinner | (3) Jim assures Della that he is not upset | (4) Della prepares her hair | (5) Della prays for Jim's reaction | (6) Jim receives his present from Della

    a. 4, 3, 2, 1, 5, 6
    b. 6, 1, 4, 3, 2, 5
    c. 4, 2, 1, 5, 3, 6
    d. 4, 2, 5, 3, 1, 6

9. In the passage, O. Henry uses several similes. Which of the following is not an example of a simile?

    a. "her head was covered with tiny, close-lying curls that made her look wonderfully like a truant schoolboy."
    b. "Jim stopped inside the door, as immovable as a setter at the scent of quail."
    c. "'I hunted all over town to find it.'"
    d. "And then Della leaped up like a little singed cat and cried, 'Oh, oh!'."

10. Which of the following best shows how O. Henry builds tension in the story?

a. "It was even worthy of The Watch. As soon as she saw it she knew that it must be Jim's."
b. "The door opened and Jim stepped in and closed it. He looked very thin and very serious."
c. "Jim looked about the room curiously. 'You say your hair is gone?' he said, with an air almost of idiocy."
d. "Jim was never late. Della doubled the fob chain in her hand and sat on the corner of the table near the door that he always entered."

11. What is the theme of this passage?

a. True love leads to the sacrifice of one's most precious possessions.
b. Christmas is the representation of the love and sacrifice needed by all.
c. The love between two people eventually leads to frustration.
d. People should not try to surprise each other gifts.

12. Who is the narrator of this passage?

a. Della
b. Jim
c. O. Henry
d. None of the above

Questions 13-23 refer to the following passage:

The Story of My Life

by Helen Keller

Have you ever been at sea in a dense fog, when it seemed as if a tangible white darkness shut you in, and the great ship, tense and anxious, groped her way toward the shore with plummet and sounding-line, and you waited with beating heart for something to happen? I was like that ship before my education began...

I felt approaching footsteps. I stretched out my hand as I supposed to my mother. Someone took it, and I was caught up and held close in the arms of her who had come to reveal all things to me, and, more than all things else, to love me.

[One afternoon] we walked down the path to the well-house, attracted by the fragrance of the honeysuckle with which it was covered. Someone was drawing water and my teacher placed my hand under the spout. As the cool stream gushed over one hand, she spelled into the other the word water, first slowly, then rapidly. I stood still; my whole attention fixed upon the motions of her fingers. Suddenly I felt a misty consciousness as of something forgotten–a thrill of returning thought; and somehow the mystery of language was revealed to me. I knew then that "w-a-t-e-r" meant the wonderful cool something that was flowing over my hand. That living word awakened my soul, gave it light, hope, joy, set it free! There were barriers still, it is true, but barriers that could in time be swept away. I left the well-house eager to learn. Everything had a name, and each name gave birth to a new thought.

I recall many incidents of the summer of 1887 that followed my soul's sudden awakening. I did nothing but explore with my hands and learn the name of every object that I touched; and the more I handled things and learned their names and uses, the more joyous and confident grew my sense of kinship with the rest of the world.

I had my first lessons in the beneficence of nature. I learned how the sun and the rain make to grow out of the ground every tree that is pleasant to the sight and good for food, how birds build their nests and live and thrive from land to land, how the squirrel, the deer, the lion and every other creature finds food and shelter. As my knowledge of things grew, I felt more and more the delight of the world I was in. Long before I learned to do a sum in arithmetic or describe the shape of the earth, Miss Sullivan had taught me to find beauty in the fragrant woods, in every blade of grass, and in the curves and dimples of my baby sister's hand. She linked my earliest thoughts with nature, and made me feel that "birds and flowers and I were happy peers."

But about this time, I had an experience which taught me that nature is not always kind. One day my teacher and I were returning from a long ramble. The morning had been fine, but it was growing warm and sultry when at last we turned our faces homeward. Two or three times we stopped to rest under a tree by the wayside. Our last halt was under a wild cherry tree a short distance from the house. The shade was grateful, and the tree was so easy to climb that with my teacher's assistance I was able to scramble to a seat in the branches. It was so cool up in the tree that Miss Sullivan proposed that we have our luncheon there. I promised to keep still while she went to the house to fetch it.

Suddenly a change passed over the tree. All the sun's warmth left the air. I knew the sky was black, because all the heat, which meant light to me, had died out of the atmosphere. A strange odour came up from the earth. I knew it, it was the odour that always precedes a thunderstorm, and a nameless fear clutched at my heart. I felt absolutely alone, cut off from my friends and the firm earth. The immense, the unknown, enfolded me. I remained still and expectant; a chilling terror crept over me. I longed for my teacher's return; but above all things I wanted to get down from that tree.

There was a moment of sinister silence, then a multitudinous stirring of the leaves. A shiver ran through the tree, and the wind sent forth a blast that would have knocked me off had I not clung to the branch with might and main. The tree swayed and strained. The small twigs snapped and fell about me in showers. A wild impulse to jump seized me, but terror held me fast. I crouched down in the fork of the tree. The branches lashed about me. I felt the intermittent jarring that came now and then, as if something heavy had fallen and the shock had traveled up till it reached the limb I sat on. It worked my suspense up to the highest point, and just as I was thinking the tree and I should fall together, my teacher seized my hand and helped me down. I clung to her, trembling with joy to feel the earth under my feet once more. I had learned a new lesson–that nature "wages open war against her children, and under softest touch hides treacherous claws."

13. What is the meaning of the word *beneficence*?
a. Kindness
b. Generosity
c. Stinginess
d. Danger

14. Paragraph 3 is mainly about the narrator...

a. Learning to write words with a pencil
b. Learning the difference between cold and hot water
c. Learning the location of the well-house
d. Learning that words have meaning

15. Why did Helen hold out her hand in paragraph 2?

a. She thought the visitor was her mother
b. She wanted to greet the visitor
c. She wanted to please her mother
d. She loved the approaching person

16. In paragraphs 7 and 8, Helen felt nervous because...

a. She was lost
b. She was alone
c. It was raining
d. It was windy

17. Which sentence best explains what Helen learned from Miss Sullivan?

a. "I learned how the sun and the rain make to grow out of the ground every tree that is pleasant to the sight..."
b. "There were barriers still, it is true, but barriers that could in time be swept away."
c. "Everything had a name, and each name gave birth to a new thought."
d. "nature wages open war against her children, and under softest touch hides treacherous claws.'"

18. Which aspect of the selection best shows the close bond between Helen and Miss Sullivan?

a. The moment when Miss Sullivan spells "w-a-t-e-r" into Helen's hand
b. When Helen learned to find beauty in nature
c. When Miss Sullivan proposed eating lunch by the cherry tree
d. The moment when Miss Sullivan pulled Helen from the tree

19. What is a major theme of the passage?

a. Family ties
b. Discovery
c. Disappointment
d. Youth

20. In paragraph 8, the narrator uses the phrase "hides treacherous claws" to explain that...

a. Miss Sullivan, beneath her kind exterior, is very mean
b. Helen continues to have violent temper tantrums
c. Climbing trees can be very dangerous.
d. Nature can be cruel.

21. By telling the story in the order that events occur, the author helps you understand...

a. The change that Helen went through after meeting Miss Sullivan
b. The way in which Helen learned to be brave
c. The strategies Miss Sullivan used to teach Helen
d. The confusion that Helen felt when she was with Miss Sullivan

22. Based on the passage, you can conclude that Helen...

a. Disliked Miss Sullivan
b. Is scared of nature
c. Didn't understand words before Miss Sullivan arrived
d. Never learned how to read or write

23. What tool of figurative language is used in the sentence: "...each name gave birth to a new thought."?

a. metaphor
b. hyperbole
c. simile
d. personification

Questions 24–29 are for the following letter:

[In 1906, Elinore Pruitt Stewart moved to Denver for housework to support her daughter, Jerrine. Her employer in Denver was Mrs. Juliet Coney. A few years later, she moved to Wyoming to be a housekeeper for a rancher. The following passage is one of many letters that Stewart wrote to Mrs. Coney on life as a homesteader in Wyoming.]

A Letter of Elinore Pruitt Stewart

January 23, 1913

When I read of the hard times among the Denver poor, I feel like urging them every one to get out and file on land. I am very enthusiastic about women homesteading. It really requires less strength and labor to raise plenty to satisfy a large family than it does to go out to wash, with the added satisfaction of knowing that their job will not be lost to them if they care to keep it. Even if improving the place does go slowly, it is that much done to stay done. Whatever is raised is the homesteader's own, and there is no house-rent to pay. This year Jerrine cut and dropped enough potatoes to raise a ton of fine potatoes. She wanted to try, so we let her, and you will remember that she is but six years old.... Any woman strong enough to go out by the day could have done every bit of the work and put in two or three times that much, and it would have been so much more pleasant than to work so hard in the city and be on starvation rations all winter.

To me, homesteading is the solution of all poverty's problems, but I realize that temperament has much to do with success in any undertaking, and persons afraid of coyotes and work and loneliness had better let ranching alone. At the same time, any woman who can stand her own company, can see the beauty of the sunset, loves growing things, and is willing to put in as much time at careful labor as she does over the washtub, will certainly succeed; will have independence, plenty to eat all the time, and a home of her own in the end.

Experimenting need cost the homesteader no more than the work, because by applying to the Department of Agriculture at Washington he can get enough of any seed and as many kinds as he wants to make a thorough trial, and it doesn't even cost postage. Also, one can always get bulletins from there and from the Experiment Station of one's own State concerning any problem or as many problems as may come up. I would not, for anything, allow Mr. Stewart to do anything toward improving my place, for I want the fun and the experience myself. And I want to be able to speak from experience when I tell others what they can do. Theories are very beautiful, but facts are what must be had, and what I intend to give some time.

24. The writer of this letter is suggesting that women should own land and farm rather than

    a. cook in a restaurant.
    b. open a bed and breakfast.
    c. do laundry for others.
    d. teach in a one-room schoolhouse.

25. Stewart mentions her daughter's potato crop. She does this to show

    a. that child labor is acceptable.
    b. that there are no schools in the area.
    c. that women work just as hard as men do.
    d. how easy it is to raise crops.

26. What do you think Mrs. Coney's reaction to the letter might have been?

    a. She was probably glad to be rid of such a lazy worker.
    b. She may be glad to know that Mrs. Stewart is enjoying her time with homesteading.
    c. She may have been sorry that she too did not homestead.
    d. She was likely angry that Mrs. Stewart had written.

27. Which of the following does Stewart NOT give as an advantage of homesteading?

    a. It takes less strength and work than doing laundry for others
    b. The worker cannot lose her job if she wants to keep it.
    c. No one has to pay rent.
    d. One can always find good company.

28. Which of the following is a risk for the poor in Denver?

    a. the possibility of losing their jobs
    b. the likelihood of a strike
    c. the probability of a landslide
    d. their shacks and apartments will burn

29. The tone of the letter is

    a. complaining and bitter.
    b. sad and lonely.
    c. positive and encouraging.
    d. hopeless and despairing.

Questions 30 – 35 come from the debate below.

Forest Manager: Salvage logging is removing dead or dying forest stands that are left behind by a fire or disease. This practice has been used for several decades. These dead or dying trees become fuel that feeds future fires. The best way to lower the risk of forest fires is to remove the dead timber from the forest floor. Salvage logging followed by replanting ensures the reestablishment of desirable tree species.

For example, planting conifers accelerates the return of fire resistant forests. Harvesting timber helps forests by reducing fuel load, thinning the forest stands, and relieving competition between trees. Burned landscapes leave black surfaces and ash layers that have very high soil temperatures. These high soil temperatures can kill many plant species. Logging mixes the soil. So, this lowers surface temperatures to more normal levels. The shade from material that is left behind by logging also helps to lower surface temperatures. After an area has been salvage logged, seedlings in the area start to grow almost immediately. However, this regrowth can take several years in areas that are not managed well.

Ecology professor: Salvage logging moves material like small, broken branches to the forest floor. These pieces can become fuel for more fires. The removal of larger, less flammable trees leaves behind small limbs and increases the risk of forest fires. In unmanaged areas, these pieces are found more commonly on the tops of trees where they are unavailable to fires. Logging destroys old forests that are more resistant to wildfires. So, this creates younger forests that are more open to fires. In old forests, branches of bigger trees are higher above the floor where fires may not reach.

Replanting after wildfires creates monoculture plantations where only a single crop is planted. This monoculture allows less biological diversity. Also, it allows plants to be less resistant to disease. So, this increases the chance of fire. Salvage logging also upsets natural forest regrowth by killing most of the seedlings that grow after a wildfire. It breaks up the soil and increases erosion. Also, it removes most of the shade that is needed for young seedlings to grow.

30. According to the professor, how are unmanaged areas helpful in spreading small, woody materials after a fire?

a. They are left on the forest floor and bring nutrients to the soil.
b. They are left on the forest floor and serve as fuel for fires.
c. They are left on the tops of trees where fires cannot reach.
d. They are spread more evenly across the forest floor.

31. What is not a supporting detail for the Forest Manager's argument?

a. "This practice has been used for decades."
b. "Logging mixes the soil. So, this lowers surface temperatures to more normal levels."
c. "After an area has been salvage logged, seedlings in the area start to grow almost immediately."
d. "Salvage logging is removing dead or dying forest stands that are left behind by a fire or disease."

32. A study compared two plots of land that were managed differently after a fire. Plot A was salvage logged. Plot B was left unmanaged. After a second fire, they compared two plant groups between Plots A and B. They found that both plant groups burned worse in Plot A than in Plot B. Which viewpoint do these results support?

a. only the manager
b. only the professor
c. both the manager and professor
d. neither the manager nor the professor

33. What is the main idea of the forest manager's argument?

a. Salvage logging is helpful because it removes dead or dying timber from the forest floor. So, this lowers the risk of future fires.
b. Salvage logging is helpful because it has been practiced for many decades.
c. Salvage logging is harmful because it raises soil temperatures above normal levels. So, this threatens the health of plant species.
d. Salvage logging is helpful because it gives shade for seedlings to grow after a wildfire.

34. According to the professor, young forests are more open to harsh fires than old growth forests. Which of the following statements does not support this view?

a. In younger forests, small branches are closer to the forest floor and more available for fires.
b. Old growth forests have larger and taller trees. So, branches are high up and fires cannot reach.
c. Younger forests have less biological diversity and less disease-resistant trees.
d. Larger trees are common in old growth forests and serve as the main fuel source for severe fires.

35. Whose viewpoints would be proven by a future study looking at the spreading out and regrowth of seedlings for many years after a wildfire in managed and unmanaged forests?

a. only the manager
b. only the professor
c. both the manager and professor
d. neither the manager nor professor

Questions 36-40 refer to the following passage:

Section 1: Improving Diets

A healthier diet is something that many people want for themselves. However, this can be a struggle to put into practice for many people. This does not mean that just because it's hard and frustrating doesn't mean that people should stop trying.

A powerful and easy approach to improving diets is to know that some foods are so good for us that we can almost think of them as medicine. Some foods help to fight heart disease, cancer, or depression. Other foods help to lower cholesterol or blood pressure. Broccoli is high in vitamin K and vitamin C which help build strong bones and fight off cancers. Avocadoes can lower cholesterol and help reduce the risk of heart disease. Sweet potatoes are full of cancer-fighting and immune system-boosting vitamin A. Garlic can slow down the growth of bacteria and has been shown to lower cholesterol and blood pressure. Spinach is a great cancer fighter and has immune-boosting antioxidants important for eye health. Beans help lower risk of heart disease and breast cancer.

At some point, people want to give themselves the full treatment: diet, exercise, and general health overhaul. In the meantime, they can take the baby step of adding in one or more healthy food a week. This step is quick, easy, and painless. It couldn't be simpler to implement. Also, it will make their switch to healthy eating much easier to accomplish when they finally get there.

Section 2: Dietary Guidelines for Americans

The Dietary Guidelines for Americans is put together by the U.S. Department of Health and Human Services and the U.S. Department of Agriculture. The guidelines offer advice to people about food choices that advance good health and lower the risk of certain diseases (e.g., hypertension, anemia, and osteoporosis). In addition, this form offers a detailed outline on the kinds of foods that people should have in their diets. The outline is given so that additional supplements or vitamins may not be necessary. The form also has information on the types of exercise that are necessary for someone to stay healthy. Also, there is information on to handle and prepare certain foods to lower the risk of foodborne illness.

The Food Pyramid gave recommendations for the number of daily servings from each group. The USDA's Food Pyramid was heavily criticized for being unclear and confusing. In 2011, MyPlate replaced the Food Pyramid. MyPlate is much easier to understand because it has a picture of a dinner plate that is divided into four sections. So, this shows how our daily diet should be spread out among the different food groups. Vegetables and grains each take up 30% of the plate. Fruits and proteins each make up 20% of the plate. In the corner of the image is a cup that is marked as Dairy.

Most experts consider MyPlate to be a great improvement over the Food Pyramid. However, some it has still come under criticism from some quarters. Many believe too much emphasis is placed on protein, and some say the dairy recommendation should be eliminated altogether. The Harvard School of Public Health created its own Healthy Eating Plate to address what it sees as shortcomings in MyPlate. Harvard's guide adds healthy plant-based oils to the mix, stresses whole grains instead of merely grains, recommends drinking water or unsweetened coffee or tea instead of milk, and adds a reminder that physical activity is important.

Section 3: Preparing Better Meals in the Food Industry

People in the food industry that want to prepare a healthy meal for their customers should first decide on the nutritional goals of their menu. Once these goals have been set up, you should continue to plan by researching foods. These foods need to meet your goals without going beyond the available time and resource limits. Then, you can put together a meal plan that list several details. These details should have what foods will be included, the average time it takes to prepare and cook each of these meals, and the cost of preparing these meals. The next step is to decide on the best way of preparing the food for these meals. Think about which foods should be prepared first and the best ways to handle or prepare your food to lower the risk of illness. Also, think about methods that can be used to lower the cooking time. Finally, you can prepare the meal according to your plans.

When you need to decide on what foods to prepare, you need to think about several things. You should consider the food's nutritional value, the time it takes to prepare each food, the number of people to be served, and the cost of preparing each food. Each food has its own cooking time and has different nutrients. So, it is important to prepare foods that meet people's nutritional goals without using too much time for cooking the meal. Since you will likely have a budget for the meal, you need to review the number of people to be served and the cost of preparing each food. If the cost is too high, some meals may not be good choices to serve to large groups. For example, you are interested in serving a good source of protein for a meal. So, steak may be a good option for a small group of people. However, that would probably be too expensive for a larger group.

36. What is the main idea of Section 1?

a. Making a change to your diet is a quick process.
b. Some foods are healthier than others.
c. With discipline and smart decisions, you can make positive changes to your diet.
d. There are some people who can make dietary changes and some who cannot.

37. What is the purpose of including Section 2 in this passage?

a. To highlight the main argumentative points of the Food Pyramid and MyPlate
b. To cover the government's influence on the dietary recommendations for Americans
c. To show that there is no perfect system for coming up with dietary recommendations
d. To share information on generally accepted nutrition guidelines for future workers in the food industry

38. What is the purpose of including Harvard's Healthy Eating Plate in Section 2?

a. It is a supporting detail of the fact that MyPlate has received criticism
b. To give a sneak peek at the next official dietary guidelines
c. It shows another option as a dietary guideline
d. To highlight the influence of an Ivy League school

39. Who is the intended audience of these three sections?

a. People who are new to dieting
b. Experienced professionals in the food industry
c. People who want to work in the food industry
d. Parents who want to improve their children's meals

40. What is the tone of the three sections?

a. Condemning
b. Informative
c. Serious
d. Pretentious

WRITING

Questions 1–9 refer to the following passage:

How Do You Prepare Your Vehicle for Winter?

A

(1) Anyone who live in a climate which brings snow during the winter knows how important it is to have a working vehicle. (2) Before winter begins, get the car or truck serviced. (3) Consider the following tips. (4) Few things are worst than being unable to see in snow or sleet. (5) Most wiper blades do not last no longer than a year. (6) Be sure that while you are at it, the windshield washer reservoir has fluid. (7) First of all, do the windshield wipers work properly? (8) Do not fill it with water because plain water won't work in the winter since it freezes.

B

(9) Now, you need to check a few things under the hood. (10) Are belts and hoses in good shape is the battery in good working order? (11) When was the last oil change? (12) Make sure you have the right blend of antifreeze and water in the radiator. (13) Add to your vehicle's emergency kit extra food water and warm clothes or a blanket. (14) In winter, carry an ice scraper and a small shovel. (15) Consider tire chains and salt, sand, or non-clumping kitty litter to give your vehicle traction if needed.

C

(16) Have a plan if you are stranded. (17) You leave only the car because you know exactly where you are and how far you are from help. (18) Following these precautions will help to keep you and your loved ones safe in winter driving.

1. Sentence (1): *"Anyone who live in a climate which brings snow during the winter knows how important it is to have a working vehicle."*

What correction should be made to sentence (1)?

a. make <u>live</u> singular
b. place commas around <u>which brings snow</u>
c. set <u>during the winter</u> off in dashes
d. change <u>which</u> to <u>that</u>

2. Sentence (4): *"Few things are worst than being unable to see in snow or sleet."*

What correction should be made to this sentence?

a. change <u>are</u> to <u>is</u>
b. change <u>Few</u> to <u>Fewer</u>
c. change <u>worst</u> to <u>worse</u>
d. no correction is necessary

3. Sentence (5): *"Most wiper blades <u>do not last no longer</u> than a year."*

Which of the following is the best way to write the underlined portion of the sentence? If you think the original is the best way to write the sentence, choose answer A.

    a. do not last no longer
    b. do not last longer
    c. do not lasted no longer
    d. have not last no longer

4. Sentence (6): *"Be sure that while you are at it the windshield washer reservoir has fluid."*

What correction should be made to this sentence?

    a. move <u>while you are at it</u> to the front of the sentence and place a comma after it
    b. move <u>Be sure</u> to the end of the sentence
    c. place a question mark at the end of the sentence
    d. no correction is necessary

5. Sentence (7): *"First of all, do the windshield wipers work properly?"*

Which revision should be made to sentence (7) to improve the organization of the paragraph?

    a. move sentence (7) to the beginning of paragraph A
    b. move sentence (7) after sentence (3).
    c. move sentence (7) to the end of paragraph A
    d. move sentence (7) to the beginning of paragraph B

6. Sentence (9): *"Now, you need to check a few things under the hood."*

What correction should be made to sentence (9)?

    a. place <u>have</u> between <u>to</u> and <u>note</u>
    b. delete <u>under the hood</u> from the sentence
    c. change <u>a few</u> to <u>one</u>
    d. no change is necessary

7. Sentence (10): *"Are belts and hoses in <u>good shape is the</u> battery in good working order?"*

Which of the following is the best way to write the underlined portion of the sentence? If you think that the original is the best way to write the sentence, choose answer A.

    a. good shape is the
    b. good shape, is the
    c. good shape and is the
    d. good shape; is the

8. Sentence (13): *"Add to your vehicle's emergency kit extra food water and warm clothes or a blanket."*

What correction should be made to this sentence?

    a. remove the apostrophe from <u>vehicle's</u>
    b. change the spelling of <u>emergency</u> to <u>emergancy</u>
    c. place commas after the words <u>food</u> and <u>water</u>
    d. no correction is necessary

9. Sentence (17): *"You leave only the car because you know exactly where you are and how far you are from help."*

What correction should be made to this sentence?

a. move <u>only</u> to come between <u>You</u> and <u>leave</u>
b. delete <u>exactly</u>
c. put a comma before <u>and</u>
d. no correction is necessary

Questions 10–18 refer to the following passage:

How Slow Is Your Food?

A

(1) A growing grassroots movement is taking place around the world. (2) Developed nations have spent the past half-century creating fast food products, which are designed more for ease and availability than for taste. (3) Today, people worry more over genetically modified crops, food safety, and the cost of shipping food across the nation. (4) So, slow foods is making a comeback.

B

(5) Slow food puts the emphasize on community and sharing. (6) A major concern is to support local farmers and artisans. (7) Examples are those who are trying to save endangered species of animals, grains, the fruits, and the vegetables. (8) A new interest in heirloom varieties has reawakened palates that were used to food which had lost nutritional appeal and flavor. (9) Slow food also seeks to fully use sustainable agriculture. (10) This way soils can be replenished without the use of chemicals.

C

(11) Slow food usa has taken the program to students in elementary and secondary schools through its Garden to Table program. (12) Focusing on pleasure, tradition, and sustainability, the projects offer young people a chance to be involved in hands-on gardening and cooking. (13) I once had a garden in my backyard. (14) Students learn where their food comes from and they find out who grows it and how to cook it and the need to share with others. (15) A similar program, Slow Food on Campus, is conducted by the college and university students. (16) All programs adhere to the basic ideas of slow food: a good, clean, and fair food system.

10. Sentence (2): *"Developed nations have spent the past half-century creating fast <u>food products, which are</u> designed more for ease and availability than for taste."*

Which of the following is the best way to write the underlined portion of the sentence? If you think that the original is the best way to write the sentence, choose answer A.

a. food products, which are
b. food products which are
c. food product, which are
d. food products, which is

11. Sentence (4): *"So, slow foods is making a comeback."*

What correction should be made to this sentence?

    a. remove the extra comma
    b. change is to are
    c. capitalize slow foods
    d. put a hyphen between *come* and *back*

12. Sentence (5): *"Slow food <u>puts the emphasize</u> on community and sharing."*

Which of the following is the best way to write the underlined portion of the sentence? If you think the original is the best way to write the sentence, choose answer A.

    a. puts the emphasize
    b. places the emphasize
    c. put the emphasize
    d. puts the emphasis

13. Sentence (7): *"Examples are those who are trying to save endangered species of animals, grains, the fruits and the vegetables."*

Which of the following is the best way to write the underlined portion of the sentence? If you think that the original is the best way to write the sentence, choose answer A.

    a. endangered species of animals, grains, the fruits and the vegetables
    b. endangered specie of animals, grains, the fruits and the vegetables
    c. endangered species of animal, grain, the fruit and the vegetable
    d. endangered species of animals, grains, fruits and vegetables

14. Sentence (9): *"Slow food also seeks to fully use sustainable agriculture."*

What correction should be made to this sentence?

    a. change <u>seeks</u> to plural
    b. put a dash between <u>replenished</u> and <u>without</u>
    c. delete <u>fully</u>
    d. no correction is needed

15. Sentence (11): *"Slow food usa has taken the program to students in elementary and secondary schools through its Garden to Table program."*

What correction should be made to this sentence?

    a. remove capital letters from <u>Garden</u> and <u>Table</u>
    b. capitalize <u>food usa</u>
    c. change the spelling of <u>through</u> to <u>thru</u>
    d. no correction is needed

16. Sentence (13): *"I once had a garden in my backyard."*

Which revision should be made to sentence (13) to improve the organization of this paragraph?

a. move the sentence to the beginning of the paragraph
b. use the sentence as the concluding statement of the article
c. delete sentence (13)
d. move the sentence to the previous paragraph

17. Sentence (14): *"Students learn where their food comes from and they find out who grows it and how to cook it and the need to share with others."*

What correction should be made to this sentence?

a. add commas
b. make the terms parallel
c. change <u>their</u> to <u>they're</u>
d. make two sentences

18. Sentence (15): *"A similar program, Slow Food on Campus, is conducted by the college and university students."*

What correction should be made to this sentence?

a. make <u>college and university students</u> the subject
b. remove the commas
c. remove the capital letters on <u>Slow, Food</u>, and <u>Campus</u>
d. change the spelling of <u>similar</u> to <u>simular</u>

Questions 19–28 refer to the following passage:

Are You SAD?

A

(1) For many healthy people, the coming of winter gets them down. (2) Some hibernation tendencies are common. (3) If you notice true depression a sense of hopelessness less energy, or anxiety, you may be suffering from seasonal affective disorder or SAD. (4) Some people experience SAD during spring and summer for most people, however, winter is the season to be SAD.

B

(5) Researchers are not certainly what causes SAD. (6) One suggestion is that having our regular body rhythms disrupted when less sunlight is available is the culprit. (7) Another study blames increased production of melatonin: a hormone related to sleep. (8) During the dark winter months, the body makes more melatonin. (9) At the same time, it makes less serotonin: the brain chemical that effects our moods. (10) Fewer sunlight means less serotonin. (11) So far, risk factors has not been identified.

C

(12) Most people with SAD just tough it out and waiting for spring. (14) If you have symptoms that last more than two weeks, it is time to see a doctor. (15) People with mild cases of SAD need to spend time outside, exercise regularly, and go to social events or travel. (16) The good news is that spring always comes?

19. Sentence (1): *"For many healthy people, the coming of winter gets them down."*

What correction should be made to this sentence?

a. delete the comma
b. change gets to plural form
c. change healthy to healthly
d. no correction is needed

20. Sentence (3): *"If you notice true depression a sense of hopelessness less energy, or anxiety, you may be suffering from seasonal affective disorder or SAD."*

What correction should be made to this sentence?

a. remove the comma after disorder
b. place a comma after hopelessness
c. capitalize seasonal affective disorder
d. no correction is needed

21. Sentence (4): *"Some people experience SAD during spring and summer for most people, however, winter is the season to be SAD."*

Which of the following is the best way to write the underlined portion of the sentence? If you think the original is the best way to write the sentence, choose answer A.

a. and summer for most
b. and summer, for most
c. and summer: for most
d. and summer. For most

22. Sentence (5): *"Researchers are not certainly what causes SAD."*

What correction should be made to this sentence?

a. change certainly to certain
b. do not use capital letters for SAD
c. end the sentence with a question mark
d. no correction is necessary

23. Sentence (8): *"During the dark winter months, the body makes more melatonin."*

What correction should be made to this sentence?

a. put a comma between dark and winter
b. change more to much
c. capitalize melatonin
d. no correction is needed

24. Sentence (9): *"At the same time, it makes less serotonin: the brain chemical that effects our moods."*

What correction should be made to this sentence?

a. change <u>effects</u> to <u>affects</u>
b. move the first phrase to after <u>serotonin</u>
c. change <u>less</u> to <u>fewer</u>
d. no correction is needed

25. Sentence (10): *"Fewer sunlight means less serotonin."*

What correction should be made to this sentence?

a. change <u>means</u> to <u>mean</u>
b. capitalize <u>serotonin</u>
c. change <u>less</u> to <u>fewer</u>
d. change <u>Fewer</u> to <u>Less</u>

26. Sentence (11): *"<u>So far, risk factors has not</u> been identified."*

What is the best way to write the underlined portion of the sentence? If you think the original is the best way to write the sentence, choose answer A.

a. So far, risk factors has not
b. so far, risk factors has not
c. So far, risk factor have not
d. So far, risk factors have not

27. Sentence (12): *"Most people with SAD just tough it out and waiting for spring."*

What correction should be made to this sentence?

a. write <u>SAD</u> as <u>sad</u>
b. change <u>tough</u> to <u>toughing</u>
c. change <u>waiting</u> to <u>wait</u>
d. no correction is necessary

28. Sentence (16): *"The good news is that spring always comes?"*

What correction should be made to this sentence?

a. change <u>good</u> to <u>well</u>
b. change the question mark to a period
c. capitalize <u>spring</u>
d. no correction is necessary

Questions 29–37 refer to the following article:

Only Temporary

A

(1) Many businesses in the United States regularly hire "temps" or temporary workers. (2) Now known as the staffing industry, temp work employs nearly 3 million people and generating more than $40 billion annually. (3) Because jobs are no longer secure, many people find that moving from job to job is a good way to

274

improve they're skills. (4) They sometimes find the perfect job and are hired as a full-time employee. (5) Businesses love temps, they save the company money because temps do not receive benefits.

B

(6) Would temp work be a good move for you? (7) If you are the kind of worker who bores quickly and needs new challenges, temping may be the way to go. (8) Temp work may offer a more flexible schedule and it gives a changing work environment. (9) On the down side, you will not get benefits like paid vacations or health insurance. (10) You may not always be treated very well because temp workers come and go.

C

(11) If you're looking for a job, temp work can add valuable experience to your résumé. (12) It also allows you time to look for and interviewing for a new and permanent job. (13) In addition, temp work is a great way to explore different careers. (14) Many temp jobs are temp-to-hire because the company needs to fill a position and is looking among temp workers for a permanant hire. (15) You may be just the employee they are seeking!

29. Sentence (1): *"Many businesses in the United States regularly hire "temps" or temporary workers."*

What correction should be made to this sentence?

    a. remove the quotation marks from <u>temps</u>
    b. remove <u>or temporary workers</u> from the sentence
    c. change the spelling of <u>temporary</u> to <u>temparary</u>
    d. place a comma after <u>temps</u>

30. Sentence (2): *"Now known as the staffing industry, temp work employs nearly 3 million people and generating more than $40 billion annually."*

What correction should be made to this sentence?

    a. change <u>industry</u> to <u>industries</u>
    b. change <u>work</u> to <u>works</u>
    c. change <u>employs</u> to <u>employing</u>
    d. change <u>generating</u> to <u>generates</u>

31. Sentence (3): *"Because jobs are no longer secure, many people find that moving from job to job is a good way to improve they're skills."*

What correction should be made to this sentence?

    a. change <u>Because</u> to <u>Since</u>
    b. remove the comma after <u>secure</u>
    c. change <u>skills</u> to <u>skill</u>
    d. change <u>they're</u> to <u>their</u>

32. Sentence (4): *"They sometimes find the perfect job and <u>are hired as a full-time employee</u>."*

Which of the following is the best way to write the underlined portion of this sentence? If you think the original is the best way to write the sentence, choose answer A.

    a. are hired as a full-time employee.
    b. are hired as full-time employees.
    c. is hired as a full-time employee.
    d. is hired as a fulltime employee.

33. Sentence (5): *"<u>Businesses love temps, they save</u> the company money, because temps do not receive benefits."*

Which of the following is the best way to write the underlined portion of this sentence? If you think the original is the best way to write the sentence, choose answer A.

    a. Businesses love temps, they save
    b. Businesses love temps, it saves
    c. Businesses love temps; they save
    d. Businesses love temps, they saves

34. Sentence (8): *"Temp work may offer a more <u>flexible schedule and it gives</u> a changing work environment."*

Which of the following is the best way to write the underlined portion of this sentence? If you think the original is the best way to write the sentence, choose answer A.

    a. flexible schedule and it gives
    b. flexible schedule and it give
    c. flexible schedules and it gives
    d. flexible schedule, and it gives

35. Sentence (11): *"If you're looking for a job, temp work can add valueable experience to your résumé."*

What correction should be made to this sentence?

    a. put a hyphen between <u>temp</u> and <u>work</u>
    b. change <u>you're</u> to <u>your</u>
    c. change <u>valueable</u> to <u>valuable</u>
    d. no correction is necessary

36. Sentence (12): *"It also allows you time to look for and interviewing for a new and permanent job."*

What correction should be made to this sentence?

    a. change <u>permanent</u> to <u>permanant</u>
    b. change <u>look</u> to <u>looking</u>
    c. change <u>interviewing</u> to <u>interview</u>
    d. no correction is necessary

37. Sentence (14): *"Many temp jobs are temp-to-hire because the company needs to fill a position and is looking among temp workers for a permanant hire."*

Which of the following is the best way to write the underlined portion of this sentence? If you think the original is the best way to write the sentence, choose answer A.

    a. workers for a permanant hire
    b. workers for a permanent hire
    c. a worker for a permanant hire
    d. workers for permanant hires

Questions 38–43 refer to the following passage:

Picking the Perfect Pet

A

    (1) Today's choices for pets go beyond the question of whether to get a cat or a dog? (2) Gerbils, rabbits, and amphibians is all popular options. (3) Before heading to an animal shelter, you need to know what pet makes sense for your home or classroom. (4) An obvious question to answer if you rent is if pets are permitted. (5) Some apartment complex places weight and size limits on pets or charge fees. (6) After gaining permission from the manager, your pet needs to be considered for other issues.

B

    (7) If allergies effect someone in your home, be sure to select a pet that will not aggravate the condition. (8) Some dog breeds like the schnauzer and the poodle are acceptable pets for those who are sensitive to fur and dander.

C

    (9) Irregardless of the pet you choose, think about other costs such as veterinary care and vaccinations, food costs, licensing, and equipment. (10) Does the pet need a special kind of home? (11) Who will be responsible for feeding and cleaning up after the animal? (12) Taking time to do a little research can save you a lot of heartache and expense later.

38. Sentence (1): *"Today's choices for pets go beyond the question of whether to get a cat or a dog?"*

What correction should be made to this sentence?

    a. change the question mark to a period
    b. change Today's to Todays
    c. change question to questions
    d. no correction is necessary

39. Sentence (2): *"Gerbils, rabbits, and amphibians is all popular options."*

What correction should be made to this sentence?

    a. remove the comma after <u>Gerbils</u>
    b. change <u>amphibians</u> to <u>amfibians</u>
    c. change <u>is</u> to <u>are</u>
    d. no correction is necessary

40. Sentence (5): *"<u>Some apartment complex places weight</u> and size limits on pets or charge fees."*

Which of the following is the best way to write the underlined portion of this sentence? If you think the original is the best way to write the sentence, choose answer A.

    a. Some apartment complex places weight
    b. Some apartment complex places wait
    c. Some apartment complexes places weight
    d. Some apartment complexes place weight

41. Sentence (6): *"After gaining permission from the manager, your pet needs to be considered for other issues."*

What correction should be made to this sentence?

    a. delete the comma
    b. change <u>permission</u> to <u>permision</u>
    c. rewrite the independent clause
    d. No correction is needed

42. Sentence (7): *"<u>If allergies effect someone</u> in your home, be sure to select a pet that will not aggravate the condition."*

Which of the following is the best way to write the underlined part of this sentence? If you think the original is the best way to write the sentence, choose answer A.

    a. If allergies effect someone
    b. If allergies affect someone
    c. If allergies affects someone
    d. If allergies effects someone

43. Sentence (9): *"Irregardless of the pet you choose, think about other costs such as veterinary care and vaccinations, food costs, licensing and equipment."*

What correction should be made to this sentence?

    a. change <u>Irregardless</u> to <u>Regardless</u>
    b. change <u>licensing</u> to <u>lisencing</u>
    c. remove the extra commas
    d. no correction is needed

Questions 44–50 refer to the following passage:

Madame President

A

(1) Before they had the right to vote, women have attempted to gain the nations highest executive office. (2) Victoria Woodhull ran as a third party candidate in 1872. (3) Although she did not win, she became the first woman who owned an investment firm on wall street. (4) In 1884 and 1888, the lawyer Belva Lockwood also ran as a third party candidate. (5) Margaret Chase Smith (who served in both houses of Congress) was the first woman nominated by a major party: the Republicans.

B

(6) Nine other women have seeked for the presidency since the 1970s. (7) Five of them were Democrats and one was a Republican and three represented third parties. (8) I think it's about time this country had a woman as president. (9) Only two women have been nominated as vice president: Democrat Geraldine Ferraro in 1984 and Republican Sarah Palin in 2008. (10) Many people believe that soon the United States will join countries such as Britain, India, Germany, Chile, and Liberia, that have women heads of state.

44. Sentence (1): *"Before they had the right to vote, women have attempted to gain the nations highest executive office."*

What correction should be made to this sentence?

a. capitalize <u>executive office</u>
b. change <u>nations</u> to <u>nation's</u>
c. put *finally* between <u>to</u> and <u>gain</u>
d. no correction is needed

45. Sentence (3): *"Although she did not win, she became the first woman who owned an investment firm on wall street."*

What correction should be made to this sentence?

a. change <u>became</u> to <u>become</u>
b. capitalize <u>wall street</u>
c. change <u>Although</u> to <u>Though</u>
d. capitalize <u>investment firm</u>

46. Sentence (5): *"Margaret Chase Smith (who served in both houses of Congress) was the first woman nominated by a major part: the Republicans."*

What correction should be made to this sentence?

a. change the parentheses to commas
b. do not capitalize <u>Republicans</u>
c. change <u>woman</u> to <u>women</u>
d. no correction is necessary

47. Sentence (6): *"Nine other women have seeked for the presidency since the 1970s."*

Which of the following is the best way to write the underlined portion of this sentence? If you think the original is the best way to write the sentence, choose answer A.

    a. women have seeked for
    b. woman have seeked for
    c. women have seek for
    d. women have sought

48. Sentence (7): *"Five of them were Democrats and one was a Republican, and three represented third parties."*

What correction should be made to this sentence?

    a. add a comma after <u>Democrats</u> and delete the <u>and</u> after <u>Democrats</u>
    b. change <u>them</u> to <u>those</u>
    c. change <u>were</u> to <u>was</u>
    d. no correction is necessary

49. Which revision would improve the overall organization of this article?

    a. switch paragraphs A and B
    b. place the final sentence at the beginning of paragraph B
    c. delete sentence (8)
    d. place sentence (2) at the end of paragraph A

50. Sentence (10): *"Many people believe that the United States will soon join countries such as Britain, India, Germany, Chile, and Liberia, that have women heads of state."*

What correction should be made to this sentence?

    a. remove the comma after <u>Liberia</u>
    b. remove the unnecessary commas
    c. change the spelling of <u>believe</u> to <u>beleive</u>
    d. no correction is necessary

EXTENDED RESPONSE

The study summary below outlines a problem that has been in America for decades. The next article gives one possible solution to the problem. Analyze the arguments made by the author of the article. Then, decide if his reasoning is sound. Be sure to give evidence from the passage. Also, give evidence from your own knowledge and experience. Explain why you would predict that his idea would succeed or fail.

Study Summary from the Education Resources Information Center

Student scores on standardized tests have steadily declined since 1965. Researchers conducted a literature review and completed data analysis to determine the reasons for this decrease, assessing trends for the period from 1965 to 1983. The reasons for the declining student scores include changes in the composition of test-takers, decreases in the quantity of schooling which students experience, curriculum changes, declines in student motivation, and deterioration of the family system and social environment. These factors, in combination, have contributed to the test score decline for more than fifteen years. Efforts to end the decreases must address the curricular and school climate factors identified.

Excerpt from an article by Roger Sipher

"So That Nobody Has To Go To School If They Don't Want To"

A decline in standardized test scores is but the most recent indicator that American education is in trouble. One reason for the crisis is that present mandatory-attendance laws force many to attend school who have no wish to be there. Such children have little desire to learn and are so antagonistic to school that neither they nor more highly motivated students receive the quality education that is the birthright of every American. The solution to this problem is simple: Abolish compulsory-attendance laws and allow only those who are committed to getting an education to attend.

Most parents want a high school education for their children. Unfortunately, compulsory attendance hampers the ability of public school officials to enforce legitimate educational and disciplinary policies and thereby make the education a good one. Private schools have no such problem. They can fail or dismiss students, knowing such students can attend public school. Without compulsory attendance, public schools would be freer to oust students whose academic or personal behavior undermines the educational mission of the institution.

Abolition of archaic attendance laws would produce enormous dividends:

- First, it would alert everyone that school is a serious place where one goes to learn. Schools are neither day-care centers nor indoor street corners. Young people who resist learning should stay away; indeed, an end to compulsory schooling would require them to stay away.
- Second, students opposed to learning would not be able to pollute the educational atmosphere for those who want to learn. Teachers could stop policing recalcitrant students and start educating.

281

- Third, grades would show what they are supposed to: how well a student is learning. Parents could again read report cards and know if their children were making progress.
- Fourth, public esteem for schools would increase. People would stop regarding them as way stations for adolescents and start thinking of them as institutions for educating America's youth.
- Fifth, elementary schools would change because students would find out early they had better learn something or risk flunking out later. Elementary teachers would no longer have to pass their failures on to junior high and high school.
- Sixth, the cost of enforcing compulsory education would be eliminated. Despite enforcement efforts, nearly 15 percent of the school-age children in our largest cities are almost permanently absent from school.

Communities could use these savings to support institutions to deal with young people not in school. If, in the long run, these institutions prove more costly, at least we would not confuse their mission with that of schools. Schools should be for education. At present, they are only tangentially so. They have attempted to serve an all-encompassing social function, trying to be all things to all people. In the process they have failed miserably at what they were originally formed to accomplish.

Mathematics

NON-CALCULATOR SECTION

Question 1 is based on the following figure:

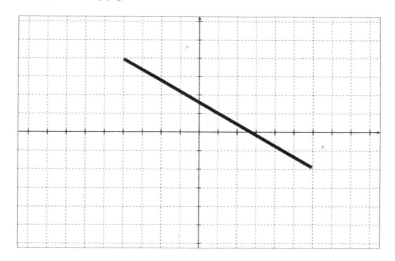

1. For each coordinate pair listed below, consider a line connecting the two coordinates. Which coordinate pairs represent a line that will intersect the line segment in the above figure? (Select all that apply.)

    a. (-8, 5) and (5,5)
    b. (-3, 2) and (1, -1)
    c. (-1, 1) and (3, 5)
    d. (0,-4) and (5, -6)
    e. (7,3) and (-1,5)
    f. (4,2) and (0,-2)

Question 2 is based on the following figure:

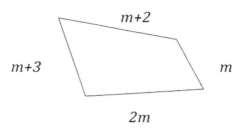

2. The figure shows an irregular quadrilateral and the lengths of its sides. Which of the following equations best shows the perimeter of the quadrilateral?

    a. $m^4 + 5$
    b. $2m^4 + 5$
    c. $4m + 5$
    d. $5m + 5$

3. If a = -6 and b = 7, then $4a(3b + 5) + 2b$ =?

    a. 638
    b. -610
    c. 624
    d. 610

4. Which of the following expressions represents the ratio of the area of a circle to its circumference?

    a. πr^2
    b. $\dfrac{\pi r^2}{2\pi}$
    c. $\dfrac{2\pi r}{r^2}$
    d. $\dfrac{r}{2}$

5. Mrs. Patterson's classroom has sixteen empty chairs. All the chairs are filled when every student is present. If 2/5 of the students are absent, how many students make up her entire class?

    a. 40
    b. 32
    c. 24
    d. 16

CALCULATOR SECTION

6. Jamie had $6.50 in his wallet when he left home. He spent $4.25 on drinks and $2.00 on a magazine. Later, his friend repaid him $2.50 that he had borrowed the previous day. How much money does Jamie have in his wallet now?

    a. $12.25
    b. $14.25
    c. $3.25
    d. $2.75

Question 7 is based on the following table:

Metric - English Equivalents

1 meter	1.094 yard
2.54 centimeter	1 inch
1 kilogram	2.205 pound
1 liter	1.06 quart

7. A building is 19 meters tall. What is its height in inches?

    a. 254
    b. 1094
    c. 4826
    d. 748

8. Rachel needs to buy extra items for her restaurant. She went to the store and spent $24.15 on vegetables. She bought 2 lbs of onions, 3 lbs of carrots, and $1\frac{1}{2}$ lbs of mushrooms. The onions cost $3.69 per lb, and the carrots cost $ 4.29 per lb. So, what is the price per pound of mushrooms?

    a. $2.60
    b. $2.25
    c. $2.80
    d. $3.10

Question 9 is based on the following figure:

9. In the figure, A, B, and C are points on the number line. Also, O is the origin. What is the ratio of the distance *BC* to distance *AB*?

    a. 3:5
    b. 8:5
    c. 8:11
    d. 3:11

10. Jesse invests $7,000 in a certificate of deposit that pays interest at the rate of 7.5% annually. How much interest (in dollars) does Jesse gain from this investment during the first year that he holds the certificate?

11. In an election in Kimball County, Candidate A gained 36,800 votes. His opponent, Candidate B, had 32,100 votes. 2,100 votes went to write-in candidates. What percentage of the vote went to Candidate A?

   a. 51.8%
   b. 53.4%
   c. 45.2%
   d. 46.8%

12. Francine can ride 16 miles on her bicycle in 45 minutes. At this speed, how many minutes would it take Francine to ride 60 miles?

Question 13 is based upon the following figure:

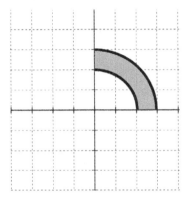

13. Marcus draws a plan for a hot tub in his backyard. He wants to put a concrete path around the tub. So, he starts with one area of the pool to find out how much material he needs. Now, the inner circle has a radius of two units. The outer circle has a radius of three units. What is the area of the shaded part?

Questions 14– 16 are based on the following table. This gives the closing prices of a number of stocks traded on the New York Stock Exchange:

Stock	Price per Share	Shares Traded
Microsoft	$45.14	89,440,000
Oracle	$19.11	12,415,000
Apple Computer	$16.90	17,953,000
Cisco Systems	$3.50	73,019,000
Garmin	$29.30	53,225,000

14. David bought 200 shares of Oracle stock yesterday and sold it today. His profit was $22.00. At what price did he buy the stock yesterday?

   a. $18.89
   b. $19.00
   c. $19.06
   d. $18.96

15. Lynn buys a package of stocks that has 100 shares each of Microsoft and Apple. Also, the package has 200 shares of Garmin at the closing prices from the table. What is the average price per share that she pays for these stocks?

16. James decides to invest $4500 in Cisco Systems stock and buys it at the price shown in the table. At what price should he sell it to have a profit of 10%?

17. Erica started work today at 7:00AM and worked until 4:30 PM. She earns $12 per hour for her regular shift which is 8 hours. Also, she works 50% more per hour for overtime. How much did Erica make today?

Question 18 is based upon the following diagram:

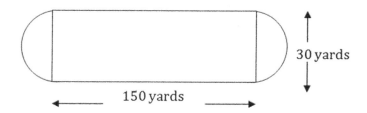

18. A company is building a track for a local high school. There are two straight sections and two semi-circular turns. Given the dimensions, which of the following most closely measures the perimeter of the entire track?
   a. 300 yards
   b. 180 yards
   c. 360 yards
   d. 395 yards

19. Elijah drove 45 miles to his job in an hour and ten minutes in the morning. On the way home, traffic was bad. So, the same trip took an hour and a half. What was his average speed in miles per hour for the round trip?
   a. 30
   b. 45
   c. $33\frac{3}{4}$
   d. $32\frac{1}{2}$

20. The distance traveled by a moving object is found with the formula: $d = rt$, where r is the rate of travel (speed) and t is the time of travel. A major league pitcher throws a fastball at a speed of 125 ft/sec. The distance from the pitching rubber to home plate is 60.5 feet. How long, in seconds, does it take a fastball to travel this distance? Write your answer to the nearest hundredth of a second.

21. Lauren had $80 in her savings account. When she received her paycheck, she put some money in her savings account. This brought the balance up to $120. By what percentage did the total amount in her account increase by putting this amount in her savings account?
   a. 50%
   b. 40%
   c. 35%
   d. 80%

Question 22 is based on the following diagram:

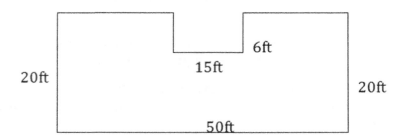

22. What is the area of the figure shown above? Give your answer in square feet.

23. Which of the following is a solution to the inequality $4x - 12 < 4$?

    a. 7
    b. 6
    c. 5
    d. 3

24. Mark is leaving a job site and moving equipment to Phoenix which is located 210 miles north. He drives the first ten miles in 12 minutes. If he continues at the same rate, how long will it take him to reach his destination?

    a. 3 hours 15 minutes
    b. 4 hours 12 minutes
    c. 3 hours 45 minutes
    d. 4 hours 20 minutes

25. An airplane leaves Atlanta at 2 PM and flies north at 250 miles per hour. A second airplane leaves Atlanta 30 minutes later and flies north at 280 miles per hour. At what time will the second airplane overtake the first?

    a. 6:00 PM
    b. 6:20 PM
    c. 6:40 PM
    d. 6:50 PM

Question 26 is based on the following diagram:

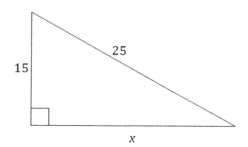

26. Find the length of the side labeled x. The triangle is a right triangle.

    a. 18
    b. 20
    c. 22
    d. 24

27. A company has been asked to design a building for an athletic event. The building is in the shape of a square pyramid. The pyramid has a height of 481 ft, and the length of each side of the base is 756 ft. What is the volume of the pyramid?

    a. $1.21 \times 10^5 \, \text{ft}^3$
    b. $4.85 \times 10^5 \, \text{ft.}^3$
    c. $9.16 \times 10^7 \, \text{ft.}^3$
    d. $2.75 \times 10^8 \, \text{ft.}^3$

28. If $x + y > 0$ when $x > y$, which of the following cannot be true?

    a. x = 3 and y = 0
    b. x = 6 and y = -1
    c. x = -3 and y = 0
    d. x = 3 and y = -3

29. Which of the following expressions is equal to $x^3 x^5$?

    a. $2x^8$
    b. x^{15}
    c. x^2
    d. x^8

30. If $\frac{12}{x} = \frac{30}{6}$, what is the value of x?

    a. 3.6
    b. 2.4
    c. 3.0
    d. 2.0

31. Which of the following could be a graph of the function $y = \frac{1}{x}$?

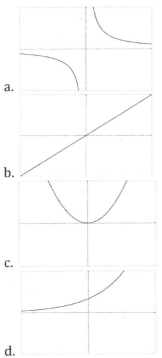

a.

b.

c.

d.

Question 32 is based on the following figure:

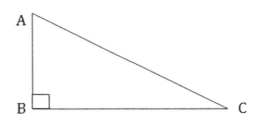

32. $\triangle ABC$ is a right triangle, and $\angle ACB = 30°$. What is the measure of $\angle BAC$?

    a. $40°$
    b. $50°$
    c. $60°$
    d. $45°$

Question 33 is based on the following table:

Hours	1	2	3
Cost	$3.60	$7.20	$10.80

33. The table shows the cost of renting a bicycle for 1, 2, or 3 hours. Which of the following equations best represents the data? Let C stand for the cost and h stand for the time of the rental.

a. $C = 3.60h$
b. $C = h + 3.60$
c. $C = 3.60h + 10.80$
d. $C = \frac{10.80}{h}$

34. Which of the following statements is true?

a. Perpendicular lines have opposite slopes
b. Perpendicular lines have the same slopes
c. Perpendicular lines have reciprocal slopes
d. Perpendicular lines have opposite reciprocal slopes

35. There are 64 squares on a checkerboard. Bobby puts one penny on the first square, two on the second square, four on the third, eight on the fourth. He continues to double the number of coins at each square until he has covered all 64 squares. How many coins must he place on the last square?

a. 2^{64}
b. $2^{64} - 1$
c. 2^{63}
d. $2^{63} + 1$

36. Carrie wants to decorate her party with bundles of balloons containing three balloons each. Balloons are available in 4 different colors. There must be three different colors in each bundle. How many different kinds of bundles can she make?

a. 18
b. 12
c. 4
d. 6

Question 37 is based on the following figure:

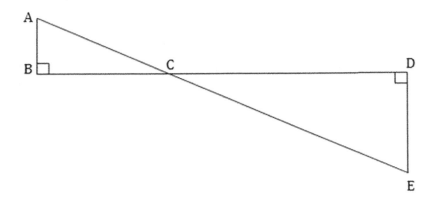

37. In the figure above, segment BC is 4 units long. Segment CD is 8 units long. Segment DE is 6 units long. What is the length of segment AC?

    a. 7 units
    b. 5 units
    c. 3 units
    d. 2.5 units

38. The expressions $y = -3x + 6$ and $y = 2x - 4$ represent straight lines. Find the coordinates of the point at which they intersect.

39. In a game of chance, 3 dice are thrown at the same time. What is the probability that all three will land with a 6?

    a. 1 in 6
    b. 1 in 18
    c. 1 in 216
    d. 1 in 30

40. Rafael has a business selling computers. He buys computers from the manufacturer for $450 each and sells them for $800. Each month, he must also pay fixed costs of $3000 for rent and utilities for his store. If he sells n computers in a month, which of the following equations can be used to find his profit?

    a. $P = n(800 - 450)$
    b. $P = n(800 - 450 - 3000)$
    c. $P = 3000\, n(800 - 450)$
    d. $P = n(800 - 450) - 3000$

41. Put the following numbers in order from the least to greatest 2^3, 4^2, 6^0, 9, 10^1.

    a. 2^3, 4^2, 6^0, 9, 10^1
    b. 6^0, 9, 10^1, 2^3, 4^2
    c. 10^1, 2^3, 6^0, 9, 4^2
    d. 6^0, 2^3, 9, 10^1, 4^2

Questions 42-43 are based on the following chart:

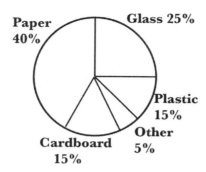

42. The Charleston Recycling Company collects 50,000 tons of recyclable material every month. The chart shows the kinds of materials that are collected by the company's five trucks. What is the second most common material that is recycled?

　a. Cardboard
　b. Glass
　c. Paper
　d. Plastic

43. About how much paper is recycled every month?

　a. 40,000 tons
　b. 50,000 tons
　c. 15,000 tons
　d. 20,000 tons

44. Dorothy is half her sister's age. Dorothy will be three fourths of her sister's age in 20 years. What is Dorothy's current age?

　a. 10
　b. 15
　c. 20
　d. 25

45. Chan receives a bonus from his job. He pays 30% in taxes, gives 30% to charity, and uses another 25% to pay off an old debt. He has $600 remaining from his bonus. What was the total amount of Chan's bonus?

Question 46 is based on the following diagram:

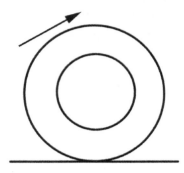

46. A tire on a car rotates at 500 RPM (revolutions per minute) when the car is traveling at 50 km/hr (kilometers per hour). What is the circumference of the tire? Give your answer in meters.

    a. $\dfrac{50,000}{2\pi}$

    b. $\dfrac{50,000}{60\times2\pi}$

    c. $\dfrac{50,000}{60}$

    d. $\dfrac{10}{6}$

47. A farmer installed a new grain silo on his property for the fall harvest. The silo is in the shape of a cylinder with a diameter of 8 m and a height of 24 m. How much grain will the farmer be able to store in the silo?

    a. 402.1 m³

    b. 1,206.4 m³

    c. 1,608.5 m³

    d. 4,825.5 m³

48. Which of the following expressions is equivalent to $(a + b)(a - b)$?

    a. $a^2 - b^2$

    b. $(a + b)^2$

    c. $(a - b)^2$

    d. $ab(a - b)$

Questions 49 and 50 are based upon the following table:

Kyle bats third in the batting order for the Badgers baseball team. The table shows the number of hits that Kyle had in the 7 consecutive games played during one week in July.

Day of Week	Number of Hits
Monday	1
Tuesday	2
Wednesday	3
Thursday	1
Friday	1
Saturday	4
Sunday	2

49. What is the mode of the numbers in the distribution shown in the table?

    a. 1

    b. 2

    c. 3

    d. 4

50. What is the mean of the numbers in the distribution shown in the table?

    a. 1

    b. 2

    c. 3

    d. 4

Science

1. A normal human sperm must have:

    a. An X chromosome
    b. A Y chromosome
    c. 23 chromosomes
    d. B and C

Questions 2 and 3 are based upon the following figures and text:

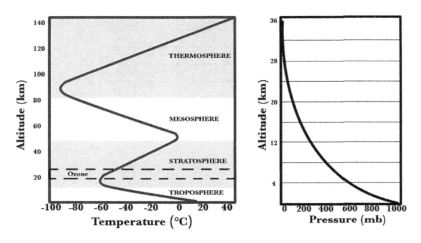

The Earth's atmosphere is comprised of multiple layers with very different temperature characteristics. Closest to the surface, the *troposphere* contains approximately 75 percent of the atmosphere's mass and 99 percent of its water vapor and aerosols. Temperature fluctuations cause constant mixing of air in the troposphere through convection, but it generally becomes cooler as altitude increases.

The *stratosphere* is heated by the absorption of ultraviolet radiation from the sun. Since its lower layers are composed of cooler, heavier air, there is no convective mixing in the stratosphere, and it is quite stable.

The *mesosphere* is the atmospheric layer directly above the stratosphere. Here, temperature decreases as altitude increases due to decreased solar heating and--to a degree--CO_2. In the lower atmosphere, CO_2 acts as a greenhouse gas by absorbing infrared radiation from the Earth's surface. In the mesosphere, CO_2 cools the atmosphere by radiating heat into space.

Above this layer lies the thermosphere. At these altitudes, atmospheric gases form layers according to their molecular masses. Temperatures increase with altitude due to absorption of solar radiation by the small amount of residual oxygen. Temperatures are highly dependent on solar activity and can rise to 1,500°C.

2. Commercial jetliners normally cruise at altitudes of 9-12 km which are the lower parts of the stratosphere. Which of the following might be the reason for this choice of cruising altitude?

a. Jet engines run more efficiently at colder temperatures.
b. There is less air resistance than at lower altitudes.
c. There is less turbulence than at lower altitudes.
d. All of the above are possible reasons.

3. The lowest temperatures in the Earth's atmosphere are recorded within the:

a. Troposphere
b. Stratosphere
c. Mesosphere
d. Thermosphere

Questions 4 and 5 are based on the following figure and paragraph:

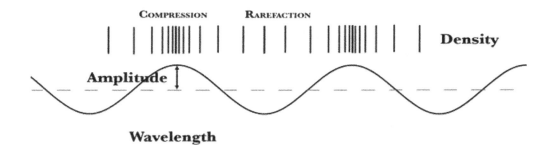

A vibrating source will produce sound by alternately forcing the air molecules in front of it closer together as it moves towards them, and then further apart as it draws away from them. In this way, alternating regions of high and low pressure, called compressions and refractions, are produced. The figure shows a typical sound wave. The volume of the sound corresponds to the magnitude of the compression, represented by the amplitude of the wave. The sound's pitch corresponds to the wave's frequency, the distance between successive compressions. Humans can hear sounds with frequencies between 20 and 20,000 Hertz. Sound waves propagate in all directions from their source. The speeds at which sound waves travel depend upon the medium they are traveling through. In dry air, sound travels at 330 m/sec at 0°C. It travels 4 times faster through water, and 15 times faster through a steel rod.

4. The sound made by a drum is much louder and lower pitched than that made by a bell. What is true about the sound wave made by a drum compared to that made by a bell?

_____

_____

_____

5. Two sound waves of exactly the same frequency and amplitude are made by sources that are in the same position. If the sound waves are out of phase by half a wavelength, what will an observer hear by standing a short distance away?

a. A sound twice as loud as either individual signal
b. A sound at twice the frequency of either individual signal
c. A sound at twice the wavelength as either individual signal
d. No sound at all

Questions 6 and 7 are based on the following figure and text:

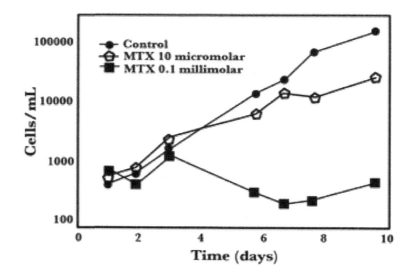

Cancer cells of the murine erythroleukemia (MEL) cell line were cultured in normal growth medium (control) and in two different concentrations of the anti-cancer drug methotrexate (MTX) for a period of ten days. Samples were removed periodically, and the number of cells per milliliter of culture was determined. Each point in the figure represents the mean of five determinations.

6. The growth of cells in the absence of drugs in this experiment can best be described as:

a. Linear
b. Exponential
c. Derivative
d. Inhibited

7. Which of the following statements is supported by the data?

a. Methotrexate does not prevent cell growth.
b. 0.1 millimolar methotrexate prevents the growth of bacteria.
c. 10 micromolar methotrexate effectively holds back cell growth.
d. 100 micromolar methotrexate effectively holds back cell growth.

8. The major advantage of sexual reproduction over asexual forms is that:

    a. It requires two individuals.
    b. It promotes diversity.
    c. It produces more offspring.
    d. It can be undertaken at any time of year.

Questions 9 and 10 are based on the following text:

Isotopes

    The nucleus of an atom contains both protons and neutrons. Protons have a single positive electric charge, while neutrons have a charge of zero. The number of protons that a nucleus contains, called the atomic number and abbreviated as Z, determines the identity of an atom of matter. For example, hydrogen contains a single proton ($Z = 1$), whereas helium contains two ($Z = 2$). Atoms of a single element may differ in terms of the number of neutrons in their atomic nuclei, however. The total number of protons and neutrons in an atom is referred to as the atomic mass, or M. Helium typically has an atomic mass equal to 4, but there is another helium isotope for which $M = 3$. This form of helium has the same number of protons but only one neutron.

    In an atomic fusion reaction, nuclei collide with one another with enough force to break them apart. The resulting nuclei may have a lower atomic mass than the reactants, with the difference being released as energy. Electric charge, however, is always conserved.

9. Two atoms of helium-3 (atomic mass = 3) collide in a fusion reaction to make a single atom of helium-4 (atomic mass = 4). What might be another product of this reaction?

    a. A neutron
    b. A proton
    c. Two electrons
    d. Two protons

10. Hydrogen atoms usually have a single nucleon (nucleon refers to either a neutron or a proton). Deuterium is an isotope of hydrogen that has two nucleons. Also, tritium is an isotope of hydrogen that has two and three nucleons. How many electrons orbit the tritium nucleus if the atom is electrically neutral?

    a. 0
    b. 1
    c. 2
    d. 3

Questions 11 and 12 are based on the following figure and text:

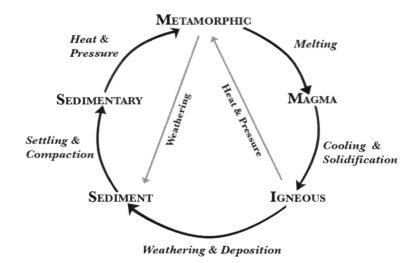

Rock Cycle

Rocks are created and destroyed in a recurrent process known as the rock cycle. Rocks are made from minerals, which are naturally occurring, crystalline solids of characteristic chemical composition. The actions of heat, pressure, and erosion can change the form of these minerals drastically. *Igneous* rocks form when molten magma flows out from the Earth's molten core, and then cools and solidifies near the surface. *Sedimentary* rocks are made of fragments of other rocks that are worn by weathering or erosion. Sand particles form sediments as they settle to the bottom, and are eventually compacted into stone by the weight above them. This is a process known as *lithification*. Heat and pressure can change the crystal structure of these minerals. This step alters them into denser *metamorphic* rocks. As these sink deeper into the hot core, they melt again into magma.

11. A process that can lead to igneous rock formation is:
   a. Weathering
   b. Sedimentation
   c. Erosion
   d. Volcanic activity

12. Which of the following rock types is made at the greatest distances below the Earth's surface?
   a. Igneous
   b. Metamorphic
   c. Sedimentary
   d. Slate

13. Which of the following animals displays the greatest fitness?
   a. A male wolf that dies young but has 4 cubs that are raised by an unrelated female
   b. A female wolf that has 3 cubs and lives to be quite old
   c. A male wolf that lives to old age and has 1 cub
   d. A female wolf that dies young after raising 3 cubs

Questions 14-19 are based upon the following figure, table, and text:

Protein Synthesis

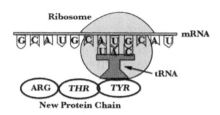

THE GENETIC CODE

First	Codon	AA	Codon	AA	Codon	AA	Codon	AA
T	TTT	Phenylalanine	TCT	Serine	TAT	Tyrosine	TGT	Cysteine
	TTC	Phenylalanine	TCC	Serine	TAC	Tyrosine	TGC	Cysteine
	TTA	Leucine	TCA	Serine	TAA	STOP	TGA	STOP
	TTG	Leucine	TCG	Serine	TAG	STOP	TGG	Tryptophane
C	CTT	Leucine	CCT	Proline	CAT	Histidine	CGT	Arginine
	CTC	Leucine	CCC	Proline	CAC	Histidine	CGC	Arginine
	CTA	Leucine	CCA	Proline	CAA	Glycine	CGA	Arginine
	CTG	Leucine	CCG	Proline	CAG	Glycine	CGG	Arginine
A	ATT	Isoleucine	ACT	Threonine	AAT	Asparagine	AGT	Serine
	ATC	Isoleucine	ACC	Threonine	AAC	Asparagine	AGC	Serine
	ATA	Isoleucine	ACA	Threonine	AAA	Lysine	AGA	Arginine
	ATG	Methionine (START)	ACG	Threonine	AAG	Lysine	AGG	Arginine
G	GTT	Valine	GCT	Alanine	GAT	Aspartate	GGT	Glycine
	GTC	Valine	GCC	Alanine	GAC	Aspartate	GGC	Glycine
	GTA	Valine	GCA	Alanine	GAA	Glutamate	GGA	Glycine
	GTG	Valine	GCG	Alanine	GAG	Glutamate	GGG	Glycine

The genetic information for making different kinds of proteins is stored in segments of DNA molecules called genes. DNA is a chain of phosphoribose molecules containing the bases guanine (G), cytosine (C), alanine (A), and thymine (T). Each amino acid component of the protein chain is represented in the DNA by a trio of bases called a codon. This provides a code which the cell can use to translate DNA into protein. The code, which is shown in the table, contains special codons for starting a protein chain (these chains always begin with the amino acid methionine) or for stopping it. To make a protein, an RNA intermediary called a messenger RNA (mRNA) is first made from the DNA by a protein called a polymerase. In the mRNA, the thymine bases are replaced by uracil (U). The mRNA then moves from the nucleus to the cytoplasm, where it locks onto a piece of protein-RNA machinery called a ribosome. The ribosome moves along the RNA molecule, reading the code. It interacts with molecules of transfer RNA, each of which is bound to a specific amino acid, and strings the amino acids together to form a protein.

14. Gene variants are called:

a. Codons
b. Alleles
c. Methionine
d. Amino acids

15. Which of the following protein sequences is encoded by the DNA base sequence GTTACAAAAAGA?

a. Valine-threonine-lysine-arginine
b. Valine-leucine-glycine-histidine
c. Valine-aspartate-proline-serine
d. Valine-serine-tyrosine-STOP

16. A polymerase begins reading the following DNA sequences with the first base shown. Which sequence specifies the end of a protein chain?

a. GTACCCCTA
b. GTACCCACA
c. GTTAAAAGA
d. GTTTAAGAC

17. The part of a DNA molecule that encodes a single amino acid is a(n):

a. Codon
b. Allele
c. Methionine
d. Phosphoribose

18. Proteins are made by:

a. Polymerases
b. Transfer RNAs
c. Ribosomes
d. DNA molecules

19. Which of the following is NOT part of a gene?

a. Codon
b. Cytosine
c. Ribosome
d. Phosphoribose

20. The pilot of an eastbound plane finds his wind speed in relation to his aircraft. He measures a wind velocity of 320 km/h with the wind coming from the east. A woman on the ground sees the plane pass overhead, and she measures its velocity as 290 km/h. What is the wind velocity in relation to the observer?

a. 30 km/h east-to-west
b. 30 km/h west-to-east
c. 320 km/h east-to-west
d. 290 km/h east-to-west

21. What causes a spring tide?

    a. The Moon being so close to the Earth
    b. The Sun and Moon are at right angles
    c. The Sun, Moon, and Earth are in a line
    d. The spin of the Earth

Question 22 is based on the following figure:

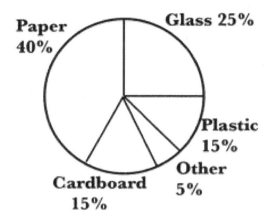

22. A recycling company collects sorted materials from its clients. The materials are weighed and processed for re-use. The chart shows the weights of different classes of materials that were collected by the company in one month. Which of the following statements is NOT supported by the data in the chart?

    a. Paper products and cardboard make up a majority of the collected materials.
    b. One quarter of the materials collected are made of glass.
    c. More plastic is collected than cardboard.
    d. The largest category of collected materials includes newspapers.

Questions 23-25 are based upon the following figure and passage:

Electrochemical Battery

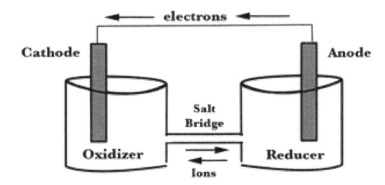

    An electrochemical battery is a device powered by oxidation and reduction reactions that are physically separated so that the electrons must travel through a wire from the reducing agent to the oxidizing agent. The reducing agent loses electrons, and is oxidized in a reaction that takes place at an electrode called the anode. The electrons flow through a wire to the other electrode: the cathode. At the cathode, an oxidizing agent gains electrons and is reduced. To maintain a net zero charge in each compartment, there is a limited flow of ions through a salt bridge. In a car battery, for example, the reducing agent is oxidized by the following reaction that involves a lead (Pb) anode and sulfuric acid (H_2SO_4). Lead sulfate ($PbSO_4$), protons (H^+), and electrons (e^-) are produced:

$$Pb + H_2SO_4 \Rightarrow PbSO_4 + 2\ H^+ + 2\ e^-$$

The cathode is made of lead oxide (PbO_2),. At the cathode, the following reaction occurs. During this reaction, the electrons produced at the anode are used:

$$PbO_2 + H_2SO_4 + 2\ e^- + 2\ H^+ \Rightarrow PbSO_4 + 2\ H_2O$$

23. Electrons are made by a chemical reaction that takes place at the:
  a. Anode
  b. Cathode
  c. Lead oxide electrode
  d. Oxidizer

24. In an oxidation reaction:
  a. An oxidizing agent gains electrons.
  b. An oxidizing agent loses electrons.
  c. A reducing agent gains electrons.
  d. A reducing agent loses electrons.

25. In a car battery, a product of the oxidation reaction that happens at the cathode is:
  a. Lead oxide
  b. Lead
  c. Electrons
  d. Water

Questions 26-27 are based upon the following figure:

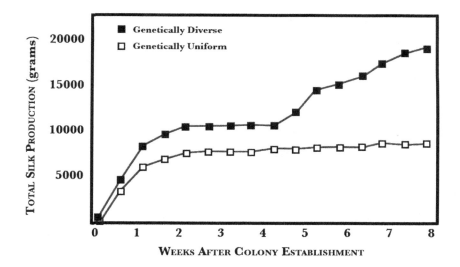

Colonies of silkworms that had the same number of genetically identical or genetically different animals were established. For several weeks after the colonies were created, silk production was estimated by removing small samples of silk from the colonies and weighing them. The results are shown in the graph. The open symbols are for the production of silk by genetically uniform worms. The closed symbols are for the production of silk by genetically diverse worms.

26. Which of the following conclusions can be drawn from the data?
    a. Genetically diverse worms produce more silk than genetically uniform worms.
    b. Genetically uniform worms produce more silk than genetically diverse worms.
    c. Genetically diverse silkworm colonies produce more silk than genetically uniform colonies.
    d. Genetically uniform silkworm colonies produce more silk than genetically diverse colonies.

27. If the generation time of a silkworm is about four weeks, what is a hypothesis that best explains the difference in silk productivity between the two colonies?

_____

_____

_____

28. The digestion of starch begins:
    a. In the mouth
    b. In the stomach
    c. In the pylorus
    d. In the duodenum

Questions 29-32 are based upon the following figure and passage:

THE WATER CYCLE

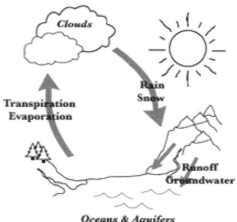

Energy from the sun heats the water in the oceans and causes it to evaporate. This makes water vapor that rises through the atmosphere. Cooler temperatures at high altitudes cause this vapor to condense and form clouds. Water droplets in the clouds condense and grow, eventually falling to the ground as precipitation. This continuous movement of water above and below ground is called the hydrologic cycle, or water cycle, and it is essential for life on our planet. All the Earth's stores of water, including that found in clouds, oceans, underground, etc., are known as the *hydrosphere.*

Water can be stored in several locations as part of the water cycle. The largest reservoirs are the oceans, which hold about 95% of the world's water, more than 300,000,000 cubic miles. Water is also stored in polar ice caps, mountain snowcaps, lakes and streams, plants, and below ground in aquifers. Each of these reservoirs has a characteristic *residence time*, which is the average amount of time a water molecule will spend there before moving on. Some typical residence times are shown in the table.

Average Reservoir Residence Times of Water

Reservoir	Residence Time
Atmosphere	9 days
Oceans	3000 years
Glaciers and ice caps	100 years
Soil moisture	2 months
Underground aquifers	10,000 years

The water cycle can change over time. During cold climatic periods, more water is stored as ice and snow, and the rate of evaporation is lower. This affects the level of the Earth's oceans. During the last ice age, for instance, oceans were 400 feet lower than today. Human activities that affect the water cycle are agriculture, dam construction, deforestation, and industrial activities.

29. Another name for the water cycle is:

    a. The hydrosphere
    b. The atmosphere
    c. The reservoir
    d. The hydrologic cycle

30. Water is stored underground. It is also stored in oceans and ice caps. These underground storage reservoirs are called:

    a. Storage tanks
    b. Aquifers
    c. Evaporators
    d. Runoff

31. Other than atmospheric water, water molecules spend the least time in:

    a. Aquifers
    b. Oceans
    c. Glaciers
    d. Soil

32. Which of the following statements is NOT true?

    a. Cutting down trees affects the water cycle.
    b. Ocean levels rise in an ice age.
    c. Oceans hold most of the world's water.
    d. Clouds are formed because of cold temperatures.

Questions 33-37 are based on the following figure and passage:

Heat and the States of Matter

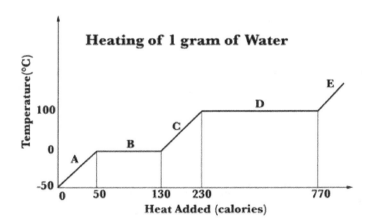

When the molecules of a substance absorb energy in the form of heat, they begin to move more rapidly. This increase in kinetic energy may be a more rapid vibration of molecules held in place in a solid, or it may be motion through molecular space in a liquid or a gas. Either way, it will be observed as either a change in temperature or a change in state. Heat has traditionally been measured in terms of calories. One calorie is equal to 4.186 Joules.

The specific heat capacity of a substance is the energy required to raise the temperature of 1 kg of the substance by 1°C. For water, this is 1000 calories. If heat continues to be applied to ice that is already at its melting point of 0°C, it remains at that temperature and melts into liquid water. The amount of energy required to produce this change in state is called the heat of fusion. For water it is equal to 80 calories per gram. Similarly, the amount of energy required to change a gram of liquid water at 100°C into steam is called the heat of vaporization which equals 540 calories.

The graph shows an experiment in calorimetry: 1 gram of water at -50°C is heated slowly from a solid state until it has all turned to gas. The temperature is monitored and reported as a function of the heat added to the system.

33. Heat is a form of:

a. Potential energy
b. Chemical energy
c. Kinetic energy
d. Temperature

34. Which of the following statements is true?

a. Adding heat to a system always increases its temperature.
b. The average speed of a gas molecule is slower than the average speed of a liquid molecule of the same substance.
c. Adding heat to a system always increases the average speed of the molecules of which it is made of.
d. Heat must be added to liquid water to make ice.

35. In which region(s) of the diagram is liquid water present? (Select all that apply.)

a. Region A
b. Region B
c. Region C
d. Region D
e. Region E

36. How much heat must be added to 1 gram of water at 1°C to raise its temperature to 101°C?

a. 100 calories
b. 540 calories
c. 770 calories
d. 640 calories

37. In the diagram, as heat is added to the system, the water in region B can be said to be:

a. Condensing
b. Melting
c. Freezing
d. Evaporating

Questions 38-40 are based on the following figure and passage:

Neurons

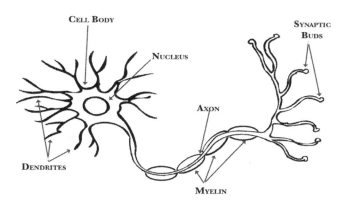

Messages travel between the brain and other parts of the body in the form of electrical impulses. A specialized cell, the neuron, produces these impulses. Neurons make up the brain and the nervous system. They number more than 100 billion in the human body.

Neurons have their own characteristic cellular anatomy consisting of three main parts. A cell body, containing a nucleus, is the center of metabolism. Dendrites project from the cell body and receive messages from neighboring neurons. At the other end, messages are sent through the *axon*, a long fiber extending from the cell body to the dendrites of other neurons, or to *effectors*, such as muscles, that perform actions based on neuronal input. Axons are sheathed in a material called myelin that helps nerve signals travel faster and farther.

At the end of the axon, messages must cross a narrow gap, the *synapse*, to reach effectors or the next neuron. Electrical impulses cannot cross this gap. The transfer of information from cell to cell occurs as a result of the release of chemical *neurotransmitters* into the space between the axon and the dendrites. The electrical impulse triggers the release of neurotransmitters into the synapse from swellings called *synaptic buds* at the axon terminal. They cross the synapse and bind to special *receptor* molecules on the dendrites of the next cell. Each neurotransmitter can bind only to a specific matching receptor, which triggers an appropriate response to the signal. This may be another electrical impulse, carrying the message along further, the contraction of a muscle, or some other effect.

38. A neuron is made of three main parts. These are: (Select all that apply.)

a. effector
b. cell body
c. axon
d. synapse
e. receptor
f. dendrite

39. Chromosomes are located within the:

    a. Cell body
    b. Dendrites
    c. Axon
    d. Synapse

40. Which of the following statements is true?

    a. Information in neurons flows in one direction: from dendrites to axon.
    b. Information in the nervous system is carried by both electrical and chemical means.
    c. Myelin assists in the transmission of electrical, but not chemical, information.
    d. All of the above statements are true.

41. Of the following, the blood vessel that has the least-oxygenated blood is:

    a. The aorta
    b. The vena cava
    c. The pulmonary artery
    d. The capillaries

42. A tsunami may be caused by:

    a. Earthquakes
    b. Volcanoes
    c. Landslides
    d. A, B, and C

Question 43 is based on the following figure:

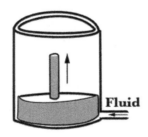

The figure shows an airtight cylinder where fluid may be injected from the bottom. In addition, the cylinder has a heavy piston. The injected fluid raises the piston until the rod on top of the piston touches the top of the cylinder container. Fluids of different densities are injected. Then, an observer records the volume needed to make the rod reach the top.

43. Which of the following fluids will need the least injected volume?

    a. Water
    b. Oil
    c. Grease
    d. The same volume will be required for all fluids.

44. Mark and Nancy both take three measurements of the length of a pencil that is 15.1 cm. Mark records 15.0, 15.0, and 15.1 cm. Nancy records 15.1, 15.2, and 15.2 cm. Which of the following statements is true about Mark and Nancy's measurements?

a. Mark's measurement is more precise.
b. Nancy's measurement is more accurate.
c. Mark's measurement is more accurate.
d. Both sets of measurements are equally accurate and precise.

45. All living organisms on Earth use:

a. Oxygen
b. Light
c. Neurotransmitters
d. A triplet genetic code

Questions 46-47 are based upon the following figure:

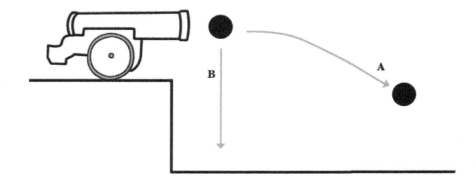

46. A cannon sits on top of a cliff that is 20 meters above an area of level ground. It fires a 5 kg cannonball horizontally (cannonball A) at 5 meters/second. At the same time, a second cannonball (cannonball B) is dropped from the same height. If air resistance is ignored, which cannonball will hit the ground first?

Note: The gravitational acceleration due to the Earth is 9.8 m/sec².

a. Cannonball A
b. Cannonball B
c. Both will hit the ground at the same time.
d. It cannot be found from the given information.

47. The cannon weighs 500 kg and is on wheels. It will recoil when firing cannonball A. If friction is ignored, what will be the recoil speed of the cannon? Note: Momentum is the product of mass and velocity.

a. 5 meters/second
b. 5000 cm/second
c. 5 cm/second
d. It cannot be found from the given information.

Questions 48-50 are based on the following figure:

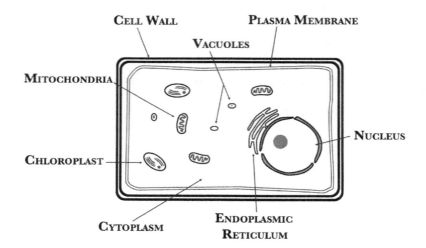

48. The cell above is a(n):

a. Animal cell
b. Plant cell
c. Bacterial cell
d. Virus

49. Which of the following structures contains DNA?

a. Cytoplasm
b. Vacuole
c. Mitochondrion
d. Nucleus

50. The mitochondria:

a. Produce energy for the cell in the form of ATP.
b. Are responsible for digesting starch.
c. Are the sites of protein synthesis.
d. Are not present in muscle cells.

Social Studies

Questions 1–3 refer to the following information:

Important Dates in the International Slave Trade

Date	Country	Event
1517	Spain	Begins regular slave trading
1592	Britain	Begins regular slave trading
1792	Denmark	Abolishes slave trade
1794	France	Abolishes slave trade
1807	Britain	Abolishes slave trade
1834	Britain	Abolishes slavery in all colonies
1865	United States	Abolishes slavery
1888	Brazil	Abolishes slavery

1. Which nation was the first to abolish slavery?

    a. Spain
    b. Britain
    c. Denmark
    d. France

2. If the United States had lost the Revolutionary War, when would slavery have been outlawed?

    a. 1792
    b. 1794
    c. 1807
    d. 1834

3. Which of the following conclusions is true? Use your prior knowledge and the information above.

    a. More slaves worked in Brazil than in any other nation.
    b. France realized its ideals of independence sooner than the United States.
    c. Denmark was the largest slave-holding country in Europe.
    d. Britain freed enslaved peoples only after losing the Asian nations of the British Empire.

Questions 4 and 5 refer to the following map:

NOTE: The year listed with each country is when the nation gained independence.

4. Which South American nations were the *last* to have independence? (Select all that apply.)

    a. Argentina
    b. Paraguay
    c. Ecuador
    d. Bolivia
    e. Venezuela
    f. Uruguay

5. Which of the following conclusions is true?

    a. The nations of North America were also fighting for independence at the same time as nations in South America.
    b. France lost most of its control in the New World because of these revolutions.
    c. Nations on the west coast gained independence first.
    d. South America had many revolutions in the first three decades of the 19th century.

Questions 6 and 7 refer to the following information:

Native Civilizations in Central and South America

Civilization	Location	Conquered by	Date Empires Ended
Maya	Central America	Internal collapse	950
Aztec	Mexico	Spanish under Hernán Cortés	1519
Inca	Peru	Spanish under Francisco Pizarro	1533

6. Mayan civilization is unlike the Aztec and Incan civilizations because

a. it collapsed without an outside conqueror.

b. it was the last empire to end.

c. it was located in North America.

d. it was taken over by the Spanish.

7. Which of the following conclusions is supported by the information above?

a. Several nations in South America were taken over by Portugal.

b. The Aztec civilization is the oldest of the three given in the table.

c. Spain had a demanding plan of taking over new lands in the 16th century.

d. Incan warriors tried to help the Aztec fight against the Spanish.

Question 8 refers to the following passage:

Islam spread to Europe during the medieval period, bringing scientific and technological insights. The Muslim emphasis on knowledge and learning can be traced to an emphasis on both in the Qur'an [Koran], the holy book of Islam. Because of this emphasis, scholars preserved some of the Greek and Roman texts that were lost to the rest of Europe. The writings of Aristotle, among others, were saved by Muslim translators. Islam scholars modified a Hindu number system. Their modification became the more commonly used Arabic system, which replaced Roman numerals. They also developed algebra. Muslim contributions also include inventing the astrolabe, a device for telling time that also helped sailors to navigate. In medicine, Muslim doctors cleaned wounds with antiseptics. They closed the wounds with gut and silk sutures. They also used sedatives.

8. Based on the information above, which of the following conclusions is likely true?

a. Muslims were braver than others when facing surgery.

b. Fewer Muslim patients died of wound infections than Europeans.

c. The silk market expanded because of the Muslim use of silk sutures.

d. Math classes would be easier without Muslim influence.

Question 9 refers to the following passage:

In July 1862, President Abraham Lincoln told his cabinet that he wanted to issue an emancipation proclamation. However, the Northern Army was not winning many battles of the Civil War that summer. Lincoln agreed with his cabinet advisers that it was a bad time to announce the plan. The following month, Horace Greeley, a respected journalist, printed an open letter criticizing Lincoln for waiting to announce the plan for the emancipation proclamation. The following is part of Lincoln's response.

" … My paramount object in this struggle is to save the Union, and it is not either to slave or destroy Slavery. If I could save the Union without freeing any slave, I would do it; and if I could save it by freeing all the slaves, I would do it; and if I could do it by freeing some and leaving others alone, I would also do that. What I do about Slavery and the colored race, I do because I believe it helps to save this Union; and what I forbear, I forbear because I do not believe it would help to save the Union...."

9. Lincoln's primary goal was to

a. free the slaves.
b. repay slave owners for their losses.
c. save the Union.
d. win the war.

Questions 10 and 11 refer to the following information:

Westward Migration

Year	Estimated Number of People Headed West
1844	2,000
1849	30,000
1854	10,000
1859	30,000
1864	20,000

10. What event caused the increase of westward movement between 1844 and 1848? Use your general knowledge to answer the question.

a. Silver was discovered in Nevada.
b. The Transcontinental Railroad was completed.
c. Roman Catholics developed missions along the California coast.
d. Gold was discovered at Sutter's Mill in California.

11. Given the increase of population, which of the following statements is most likely to be true?

a. More children were being born in 1849 and 1858.
b. Most of the new migrants were women who wanted to open businesses.
c. The Civil War increased the westward migration.
d. Cities and towns in the West grew and supported many businesses.

Questions 12 and 13 refer to the following information:

Time Needed to Ship Freight from Cincinnati, Ohio, to New York City

Date	Route	Average Amount of Time
1817	Ohio River keelboat to Pittsburgh, wagon to Philadelphia, wagon or wagon and river to New York	52 days
1843–1851	Ohio River steamboat to Pittsburgh, canal to Philadelphia, railroad to New York	18–20 days
1852	Canal across Ohio, Lake Erie, Erie Canal, and Hudson River	18 days
1852	All rail via Erie Railroad and connecting lines	6–8 days
1850s	Steamboat to New Orleans and packet ship to New York	28 days

12. Think about a business owner in Cincinnati during the 1850s. Which kind of transportation would you be most likely to choose?

    a. steamboat
    b. railroad
    c. canal
    d. keelboat

13. Which change in transportation caused the *most* time saved over its predecessor?

    a. railroad over steamboat and packet
    b. railroad over canals
    c. canal over steamboat and packet
    d. steamboat, canal, and railroad over keelboat and wagon

Question 14 refers to the following information:

Group	Arrived in New World	Settled in
British Catholics	1632	Maryland
British Pilgrims	1620	Plymouth Colony, Massachusetts
British Puritans	1607	Virginia
British Quakers	1681	Pennsylvania
Dutch traders	1625	Manhattan Island
French traders	1608	Quebec

14. Which of the following conclusions can you draw from the information above?

    a. Religious influences strongly affected the growth of the North American colonies.
    b. The French had large settlements in what became the eastern United States.
    c. The Dutch did not get a fair deal for the land they purchased.
    d. The Spanish were the first to settle in North America.

Question 15 refers to the following passage:

In 1917, Orville Wright wrote of the invention of the airplane: "When my brother and I built and flew the first man-carrying flying machine, we thought that we were introducing into the world an invention which would make further wars practically impossible. That we were not alone in this thought is evidenced by the fact that the French Peace Society presented us with medals on account of our invention. We thought governments would realize the impossibility of winning by surprise attacks, and that no country would enter into war with another when it knew it would have to win by simply wearing out the enemy."

15. Which of the following statements do you think best expresses what the Wright brothers thought of World War I?

a. "Ah, that splendid little war!"
b. "How exciting to see airplanes extending fighting into the air!"
c. "Using airplanes in war is unacceptable."
d. "We can't wait to join the fight."

Question 16 refers to the following passage:

In 1988, the federal government, as part of the Clean Air Act, began to monitor visibility in national parks and wilderness areas. Eleven years later, the Environmental Protection Agency set forth an attempt to improve the air quality in wilderness areas and national parks.

16. Who of the following historical persons would NOT have agreed with this effort?

a. President Richard M. Nixon, who signed the act in 1970.
b. Rachel Carson: environmentalist and author of Silent Spring.
c. President Theodore Roosevelt, who set aside land for public parks.
d. the senator who campaigned in the early 1900s on the promise "Not one penny for scenery!"

Question 17 refers to the following passage:

Mother Jones, who was a labor activist, wrote the following about children working in cotton mills in Alabama: "Little girls and boys, barefooted, walked up and down between the endless rows of spindles, reaching thin little hands into the machinery to repair snapped threads. They crawled under machinery to oil it. They replaced spindles all day long; all night through...six-year-olds with faces of sixty did an eight-hour shift for ten cents a day; the machines, built in the North, were built low for the hands of little children."

17. Which of the following do you think happened after this was published?

a. More children signed up to work in the factories.
b. Cotton factories in the South closed.
c. Laws were passed to prevent child labor.
d. The pay scale for these children was increased.

18. Why was the city of Antwerp in Belgium building so many forts in 1914?

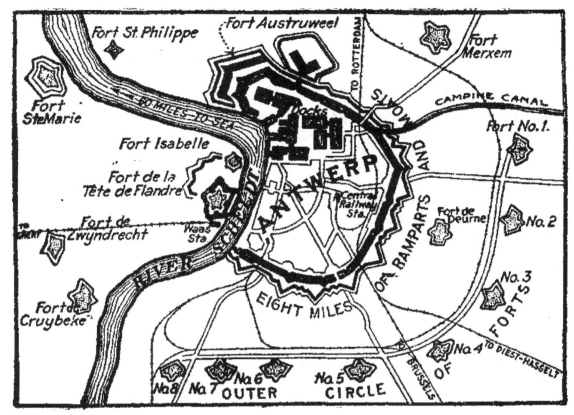

ANTWERP AND ITS FORTIFICATIONS

a. World War I had started. Germany had invaded other Belgian cities and was moving to invade Antwerp.

b. World War I had started. Italy had invaded other Belgian cities and was moving to invade Antwerp.

c. Antwerp was fortifying against possible British air attacks in World War I.

d. Antwerp feared a Russian invasion after the start of World War I.

Question 19 refers to the following passage:

In 1781, a county court in Massachusetts heard the case Brom & Bett v. Ashley. What was unusual about the case was that the plaintiffs were both enslaved by John Ashley's family. They had walked out and appealed to a lawyer for help after Mrs. Ashley tried to hit Mum Bett's sister. Mum Bett, whose real name was Elizabeth Freeman, claimed that if all people were free and equal, as she had heard while serving at the Ashley table, slaves too were equal. The court agreed by basing their decision on the Massachusetts constitution of the previous year. The decision, affirmed in subsequent cases, led to the abolishing of slavery in that state.

19. Which of the following statements is most accurate?

a. Mrs. Ashley was probably just having a bad day when she tried to strike another person.
b. Elizabeth Freeman's actions helped to gain women the right to vote.
c. White people in Southern states applauded the court's decision.
d. The ideals of the American Revolution reached farther than the founders may have intended.

Question 20 refers to the following passage:

In 1949, the National Parks Service added the Effigy Mounds National Monument in northeast Iowa to its list of protected parks. Effigy mounds, which are shaped like animals, were built by Native Americans. Of the more than 200 mounds created by the Mississippian Culture at the park, 31 are in the shape of animals. Most famous are the so-called Marching Bears, clearly visible from an airplane. Other mounds are bird effigies or shaped in cones or lines. The mounds were created over a period of at least 1,500 years. This is just one of the moundbuilders' sites in the eastern third of North America. Historians speculate that the mounds were used for religious purposes and were burial places.

20. Which of the following is NOT accurate?

a. The Effigy Mounds were built by Native Americans in 1949.
b. Mounds are also found in other states.
c. President Harry S. Truman signed the law that made the mounds a national monument.
d. Effigy mounds are shaped like animals.

Questions 21 and 22 refer to the following information:

United States Foreign Trade 1960–1970

(by Category Percentages)

Category	1960		1970	
	Exports	Imports	Exports	Imports
Chemicals	8.7	5.3	9.0	3.6
Crude materials (except fuel)	13.7	18.3	10.8	8.3
Food and beverages, including tobacco	15.6	22.5	11.8	15.6
Machinery and transport	34.3	9.7	42.0	28.0
Mineral fuels and related materials	4.1	10.5	3.7	7.7

21. From 1960 to 1970, which of the following categories had the greatest difference between percentage of exports and imports?

a. chemicals
b. crude materials
c. food and beverages
d. machinery and transport

22. Which category saw the greatest percentage decrease in imports between 1960 and 1970?

    a. chemicals

    b. crude materials

    c. food and beverages

    d. machinery and transport

Questions 23 and 24 refer to the following information:

Per Capita National Debt

Year	Historical Context	Amount
1790	Following American Revolution at the beginning of the national government	$19
1816	After the War of 1812	$15
1866	Following the Civil War	$78
1919	After World War I	$240
1948	Three years after World War II ended	$1,720
1975	After the Vietnam War	$2,475
1989	Near the close of Reagan's administration	$11,545

23. Which of the following armed conflicts increased the per capita national debt by the largest *percentage* over the previous conflict listed?

    a. War of 1812

    b. Civil War

    c. World War I

    d. World War II

24. What does the change of per capita national debt between 1790 and 1816 likely indicate?

    a. The United States borrowed more money to pay for the War of 1812.

    b. The new nation worked hard to pay off debts owed from the Revolutionary War.

    c. People did not spend very much money between those wars.

    d. More citizens bought Treasury bonds in those days.

Questions 25 and 26 refer to the following information:

Women in the Labor Force, Selected Years

Year	Women in Labor Force (thousands)	Percentage of Total Labor Force
1900	5,114	18.1
1920	8,430	20.4
1940	12,845	24.3
1950	18,412	28.8
1970	31,560	36.7

25. In what year did women first make up more than 25 percent of the total labor force?

    a. 1900

    b. 1920

    c. 1940

    d. 1950

26. **How could you express the change in percentage of women as part of the total labor force from 1900 to 1970?**

    a. The percentage rate declined by half.
    b. The percentage rate stayed constant.
    c. The percentage rate doubled.
    d. The percentage rate fluctuated up and down over the years.

27. **When the euro was introduced in January 2002, a single euro was valued at 88 cents in United States currency. In the summer of 2008, at one point it required $1.60 U.S. to buy 1 euro. In late October 2008, the euro fell to its lowest level against the dollar in two years. Which of the following statements is a correct conclusion?**

    a. The global economy in 2008 was headed for another Great Depression.
    b. The dollar regained strength after much devaluing against the euro.
    c. The euro is the world's strongest currency.
    d. Investors need to keep buying stocks.

Questions 28 and 29 refer to the following information:

Revenue Sources: 2004

Source	Amount in Millions	Percentage of Budget
Corporation income taxes	$189.3	10.1
Excise [sales] taxes	$69.9	3.7
Individual income taxes	$809.0	43.0
Social insurance and retirement receipts	$733.4	39.0
Other	$78.4	4.2

28. **If the government ended the use of offshore tax havens for corporations, how would the above information change?**

    a. Corporate income taxes would decrease.
    b. Retirement receipts would increase.
    c. Individuals would pay less in income taxes.
    d. The share of corporate income taxes would increase.

29. **Which category of taxpayer gives the most to the federal budget?**

    a. individuals
    b. corporations
    c. businesses paying Social Security tax
    d. federal government agencies

Question 30 refers to the following information:

Number of Small Business Administration Loans

to Minority-Owned Small Businesses in 2000 and 2005

Minority Group	2000	2005
African American	2,120	6,635
Asian American	5,838	3,456
Hispanic American	3,500	8,796
Native American	541	835

30. Which of the following statements is accurate?

a. The number of loans increased in every ethnic group category.
b. The number of loans to African Americans doubled in five years.
c. Native Americans represent the smallest number of loans.
d. The greatest number of loans in 2000 was to Hispanic Americans.

Question 31 refers to the following voter issue from 2008:

ISSUE 3: PROPOSED CONSTITUTIONAL AMENDMENT TO AMEND THE CONSTITUTION TO PROTECT PRIVATE PROPERTY RIGHTS IN GROUND WATER, LAKES AND OTHER WATERCOURSES (Proposed by Joint Resolution of the General Assembly of Ohio) To adopt Section 19b of Article I of the Constitution of the State of Ohio A YES vote means approval of the amendment. A NO vote means disapproval of the amendment. A majority YES vote is required for the amendment to be adopted. If approved, this amendment shall take effect December 1, 2008.

League Explanation of Issue 3: This proposed amendment resulted from the Ohio legislature's passage of the Great Lakes Water Compact this past spring. Some lawmakers feared final approval of the Compact might limit private water rights. The constitutional amendment is intended to recognize that:

- Property owners have a protected right to the "reasonable use" of the ground water flowing under their property, and of the water in a lake or watercourse that is on or flows through their property.
- An owner has the right to give or sell these interests to a governmental body.
- The public welfare supersedes individual property owners' rights. The state and political subdivisions may regulate such waters to the extent state law allows.
- The proposed amendment would not affect public use of Lake Erie and the state's other navigable waters.
- The rights confirmed by this amendment may not be limited by sections of the Ohio Constitution addressing home rule, public debt and public works, conservation of natural resources, and the prohibition of the use of "initiative" and "referendum" on property taxes.

31. Which of the following conclusions is correct?

a. The state of Ohio will give up rights to the control of Lake Erie in favor of public rights.
b. People who own property with water on it cannot sell that land to the state.
c. The state considers the public's welfare to be more important than an individual property owner's rights.
d. This issue was created without input from any lawmakers or organization.

32. The United States Congress funds Amtrak, a national railroad system. Railroads did not exist when the framers wrote the Constitution. However, this use of money is legal and is covered in Article 1 of the Constitution as

a. a delegated power.
b. a denied power.
c. an expressed power.
d. an implied power.

33. In 1957, President Dwight Eisenhower sent federal troops to Little Rock, Arkansas. They were to enforce integration at Little Rock Central High School. The reason was that the governor of the state had tried to prevent integration. Eisenhower's action is an example that shows how

a. acting like a dictator with power he did not legally have.
b. trying to keep federal troops out of Vietnam.
c. states' rights being more important than federal law.
d. upholding federal law if state or local officials will not.

34. In two referendums, citizens of New York City voted to limit key office holders (e.g., the mayor, the City Council members, and the comptroller) to two consecutive four-year terms. In November 2008, however, Mayor Michael Bloomberg signed into law a proposal that removed these limits. Which of the following conclusions might you draw?

a. The referendum votes were improperly counted.
b. Mayor Bloomberg was nearing the completion of his two terms in office.
c. People petitioned to have the earlier referendums revoked.
d. City Council members pressured the mayor.

35. Increasing border patrols at the U.S.-Canada border was part of which legislation?

a. USA PATRIOT Act of 2001
b. Trade Act of 2002
c. Protection of Lawful Commerce in Arms Act of 2005
d. Secure Fence Act of 2006

36. In 1983, Dianne Feinstein was mayor of San Francisco. She called for a women-mayors' caucus to be part of the U.S. Conference of Mayors. The organization exists to encourage women to run for mayor and to be more involved in the larger organization. This goal is an example of:

a. cronyism
b. networking
c. lobbying
d. patronage

324

Questions 37–39 refer to the following information:

Issues and Compromises in the United States Constitution

Issue	New Jersey Plan	Virginia Plan	Constitution
Legislative branch	A single house with members appointed by state legislatures	Two houses: Upper House with members elected by the people; Lower House elected by Upper House	Two houses: originally Senate members were elected by state legislatures, and representatives were and are still elected by the people.
Executive branch	Congress to choose an executive committee	Congress to choose a single president	President chosen by Electoral College, with electors selected by each of the states.
Judicial branch	Executive committee to appoint national judges	Congress chooses national judges	President appoints and Senate confirms Supreme Court judges.
Representation	Each state receives equal number of representatives	Representation to be based on wealth or population	Two houses created: House of Representatives based on population; Senate has two delegates from each state.

37. Which of the following conclusions can you draw on the issue of representation?

a. Virginia's people were very poor.
b. New Jersey started using the phrase "Liberty, Equality, and Fraternity."
c. Virginia was probably a state with many people.
d. Many wealthy citizens lived in New Jersey.

38. The Virginia Plan for the legislative branch closely mirrors

a. the Mayflower Compact.
b. Britain's Parliament.
c. the government of the Sioux.
d. France's monarchial system.

39. The Electoral College was created to resolve the issue of

a. how the wealthiest people would be represented.
b. who would appoint the Supreme Court members.
c. how to elect senators.
d. who would elect the chief executive.

Questions 40 and 41 refer to the following passage:

In 1969, 13 African American members of the House of Representatives gathered to form the Congressional Black Caucus (CBC). They felt that a unified voice for minorities was needed. President Richard Nixon met with the group two years later; his weak response to their list of 60 recommendations increased their efforts. These efforts included ending apartheid in South Africa, reforming welfare, expanding educational opportunities, and developing of businesses by minorities. For nearly 20 years, the CBC has proposed an alternative annual budget; it generally varies widely from the budget that the president submits. In 2008, the organization has 43 members from urban and rural areas. The CBC is sometimes called the conscience of Congress.

40. Which of the following statements is true?

a. The Congressional Black Caucus was started right after the Civil War.
b. The major goal of the CBC is to elect an African American president.
c. Since its beginning, the organization has grown by about 30 members.
d. The president usually implements the budget recommendations of the CBC.

41. Which of the following statements is an opinion?

a. The Congressional Black Caucus began in 1969.
b. Every year for two decades, the CBC has proposed a national budget.
c. In 2008, there were 43 members of the Congressional Black Caucus.
d. Apartheid was the worst political system of the twentieth century.

Question 42 refers to the following passage:

ARTICLE XXVII (Ratified July 1, 1971)

Section 1. The right of citizens of the United States, who are eighteen years of age or older, to vote shall not be denied or abridged by the United States or by any State on account of age.

42. This amendment to the Constitution was ratified in part because of what historic moment?

a. Women gained the right to vote.
b. Suffrage was extended to all African Americans.
c. Young men were being drafted to serve in the Vietnam War.
d. The number of people under 21 years of age increased.

Questions 43–45 refer to the following information:

Ethnic Groups in Selected Central American Countries

	Honduras	Nicaragua	El Salvador	Costa Rica	Belize
Mestizo [European and Native American]	90%	69%	90%		49%
Amerindian	7%	5%	1%	1%	
Black	2%	9%		3%	
White	1%	17%	9%	94% [includes Mestizo]	
Chinese				1%	
Creole [African and European]					25%
Mayans					11%

43. To which nation would you go to study the living traditions of the Mayans?

a. Honduras
b. Costa Rica
c. Belize
d. Nicaragua

44. Which of the following conclusions is correct?

a. The Creole population is the largest ethnic group in Latin America.
b. The Mayans have completely died out.
c. Costa Rica used Chinese labor to build the canal.
d. The Amerindian population of many Central American countries was destroyed by war and disease.

45. How do you explain the large Creole population of Belize? Use your own general knowledge.

a. Belize is near the Caribbean, where many Africans were once enslaved.
b. Belize has long been a trading partner with West African nations.
c. Many Creole who once lived in New Orleans left after Hurricane Katrina.
d. The Creole came to Belize to start new restaurants.

Question 46 is for the following map:

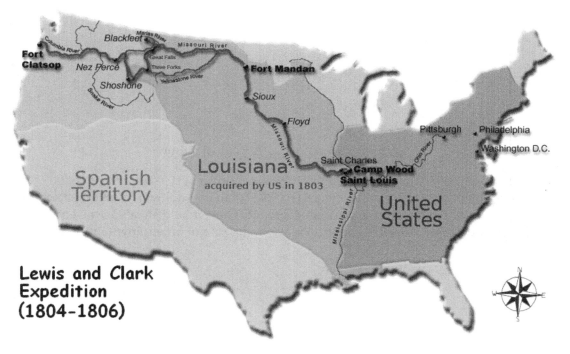

46. The Lewis and Clark expedition of 1803 set out from

a. Washington, D.C.
b. the Rocky Mountains.
c. Fort Mandan.
d. the Mississippi River.

47. What is one conclusion that can be made from this chart?

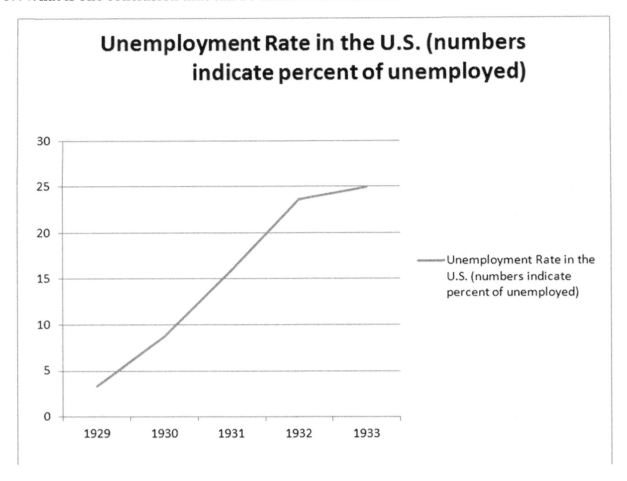

Statistics from the U.S. Bureau of Labor

a. High U.S. unemployment that started in 1929 was a cause of the Great Depression
b. U.S. unemployment was higher in the early 1930s than unemployment in other countries
c. High U.S. unemployment showed a small decrease. Then, it held steady in the early 1930s
d. The Great Depression caused a sharp increase in the rate of unemployment in the U.S.

Questions 48–50 refer to the following map:

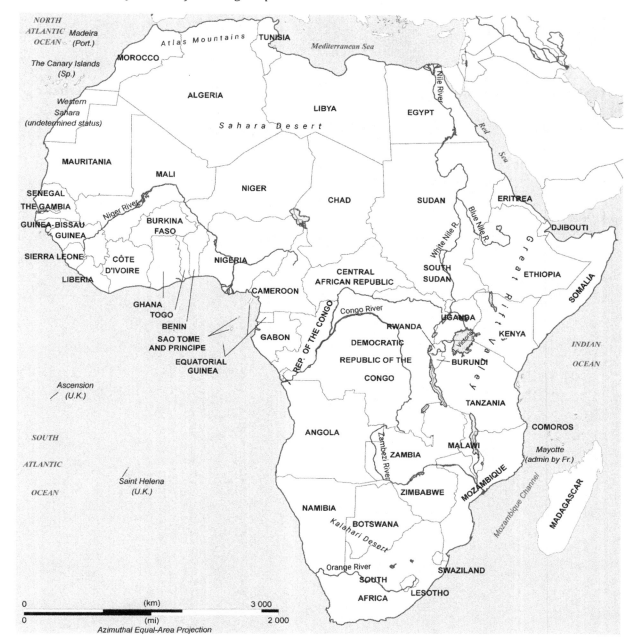

48. In Sudan, the Nile River splits into which bodies of water?

a. Gulf of Aden and Red Sea
b. Congo River and Lake Chad
c. Lake Victoria and the White Nile
d. The Blue Nile and the White Nile

49. What major geographical feature is located in Botswana?

a. Zambezi River
b. Lake Tanganyika
c. Kalahari Desert
d. Congo River

50. Which of the following countries are located along the Indian Ocean? (Select all that apply.)

a. Somalia
b. Cameroon
c. Mozambique
d. Chad
e. Kenya
f. Angola

Answer Explanations

Reasoning Through Language Arts

READING

1. D: The correct answer is D because the author says that the ancient Britons were divided into many tribes and each had a king. The author implies that these tribes fought among each other. The passage does say that the ancient Britons had many weapons. However, it doesn't say that the weapons were the reason that they fought. Instead, it just says that they fought with the weapons. Choice B is incorrect because paragraph 7 says that the ancient Britons constantly fought. However, the passage stops discussing the Phoenicians after paragraph 4. Choice C is incorrect because paragraph 6 says that there were no roads or bridges. The author gives this detail in order to describe the land. This detail does not support paragraph 7 which says that the ancient Britons regularly fought.

2. D: The correct answer is D because the word *grew* shows that the ancient Britons changed after the Phoenicians arrived. Choice A is incorrect because the answer choice only shows something that the Phoenicians did with the Britons; however, it does not describe how the Britons changed. Choice B is incorrect because the sentence only talks about the Phoenicians and does not mention the ancient Britons. Choice C is incorrect because it refers to the French and Belgians who moved to England. Moreover, there is no mention of the ancient Britons.

3. B: The word *solitary* refers to isolation or being alone. Also, the sentence says that the islands are alone in a great expanse of water. So, this shows that other lands do not surround the islands. Choice A is incorrect because the sentence only talks about the size of the small islands around Scotland. It does not talk about where the islands are in relation to larger lands. Choice C is incorrect because it shows the islanders' relationship with the sea. However, it does not talk about the separation that the islanders have with other people. Choice D is incorrect because it shows the opposite of isolation; the sentence shows how the people who came to the islands (e.g., the French, Belgians, and Spanish) mixed with the ancient Britons.

4. B: The correct answer is B because the first part of the sentence describes the boats that the ancient Britons built. However, the phrase "But seldom, if ever, ventured far from the shore" means that the boats didn't go far from shore. This implies that the boats may not have been used much. Choice A is incorrect because the phrase does not talk about specific ways that the ancient Britons used the boats. The author does describe weapons in the same paragraph. However, the phrase in the question focuses on the boats that the people made. The paragraph only moves onto weapons in the second sentence. Choice D is incorrect because the author does not connect the boats (discussed in paragraph 7) to the fortresses (discussed at the end of paragraph 6).

5. A: Choice A is the best answer because the first paragraph describes the location of the islands on the map. With this description: "you can find the islands by looking in the left-hand upper corner of the Eastern Hemisphere." Choice B is incorrect because there were no roads that ran through England, Scotland, or Ireland during the time period that the passage is describing. Choice C is incorrect because the details about the small islands are only a small part of the first paragraph. Most of the paragraph describes how the islands appear on the map. Choice D is incorrect because the paragraph does not mention the size of the main islands. Also, the paragraph does not mention France or Belgium. Those countries are first mentioned in paragraph 4.

6. C: Choice C is the correct answer because this answer choice describes the lands by mentioning swamps and forests. Choice A is incorrect because it does not give details of the lands. Also, there is no mention of the interior of the islands which is first mentioned in paragraph 5. Choice B does mention the interior. However, it is incorrect because it only says that it is away from the sea. There are no details about the lands. Choice D is incorrect because it discusses the tribes and the people rather than the features of the lands (e.g., the swamps and forests).

7. B: The word *ardent* means passionate or devoted. Look at the word in the context of the sentence: "The dull precious metal seemed to flash with a reflection of her bright and <u>ardent</u> spirit," and think about Della's actions. Choice A is not correct because Della has planned and saved to buy her husband a Christmas present. So, she has not procrastinated (i.e., waited too long to start on something). Choices C and D are synonyms. They are wrong because Della shows over and over again that she cares very much for her husband.

8. D: The first event in the story is Della preparing her hair (4). The next event in the story is Della preparing a meal for the night (2). Then, Della prays about the reaction that Jim will have to her hair (5). The next event is Jim assuring Della that he is not upset about her decision to cut her hair (3). Then, Jim gives the combs to Della (1). Finally, Della gives the fob chain to Jim (6).

9. C: The sentence "'I hunted all over town to find it.'" is an exaggeration or hyperbole. The other answer choices have similes.

10. C: In the beginning of the story, Della has her hair cut off. She does this so she can get money for Jim's gift. However, she is worried about how she will appear to her husband and is concerned that he will be very angry or worse. When Jim keeps asking about Della's hair, it almost seems as if he is angry about it.

11. A: The entire story is about how Della and Jim are deeply in love. They sell a prized possession to buy a present for the other. Choice B is wrong because the overall meaning of this passage is not about a holiday. Choice C is wrong because it fails to recognize how Della and Jim overcome difficulty and have a deeper love for each other after giving their gifts. Choice D is wrong because the focus of the passage is not on buying the right gift for a loved one. Instead, the focus is on giving up a thing that you care about to show how much you love someone.

12. D: The narrator of the passage is not named. Della and Jim are simply characters in the story. O. Henry is the author of the story, not the narrator.

13. B: The word *beneficence* is used to show how nature helps the plants and animals on Earth. For example, nature provides sunlight and rain that helps the trees grow. Choice A is incorrect because *beneficence* refers to how nature helps life grow. Choice C is incorrect because nature gives the sunlight and the rain. So, this makes it the opposite of stingy. Later, Keller experiences the dangers of nature. However, choice D is incorrect because paragraph 5 is about the generosity of nature.

14. D: The paragraph shows the narrator's discovery that words have meaning. Choice A is incorrect because the narrator and Miss Sullivan do not use a pencil. Instead, Miss Sullivan uses her fingers to spell words into the narrator's hand. The narrator does learn about cool water. However, choice B is incorrect because the main idea of the paragraph is that the narrator learns that words have meaning. Choice C is incorrect because the focus of the paragraph is not on learning the location of places.

15. A: Helen says in the second sentence that she stretched out her hand "as I supposed to my mother." Choice B is incorrect because Helen is not aware that a visitor is coming. Choice C is incorrect because there is no mention that she wants to please her mother. Choice D is incorrect because Helen does not yet know who is walking up to her.

16. B: Helen is alone and defenseless as the storm approaches. Choice A is incorrect because Helen is not lost. She knows where she is, but she is unable to get out of the tree to go home. The wind and approaching rain make Helen feel uncomfortable. However, choices C and D are incorrect because Helen's main nervousness comes from being alone. She wants the presence of her teacher.

17. C: Miss Sullivan opened up Helen's world by showing her that words have meaning and every object has a name. Choice A is incorrect because the specific words that Miss Sullivan taught Helen are not as important as the overall concept of words. Choice B is incorrect because the observation about barriers is not what she learned from Miss Sullivan. Choice D is incorrect because the sentence is not about what Helen learned. Instead, it is about the idea of learning.

18. D: Helen's relief at feeling Miss Sullivan's arms shows her reliance on and love for Miss Sullivan. Choice A is incorrect because Miss Sullivan spells "w-a-t-e-r" near the beginning of their relationship. So, they have not yet developed a very close bond. Choice B is incorrect because that is a personal growth in Helen, not a growth in the relationship of Helen and Miss Sullivan. Choice C is incorrect because it does not show the bond between Helen and Miss Sullivan. Instead, this moment simply shows something Helen and Miss Sullivan are doing together.

19. B: The passage shows Helen's discovery of language and communication. While Helen develops a close tie with Miss Sullivan, Miss Sullivan is not Helen's family. So, choice A is incorrect. Choice C is incorrect because the passage is about Helen's joy of learning and close bond with Miss Sullivan. The theme of the passage is not on any disappointment. Choice D is incorrect because the passage is about relationships and learning rather than youth.

20. D: This is correct because the paragraph is about the way that nature is turning on Helen and becoming cruel. Choice A is incorrect because Miss Sullivan does not show any cruelty towards Helen. Choice B is incorrect because this paragraph shows Helen feeling nervous but does not show her having a temper tantrum. Choice C is incorrect because Helen was in danger from being alone in the tree as the storm approached. The phrase "treacherous claws" is about the danger of being alone in the tree rather than the danger of climbing the tree.

21. A: The story shows Helen just before meeting Miss Sullivan. Then, it shows the effect that Miss Sullivan has on Helen's life. Helen may have learned some bravery in her time with Miss Sullivan. However, the order of events in the story is meant to show Helen's growing relationship with Miss Sullivan. So, this makes choice B incorrect. Choice C is incorrect because only part of the passage shows the strategies that Miss Sullivan used to teach Helen. Choice D is incorrect because Helen feels security rather than confusion when she is with Miss Sullivan.

22. C: The passage is about how Miss Sullivan taught Helen that words have meaning. Choice A is incorrect because Helen explains that she loves Miss Sullivan. Choice B is incorrect because Helen is not scared of nature; rather, she realizes that nature can be generous and dangerous. The passage does not clearly say that Helen learns to read or write. Instead, it shows the beginning of her relationship with words and implies that Helen will continue to learn.

23. D: A non-human thing (e.g., a name) is described with a human quality or action (e.g., birth). Choice A is not correct because there is not a comparison being made. Choice B is not correct because there is no exaggeration in the sentence. Choice C is not correct because there is not a comparison being made with the words *like* or *as*.

24. C: The question asks what job would be less desirable than homesteading. Choice C is correct because Stewart speaks of going out to wash as less preferable than homesteading. Choice A is incorrect because the letter does not mention cooking or restaurants. Choice B is also incorrect. The reason is that there is no mention of opening a bed and breakfast in the letter. Choice D is also wrong because the letter shares nothing about teaching.

25. D: Growing potatoes is so simple that her six-year-old can do so with little help. The issue is not child labor. So, choice A is incorrect. Stewart does not mention schooling. So, this makes choice B incorrect. Stewart's point has nothing to do with whether women work as hard as men. So, choice C is not the correct response.

26. B: Stewart mentions the hard work of laundry, but she does not speak of any enjoyment of it as she does about homesteading. Choice A cannot be correct because Stewart does not seem to be lazy. Choice C is possible, but there is no evidence to support that idea. Choice D cannot be correct because no reason for anger is given.

27. D: Stewart says that homesteading is a lonely task. For example, she mentions that "persons afraid of ...loneliness had better let ranching alone." Stewart explains in the letter that her work uses less strength than washing. So, choice A is wrong. Choice B is also incorrect because it is addressed in the first paragraph of the letter. Choice C is incorrect because it is mentioned as an advantage in the first paragraph.

28. A: Stewart directly states that women would have "the added satisfaction of knowing that their job will not be lost to them if they care to keep it." Although going on strike was common at the time, Stewart does not mention it. So, choice B is incorrect. Denver is in the Rocky Mountains, but landslides are not mentioned as a risk. So, choice C cannot be the correct answer. Fire is always a risk, but Stewart does not bring it up in the letter. So, choice D is not the correct answer.

29. C: The letter is very positive and full of reasons on why homesteading is a good choice. Choice A is incorrect. The reason is that there is no complaint of hard work, weather, or loneliness. Choice B is also not correct because the letter does not speak of sadness or loneliness. Instead, Stewart rejoices in the good success of the homestead. Also, choice D is not correct because there is no hopelessness expressed in the letter.

30. C: The professor argues that small, woody material is left on the tops of trees where a fire cannot reach. So, the material cannot be fuel for future fires.

31. D: Choice D is not a supporting detail because it is a definition of salvage logging. The other choices are supporting details of the Forest Manager's argument.

32. B: Plot A was salvage logged and burned worse than the unmanaged plot (Plot B). So, this study supports the professor's view that salvage logging raises the risk and energy of the fire.

33. A: The forest manager thinks that less fuel is open to future fires by removing dead or dying material through salvage logging.

34. D: The professor says that larger trees found in old growth forests are better at holding back fires than small, younger trees.

35. C: A study looking at the regrowth of seedlings in logged and unmanaged forests would help to explain and/or prove both arguments. The reason is that the manager and the professor talk on the importance of seedling growth after a fire.

36. C: The first section covers how people want to change and the options that are available to them. As people move towards a healthier lifestyle, they can work at small steps on their way to better health. Choice A is not correct because the process takes a lot of time to change habits and choose healthier options. Although there is a paragraph on benefits of certain foods, the focus of the section is on making better choices with food. Choice D is incorrect because the passage mentions that the process is a struggle for many, not an impossible task.

37. D: The overall passage is information for someone who is interested in the food industry. So, choice A is not correct. The reason is that there is not much of a comparison or contrast between the Food Pyramid and MyPlate. Choice B is incorrect because the focus of the passage is not on government involvement. Choice C is wrong as well. It is true that there is not a perfect system of dietary recommendations. However, that is not the purpose of including that section in the passage.

38. A: Choice B is wrong because there is no mention of Harvard's guidelines replacing MyPlate. Choice C is also not correct. It is another approach to dietary guidelines; however, that is not the reason that it was included in Section 2. Choice D is wrong because Harvard is an influential school, but it is not mentioned in the section for that reason.

39. C: This passage was written for people who have an interest in the food industry. So, choice A is wrong because the passage is not meant for those who are new to dieting. Choice B is wrong because experienced professionals don't need introductory-level material on preparing food. Choice D is incorrect because there is no mention of parents or children in the passage.

40. B: Each section of the passage has the tone of educating readers. So, choice A is wrong because the tone is not blaming readers. Choice C is close, but it is not the best answer choice. Overall, the passage is more serious than entertaining. However, the main tone of the passage is informative. Choice D is wrong because the tone of the material is not snobbish or cocky.

WRITING

1. A: The problem in this sentence is subject-verb agreement. Remember that the indefinite pronouns are always singular. Choice B is incorrect because the clause is essential to the sentence. So, commas are not needed. Choice C is wrong because the prepositional phrase does not need punctuation. Choice D is incorrect because there is no need to change *which* to *that*.

2. C: The question tests you on the correct word for comparison with adjectives. The correct adjective is the comparative form of the adjective *bad* which is *worse*, not the superlative form *worst*. Choice A will create a problem with subject-verb agreement. So, it is incorrect. Choice B is wrong as well. The reason is that it creates an adjective comparison problem, and this is the problem you want to correct. Choice D is incorrect because there is a problem that needs to be corrected.

3. B: The sentence is written as a double negative. Choice B is the only choice that corrects the problem. So, choice A is incorrect because the sentence needs to be changed. Choice C is incorrect because it does not solve the problem of the double negative and makes another problem with verb tense. Also, choice D does not solve the problem of the double negative. So, it can be eliminated.

4. A: The sentence has a clarity problem. The dependent clause should come at the beginning of the sentence rather than interrupting the independent clause. Choice B does not make a correction to the sentence. Choice C makes the sentence into a question which is not necessary. Choice D is incorrect because the sentence needs to be reworded to have clarity.

5. B: This sentence should come after the third sentence because it is the first "tip" to consider. Choice A is incorrect because this sentence is only one part to a working vehicle. Choice C is not correct because a sentence that begins with *First of all* should not be the concluding sentence. Choice D is wrong because the sentence belongs with paragraph A. In paragraph B, the focus is on working under the hood and the inside of the vehicle.

6. D: The sentence is written correctly. Choice A is incorrect because splitting the infinitive will be a mistake, not a correction. Choice B is not correct because you need to which area of the car that needs to be checked. Choice C is incorrect because that would only create a problem in agreement.

7. D: Sentence (10) is a run-on sentence and needs correct punctuation. The use of a semicolon between two sentences that are connected in thought is the only acceptable answer choice. You cannot leave the sentence alone. So, choice A is not the correct choice. Choice C places a conjunction between the two sentences. However, it does not include the necessary comma before the conjunction. So, it is an incorrect choice.

8. C: These words are three items in a series. So, commas are needed to separate them. Choice A is not correct because the apostrophe shows possession, and it is used correctly. Choice B is also wrong because the word *emergency* is spelled correctly in the sentence. Choice D is incorrect because the sentence needs commas.

9. A: This sentence has a misplaced modifier. Currently, you can read the sentence and think that you should take everything with you except the car. When you move the word, you understand the reason that you are leaving the car is that you know where you are going and what you are doing. Choice B is not correct because the word is important to the sentence. Choice C is wrong because there is no need for a comma. Choice D is not correct as well. The reason is that there is an error in the sentence.

10. A: There is nothing wrong with the sentence. So, choice A is the correct choice. Everything after the comma could be removed without harming the independent clause at the beginning of the sentence. So, the nonessential adjective clause needs a comma. Choice B is incorrect because it suggests removing the comma. Choice C makes *products* singular. This is incorrect because it creates a problem with subject-verb agreement. The same problem is in choice D; however, the verb is singular.

11. B: This question is about subject-verb agreement. *Slow foods* is plural and needs the plural form of *to be* which is *are*. When you change *is* to *are*, the sentence is corrected. Choice A is not correct because there is not an extra comma in the sentence. Choice C is also wrong because *slow foods* is not a proper noun. So, it does not need capitalization. Choice D is incorrect because *comeback* is one word.

12. D: The question reviews correct spelling. *Emphasize* is the verb, and *emphasis* is the noun which is needed here. Choice A is incorrect because it does not address the problem. Choice B changes the verb from *puts* to *places*, yet there is no problem with the verb choice. Choice C makes the verb plural, but this only adds to the problem.

13. D: This question is about parallel structure. Placing the definite article *the* in front of the final two terms in the series hurts the structure. Removing *the* makes all the items parallel. So, choice A is incorrect. Choice B is also wrong. By making *species* singular, another problem is introduced. Choice C is incorrect because making all nouns singular does not correct the problem.

14. C: The error in this sentence is a split infinitive. The adverb *fully* comes between the words *to* and *use*, and this is not correct grammar. Choice A is incorrect because the change would cause a subject-verb disagreement. Choice B is wrong because the prepositional phrase is not an aside. Also, choice D is wrong because there is an error in the sentence.

15. B: *Slow Food USA* is the name of an organization. So, this makes it a proper noun that needs capitalization. Choice A is not correct because this is the proper name of a specific program. So, the capital letters are correct. Choice C is also wrong because *thru* is a shortcut spelling, but *through* is Standard English. Choice D is incorrect because the sentence has an error.

16. C: Sentence (13) is not important to the article. The writer's garden is not a concern. Choice A is wrong. The reason is that placing the sentence at the beginning of the paragraph makes readers think that the paragraph will be a narrative about the writer's garden. Choice B is incorrect because the last sentence of an essay should be related to the rest of the essay. Choice D is not correct because the sentence should be removed from this passage.

17. D: The sentence is a run-on. So, the best answer choice is to make two sentences of the run-on sentence. Choice A is incorrect because adding commas does not correct the run-on. For choice C, the original word is the correct word. So, this is not correct. Choice B is incorrect because it suggests that the terms are not parallel.

18. B: The proper noun *Slow Food on Campus* is an essential appositive. So, the commas can be removed. Now, the sentence is in passive voice. Choice A would help move the sentence to active voice which is preferred over passive voice. However, this is not the error of the sentence. So, choice A is incorrect. Choice C is wrong because *Slow Food on Campus* is a proper noun that needs capital letters. Choice D is also wrong because *similar* is the correct spelling.

19. D: This sentence is written correctly. Choice A is wrong because the introductory prepositional phrase needs a comma. Choice B is not correct because the verb needs to stay in singular form. Choice C is incorrect because *healthy* is spelled correctly.

20. B: Items in a series need commas between each item. Choice A is wrong because there are no commas for this series. There is no need to capitalize the name of a disease. So, choice C is incorrect. There is an error in the sentence. So, choice D cannot be correct.

21. D: This sentence is a run-on. The sentence has two independent clauses. So, you can place a period between them and capitalize the word *for*. Choice A is wrong because the original sentence is not correct. Choice B is wrong as well. The reason is that a comma between two independent clauses does not correct the problem. Choice C is wrong because a colon cannot be used to separate independent clauses.

22. A: The sentence does not need an adverb. Instead, it needs a predicate adjective to modify the subject *researchers*. Choice B is incorrect because SAD is an acronym that should have capital letters. The sentence is not a question. So, choice C is wrong because it does not need a question mark. Choice D is not correct because there is a mistake in the sentence.

23. D: The sentence is written correctly. So, choice A is not correct because the adjectives are not coordinate. Choice B is not correct because the sentence is making a comparison to months that are not during the winter. In other words, the body makes less melatonin in the summer months. Choice C is wrong because *melatonin* does not need to be capitalized.

24. A: The question tests on the use of *effect* and *affect*. In this sentence, you are looking for the verb that means *influence*. So, affect is the correct word in this sentence. Choice B is wrong because the prepositional phrase should not come after *serotonin*. Choice C is incorrect because *Less* is for amounts which is true for this sentence. *Fewer* is for numbers and applies to things that can be counted. So, the correct adverb is being used in this sentence. Choice D is wrong because the sentence has an error.

25. D: Again, *fewer* is for numbers and applies to things that can be counted. Sunlight cannot be counted. *Less* is for an amount which is true for this sentence. Also, making the change brings back the intended parallelism of the sentence. Choice A is incorrect because the subject and verb agree as they are written. Choice B is also incorrect because the word is not a proper noun and does not need capitalization. Choice C is incorrect. The reason is given in the explanation above for choice D.

26. D: *Factors* is plural and needs a plural verb. The verb *has* is singular. So, this makes a disagreement between subject and verb. *Have* is the plural form of *has* and needs to be used here. Choice A is incorrect because the sentence has an error with subject-verb agreement. Choice B is wrong because removing the capital letter causes another error. Choice C is incorrect. The change simply switches the problem in agreement rather than eliminating it.

27. C: The sentence has a problem with parallel structure. The verbs *tough* and *wait* need to be parallel. Choice A is incorrect because SAD is an acronym and needs capital letters. Choice B is also incorrect. There is an attempt to correct the problem of parallelism. However, *toughing* needs an auxiliary verb. Choice D is wrong because there is an error that needs to be corrected.

28. B: The sentence is not interrogative; it is declarative. In other words, it needs a period at the end, not a question mark. Choice A is incorrect because *well* is an adverb, and the noun *news* needs an adjective modifier. Choice C is incorrect because the seasons are not capitalized. Choice D is wrong because there is an error that needs to be corrected.

29. A: Choice A is correct because the word is not being used in a different way from a dictionary definition. Choice B is not correct because readers need an explanation of the word *temp*. Choice C is wrong because *temporary* is spelled correctly. Choice D is incorrect because a comma is not needed.

30. D: This question is about parallel structure. *Employs* and *generating* are verbs that need to be changed to be parallel. The best way to make them parallel is by putting both in the present tense. Choice A is incorrect because *the staffing industry* is a single unit. So, it does not need the plural form. Choice B is incorrect because the noun is singular and needs a singular verb. Choice C cannot be done without adding more words.

31. D: The problem in the sentence is the wrong homonym. The word *their* is possessive and is needed in this sentence. *They're* is a contraction of *they are*. So, this is the wrong word. In this sentence, *because* is used correctly. So, this makes choice A incorrect. Choice C makes *skills* singular; however, this is not the correct choice. After all, an employer wants a worker who has more than one skill.

32. B: The problem in this question is with antecedent agreement. The pronoun *they* needs a plural noun: *employees*. Choice A is incorrect because of the problem with antecedent agreement. Choice C is incorrect because it has disagreement between subject and verb. Choice D is also wrong. The hyphen in *full-time* does not need to be removed. Also, choice D has disagreement between subject and verb. So, choice D is not correct.

33. C: The problem with the sentence is a comma splice. A semicolon shows that the thoughts of both sentences are related. So, the problem is corrected with the semicolon. Choice A cannot be correct because the original has a comma splice. Choice B is also wrong. The reason is that it has a pronoun-antecedent agreement problem. Choice D is incorrect because it creates a subject-verb agreement problem.

34. D: Adding a comma eliminates the problem of the run-on sentence. Choice A is wrong because there is an error in the sentence. Choice B is also incorrect because it creates a problem with subject-verb agreement. Choice C is incorrect because it creates a subject-verb disagreement in a different part of the sentence.

35. C: The problem in this sentence is a misspelling of valuable. Choice A is wrong because a hyphen is not needed to connect the two words. Choice B cannot be correct because *you're* is the right homonym. Choice D is not correct because there is an error in the sentence.

36. C: This sentence has no parallelism. *To look for* and *interviewing* can be made parallel by making this change. Choice A is not correct because the word *permanent* is spelled correctly. Choice B is not correct. The reason is that it tries to correct the problem, but it fails. Choice D cannot be correct because of the error with parallel structure in the sentence.

37. B: The problem is a misspelled word. Choice B corrects the problem. So, choice A cannot be correct because of the spelling error. Choice C is incorrect because the preposition *among* suggests that there is more than one worker who is being considered for a position. Choice D corrects the spelling error. However, it changes *workers* from plural to singular. So, it is incorrect.

38. A: The sentence is declarative, not interrogative. So, the sentence needs a period as the end mark. Choice B is not correct because the apostrophe is needed to show possession. Choice C is incorrect because it does not solve the problem, and it creates a problem of agreement. Choice D is incorrect as well. The reason is that the sentence has an error that needs to be corrected.

39. C: The sentence has disagreement between the compound subject and the singular verb. Changing *is* to *are* solves the problem. Choice A is incorrect because the comma is needed for items in a series. Choice B is not correct because the word is spelled correctly. Choice D is incorrect because the sentence has an error that should be corrected.

40. D: The problem in the sentence is subject-verb agreement. *Some* suggests that more than one apartment complex is being discussed. So, it is necessary to change the subject and verb to plural. Choice A is incorrect because the sentence has an error that needs to be fixed. Choice B is not correct because the correct homonym is being used in this sentence. Choice C is incorrect because it creates a different subject-verb agreement problem.

41. C: The problem in this sentence is a dangling modifier. To correct the problem, you can write the independent clause as "*you need to consider the other issues about keeping your pet at your apartment.*" Choice A is wrong because the comma needs to come after the introductory prepositional phrase. Choice B is not correct because the word is spelled correctly. Choice D cannot be correct because there is an error in the sentence.

42. B: This question is on the use of *affect* and *effect*. *Affect* is the verb that means to influence, and it is needed here. *Effect* is the noun that points to the influence. Choice A is incorrect because there is a problem in the sentence. Choice C is also incorrect because it creates a subject-verb agreement problem. Choice D is not correct because it does not address the word choice and creates a subject-verb agreement problem.

43. A: *Irregardless* is used very often in informal communication. However, it is not an acceptable word in Standard English. The correct word is *regardless*. Choice B is not correct because the word *licensing* is spelled correctly. Choice C is not correct because the sentence does not have extra commas. The first comma separates the dependent clause. The other commas are needed for the items in a series. Choice D is incorrect as well because the sentence does have an error.

44. B: The apostrophe is needed in *nations* to show possession of the *highest executive office*. Choice A is not correct because executive office is not a proper noun that needs capitalization. Choice C is wrong because you do not want to separate an infinitive. Also, choice D is wrong because there is an error in the sentence.

45. B: *Wall Street* is the name of a street in New York. So, it needs capitalization. Choice A is wrong because this would make an error in verb tense. Choice C is incorrect because the words *although* and *though* are nearly synonyms. So, choosing *although* is not an error. Choice D is incorrect as well because *investment firm* is a common noun. It is not the name of a certain investment firm. So, no capitalization is needed.

46. A: The information in the parentheses is not necessary information. However, the information is closely connected to the sentence. So, commas should be used instead of parentheses. Choice B is wrong because *Republicans* is the name of a certain political party and needs capitalization. Choice C is incorrect because the sentence needs a singular noun for *Margaret Chase Smith*. Choice D is not correct because there is a mistake in the sentence.

47. D: The question tests on irregular verb forms. The sentence needs the past participle of *seek* which is *sought*. So, choice A is incorrect. Choice B is also wrong because the singular subject causes a problem with subject-verb agreement. Choice C is incorrect because the problem is not with the verb tense.

48. A: This is a run-on sentence that can be corrected with a comma between the short independent clauses. Choice B is not correct because the pronoun *them* is correct. Choice C is incorrect. If you made the change, then you would have an error in subject-verb agreement. Choice D is wrong because there is an error in the sentence.

49. C: Sentence (8) is a personal opinion that does not help this passage. Choice A is incorrect. Changing the order of the paragraphs only hurts the chronological order of the passage. Choices B and D are incorrect. The reason is that moving these sentences upsets the unity and coherence of the piece.

50. A: The sentence places a comma after each country correctly because they are items in a series. However, a comma is not needed after Liberia because it is the last item in the series. Choice B is incorrect because the commas are necessary for the items in the series. The exception is the comma after Liberia. Choice D is incorrect because believe is spelled correctly and there is an error in the sentence.

Mathematics

1. C and F: The other coordinates make lines that are not perpendicular to the line in the figure.

2. D: The perimeter (P) of the quadrilateral is simply the sum of its sides:

$$P = m + (m + 2) + (m + 3) + 2m$$

340

Put together like terms by adding the variables (m terms) together. Then, add the constants. This gives you: $P = 5m + 5$

In this problem, it seems that some of the variables do not have a number in front of them. However, when there is no coefficient, this means multiplication by 1. So, $m = 1m$, $x = 1x$, and so on.

3. B:

Substitute the given values for the variables into the expression

4·**-6** (3 · **7** +5) + 2· **7**

Using order of operations, find the expression in the parentheses first.

Remember that first you must multiply 3 by 7. Then, add 5 to follow the steps of order of operations

= 4·**-6** (21 +5) + 2· **7**   Next add the values in the parenthesis.

= 4·**-6** (26) + 2· **7**   Simplify by multiplying the numbers outside the parenthesis.

=-24(26) +14   Multiply -24 by 26

=-624 +14   Add.

=-610 is your final answer.

4. D: The area of the circle is πr². The circumference is 2πr. First, take the ratio of these two expressions: Ratio=$\frac{\pi r^2}{2\pi r}$. Then, reduce it to: $\frac{r}{2}$.

5. A: There are 16 empty chairs. This gives 2/5 of the total enrollment. So, the full class must be:

Class = $\frac{5}{2}$ × 16 = 40 students

Another option is to use proportions:

$$\frac{2}{5} = \frac{16}{x}$$

First, cross multiply to get: $2x = 80$. Then, divide each side by 2 to solve for x. So, $x = 40$ students

6. D: Jamie had $2.75 in his wallet. To solve this problem, you subtract $4.25 and $2.00 from the first sum of $6.50. So, you are left with $0.25. Then, you add $2.50. So, you come to the final answer of $2.75.

7. D: There are two ways to solve this problem. First, you can convert meters to centimeters. Then, use the conversion factor in the table to convert centimeters to inches. Second, use the table to convert meters to yards. Then, convert to inches.

For the first way, remember that there are 100 centimeters in a meter (*centi* means "hundredth").

So, $19m = 1900cm = \left(\frac{1900}{2.54}\right) = 748$ inches.

In the second way to solve the problem, remember that there are 36 inches in a yard.

So, 19m = 19 x 1.094 = 20.786 yd = 20.786 x 36 = 748 inches.

Often, proportions are used for conversions. After converting meters to centimeters, you set up proportions to solve for an unknown variable, x.

$$\frac{1900\ cm}{x\ in} = \frac{2.54\ cm}{1\ in}$$

Cross multiply to get: 1900 = 2.54x. Then, divide each side by 2.54 to solve for x. So, x = 748

8. A: You know price for each pound of onions and carrots. So, start by finding the total cost of the onions and carrots. This will equal (2 x $3.69) + (3 x $4.29) = $20.25. Next, this sum is subtracted from the total cost of the vegetables. This is done to find the cost of the mushrooms: $24.15 - $20.25 = $3.90. Finally, the cost of the mushrooms is divided by the quantity (lbs) to find the cost per pound:

Cost per pound lb = $\frac{\$3.90}{1.5}$ = $2.60

9. D: The figure is a number line. So, the distance from point A to point B will be the difference of B-A. This is 5 − (-6) = 11. Also, the distance from point B to point C will be the difference of C-B. This is 8 − 5 = 3. So, the ratio $BC{:}AB$ will be 3:11.

10. The correct answer is $525. In the first year that he holds the certificate, Jesse's income will be equal to 7.5% of the principal that he has invested which was $7,000. Remember the formula: I = Prt where I is interest, P is principal, r is rate (given as a decimal) and t is time (in years).

So, I = $7,000 × .75 × 1. This equals $525.

11. A: Candidate A's vote percentage is the number of votes that he obtained divided by the total number of votes cast. Then, multiply that decimal by 100 to convert the decimal into a percentage. Now, Candidate A's vote is: Percentage = $\frac{36800}{36800+32100+2100}$ × 100. So, you have a percentage of 51.8%

12. The correct answer is 168.75 minutes. First, find the time that is needed to ride 1 mile.

This is equal to 45 / 16 or 2.8125 minutes. Next, multiply this by the total number of miles to be ridden, or 60, to have the final answer. When you put all of this together, you have:

Time = $\frac{45}{16}$ × 60 = 168.75 minutes

Another way is to use proportions. To begin set up your proportions:

$$\frac{16\ miles}{45\ min} = \frac{60\ miles}{x\ min}$$

Then, cross multiply to get: 16x = 2700. Now, divide each side by 16. So, you have x = 168.75 minutes

13. The area is 3.93 square units. Note that the shaded area is one fourth of the difference between the areas of the inner and outer circles. The formula for finding the area of a circle is: Area

$= \pi r^2$. The radius (r) of the outer circle is 3. So, you have $A_{out} = \pi \times 3^2$, or 9π. The radius of the inner circle is $A_{in} = \pi \times 2^2$, or 4π. So, the area of the shaded part must be found as follows:

$Area = (9\pi - 4\pi)$ Then, factor out π.

So, you have: $Area = \frac{1}{4}\pi(9-4) = \frac{5\pi}{4} = 3.93$

14. B: $19.00 per share. Divide David's total profit of $22.00 by the number of shares he purchased (200) to find David's profit per share:

$P = \$22.00 \div 200 = \$.11$ per share. So, the price he paid was 11¢ lower than the closing price given in the table. The table shows that Oracle closed at $19.11 per share today. So, the price David paid was $19.11 - $0.11 = $19.00 per share.

15. The correct answer is $30.16 per share. To find this weighted average, you multiply the number of shares purchased per stock by the stock price. Then, add these totals together and divide by the total number of shares. Lynn bought 100 shares of Microsoft at $45.14, 100 shares of Apple Computer at $16.90, and 200 shares of Garmin at $29.30. So, the total amount that she spent was:

$$Total = (100 \times \$45.14) + (100 \times \$16.90) + (200 \times \$29.30) = \$12064$$

She gained a total of 400 shares of stock. So, the average cost per share is $Avg = \frac{Total}{shares} = \frac{\$12064}{400} \approx \$30.16$

16. The correct answer is $3.85. To make a profit of 10%, James must sell the stock at a price that is 10% higher than what he paid for it. So, he must sell it at 110% of the purchase price. He buys the stock at $3.50 per share. So, he must sell it at a price (P) as follows:

$$P = \frac{110 \times \$3.50}{100} = \$3.85$$

17. The correct answer is $123. To calculate this, first find the total number of hours worked. From 7AM until noon is 5 hours. From noon until 4:30 PM is 4.5 hours. So, the total number of hours worked is:

5+4.5 = 9.5 hours. Next, find the number of hours paid at the overtime rate. This is 9.5 – 8 or 1.5 hours. The overtime pay rate is 50% greater than the regular rate of $12 per hour or 1.5 x $12 = $18 per hour. Finally, calculate the amount of pay at each rate, regular and overtime. Then, add these together to find the total pay: $Total = (8 \times \$12) + (1.5 \times \$18) = \$123$

18. D: First, add the two straight 150-yard portions. Also, note that the distance for the two semi-circles put together is the circumference of a circle. The radius (r) of that circle is half of the dimension given as the width of the track. In other words, it is 15 yards. Now, use the formula for the circumference of a circle: $2\pi r$. Then, add it to the length of the two straight portions of the track. So, you have:

$Length = (2\pi \times 15) + (2 \times 150) = 394.25$

Choice D is the closest to this calculated answer.

19. C: First, find the total distance of the round trip. This is twice the 45 miles of the one-way trip to work in the morning. So, that equals 90 miles. Then, find the total amount of time that Elijah spent on his round trip by converting his travel times into minutes. One hour and ten minutes equals 70 minutes, and one and a half hours equals 90 minutes. So, Elijah's total travel time was 70 + 90 = 160 minutes. Elijah's average speed can now be found in miles per minute:

$$Speed = \frac{90\ miles}{160\ min.} = 0.5625 \text{ miles per minute}$$

Finally, to convert this average speed into miles per hour, you need to multiply by 60. The reason is that there are 60 minutes in an hour:

$$Avg.\ Speed(mph) = 60 \times 0.5625 = 33.75 \text{ miles per hour}$$

20. The correct answer is 0.48 seconds. Modify the relationship given in the question to solve for the time. You know that the distance is the product of the rate and time: $d = rt$. To change the relationship for this problem, you need to put time (t) by itself. So, this will look like: $t = \frac{d}{r} = \frac{60.5ft}{125\ ft/sec} = 0.484\ sec$. When you round to the nearest hundredth of a second, you have the answer of 0.48 seconds.

21. A: The rate of increase equals the change in the account balance divided by the original amount: $80. Multiply that decimal by 100 to know the percentage of increase. So, to find the change in the balance, subtract the original amount from the new balance: Change = $120 - $80 = $40 Now, you can find the percentage of increase: $Percent = \frac{\$40}{\$80} \times 100 = 50\%$

22. The correct answer is 910 square feet. The answer is found by computing the area of the large rectangle and the area of the rectangular cutout. Then, the area of the cutout is subtracted from the larger rectangle. The area of the rectangle is the product of its length and width, $A_{rect} = 20 \times 50 = 1000$ square feet. The cutout is a rectangle as well. So, its area is computed in the same way: $A_{cutout} = 6 \times 15 = 90$ square feet. Then, subtracting gives you the answer: $Area = A_{rect} - A_{cutout} = 1000 - 90 = 910$ square feet.

23. D: Begin as you would with a regular equation: 4x – 12 > 4.

> Add 12 to each side: 4x – 12 + 12 > 4 + 12. This gives you: 4x > 16.

> Divide each side by 4: 4x/4 > 16/4. This gives you: x > 4.

Note that the inequality does not change. The reason is that the division was by a positive 4.

Only choice D follows the condition that it needs to be less than 4.

24. B: The rate, miles per minute, is constant. So, this can be solved by setting up a proportion:

$\frac{miles}{min} = \frac{10}{12} = \frac{210}{x}$. Now, solve for time: $t = \frac{210 \times 12}{10} = 252$ minutes. Finally, convert to hours by dividing this total by 60. The reason is that there are 60 minutes in an hour: $t = \frac{252}{60} = 4$ hours and 12 minutes.

Note: When dividing 252 by 60, you get a decimal answer of 4.2 hours. However, the answers are given in a different unit of measurement. 4.2 hours is not the same as 4 hours and 2 minutes. In order to find the number of minutes, the decimal (.2) has to be converted into minutes. To convert, multiply .2 by 60 which becomes 12 minutes.

25. C: Define the variable t as the passed time (in hours) from the time the first airplane takes off. Then, at any time the distance traveled by the first plane is $d_1 = 250t$. The second plane takes off 30 minutes later. So, at any time the distance that it has traveled is $d_2 = 280(t - 30)$. This plane will overtake the first when the two distances are equal: $d_1 = d_2$ or $250t = 280(t - 30)$.

First use the distributive property to solve for t: $250t = 280t - 8400$.

Next, add 8400 to each side of the equation: $250t + 8400 = 280t$

Next, subtract $250t$ from each side of the equation: $8400 = 30t$

Next, divide both sides by 30: $280 = t$.

This gives the value of t in minutes. Convert to hours by dividing 280 by 60 minutes per hour. So, you have the found an elapsed time of 4 hours and 40 minutes. Remember to multiply the decimal (.66...) by 60 to convert the decimal into minutes (40 min). The first plane left at 2 PM. So, 4 hours and 40 minutes later is 6:40 PM.

26. B: The figure is a right triangle. So, the Pythagorean Theorem can be used. The side that is 25 units long is the hypotenuse. Its square will equal the sum of the squares of the other two sides.

That is $25^2 = 15^2 + x^2$. Solve for x^2 by subtracting 15^2 from each side of this equation. Then, take the square root to find x.

$$x = \sqrt{25^2 - 15^2} = \sqrt{625 - 225} = \sqrt{400} = 20$$

27. C: The formula for the volume of a pyramid is $V = \frac{1}{3}BH$, where B is the area of the base and H is the height of the pyramid. The base is a square with a length of 756 ft on each side. So, the area of the base is

$A = s^2 = (756 \text{ ft})^2 = 571{,}536 \text{ ft}^2$. With a base of 571,536 ft² and a height of 481 ft, the volume of the pyramid is $V = \frac{1}{3}(571{,}536 \ ft^2)(481 \ ft) = 9.16 \times 10^7 ft.^3$

28. D: First, test each expression to see which follows the condition $x > y$. This condition is met for all the answer choices except choice C. Next, test the remaining choices to see which follows the inequality $x + y > 0$. It can be seen that this inequality holds for choice A and choice B. However, this does not hold for choice D. The reason is that $x + y = 3 + (-3) = 3 - 3 = 0$. In this case, the sum $x + y$ is not greater than 0.

29. D: To multiply two powers that have the same base, you need to add their exponents.

So, $x^3 x^5 = x^{3+5} = x^8$. Also note that $x^3 = x \cdot x \cdot x$. So, the expression equals $x \cdot x \cdot x \cdot x \cdot x \cdot x \cdot x \cdot x$

30. B: Take the cross product of the numerators and denominators from either side for this proportion.

$$\frac{12}{x} = \frac{30}{6}$$

Cross multiply to get: 30x = 72. Then, divide each side by 30. So, you are left with $x = 2.4$

31. A: This is a typical plot of an inverse variation where the product of the dependent and independent variables, x and y, is always equal to the same value. In this case, the product is always equal to 1. So, the plot is in the first and third quadrants of the coordinate plane. As x increases and goes to infinity, y decreases and goes to zero while keeping the constant product. In contrast, choice B is a linear plot for an equation of the form $y = x$. Choice C is a quadratic plot for the equation $y = x^2$. Choice D is an exponential plot for the equation $y = 2x$.

32. C: The internal angles of a triangle always add up to 180°. Since $\triangle ABC$ is a right triangle, then $\angle ABC = 90°$ and $\angle ACB$ is given as 30°. The middle letter is for the vertex. By using the triangle addition theorem, the answer must be: $\angle BAC = 180 - (90+30)$. This equals 60°.

33. A: This equation is a linear relationship that has a slope of 3.60 and passes through the origin. The table shows that for each hour of rental, the cost increases by $3.60. This matches with the slope of the equation. Of course, if the bicycle is not rented at all (0 hours), there will be no charge ($0). If plotted on the Cartesian plane, the line would have a y intercept of 0. Choice A is the only one that follows these requirements.

34. D: The slopes of perpendicular lines are reciprocals and have the opposite sign. In the figure below, line A has a slope of -1/2, and line B has a slope of 2.

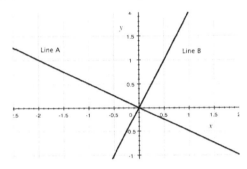

35. C: This table shows the numbers of coins added to the first few squares and the equivalent powers of 2:

Square	1	2	3	4
Coins	1	2	4	8
Power of 2	2^0	2^1	2^2	2^3

In this series, the number of coins on each is the consecutive powers of 2. The reason is that the number doubles with each consecutive square. However, the series of powers begins with 0 for the first square. For the 64th square, the number of coins will be 2^{63}.

36. C: There are four different colors. So, one color must be held back from each balloon bundle. So, there is one color set for each excluded color or four in all.

When the order of the individual parts is not important, this is called a combination. The number of combinations of n objects taken k at a time is given by $C = \dfrac{n!}{(n-k)!k!}$. The ! notation is for a *factorial* product where $n! = 1 \times 2 \times 3 \times \ldots \times (n-1) \times n$. In this case, $n = 4$ colors, and $k = 3$ balloons per bundle. Then, substitute into the equation above and simplify:

$$C = \frac{4!}{(4-3)! \times 3!} = \frac{1 \times 2 \times 3 \times 4}{(1)(1 \times 2 \times 3)} = 4$$

37. B: The two right triangles are similar because they share a pair of vertical angles. Vertical angles are always congruent (e.g., angle ACB and angle DCE). Obviously, both right angles (e.g., angle B and angle D) are congruent. So, angles A and E are congruent because of the triangular sum theorem.

With similar triangles, corresponding sides will be proportional. Segment BC is $\frac{1}{2}$ the length of segment CD. So, AC will be $\frac{1}{2}$ the length of CE. The length of CE can be computed from the Pythagorean theorem. The reason is that it is the hypotenuse of a right triangle, and the lengths of the other two sides are known: $CE = \sqrt{6^2 + 8^2} = \sqrt{100} = 10$.

The length of segment AC will be $\frac{1}{2}$ of this value or 5 units.

38. The correct answer is (2,0). To come to this answer, set the two expressions to be equal and solve for the variable x. This is the substitution method:

$$-3x + 6 = 2x - 4$$

Gather like terms on each side of the equation and isolate the variable. This gives you $10 = 5x$.

Finally, divide each side by 5. So, you have $x = 2$.

Now, substitute this value of x into either of the original equations to find the y coordinate

$$y = -3x + 6 = -6 + 6 = 0$$

39. C: For each die there is 1 in 6 chance that a 6 will be on top. The reason is that the die has 6 sides. The probability that a 6 will show for each die is not affected by the results from another roll of the die. In other words, these probabilities are independent. So, the overall probability of throwing 3 sixes is the product of the individual probabilities: $P = \frac{1}{6} \times \frac{1}{6} \times \frac{1}{6} = \frac{1}{6^3} = \frac{1}{216}$

40. D: Rafael's profit on each computer is the difference between the price he pays and the price he charges his customer: \$800-\$450. If he sells n computers in a month, his total profit will be n times this difference: $n(800 - 450)$. However, it is necessary to subtract his fixed costs of \$3000 from $n(800 - 450)$ to find his final profit per month.

41. D: When a number is raised to a power, you multiply the number by itself by the number of times of the power. For example, $2^3 = 2 \times 2 \times 2 = 8$. A number raised to the power of 0 is always equal to 1. So, 6^0 is the smallest number shown. Similarly, for the other numbers: $9^1 = 9$; $10^1 = 10$; $4^2 = 4 \times 4 = 16$

42. B: This pie chart shows the relative amounts of each variable as a slice of the whole circle. The larger variables have larger slices. Also, the percentage of each variable (e.g., recycled material) is shown next to each slice. In this chart, paper is the most common recycled material (i.e., the largest variable). This is 40% of the total. The next largest is glass at 25% of the total. All of the other materials stand for smaller portions of the total.

43. D: The chart indicates that 40% of the total recycled material is paper. Since 50,000 tons of material are recycled every month, the total amount of paper will be 40% of 50,000 tons, or $\frac{40}{100} \times 50,000 = 20,000$ tons.

44. A: Let D represent Dorothy's age, and S her is sister's age. Since she is half her sister's age today, we have, $D = \frac{S}{2}$ or $S = 2D$. In twenty years, her age will be $D + 20$ years. Her sister's age will be $S + 20$ years. At that time, Dorothy will be $\frac{3}{4}$ of her sister's age. So, $D + 20 = \frac{3\times(S+20)}{4}$ Substituting $2D$ for S in this equation gives

$$D + 20 = \frac{3(2D + 20)}{4}$$

$$D + 20 = \frac{6D + 60}{4}$$

Use the distributive property and reduce.

$$D + 20 = \frac{3}{2}D + 15$$

$$D + 20 = \frac{3D}{2} + 15$$

Gather like terms:

$20 - 15 = \frac{3D}{2} - D$ which is equal to $5 = \frac{D}{2}$

Therefore, $D = 10$ years old. Dorothy is ten years old today. Her sister is twenty years old. In twenty years, Dorothy will be 30 years old, and her sister will be 40.

45. The correct answer is $4000. Chan has paid out a total of 85% (30% + 30% +25%) of his bonus for the items in the question. So, the $600 is the remaining 15%. To find out his total bonus, solve $\frac{100}{15} \times 600 = \$4000$.

46. D: It is not necessary to use the circle formula to solve the problem. Note that 50 km/hr matches with 50,000 meters per hour. You have the car's revolutions per minute, and the answer must be given in meters. So, the speed must be converted to meters per minute. This matches with a speed of $\frac{50,000}{60}$ meters per minute. The reason is that there are 60 minutes in an hour. In any given minute, the car travels at $\frac{50,000}{60}$ meters/min. The tires rotate 500 times around. So, this is 500 times its circumference. This matches with $\frac{50,000}{60\times500} = \frac{10}{6}$ meters per revolution. This is the circumference of the tire.

47. B: The volume of the cylinder is the amount of grain that the farmer will be able to store in the silo. The formula for the volume of a cylinder is $V = \pi r^2 h$, where r is the radius and h is the height. The cylinder has a diameter of 8 m. So, the radius is half of the diameter or 4 m. The height is 24 m. So, your equation becomes $V = \pi(4\ m)^2(24\ m)$= 1,206.4 m³.

48. A: Find the product using the FOIL method. As a result, $(a + b)(a - b) = a^2 + ba - ab - b^2$. Since ab is equal to ba, the middle terms cancel each other. This leaves you with $a^2 - b^2$.

49. A: The mode is the number that appears most often in a set of data. If no item appears most often, then the data set has no mode. In this case, Kyle had one hit for a total of three times. There were two times that he had two hits. Also, on one day, he had three hits. Then, on another day, he had four hits. One hit happened the most times. So, the mode of the data set is 1.

50. B: The mean, or average, is the sum of the numbers in a data set. Then, the sum is divided by the total number of items. This data set has seven items (i.e., one for each day of the week). The total number of hits that Kyle had during the week is the sum of the numbers in the right-hand column. The sum is 14. So, to find the average: $Mean = \frac{14}{7} = 2$.

Science

1. C: A normal sperm must have one of each of the human chromosome pairs. There are 23 chromosome pairs in all. Twenty-two of these are *autosomal* chromosomes. They do not play a role in deciding gender. The remaining pair has two X chromosomes in the case of a female. In the case of a male, there is an X and a Y chromosome. So, a normal sperm cell will have 22 autosomal chromosomes and either an X or a Y chromosome, not both.

2. D: The graph shows that temperatures in the lower stratosphere are -50°C or lower. This allows more efficient engine operation. The paragraph explains that 75% of the Earth's atmosphere is in the troposphere which is below the stratosphere. It also says that the convective mixing of air and the effects of weather are characteristic of the troposphere. In the stratosphere, temperature-based layering of air leads to a stable environment. All of these effects combine to allow jets to operate with the best fuel efficiency possible in the lower stratosphere.

3. D: This can be read from the graph. The thermosphere has both the coldest and the highest temperatures in the atmospheric regions beneath outer space. In the thermosphere, atmospheric gases make layers of nearly pure molecular species. In its lower areas, carbon dioxide adds to cooling through radiative emission. An example is the mesosphere. In its upper areas, molecular oxygen absorbs solar radiation and causes much warming.

4. Sample Response: The amplitude is greater and the wavelength is longer.

The pitch of a sound depends on the frequency of the sound wave. As the frequency rises, the sound's pitch will rise as well. Frequency varies inversely with wavelength. So, a higher pitched sound with a higher frequency will have a longer wavelength. The volume of a sound depends on the degree that the molecules of air (or any other medium through which the sound travels) are compressed. This compression is represented by the wave amplitude. As the amplitude becomes greater, the sound becomes louder.

5. D: The two sound waves are added together. This means that the values of the two waves at each point are combined or added together. Since the two waves are out of phase by exactly half a wavelength, this means that when one wave has a positive value, the other has a negative value. Being out of phase by half a wavelength is the same as being perfectly out of phase. Since they are perfectly out of phase, they will cancel one another out. In other words, the amplitude peak of one wave will match in space with the amplitude trough of the other. This event is called cancellation. The opposite is also possible. If the waves were perfectly in phase, their peaks and troughs would match each other. So, instead of canceling out, the sum of the two waves would be twice as strong as each individual wave. This would make a much louder sound.

6. B: The vertical axis of this graph is an exponential scale. Each tick mark for a day matches with an increase in the number of cells per mL. The curve for the control cells (i.e., those grown in the absence of the drug) shows a cell concentration of about 500 cells/mL at the start. Then, there are 5000 cells/mL after 4 days, and 50,000 cells per mL after 8 days. This shows an exponential growth pattern where the number of cells increases by a factor of ten every four days.

7. D: The effects of two concentrations of methotrexate (MTX) on the growth of cancer cells are shown by the open pentagons and solid squares in the figure. These growth curves may be compared to the growth of untreated cells (the control) shown by the solid circles. At a concentration of 10 micromoles per liter (10 micromolar), cell growth is slightly inhibited when compared to the control. At the greater concentration of 100 micromoles per liter (i.e., equivalent to 0.1 millimolar), the cells do not grow at all. Also, the experiment is concerned with cancer cells, not bacteria. So, choice B cannot be correct.

8. B: Sexual reproduction allows the genetic information from two parents to mix. Recombination events between the two parental copies of individual genes can happen. So, this will create new genes. The production of new genes and of new gene combinations leads to an increase in diversity in the population. This is a great advantage for adapting to changes in the environment.

9. D: The charge must be conserved in the reaction. Each reactant (i.e., two helium atoms) has two protons. So, they will have a total electric charge of +4. The reaction product (i.e., helium-4) also has two protons. Thus, it has a total charge of +2. Two positive charges are lacking to balance the reaction. Choice D with two protons has a charge of +2.

10. B: Tritium is an isotope of hydrogen. So, the nucleus has a single proton that has a charge of +1. The extra neutrons do not add to the charge. Electrons have a charge of -1. In order to neutralize the single positive charge of the nuclear proton, one electron is needed.

11. D: Volcanic activity allows molten magma to reach the surface of the Earth. This is where it cools and solidifies into rock. The diagram and paragraph show that these types of rocks are known as *igneous* rocks. Examples of igneous rocks are obsidian and basalt. The type of igneous rock that is made depends on the chemical makeup of the magma.

12. B: A metamorphic rock is a rock with a changed form. These rocks are made at great depths. Usually, they come from previous sedimentary rocks. As more sediment builds above them, there is increased pressure and heat. This forces the relatively open crystal structure of the sedimentary rocks to collapse. Then, they take on a denser structure. Examples of metamorphic rocks are quartz and gneiss.

13. A: Evolutionary fitness measures the ability to pass on genes to future generations. So, it is marked by the ability to have offspring. The male wolf in choice A died young. However, he lived long enough to have 4 offspring. As you can see, this is more than any other wolf described in the other choices. So, his genes have the greatest chance of being passed on. It is important to know that evolutionary fitness simply requires an organism to live long enough to reproduce. This is measured only by reproductive success.

14. B: An allele is a variant of the original DNA sequence for a gene. It may differ from the original by a single base. For example, it may have a C in place of a G. Also, it may differ by a whole region where the sequence of bases is different. It may have extra bases in it (i.e., insertions) or be missing some material (i.e., deletions). Whatever the difference, it will result in RNA and a protein. This RNA sequence differs from the original. Sometimes, these differing proteins are broken. They may result in disease or developmental anomalies. Sometimes they are mild. An example is the difference between blue and brown eyes in humans.

15. A: The sequence can be read directly from the table. It is read three bases at a time. Three bases makeup a codon and give the information needed to specify one amino acid. In the sequence given, the first codon is GTT. The table shows that this matches with the amino acid *valine*. Similarly, the second codon is ACA. So, this matches with threonine. The third codon (i.e., AAA) matches with lysine. The fourth (i.e., AGA) goes with arginine. Each sequence of amino acids makes a specific protein.

16. D: Begin by looking over each sequence from the first base. Then, break it into triplets for each codon. The sequence in choice A is GTA CCC CTA. This is for valine-proline-leucine. Only the sequence in choice D has one of the three STOP codons. The STOP codons are TGA, TAA, and TAG. In choice D, the second codon is TAA. When the polymerase reaches this codon, it will start the process of disengaging from the DNA. This process ends the mRNA copy and ultimately the protein product of the gene.

17. A: The DNA molecule is a long chain of phosphoribose that has attached bases. The sequence of bases defines the individual amino acids that are connected to make a protein. There are 4 different bases and 23 different amino acids. Each amino acid is specified by a three-base "word." This "word" is known as a codon in the language of DNA. The four bases can be put together in 64 different ways to encode the 23 different amino acids and STOP signals. Some amino acids are defined by more than one codon.

18. C: Proteins are *encoded* in the DNA. However, they are *made* by ribosomes that string the proteins together from amino acids in the cell's cytoplasm. The information needed to string proteins into the correct sequence comes from mRNAs that are made by polymerases. These polymerases read the codons in the DNA. Transfer RNAs bring the amino acids to the ribosomes where they are built into proteins.

19. D: Phosphoribose gives the backbone of the DNA chain which makes up genes. In this area, bases like cytosine and guanine are strung together. Then, they are organized into triplets known as codons. These codons encode the protein to be made. The protein itself will be put together far away from the gene that is in the cell's nucleus. The ribosome is in the cytoplasm of the cell and will help to build the protein.

20. A: Vectors can show the velocities of the wind and the aircraft. The length of the vector can be for the speed. The direction of the vector can be for the direction of either the wind or the airplane.

The wind speed is going against the plane. The pilot will measure the sum of the actual wind speed plus the speed of his aircraft:

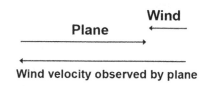

21. C: Spring tides happen when the Sun, Moon, and Earth are in a line. Neap tides happen when the Sun and Moon are at right angles.

22. C: The chart shows that plastic and cardboard materials are made of 15% of the collected materials. So, it is incorrect to say that there is more plastic than cardboard. They are present in equal amounts.

23. A: The reactions described in the paragraph happen when electrons are made by a reaction that reduces the positively-charged lead anode. The reducing agent, in turn, is oxidized by this reaction. These electrons travel through the wire to the negatively-charged cathode where they react with the sulfuric acid oxidizer and reduce it. This makes a lead sulfate. In a car battery, the anode is the positively-charged electrode. Normally, you can find it with the red marking on the battery.

24. A: In an oxidation reaction, an oxidizing agent gains electrons from a reducing agent. By adding electrons, the reducing agent reduces (i.e., makes more negative) the charge on the oxidizer. In the car battery, reduction of the positively-charged anode provides electrons. Then, these electrons flow to the cathode where an oxidation takes place. In an oxidation, an oxidizing agent increases (i.e., makes more positive) the charge on a reducer. In this way, the extra electrons in the negatively charged cathode are neutralized by the surrounding oxidizing agent.

25. D: The reaction described in the paragraph happens when two water molecules (H_2O) are made for each lead oxide (PbO_2) molecule that reacts at the cathode.

26. C: The data shows that up until about 4 weeks, the silk production from both colonies was similar. This suggests that the worms from each colony made the same amount of silk. So, choices A and B are incorrect. Over the long term, the data shows that the silk made by the entire colony of genetically diverse worms was greater than the silk made by the entire colony of genetically uniform worms. This might be because the worms made silk for a longer time. This could be due to some other mechanism. The experiment does not give information on that mechanism.

27. Sample Response: *Genetically diverse silkworms reproduce more than genetically uniform worms.* The increase in productivity from the diverse culture happens at about 4 weeks. This comes at the same time when new worms are hatched and start to make silk.

28. A: The digestion of starch starts with its exposure to the enzyme amylase that is found in the saliva. Amylase attacks the glycosidic bonds in starch. This attack separates them to release sugars. This is the reason why some starchy foods may taste sweet if they are chewed for a long time. Another form of amylase is made by the pancreas. This amylase continues the digestion of starches in the upper intestine. The di- and tri-saccharides are the first products of this digestion. Later, they are converted to glucose. The glucose is a monosaccharide that is easily absorbed through the intestinal wall.

29. D: The term *hydrologic cycle* is defined in the first paragraph. It is described as being equal to the *water cycle*. It comes from the Greek root *hydros* which means "water."

30. B: The second paragraph gives examples of different storage reservoirs for water in the water cycle. An underground aquifer is one example. An *aquifer* is any geologic formation that has ground water. The word comes from the Latin root *aqua* which means "water."

31. D: According to the table, the average residence time of water in soil is only two months. Only its residence time in the atmosphere (9 days) is shorter. *Residence time* is the average amount of time that a water molecule spends in each of the reservoirs before it moves on to the next reservoir of the water cycle.

32. B: According to the final paragraph, ocean levels actually fall during an ice age. The reason is that more water is stored in ice caps and glaciers when the temperatures are very cold. So, there is less water that stays in the oceans as liquid water.

33. C: Adding heat causes the molecules of a substance to increase their rate of motion. This is why heat is known as a form of kinetic energy. The temperature of a substance is proportional to the kinetic energy of the molecules that make up the substance. Adding heat to a system usually raises the temperature. However, temperature is not a form of heat. Instead, temperature measures the amount of heat that is in a system.

34. C: Energy in the form of heat is always absorbed by the molecules of a substance to make them move faster. During a change of state, some molecules absorb energy and escape the solid phase to become liquid. Others escape the liquid phase to become gas. Since molecules in a gas move faster than those in a liquid and molecules in a liquid move faster than those in a gas, the average speed increases.

35. B, C, and D: In region B of the graph, the water is at 0°C. Heat is being added to it, and it is slowly changing to a liquid. In region C, the temperature is climbing from 0°C to 100°C, and all of the water is in a liquid phase. In region D, the water is at 100°C. So, it is slowly changing to a gas as more energy is added. Once it has all changed to a gas, the temperature will increase again as more heat is added (region E).

36. D: Water at 1°C is in the liquid phase. Using the definition of the specific heat capacity, it will take 99 calories to raise the temperature of 1 gm of liquid water to 100°C. Using the definition of the heat of vaporization given in the text, it will take an additional 540 calories to turn it into the gaseous phase as it reaches 100°C. Finally, an additional calorie must be added to bring the temperature of the gas up to 101°C. So, the total amount of heat which must be added is 640 calories.

37. B: Region B of the graph is the transition between the solid and liquid phases of water. If heat is added to the system, solid ice melts into liquid. Conversely, if heat is removed from the system, liquid water will freeze in this area of the graph. Similarly, region D is the transition between liquid and gaseous water. In this region, water either evaporates or condenses. This depends on whether heat is added to or removed from water.

38. B, C, and F: The cell body has the nucleus. This is the control center of the cell and the site of its metabolic activity. Dendrites extend from this cell body. The dendrites receive signals from other cells in the form of neurotransmitters. This triggers an electrical impulse that travels down the axon to the next cell on the route of the signal. At the end of the axon, neurotransmitters are released again. Then, they cross the synapse and act on the following cell.

39. A: The cell body has the nucleus as shown in the diagram. *Eukaryotic* cells have a nucleus. The nucleus is where the chromosomes stay. The chromosomes carry the genes and manage the activities of the neuron.

40. D: Information flow is in one direction and moves from dendrite to axon in a neuron. Then, it crosses from axon to dendrite to move from cell to cell at the synapse. The electrical impulse that carries information along the axon is helped by myelin. However, there is no myelin at the synapse. So, it can have no role there. The flow of information across the synapse is done through the medium of neurotransmitters. These neurotransmitters spread out across the synapse to interact with dendritic receptors on the other side.

41. C: The pulmonary artery carries oxygen-drained blood from the heart to the lungs. Then, carbon dioxide is released, and the supply of oxygen is filled again. Next, this blood returns to the heart through the pulmonary artery. Then, it is carried through the aorta and a series of branching arteries to the capillaries. At the capillaries, much of the gas exchange with the tissues happens. Oxygen-drained blood returns to the heart through branching veins into the vena cava. Then, the vena cava carries the blood again to the heart. The pulmonary artery is the last step before replenishment of the blood's oxygen content. So, it has blood with very small amounts of oxygen.

42. D: A tsunami is a large wave or series of waves caused by the displacement of a large volume of water. The most common cause is an earthquake. However, large landslides or explosive volcanic action may also cause a tsunami. Tsunamis look like very high, sustained tides. They can move water very far inland. Large storms (e.g., cyclones or hurricanes) may also move large amounts of water. This can cause a high tide known as a storm surge that looks like a tsunami.

43. D: Since the cylinder is airtight, the piston cannot sink into the injected fluids. So, it will not displace a volume of fluid equal to its weight. Since liquids are not compressible, the density of the injected fluid does not make a difference in this experiment. Equal volumes of any fluid will raise the cylinder by an equal amount.

44. D: The terms accuracy and precision are used in place of each other in informal speech. However, they have specific meanings as scientific terms. Accuracy is how close a measurement is to the actual target. Precision is how many times that you have the same measurement. In this case, both sets of measurements have the same accuracy and the same precision. One measurement in each set is exactly correct and two are off by one millimeter.

45. D: All living organisms on Earth use the same triplet genetic code. This code has a three-nucleotide sequence called a codon. This codon gives information that matches to an amino acid that will be added to a protein. In contrast, many organisms-- especially certain types of bacteria-- do not use oxygen. These organisms live in oxygen-poor environments and may make energy through fermentation. Other organisms may live in dark environments (e.g., caves or deep underground). Only the most evolutionarily-advanced organisms use neurotransmitters in their nervous systems.

46. C: Both cannonballs will be subject to a vertical acceleration due to the force of gravity. There is an additional horizontal component to the velocity of cannonball A. However, its vertical velocity will be the same. In each case, the height of the object at time t seconds will be $h = -\frac{1}{2}t^2 + 20$.

47. C: First, note that 5 meters equals 500 cm. So, the horizontal speed of the cannonball is 500 cm/sec. Momentum must be conserved in the recoiling system. The vertical motion due to gravity can be ignored. The reason is that it involves the conservation of momentum between the cannonball and the Earth rather than the cannon. In the horizontal dimension, conservation of momentum says that $MV = mv$, where M and V are for the mass and the velocity of the cannon. Also, m and v are for the mass and the velocity of the cannonball. Solving for V gives $V = \frac{1}{M} \times mv = \frac{1}{500} \times 5 \times 500 = 5cm/sec$

48. B: This cell has chloroplasts and a cell wall. This is characteristic of plant cells. They are not found in the other cell types listed as answer choices. Chloroplasts have the pigment known as chlorophyll. They are the engines of photosynthesis. Also, they bring energy to the cell from sunlight. The cell wall is made of cellulose and gives a protective covering.

49. D: The nucleus is the home for the chromosomes. These chromosomes are made of DNA and a protein component. The chromosomes have the genetic code in a certain sequence of bases that make up the DNA chain.

50. A: Mitochondria give chemical energy for the cell in the form of ATP (i.e., adenosine triphosphate). They give energy by converting nutritional energy sources (e.g., glucose) through a complex series of chemical reactions. These reactions take place on the extensive membrane system located in the mitochondria's outer membranes.

Social Studies

1. C: Denmark abolished slavery in 1792. France did not abolish slavery for another two years. The chart does not include information on Spain abolishing slavery. Britain was the third European nation to abolish slavery in 1807.

2. D: The United States was a British colony before winning independence. So, they would have been required to end slavery in 1834 with all British colonies. Denmark abolished slavery in 1792, but the American colonies did not have a major relationship with Denmark. In 1794, France banned slavery. However, most of the colonies were not French possessions by the time of the American Revolution. In 1807, Britain ended slavery. However, that rule was not for the colonies.

3. B: France's Revolution began in 1789. Only five years later, the slave trade was abolished. This seems to show an understanding and spreading out of the ideals of independence. The United States Revolution began in 1776. Then, almost a century passed before slavery finally ended in 1865. None of the other conclusions can be supported from the chart. Brazil was a large slave-holding nation, but that information is not given in the chart. It is unlikely that Denmark, a small nation with few colonies, would have been a large slave-holding state. The Asian nations stayed in Britain's empire until the mid-twentieth century.

4. C and E: Ecuador and Venezuela did not have independence from Spain until 1830. Argentina received independence from Spain in 1810, and Paraguay declared independence in 1811. So, choice A and choice B cannot be correct answer choices. Bolivia became independent from Spain in 1825, and Uruguay followed three years later.

5. D: Ten nations received independence in the first thirty years of the nineteenth century. Choice A is incorrect because the American Revolution was fought during the latter 1770s and early 1780s. This was decades before the independence movements in South America. In fact, the American Revolution inspired some of the movements. France did not have many possessions in South America. So, choice B is wrong. Nations on the west coast were among the last to gain independence. So, that makes choice C incorrect.

6. A: The Mayan Empire collapsed from the inside. The other civilizations were taken over by the Spanish. The Incan Empire was the last to fall. So, this makes choice B an incorrect answer. None of the empires was located in North America. The title of the chart makes this clear. So, choice C is not correct. The Mayans were not taken over by Spain like the Aztecs and the Incans. This makes choice D incorrect.

7. C: The Spanish conquistadors were active in Central and South America in the sixteenth century. Choice A is incorrect. The reason is that Portugal was active in Brazil, but that location is not mentioned in the chart. The Mayan empire is older than the Aztec and Incan civilizations. So, this makes choice B incorrect. There is no sign that the Incan warriors in Peru tried to help the Aztec of Mexico.

8. B: Antiseptics kept infections down. By using antiseptics, Muslim doctors prevented infections that often led to loss of limbs or life for Europeans. The other choices are opinions or statements that are not supported by the paragraph. There is no way to compare the bravery of Muslims with the bravery of other faiths when facing surgery. So, choice A can be eliminated. Also, choice C is incorrect. There would not be a noticeable rise in silk use for sutures to explain a larger silk market. Choice D is an opinion, not a fact.

9. C: Lincoln repeats the phrase "save the Union" four times. He explains that slavery is not his primary issue. So, he explains all the ways that he would manipulate that institution to preserve the Union. Lincoln says directly that his object is neither to free the slave nor to destroy slavery. So, this makes choice A incorrect. Choice B is also incorrect. There is no mention of payment to the slave owner in this passage. He does not mention winning the war. So, choice D is not correct.

10. D: In 1848, gold was discovered in California at John Sutter's mill. This event led to the migration of people known as the Forty-Niners. The silver rush in Nevada came later. So, this makes choice A incorrect. The transcontinental railroad was finished in 1869. This date is not included in the chart. So, choice B cannot be correct. Choice C is also incorrect. The reason is that the founding of Spanish missions in California and the Southwest happened several centuries earlier.

11. D: With an increasing population, cities and towns were made. These places became the sites of hotels, brothels, laundries, and saloons. Choice A is not likely. Most of the migration was men coming to seek their fortunes and planning to return to the East. The key term in choice B is *most*. Many of the women who went west set up businesses. However, most of the new migrants were men. The Civil War did not begin until 1860. That is more than a decade after the Gold Rush.

12. B: The railroad required only 6 to 8 days. So, this was a 20-day advantage over all the other ways of moving goods or people. Choice A is an incorrect choice. The reason is that a steamboat to New Orleans that is combined with a packet ship to New York needed 28 days. The route across the Erie Canal needed 18 days. So, this makes choice C incorrect. The keelboat was used in the earliest part of the nineteenth century. This boat was only part of the difficult 52-day route that needed water and overland travel to reach New York.

13. D: Using the keelboat and the wagon called for 52 days of travel. Combining steamboat, canal, and railroad cut the time by more than 30 days. This was a larger amount of time saved than any other new development. Steamboat and packet needed 28 days of travel, and the railroad took 6 to 8 days. This was a savings of 20 to 22 days. So, this makes choice A incorrect. Also, choice B is wrong. The canal took 18 days, and the railroad took 6 to 8 days. So, this was a savings of 10 to 12 days. The canal route took 18 days, and the steamboat and packet needed 28 days. So, this saved 10 days and makes choice C wrong.

14. A: Catholics, Pilgrims, Puritans, and Quakers were important in developing new colonies. So, this shows you the importance of religion to these people. Choice B is incorrect because the French did not hold much territory in the eastern United States. They did have land in areas west of the Appalachians and in what became Canada. Choice C is incorrect because there is nothing on the chart to confirm this information. Choice D is true. However, that information cannot be known from the chart.

15. C: The men had expected their invention to end war. Instead, it became a new weapon. Choice A is often cited as a reference to the Spanish-American War of 1898. So, it is incorrect. The Wright brothers hoped that their invention would put an end to war. So, choice B is the opposite idea. Rickenbacker was a famous World War I ace pilot. Since the Wright brothers wanted peace, they probably would not be interested in fighting. So, choice D is incorrect.

16. D: A politician who did not want to give even a penny for "scenery" would likely not have favored the Clean Air Act. All others would have favored the measures. Choice A is not the right answer because Nixon signed the bill. In 1970, he was still a popular president. So, he did not need to sign it to create goodwill. Rachel Carson sounded an early warning about the effects of DDT. So, she would likely have been excited about the act. Theodore Roosevelt was a strong supporter of environmental causes and would have championed the bill.

17. C: Mother Jones wanted laws to protect child workers. Legislators finally responded to appeals from her and others. None of the other answer choices would logically follow. The words would not have been an encouragement for children to work in factories. So, choice A is incorrect. Choice B is also not right. The South continued to be a major textile region. Increasing pay for child labor was not the solution to the problem. So, choice D is incorrect.

18. A: The other choices are incorrect because Italy, Russia, and England were not invading Belgium.

19. D: Many of the founders were also slaveholders, yet they believed that the practice was wrong. Choice A is an assumption that cannot be supported. Choice B is false. Freeman's actions had no effect on women's suffrage. However, it did have an impact on slavery. Many white Southerners wanted slavery to continue. Thus, they were unlikely to applaud the decision of the court. This makes choice C incorrect.

20. A: The mounds were built much earlier. 1949 is the date that they came under the protection of the National Park Service. Mounds are located in other places in the United States. So, choice B is not the right choice. In 1949, Truman was president, and he would have signed the bill into law. So, choice C is not a correct answer. Effigy mounds are shaped like animals. So, choice D is not correct.

21. D: Machinery and transport jumped from 34.3 to 42.0 percent in exports. Also, they went from 9.7 to 28.0 percent in imports. Chemicals increased exports from 8.7 to 9.0. Imports declined from 5.3 to 3.6. So, choice A is incorrect. Crude material exports declined from 13.7 to 10.8. For imports, they declined from 18.3 to 8.3. So, this makes choice B incorrect. The decline in exports of food and beverages was just under 4 percent, and imports declined 7 percent. So, choice C is not correct.

22. B: Crude material imports declined by 10 percentage points. All other categories saw imports that declined less than 10 points over the decade. Chemicals decreased in that time by only 1.7 percent. So, this makes choice A incorrect. Choice C is also incorrect. Food and beverages decreased during those ten years by just over 7 percent. Imports of machinery and transport nearly tripled, rather than decreased. This means that choice D is incorrect.

23. C: After World War I, the per capita national debt increased by 32 percent during the Civil War. Choice A is not an accurate choice; the amount of debt per capita actually decreased between the American Revolution and the War of 1812. Between the War of 1812 and the Civil War, the percentage of debt increased by almost 14 percent. So, choice B is also incorrect. The per capita national debt increased after World War I by nearly 14 percent. So, this makes choice D wrong as well.

24. B: The only time that the national debt level fell after a war was after the American Revolution. One conclusion is that the new government felt the need to show fiscal responsibility to the world. Choice A is incorrect. To borrow more money would increase the debt, not lower it. Choice C is not correct. The amount of money that people spent had nothing to do with the per capita national debt. Purchase of Treasury bonds would show a growing debt. This was the opposite of what was actually happening. So, this makes choice D incorrect.

25. D: By 1950, the number of women in the workforce had climbed to 28.8 percent. This was the first time that the percentage was above 25 percent. Choice A is incorrect because women in 1900 made up only 18 percent of the workforce. By 1920, women still made up only 20.4 percent of the

357

workforce. So, choice B is not correct. In 1940, 24.3 percent of women were in the labor force, but the question asks for a percentage higher than 25.

26. C: The percent of women in the workforce steadily increased through seven decades and beyond. By 1970, it reached 36.7 percent. This was double the 18.1 percent of 1900. Choice A is wrong because the rate did not decline. Choice B is also incorrect. The reason is that the rate climbed. Choice D is not correct because the rate did not go up and down. Instead, it increased steadily.

27. B: Although the nation faced recession, the U.S. dollar made a comeback in world currency during the fall of 2008. Choice A cannot be concluded from the information which is about the dollar and the euro, not the whole world. Choice C is incorrect as well; the euro fell in 2008 against the dollar. The wisdom of buying stocks cannot be known from the information given. So, choice D is not correct.

28. D: Corporate taxes would be paid in greater amounts because businesses would no longer be able to use offshore havens. Choice A suggests the opposite situation. So, it is clearly incorrect. The offshore tax havens have nothing to do with retirement receipts. So, choice B is also incorrect. Again, individual income tax is not related to the problem of offshore tax havens. So, choice C is incorrect as well.

29. A: Individuals give the largest part of the total revenue at 43 percent. Choice B is incorrect. The reason is that corporations were adding only 10.1 percent of the revenue in 2004. Social Security is part of the 39 percent of the amount that comes from social insurance and retirement receipts. So, this makes choice C incorrect. Choice D is also wrong. Government agencies do not pay taxes and do not appear on the chart.

30. C: Loans to Native Americans remain fewer than a thousand and are the smallest category represented. Choice A is incorrect; the number of loans to Asian Americans decreased during this five-year period. The number of loans to African Americans more than doubled during this period. So, this makes choice B incorrect. In 2000, the highest number of loans went to Asian Americans, not to Hispanic Americans. So, choice D is incorrect.

31. C: Public welfare overrides private rights. Choice A is incorrect. The reason is that the proposal does not suggest that Ohio will lose rights to the control of the lake. Choice B is also incorrect. The property owners are said to have a protected right to their land and to be able to give or sell those rights. Choice D is wrong. The reason is that the amendment clearly refers to the lawmakers' response to passing the Great Lakes Water Compact.

32. D: Implied powers in Article I, Clause 18, Section 8. This section has the "necessary and proper" clause. An example of this clause being used is when Congress funds a national railroad system. Choice A is incorrect. The reason is that the delegated powers did not include funding for a railroad. Choice B is incorrect because the power to support rail travel was not a denied power. This power is not expressed directly in the Constitution. So, choice C is not correct.

33. D: The president makes sure that laws are carried out. National laws are not subject to state laws or interpretations. Choice A is not correct because Eisenhower had the legal power to send federal troops. The conflict in Vietnam had nothing to do with the event in Arkansas. So, choice B is not correct. Choice C cannot be correct because Eisenhower would not have been able to send troops into the state.

34. B: Bloomberg's term ended in 2009. A majority of City Council members who approved the measure finished their terms as well. Now, choice A is not discussed in the question. So, it is unlikely to have happened twice. There is no mention of a voter initiative to overturn the earlier referendums. So, choice C is not correct. Also, there is no mention of action by the City Council that would be thought of as pressuring him. So, this makes choice D wrong.

35. A: Increasing border controls on the Canada-U.S. border was part of the USA PATRIOT Act of 2001 and affected the private and public sectors of people traveling between those two countries. The other choices sound like they could be related to events between the U.S. and Canada. For example, lawful commerce in arms could relate to guns sold between countries, but it was for guns within the United States. So, choice C is incorrect. Choice B is wrong because a Trade Act might apply to U.S.-Canada trade, but not to border patrols. Choice D is wrong because the "Fence" Act applied to the Mexico-U.S. border, not the Canada-U.S. border.

36. B: Women in the organization have the opportunity to meet others and bring their involvement into the larger organization. Choice A is wrong because cronyism is using power to place your friends and associates in power. Choice C is also incorrect because lobbyists are not mayors. Instead, they are people who try to influence legislators. Patronage is a system of supporting worthy persons or causes. So, this makes choice D incorrect.

37. C: Virginia's plan called for representation based on population. So, that plan would help states with larger populations. Choice A is incorrect because Virginia would not want representation based on wealth if it were a poor state. Choice B uses the motto of the French Revolution. So, this has nothing to do with the U.S. Constitution. Choice D is incorrect because the New Jersey plan did not ask for representation to be based on wealth.

38. B: Britain's Parliament has a two-house system. So, this may have been a model for the Virginia Plan. Choice A is not correct because the Mayflower Compact set up a more theocratic system of government. Choice C is also wrong because some historians believe that the Iroquois system of government influenced the framers' ideas. However, there is no sign that the Sioux system had an influence. Choice D is clearly incorrect because the legislature is not a monarchy.

39. D: The Electoral College was a compromise for a way to elect the president. Choice A is incorrect because wealth has nothing to do with the role of the Electoral College. Choice B is wrong as well. The appointment of Supreme Court justices is not part of the Electoral College. That is a job for the chief executive. Electing senators is also not the responsibility of the Electoral College. So, this makes choice C incorrect.

40. C: In 1969, there were 13 members. In 2008, there were 43. So, this is an increase of 30. Choice A is not correct because the CBC was set up 100 years after the Civil War. Choice B is also incorrect because there is nothing in the passage about a goal of a black president. Choice D is wrong as well. The reason is that the passage clearly says that the alternative budget has many differences from the president's budget.

41. D: When you see a superlative in a sentence, you may have an opinion. Choice D says that apartheid was the worst political system. That sentence is an opinion that can be challenged. The other answer choices can be proven as fact. The passage clearly says that the founding of the CBC was in 1969. So, this makes choice A incorrect. Choice B can also be found in the passage as a fact. Choice C is confirmed in the passage as well.

42. C: Young people protested that they were old enough to fight and die for their country, yet they could not vote. Choice A is incorrect because women had the right to vote after the Nineteenth

Amendment passed in 1920. Choice B is also wrong. African American males were able to vote after the Civil War. African American females gained the right in 1920. The baby boom ended in 1964. So, choice D is not correct.

43. C: The Mayan population of Belize stands at about 10 percent. The other answers do not have much of a Mayan population according to the table.

44. D: Choice A is incorrect because the Creole population is not the largest ethnic group in the entire region. Choice B is also wrong because the Mayans make up about 10 percent of the Belize population. Choice C is incorrect. The reason is that Costa Rica does not have a canal, and the chart does not explain how Chinese people came to Costa Rica.

45. A: Belize is close to Haiti and Jamaica. These countries have many people of African heritage. There is no evidence of trade between Belize and the nations of West Africa. So, choice B is wrong. It is possible that many Creole in New Orleans left after Hurricane Katrina. However, there is no evidence that they went to Belize. So, choice C cannot be correct. Choice D cannot be supported.

46. D: The route began at the Mississippi River. Choice A is incorrect because the order came from President Jefferson in Washington, D.C. However, the journey did not start from that city. Instead, St. Louis was the starting point. Choice B is also incorrect. The reason is that the group had to cross the Rockies, but they did not start their journey from that area. Fort Mandan was one of the forts built farther west. So, choice C cannot be the correct answer.

47. D: The rate was not high in 1929. However, it did steadily increase in the years after 1929. You may think that the graph shows the rate as "steady" at one point. However, it is still going up between 1932 and 1933. The unemployment rate of other countries is not shown on the graph. So, choice B cannot be correct.

48. D: Khartoum is Sudan's capital. At this point, the Nile splits into the White and Blue Nile rivers. Choice A is not correct. The Gulf of Aden and the Red Sea is north of Somalia. Choice B is incorrect because the Congo River and Lake Chad are not in Sudan. Also, they do not come from the Nile. Choice C is not correct because Lake Victoria is not in Sudan at all.

49. C: The Kalahari Desert is located in the middle western part of Botswana. Choice A is not correct because the Zambezi River runs through Zambia and Angola. These are countries that are north of Botswana. Choice B is also wrong. The reason is that Lake Tanganyika is northeast of Botswana which is along Tanzania's western border. Choice D is not correct because the Congo River is in the Democratic Republic of the Congo which is north of Botswana.

50. A, C, and E: Somalia, Mozambique, and Kenya are bordered by the Indian Ocean. The other answer choices are not bordered by the Indian Ocean.

How to Overcome Test Anxiety

Just the thought of taking a test is enough to make most people a little nervous. A test is an important event that can have a long-term impact on your future, so it's important to take it seriously and it's natural to feel anxious about performing well. But just because anxiety is normal, that doesn't mean that it's helpful in test taking, or that you should simply accept it as part of your life. Anxiety can have a variety of effects. These effects can be mild, like making you feel slightly nervous, or severe, like blocking your ability to focus or remember even a simple detail.

If you experience test anxiety—whether severe or mild—it's important to know how to beat it. To discover this, first you need to understand what causes test anxiety.

Causes of Test Anxiety

While we often think of anxiety as an uncontrollable emotional state, it can actually be caused by simple, practical things. One of the most common causes of test anxiety is that a person does not feel adequately prepared for their test. This feeling can be the result of many different issues such as poor study habits or lack of organization, but the most common culprit is time management. Starting to study too late, failing to organize your study time to cover all of the material, or being distracted while you study will mean that you're not well prepared for the test. This may lead to cramming the night before, which will cause you to be physically and mentally exhausted for the test. Poor time management also contributes to feelings of stress, fear, and hopelessness as you realize you are not well prepared but don't know what to do about it.

Other times, test anxiety is not related to your preparation for the test but comes from unresolved fear. This may be a past failure on a test, or poor performance on tests in general. It may come from comparing yourself to others who seem to be performing better or from the stress of living up to expectations. Anxiety may be driven by fears of the future—how failure on this test would affect your educational and career goals. These fears are often completely irrational, but they can still negatively impact your test performance.

Review Video: 3 Reasons You Have Test Anxiety
Visit mometrix.com/academy and enter code: 428468

361

Elements of Test Anxiety

As mentioned earlier, test anxiety is considered to be an emotional state, but it has physical and mental components as well. Sometimes you may not even realize that you are suffering from test anxiety until you notice the physical symptoms. These can include trembling hands, rapid heartbeat, sweating, nausea, and tense muscles. Extreme anxiety may lead to fainting or vomiting. Obviously, any of these symptoms can have a negative impact on testing. It is important to recognize them as soon as they begin to occur so that you can address the problem before it damages your performance.

> **Review Video: 3 Ways to Tell You Have Test Anxiety**
> Visit mometrix.com/academy and enter code: 927847

The mental components of test anxiety include trouble focusing and inability to remember learned information. During a test, your mind is on high alert, which can help you recall information and stay focused for an extended period of time. However, anxiety interferes with your mind's natural processes, causing you to blank out, even on the questions you know well. The strain of testing during anxiety makes it difficult to stay focused, especially on a test that may take several hours. Extreme anxiety can take a huge mental toll, making it difficult not only to recall test information but even to understand the test questions or pull your thoughts together.

> **Review Video: How Test Anxiety Affects Memory**
> Visit mometrix.com/academy and enter code: 609003

Effects of Test Anxiety

Test anxiety is like a disease—if left untreated, it will get progressively worse. Anxiety leads to poor performance, and this reinforces the feelings of fear and failure, which in turn lead to poor performances on subsequent tests. It can grow from a mild nervousness to a crippling condition. If allowed to progress, test anxiety can have a big impact on your schooling, and consequently on your future.

Test anxiety can spread to other parts of your life. Anxiety on tests can become anxiety in any stressful situation, and blanking on a test can turn into panicking in a job situation. But fortunately, you don't have to let anxiety rule your testing and determine your grades. There are a number of relatively simple steps you can take to move past anxiety and function normally on a test and in the rest of life.

> **Review Video: How Test Anxiety Impacts Your Grades**
> Visit mometrix.com/academy and enter code: 939819

Physical Steps for Beating Test Anxiety

While test anxiety is a serious problem, the good news is that it can be overcome. It doesn't have to control your ability to think and remember information. While it may take time, you can begin taking steps today to beat anxiety.

Just as your first hint that you may be struggling with anxiety comes from the physical symptoms, the first step to treating it is also physical. Rest is crucial for having a clear, strong mind. If you are tired, it is much easier to give in to anxiety. But if you establish good sleep habits, your body and mind will be ready to perform optimally, without the strain of exhaustion. Additionally, sleeping well helps you to retain information better, so you're more likely to recall the answers when you see the test questions.

Getting good sleep means more than going to bed on time. It's important to allow your brain time to relax. Take study breaks from time to time so it doesn't get overworked, and don't study right before bed. Take time to rest your mind before trying to rest your body, or you may find it difficult to fall asleep.

Review Video: <u>The Importance of Sleep for Your Brain</u>
Visit mometrix.com/academy and enter code: 319338

Along with sleep, other aspects of physical health are important in preparing for a test. Good nutrition is vital for good brain function. Sugary foods and drinks may give a burst of energy but this burst is followed by a crash, both physically and emotionally. Instead, fuel your body with protein and vitamin-rich foods.

Also, drink plenty of water. Dehydration can lead to headaches and exhaustion, especially if your brain is already under stress from the rigors of the test. Particularly if your test is a long one, drink water during the breaks. And if possible, take an energy-boosting snack to eat between sections.

Review Video: <u>How Diet Can Affect your Mood</u>
Visit mometrix.com/academy and enter code: 624317

Along with sleep and diet, a third important part of physical health is exercise. Maintaining a steady workout schedule is helpful, but even taking 5-minute study breaks to walk can help get your blood pumping faster and clear your head. Exercise also releases endorphins, which contribute to a positive feeling and can help combat test anxiety.

When you nurture your physical health, you are also contributing to your mental health. If your body is healthy, your mind is much more likely to be healthy as well. So take time to rest, nourish your body with healthy food and water, and get moving as much as possible. Taking these physical steps will make you stronger and more able to take the mental steps necessary to overcome test anxiety.

Review Video: <u>How to Stay Healthy and Prevent Test Anxiety</u>
Visit mometrix.com/academy and enter code: 877894

Mental Steps for Beating Test Anxiety

Working on the mental side of test anxiety can be more challenging, but as with the physical side, there are clear steps you can take to overcome it. As mentioned earlier, test anxiety often stems from lack of preparation, so the obvious solution is to prepare for the test. Effective studying may be the most important weapon you have for beating test anxiety, but you can and should employ several other mental tools to combat fear.

First, boost your confidence by reminding yourself of past success—tests or projects that you aced. If you're putting as much effort into preparing for this test as you did for those, there's no reason you should expect to fail here. Work hard to prepare; then trust your preparation.

Second, surround yourself with encouraging people. It can be helpful to find a study group, but be sure that the people you're around will encourage a positive attitude. If you spend time with others who are anxious or cynical, this will only contribute to your own anxiety. Look for others who are motivated to study hard from a desire to succeed, not from a fear of failure.

Third, reward yourself. A test is physically and mentally tiring, even without anxiety, and it can be helpful to have something to look forward to. Plan an activity following the test, regardless of the outcome, such as going to a movie or getting ice cream.

When you are taking the test, if you find yourself beginning to feel anxious, remind yourself that you know the material. Visualize successfully completing the test. Then take a few deep, relaxing breaths and return to it. Work through the questions carefully but with confidence, knowing that you are capable of succeeding.

Developing a healthy mental approach to test taking will also aid in other areas of life. Test anxiety affects more than just the actual test—it can be damaging to your mental health and even contribute to depression. It's important to beat test anxiety before it becomes a problem for more than testing.

> **Review Video: Test Anxiety and Depression**
> Visit mometrix.com/academy and enter code: 904704

Study Strategy

Being prepared for the test is necessary to combat anxiety, but what does being prepared look like? You may study for hours on end and still not feel prepared. What you need is a strategy for test prep. The next few pages outline our recommended steps to help you plan out and conquer the challenge of preparation.

STEP 1: SCOPE OUT THE TEST

Learn everything you can about the format (multiple choice, essay, etc.) and what will be on the test. Gather any study materials, course outlines, or sample exams that may be available. Not only will this help you to prepare, but knowing what to expect can help to alleviate test anxiety.

STEP 2: MAP OUT THE MATERIAL

Look through the textbook or study guide and make note of how many chapters or sections it has. Then divide these over the time you have. For example, if a book has 15 chapters and you have five days to study, you need to cover three chapters each day. Even better, if you have the time, leave an extra day at the end for overall review after you have gone through the material in depth.

If time is limited, you may need to prioritize the material. Look through it and make note of which sections you think you already have a good grasp on, and which need review. While you are studying, skim quickly through the familiar sections and take more time on the challenging parts. Write out your plan so you don't get lost as you go. Having a written plan also helps you feel more in control of the study, so anxiety is less likely to arise from feeling overwhelmed at the amount to cover.

STEP 3: GATHER YOUR TOOLS

Decide what study method works best for you. Do you prefer to highlight in the book as you study and then go back over the highlighted portions? Or do you type out notes of the important information? Or is it helpful to make flashcards that you can carry with you? Assemble the pens, index cards, highlighters, post-it notes, and any other materials you may need so you won't be distracted by getting up to find things while you study.

If you're having a hard time retaining the information or organizing your notes, experiment with different methods. For example, try color-coding by subject with colored pens, highlighters, or post-it notes. If you learn better by hearing, try recording yourself reading your notes so you can listen while in the car, working out, or simply sitting at your desk. Ask a friend to quiz you from your flashcards, or try teaching someone the material to solidify it in your mind.

STEP 4: CREATE YOUR ENVIRONMENT

It's important to avoid distractions while you study. This includes both the obvious distractions like visitors and the subtle distractions like an uncomfortable chair (or a too-comfortable couch that makes you want to fall asleep). Set up the best study environment possible: good lighting and a comfortable work area. If background music helps you focus, you may want to turn it on, but otherwise keep the room quiet. If you are using a computer to take notes, be sure you don't have any other windows open, especially applications like social media, games, or anything else that could distract you. Silence your phone and turn off notifications. Be sure to keep water close by so you stay hydrated while you study (but avoid unhealthy drinks and snacks).

Also, take into account the best time of day to study. Are you freshest first thing in the morning? Try to set aside some time then to work through the material. Is your mind clearer in the afternoon or evening? Schedule your study session then. Another method is to study at the same time of day that you will take the test, so that your brain gets used to working on the material at that time and will be ready to focus at test time.

STEP 5: STUDY!

Once you have done all the study preparation, it's time to settle into the actual studying. Sit down, take a few moments to settle your mind so you can focus, and begin to follow your study plan. Don't give in to distractions or let yourself procrastinate. This is your time to prepare so you'll be ready to fearlessly approach the test. Make the most of the time and stay focused.

Of course, you don't want to burn out. If you study too long you may find that you're not retaining the information very well. Take regular study breaks. For example, taking five minutes out of every hour to walk briskly, breathing deeply and swinging your arms, can help your mind stay fresh.

As you get to the end of each chapter or section, it's a good idea to do a quick review. Remind yourself of what you learned and work on any difficult parts. When you feel that you've mastered the material, move on to the next part. At the end of your study session, briefly skim through your notes again.

But while review is helpful, cramming last minute is NOT. If at all possible, work ahead so that you won't need to fit all your study into the last day. Cramming overloads your brain with more information than it can process and retain, and your tired mind may struggle to recall even previously learned information when it is overwhelmed with last-minute study. Also, the urgent nature of cramming and the stress placed on your brain contribute to anxiety. You'll be more likely to go to the test feeling unprepared and having trouble thinking clearly.

So don't cram, and don't stay up late before the test, even just to review your notes at a leisurely pace. Your brain needs rest more than it needs to go over the information again. In fact, plan to finish your studies by noon or early afternoon the day before the test. Give your brain the rest of the day to relax or focus on other things, and get a good night's sleep. Then you will be fresh for the test and better able to recall what you've studied.

STEP 6: TAKE A PRACTICE TEST

Many courses offer sample tests, either online or in the study materials. This is an excellent resource to check whether you have mastered the material, as well as to prepare for the test format and environment.

Check the test format ahead of time: the number of questions, the type (multiple choice, free response, etc.), and the time limit. Then create a plan for working through them. For example, if you have 30 minutes to take a 60-question test, your limit is 30 seconds per question. Spend less time on the questions you know well so that you can take more time on the difficult ones.

If you have time to take several practice tests, take the first one open book, with no time limit. Work through the questions at your own pace and make sure you fully understand them. Gradually work up to taking a test under test conditions: sit at a desk with all study materials put away and set a timer. Pace yourself to make sure you finish the test with time to spare and go back to check your answers if you have time.

After each test, check your answers. On the questions you missed, be sure you understand why you missed them. Did you misread the question (tests can use tricky wording)? Did you forget the information? Or was it something you hadn't learned? Go back and study any shaky areas that the practice tests reveal.

Taking these tests not only helps with your grade, but also aids in combating test anxiety. If you're already used to the test conditions, you're less likely to worry about it, and working through tests until you're scoring well gives you a confidence boost. Go through the practice tests until you feel comfortable, and then you can go into the test knowing that you're ready for it.

Test Tips

On test day, you should be confident, knowing that you've prepared well and are ready to answer the questions. But aside from preparation, there are several test day strategies you can employ to maximize your performance.

First, as stated before, get a good night's sleep the night before the test (and for several nights before that, if possible). Go into the test with a fresh, alert mind rather than staying up late to study.

Try not to change too much about your normal routine on the day of the test. It's important to eat a nutritious breakfast, but if you normally don't eat breakfast at all, consider eating just a protein bar. If you're a coffee drinker, go ahead and have your normal coffee. Just make sure you time it so that the caffeine doesn't wear off right in the middle of your test. Avoid sugary beverages, and drink enough water to stay hydrated but not so much that you need a restroom break 10 minutes into the test. If your test isn't first thing in the morning, consider going for a walk or doing a light workout before the test to get your blood flowing.

Allow yourself enough time to get ready, and leave for the test with plenty of time to spare so you won't have the anxiety of scrambling to arrive in time. Another reason to be early is to select a good seat. It's helpful to sit away from doors and windows, which can be distracting. Find a good seat, get out your supplies, and settle your mind before the test begins.

When the test begins, start by going over the instructions carefully, even if you already know what to expect. Make sure you avoid any careless mistakes by following the directions.

Then begin working through the questions, pacing yourself as you've practiced. If you're not sure on an answer, don't spend too much time on it, and don't let it shake your confidence. Either skip it and come back later, or eliminate as many wrong answers as possible and guess among the remaining ones. Don't dwell on these questions as you continue—put them out of your mind and focus on what lies ahead.

Be sure to read all of the answer choices, even if you're sure the first one is the right answer. Sometimes you'll find a better one if you keep reading. But don't second-guess yourself if you do immediately know the answer. Your gut instinct is usually right. Don't let test anxiety rob you of the information you know.

If you have time at the end of the test (and if the test format allows), go back and review your answers. Be cautious about changing any, since your first instinct tends to be correct, but make sure you didn't misread any of the questions or accidentally mark the wrong answer choice. Look over any you skipped and make an educated guess.

At the end, leave the test feeling confident. You've done your best, so don't waste time worrying about your performance or wishing you could change anything. Instead, celebrate the successful

completion of this test. And finally, use this test to learn how to deal with anxiety even better next time.

Important Qualification

Not all anxiety is created equal. If your test anxiety is causing major issues in your life beyond the classroom or testing center, or if you are experiencing troubling physical symptoms related to your anxiety, it may be a sign of a serious physiological or psychological condition. If this sounds like your situation, we strongly encourage you to seek professional help.

How to Overcome Your Fear of Math

The word *math* is enough to strike fear into most hearts. How many of us have memories of sitting through confusing lectures, wrestling over mind-numbing homework, or taking tests that still seem incomprehensible even after hours of study? Years after graduation, many still shudder at these memories.

The fact is, math is not just a classroom subject. It has real-world implications that you face every day, whether you realize it or not. This may be balancing your monthly budget, deciding how many supplies to buy for a project, or simply splitting a meal check with friends. The idea of daily confrontations with math can be so paralyzing that some develop a condition known as *math anxiety*.

But you do NOT need to be paralyzed by this anxiety! In fact, while you may have thought all your life that you're not good at math, or that your brain isn't wired to understand it, the truth is that you may have been conditioned to think this way. From your earliest school days, the way you were taught affected the way you viewed different subjects. And the way math has been taught has changed.

Several decades ago, there was a shift in American math classrooms. The focus changed from traditional problem-solving to a conceptual view of topics, de-emphasizing the importance of learning the basics and building on them. The solid foundation necessary for math progression and confidence was undermined. Math became more of a vague concept than a concrete idea. Today, it is common to think of math, not as a straightforward system, but as a mysterious, complicated method that can't be fully understood unless you're a genius.

This is why you may still have nightmares about being called on to answer a difficult problem in front of the class. Math anxiety is a very real, though unnecessary, fear.

Math anxiety may begin with a single class period. Let's say you missed a day in 6th grade math and never quite understood the concept that was taught while you were gone. Since math is cumulative, with each new concept building on past ones, this could very well affect the rest of your math career. Without that one day's knowledge, it will be difficult to understand any other concepts that link to it. Rather than realizing that you're just missing one key piece, you may begin to believe that you're simply not capable of understanding math.

This belief can change the way you approach other classes, career options, and everyday life experiences, if you become anxious at the thought that math might be required. A student who loves science may choose a different path of study upon realizing that multiple math classes will be required for a degree. An aspiring medical student may hesitate at the thought of going through the necessary math classes. For some this anxiety escalates into a more extreme state known as *math phobia*.

Math anxiety is challenging to address because it is rooted deeply and may come from a variety of causes: an embarrassing moment in class, a teacher who did not explain concepts well and contributed to a shaky foundation, or a failed test that contributed to the belief of math failure.

These causes add up over time, encouraged by society's popular view that math is hard and unpleasant. Eventually a person comes to firmly believe that he or she is simply bad at math. This belief makes it difficult to grasp new concepts or even remember old ones. Homework and test grades begin to slip, which only confirms the belief. The poor performance is not due to lack of ability but is caused by math anxiety.

Math anxiety is an emotional issue, not a lack of intelligence. But when it becomes deeply rooted, it can become more than just an emotional problem. Physical symptoms appear. Blood pressure may rise and heartbeat may quicken at the sight of a math problem – or even the thought of math! This fear leads to a mental block. When someone with math anxiety is asked to perform a calculation, even a basic problem can seem overwhelming and impossible. The emotional and physical response to the thought of math prevents the brain from working through it logically.

The more this happens, the more a person's confidence drops, and the more math anxiety is generated. This vicious cycle must be broken!

The first step in breaking the cycle is to go back to very beginning and make sure you really understand the basics of how math works and why it works. It is not enough to memorize rules for multiplication and division. If you don't know WHY these rules work, your foundation will be shaky and you will be at risk of developing a phobia. Understanding mathematical concepts not only promotes confidence and security, but allows you to build on this understanding for new concepts. Additionally, you can solve unfamiliar problems using familiar concepts and processes.

Why is it that students in other countries regularly outperform American students in math? The answer likely boils down to a couple of things: the foundation of mathematical conceptual understanding and societal perception. While students in the US are not expected to *like* or *get* math, in many other nations, students are expected not only to understand math but also to excel at it.

Changing the American view of math that leads to math anxiety is a monumental task. It requires changing the training of teachers nationwide, from kindergarten through high school, so that they learn to teach the *why* behind math and to combat the wrong math views that students may develop. It also involves changing the stigma associated with math, so that it is no longer viewed as unpleasant and incomprehensible. While these are necessary changes, they are challenging and will take time. But in the meantime, math anxiety is not irreversible—it can be faced and defeated, one person at a time.

False Beliefs

One reason math anxiety has taken such hold is that several false beliefs have been created and shared until they became widely accepted. Some of these unhelpful beliefs include the following:

There is only one way to solve a math problem. In the same way that you can choose from different driving routes and still arrive at the same house, you can solve a math problem using different methods and still find the correct answer. A person who understands the reasoning behind math calculations may be able to look at an unfamiliar concept and find the right answer, just by applying logic to the knowledge they already have. This approach may be different than what is taught in the classroom, but it is still valid. Unfortunately, even many teachers view math as a subject where the best course of action is to memorize the rule or process for each problem rather than as a place for students to exercise logic and creativity in finding a solution.

Many people don't have a mind for math. A person who has struggled due to poor teaching or math anxiety may falsely believe that he or she doesn't have the mental capacity to grasp mathematical concepts. Most of the time, this is false. Many people find that when they are relieved of their math anxiety, they have more than enough brainpower to understand math.

Men are naturally better at math than women. Even though research has shown this to be false, many young women still avoid math careers and classes because of their belief that their math abilities are inferior. Many girls have come to believe that math is a male skill and have given up trying to understand or enjoy it.

Counting aids are bad. Something like counting on your fingers or drawing out a problem to visualize it may be frowned on as childish or a crutch, but these devices can help you get a tangible understanding of a problem or a concept.

Sadly, many students buy into these ideologies at an early age. A young girl who enjoys math class may be conditioned to think that she doesn't actually have the brain for it because math is for boys, and may turn her energies to other pursuits, permanently closing the door on a wide range of opportunities. A child who finds the right answer but doesn't follow the teacher's method may believe that he is doing it wrong and isn't good at math. A student who never had a problem with math before may have a poor teacher and become confused, yet believe that the problem is because she doesn't have a mathematical mind.

Students who have bought into these erroneous beliefs quickly begin to add their own anxieties, adapting them to their own personal situations:

I'll never use this in real life. A huge number of people wrongly believe that math is irrelevant outside the classroom. By adopting this mindset, they are handicapping themselves for a life in a mathematical world, as well as limiting their career choices. When they are inevitably faced with real-world math, they are conditioning themselves to respond with anxiety.

I'm not quick enough. While timed tests and quizzes, or even simply comparing yourself with other students in the class, can lead to this belief, speed is not an indicator of skill level. A person can work very slowly yet understand at a deep level.

If I can understand it, it's too easy. People with a low view of their own abilities tend to think that if they are able to grasp a concept, it must be simple. They cannot accept the idea that they are capable of understanding math. This belief will make it harder to learn, no matter how intelligent they are.

I just can't learn this. An overwhelming number of people think this, from young children to adults, and much of the time it is simply not true. But this mindset can turn into a self-fulfilling prophecy that keeps you from exercising and growing your math ability.

The good news is, each of these myths can be debunked. For most people, they are based on emotion and psychology, NOT on actual ability! It will take time, effort, and the desire to change, but change is possible. Even if you have spent years thinking that you don't have the capability to understand math, it is not too late to uncover your true ability and find relief from the anxiety that surrounds math.

Math Strategies

It is important to have a plan of attack to combat math anxiety. There are many useful strategies for pinpointing the fears or myths and eradicating them:

Go back to the basics. For most people, math anxiety stems from a poor foundation. You may think that you have a complete understanding of addition and subtraction, or even decimals and percentages, but make absolutely sure. Learning math is different from learning other subjects. For example, when you learn history, you study various time periods and places and events. It may be important to memorize dates or find out about the lives of famous people. When you move from US history to world history, there will be some overlap, but a large amount of the information will be new. Mathematical concepts, on the other hand, are very closely linked and highly dependent on each other. It's like climbing a ladder – if a rung is missing from your understanding, it may be difficult or impossible for you to climb any higher, no matter how hard you try. So go back and make sure your math foundation is strong. This may mean taking a remedial math course, going to a tutor to work through the shaky concepts, or just going through your old homework to make sure you really understand it.

Speak the language. Math has a large vocabulary of terms and phrases unique to working problems. Sometimes these are completely new terms, and sometimes they are common words, but are used differently in a math setting. If you can't speak the language, it will be very difficult to get a thorough understanding of the concepts. It's common for students to think that they don't understand math when they simply don't understand the vocabulary. The good news is that this is fairly easy to fix. Brushing up on any terms you aren't quite sure of can help bring the rest of the concepts into focus.

Check your anxiety level. When you think about math, do you feel nervous or uncomfortable? Do you struggle with feelings of inadequacy, even on concepts that you know you've already learned? It's important to understand your specific math anxieties, and what triggers them. When you catch yourself falling back on a false belief, mentally replace it with the truth. Don't let yourself believe that you can't learn, or that struggling with a concept means you'll never understand it. Instead, remind yourself of how much you've already learned and dwell on that past success. Visualize grasping the new concept, linking it to your old knowledge, and moving on to the next challenge. Also, learn how to manage anxiety when it arises. There are many techniques for coping with the irrational fears that rise to the surface when you enter the math classroom. This may include controlled breathing, replacing negative thoughts with positive ones, or visualizing success. Anxiety interferes with your ability to concentrate and absorb information, which in turn contributes to greater anxiety. If you can learn how to regain control of your thinking, you will be better able to pay attention, make progress, and succeed!

Don't go it alone. Like any deeply ingrained belief, math anxiety is not easy to eradicate. And there is no need for you to wrestle through it on your own. It will take time, and many people find that speaking with a counselor or psychiatrist helps. They can help you develop strategies for responding to anxiety and overcoming old ideas. Additionally, it can be very helpful to take a short course or seek out a math tutor to help you find and fix the missing rungs on your ladder and make sure that you're ready to progress to the next level. You can also find a number of math aids online: courses that will teach you mental devices for figuring out problems, how to get the most out of your math classes, etc.

Check your math attitude. No matter how much you want to learn and overcome your anxiety, you'll have trouble if you still have a negative attitude toward math. If you think it's too hard, or just have general feelings of dread about math, it will be hard to learn and to break through the anxiety. Work on cultivating a positive math attitude. Remind yourself that math is not just a hurdle to be cleared, but a valuable asset. When you view math with a positive attitude, you'll be much more likely to understand and even enjoy it. This is something you must do for yourself. You may find it helpful to visit with a counselor. Your tutor, friends, and family may cheer you on in your endeavors. But your greatest asset is yourself. You are inside your own mind – tell yourself what you need to hear. Relive past victories. Remind yourself that you are capable of understanding math. Root out any false beliefs that linger and replace them with positive truths. Even if it doesn't feel true at first, it will begin to affect your thinking and pave the way for a positive, anxiety-free mindset.

Aside from these general strategies, there are a number of specific practical things you can do to begin your journey toward overcoming math anxiety. Something as simple as learning a new note-taking strategy can change the way you approach math and give you more confidence and understanding. New study techniques can also make a huge difference.

Math anxiety leads to bad habits. If it causes you to be afraid of answering a question in class, you may gravitate toward the back row. You may be embarrassed to ask for help. And you may procrastinate on assignments, which leads to rushing through them at the last moment when it's too late to get a better understanding. It's important to identify your negative behaviors and replace them with positive ones:

Prepare ahead of time. Read the lesson before you go to class. Being exposed to the topics that will be covered in class ahead of time, even if you don't understand them perfectly, is extremely helpful in increasing what you retain from the lecture. Do your homework and, if you're still shaky, go over some extra problems. The key to a solid understanding of math is practice.

Sit front and center. When you can easily see and hear, you'll understand more, and you'll avoid the distractions of other students if no one is in front of you. Plus, you're more likely to be sitting with students who are positive and engaged, rather than others with math anxiety. Let their positive math attitude rub off on you.

Ask questions in class and out. If you don't understand something, just ask. If you need a more in-depth explanation, the teacher may need to work with you outside of class, but often it's a simple concept you don't quite understand, and a single question may clear it up. If you wait, you may not be able to follow the rest of the day's lesson. For extra help, most professors have office hours outside of class when you can go over concepts one-on-one to clear up any uncertainties. Additionally, there may be a *math lab* or study session you can attend for homework help. Take advantage of this.

Review. Even if you feel that you've fully mastered a concept, review it periodically to reinforce it. Going over an old lesson has several benefits: solidifying your understanding, giving you a confidence boost, and even giving some new insights into material that you're currently learning! Don't let yourself get rusty. That can lead to problems with learning later concepts.

Teaching Tips

While the math student's mindset is the most crucial to overcoming math anxiety, it is also important for others to adjust their math attitudes. Teachers and parents have an enormous influence on how students relate to math. They can either contribute to math confidence or math anxiety.

As a parent or teacher, it is very important to convey a positive math attitude. Retelling horror stories of your own bad experience with math will contribute to a new generation of math anxiety. Even if you don't share your experiences, others will be able to sense your fears and may begin to believe them.

Even a careless comment can have a big impact, so watch for phrases like *He's not good at math* or *I never liked math*. You are a crucial role model, and your children or students will unconsciously adopt your mindset. Give them a positive example to follow. Rather than teaching them to fear the math world before they even know it, teach them about all its potential and excitement.

Work to present math as an integral, beautiful, and understandable part of life. Encourage creativity in solving problems. Watch for false beliefs and dispel them. Cross the lines between subjects: integrate history, English, and music with math. Show students how math is used every day, and how the entire world is based on mathematical principles, from the pull of gravity to the shape of seashells. Instead of letting students see math as a necessary evil, direct them to view it as an imaginative, beautiful art form – an art form that they are capable of mastering and using.

Don't give too narrow a view of math. It is more than just numbers. Yes, working problems and learning formulas is a large part of classroom math. But don't let the teaching stop there. Teach students about the everyday implications of math. Show them how nature works according to the laws of mathematics, and take them outside to make discoveries of their own. Expose them to math-related careers by inviting visiting speakers, asking students to do research and presentations, and learning students' interests and aptitudes on a personal level.

Demonstrate the importance of math. Many people see math as nothing more than a required stepping stone to their degree, a nuisance with no real usefulness. Teach students that algebra is used every day in managing their bank accounts, in following recipes, and in scheduling the day's events. Show them how learning to do geometric proofs helps them to develop logical thinking, an invaluable life skill. Let them see that math surrounds them and is integrally linked to their daily lives: that weather predictions are based on math, that math was used to design cars and other machines, etc. Most of all, give them the tools to use math to enrich their lives.

Make math as tangible as possible. Use visual aids and objects that can be touched. It is much easier to grasp a concept when you can hold it in your hands and manipulate it, rather than just listening to the lecture. Encourage math outside of the classroom. The real world is full of measuring, counting, and calculating, so let students participate in this. Keep your eyes open for numbers and patterns to discuss. Talk about how scores are calculated in sports games and how far apart plants are placed in a garden row for maximum growth. Build the mindset that math is a normal and interesting part of daily life.

Finally, find math resources that help to build a positive math attitude. There are a number of books that show math as fascinating and exciting while teaching important concepts, for example: *The Math Curse; A Wrinkle in Time; The Phantom Tollbooth;* and *Fractals, Googols and Other Mathematical Tales*. You can also find a number of online resources: math puzzles and games,

374

videos that show math in nature, and communities of math enthusiasts. On a local level, students can compete in a variety of math competitions with other schools or join a math club.

The student who experiences math as exciting and interesting is unlikely to suffer from math anxiety. Going through life without this handicap is an immense advantage and opens many doors that others have closed through their fear.

Self-Check

Whether you suffer from math anxiety or not, chances are that you have been exposed to some of the false beliefs mentioned above. Now is the time to check yourself for any errors you may have accepted. Do you think you're not wired for math? Or that you don't need to understand it since you're not planning on a math career? Do you think math is just too difficult for the average person?

Find the errors you've taken to heart and replace them with positive thinking. Are you capable of learning math? Yes! Can you control your anxiety? Yes! These errors will resurface from time to time, so be watchful. Don't let others with math anxiety influence you or sway your confidence. If you're having trouble with a concept, find help. Don't let it discourage you!

Create a plan of attack for defeating math anxiety and sharpening your skills. Do some research and decide if it would help you to take a class, get a tutor, or find some online resources to fine-tune your knowledge. Make the effort to get good nutrition, hydration, and sleep so that you are operating at full capacity. Remind yourself daily that you are skilled and that anxiety does not control you. Your mind is capable of so much more than you know. Give it the tools it needs to grow and thrive.

Thank You

We at Mometrix would like to extend our heartfelt thanks to you, our friend and patron, for allowing us to play a part in your journey. It is a privilege to serve people from all walks of life who are unified in their commitment to building the best future they can for themselves.

The preparation you devote to these important testing milestones may be the most valuable educational opportunity you have for making a real difference in your life. We encourage you to put your heart into it—that feeling of succeeding, overcoming, and yes, conquering will be well worth the hours you've invested.

We want to hear your story, your struggles and your successes, and if you see any opportunities for us to improve our materials so we can help others even more effectively in the future, please share that with us as well. **The team at Mometrix would be absolutely thrilled to hear from you!** So please, send us an email (support@mometrix.com) and let's stay in touch.

> **If you'd like some additional help, check out these other resources we offer for your exam:**
> http://mometrixflashcards.com/GED

Additional Bonus Material

Due to our efforts to try to keep this book to a manageable length, we've created a link that will give you access to all of your additional bonus material.

Please visit https://www.mometrix.com/bonus948/ged to access the information.

Made in the USA
Middletown, DE
14 January 2021